The Working Class in American History

Editorial Advisors
David Brody
Alice Kessler-Harris
David Montgomery
Sean Wilentz

A list of books in the series appears at the end of this volume.

Producers, Proletarians, and Politicians

Producers, Proletarians, and Politicians

Workers and Party Politics in Evansville and New Albany, Indiana, 1850–87

Lawrence M. Lipin

University of Illinois Press
Urbana and Chicago

Library of Congress Cataloging-in-Publication Data

Lipin, Lawrence M., 1956–
    Producers, proletarians, and politicians : workers and party
politics in Evansville and New Albany, Indiana, 1850–87 / Lawrence
M. Lipin.
        p.   cm. — (The working class in American history)
    Includes bibliographical references and index.
    ISBN 0-252-02019-7
    1. Working class—Indiana—New Albany—Political activity—
History—19th century. 2. Working class—Indiana—Evansville—
Political activity—History—19th century. I. Title. II. Series.
HD8079.N39L57   1994
322′.2′0977219—dc20

92-41298
CIP

For Rosa and Ella

Contents

Acknowledgments

Eugene Lunn's European intellectual history course at UC Davis challenged me and other undergraduates to rethink old formulations and to "ask the right questions." I chose to become a historian because of Gene's example. I only regret that he is no longer alive to judge whether or not the right questions have been asked.

In preparing this book, I have benefited from the help of many. Travel for this project was funded by grants from the Indiana Historical Society and the UCLA Graduate Division. Materials were made available by a number of particularly helpful individuals, notably, Byron Swanson of the Indiana State Library; Eric Pumroy of the Indiana Historical Society Library; Don Baker, Joan Elliot, and Frank Chandler of the Willard Library in Evansville; and Lee Fletcher and Mona Leitner of the New Albany Public Library. Additional thanks are due Ruth Ann Kramer of the latter institution for her efforts to find ever more interesting and obscure sources that helped define this project and for the friendship she offered me and my family.

At the dissertation stage, this work was guided by my advisor, John Laslett, who constantly worked to force greater precision on my part. Eric Monkkonen served as a helpful resource on my committee, providing detours where I saw dead ends. In revising this work for publication, all or parts of the manuscript have received generous readings from Gary Nash, Katy Clay, Alan Heskin, and Jane Hunter, and their suggestions have improved it considerably. A still greater debt is owed David Montgomery, who more than once has brought his considerable knowledge and powers of perceptions to bear on this manuscript, precisely identifying the issues I had long avoided. And many long-standing violations against the English language have been removed by manuscript editor Rita D. Disroe. This book is what it is because of the efforts of all who have read it and worked to make it better.

I am doubly fortunate, for beside generous professional assistance, this project was blessed with the emotional support of friends and family. My brother, Eric Lipin, my sister, Lisa Boks, and my sister-in-law, Rikki Horne, have all demonstrated unwavering support for the decade-long quest to complete this work. My parents, Irma and Allen Lipin, have encouraged me to continue, even at times when I thought it best to quit. In addition, Terry Marcelle, whom I met in Gene Lunn's class, has been helping me to ask the right questions ever since.

Finally, Sylvie Horne has read all my prose and, not without cause, has found it lacking plot and character development. Without typing this manuscript, without serving as my strongest critic (at least not with regard to this book), and without a deep passion for history, she has given me the strength to start and finish this project, all the while keeping me honest. I cannot begin to sort out the effect she has had, and continues to have, on me, but I know I am better for it.

The Ballot Box and Industrialization: The Salience of Class in Local Politics

1 In 1886, Friedrich Engels viewed the meteoric rise of the Knights of Labor as evidence that proletarianized workers in the United States were on the verge of challenging their employers for economic and political power. In a letter to Florence Kelley, he remarked that American workers now "appeal all of a sudden in such organized masses as to strike terror into the whole capitalist class."[1] However, prominent Gilded Age observers had long recognized the dangers of working-class power. Noted liberals like E. L. Godkin viewed the general strikes surrounding the railroad workers' revolt in 1877 as American versions of the "commune" and as evidence that the United States would not escape the violent clashes between classes that so often immersed European society.[2] And the problem was broader than the exceptional event. In the context of debates over state activity in Reconstruction, Godkin and others had expressed fears that the labor question "contains the disease of which this Christian civilization of ours is to perish."[3] Across the urban landscape, bourgeois "reformers" expressed disenchantment with a political democracy that seemed too responsive to the aspirations of immigrant working-class communities. In many smaller mining and manufacturing towns, industrialists faced a hostile community and a militant labor movement. To such contemporary observers, the early extension of the full rights of political citizenship to all white men and the rise of a party system dependent on the active participation of the masses did not appear to accommodate workers to the authority of a class of employers.[4]

Twentieth-century commentators have, with hindsight, found that such hopes or fears were unwarranted. Early in the century, academic observers stressed the nonrevolutionary character of the working class. Labor economists John Commons and Selig Perlman argued that the aims of the American worker were modest, job oriented, and politically reformist.[5] Others have argued that the liberal political culture of the United States moderated worker demands.[6] More recently, labor historians dedicated to uncovering patterns of culture and community have argued that American workers often responded with a militancy rooted in patterns of work and social life, but which was often defused by electoral politics. In this way, they have conceded the political ground to quantitative historians who have argued that elections turned not on questions of class, but rather on ethnic and religious antagonisms.[7]

However, the twentieth-century understanding of class and politics is mediated by a political culture that is, in very significant particulars, distinct from that of the earlier era. In his recent work, Michael McGerr has done much to uncover the nature and meaning of the transformation that bridges the two centuries. In the nineteenth century, politicians depended on the active involvement of a large cadre of party workers in conventions at the city, county, and state levels, as well as in myriad barbecues, torchlight parades, and rallies. McGerr argues that the disappearance of a politics of mass participation in favor of one in which candidates are marketed like commodities was the result of a successful intervention by elite reformers who saw in popular support of machine politicians a dangerous relationship.[8] Whether McGerr has uncovered the sources of this change in style or not, it is important to recognize that in the nineteenth century political party structures never seemed as bureaucratic and removed from the concerns of common people as they do in our day. It is the objective of this work to examine the importance that this popular style had in the shaping of working-class militancy in the nineteenth century and at the same time in understanding the sources of local support that labor often enjoyed in the small industrial city. I contend that these two matters are closely related.

Thanks to a series of essays by Herbert Gutman, we know that in small nineteenth-century cities labor did not always stand alone in industrial conflict. In places where face-to-face relations still bound together members of the community, Gutman found numerous instances of broad-based support by shopkeepers, professionals, and small manufacturers for unions engaged in strikes against large employers.[9] Class lines were unlikely to be rigid in these places; the skilled worker who succeeded in establishing a small factory was likely to have relatives and friends within the city who still were counted among the laboring class. As a result, employer and employee often shared values about economic conduct that opposed the logic of the market and were shaped by moral and community-minded considerations of "justice" and "equality."[10] Because this opposition was rooted in a broad-based tradition, nonworkers were frequently willing to aid striking workers in conflict with industrialists. Out of this cultural matrix came the impetus for local editors to lecture intransigent capitalists to "put conscience as well as capital" into their enterprises.[11]

The uncovering of this value system has stimulated a generation of labor historians to seek the material and cultural sources of worker militancy. Much of the literature they have produced emphasizes the relations of the preindustrial artisanal workshop. There, production was normally undertaken in small settings where the master craftsman, aided by a few journeymen and perhaps an apprentice, manually worked raw material into a finished product, usually on a custom basis. Since markets were local, the invisible hand of the market had not yet encouraged masters to transform traditional work practices to gain a competitive advantage. Out of this context arose a worldview identified by historians as "producerism." Located at its heart was the labor theory of value, which insisted that those who produced wealth were entitled to the full product of their labor, contrary to market logic. Producerism celebrated the virtue of manual producers while vilifying those who accumulated wealth through exchange. By focusing on the exploitation of the productive population by bankers, merchants, and lawyers, it united employers and employees in the workshops and the farms against those who, as they perceived, lived off the fruits of their labor.[12]

Nevertheless, there was room for distinctions between employers in the producerist drama. The employer wore two masks, each exposing a side of his character, only one of which was apparent at any one time to himself or his fellow actors. The first portrayed him as the bearer of employment, by which workers earned the means to provide sustenance for their families. The "good" employer, accordingly, reinvested his profits into larger industrial plants and created more jobs. At less-optimistic moments, characterized by declining earnings and rising competitive pressures, however, the capitalist discarded this beneficent mask for another that revealed a darker, and perhaps more essential, side of his character. He was now the exploiter who amassed profits at the expense of his workers, either by cutting wages, breaking down the work process, or increasing the hours and the pace of labor, all of which threatened the independence of the worker, at work and in the community. Jacksonian-era politicians affirmed the power of these images by using them to seek the working-class vote—Democrats more often availing themselves of the darker vision, Whigs more commonly of the optimistic side.[13] Thus it is critically important to note that producerism, especially in the hands of politicians, was a flexible ideological construct that provided the emerging industrialist with some breathing space.

Workers also drew on a form of republicanism with origins in the political arena of revolutionary America. Rooted in an organic theory of development in which societies passed through a cycle of birth, maturity and decay, republicanism came to embody the characteristics distinguishing the new republic from England. Americans perceived England as a decaying society dominated by a corrupt aristocracy accustomed to luxury and vice while they saw their own as newer, freer, and peopled by a citizenry that lived simply and independently. It was believed that only in such a society, dominated by an educated, hard working and prosperous citizenry, could a republic survive.[14] At the core of republican thought resided the fear that future economic development might lead to the rise of an impoverished and dependent population that would be at the mercy of the rich. By controlling the poor, the wealthy and powerful could usurp liberty and establish themselves as a new aristocracy. Such fears motivated Americans to maintain a constant and vigilant watch for threats to the republican form of government which might come from a capitalist "aristocracy." Thus, opposition to the "aristocratic pretensions of capital" had politico-cultural as well as material sources.

For American working-class activists, republicanism came to be inseparably associated with equal rights. Workers cherished their position as free laborers with full political rights, and they feared in the rise of large-scale capitalist enterprise a threat to their independence. It was this fear of dependence, proletarianization, and the centralization of power, Gutman suggests, that led workers to perceive in industrial capitalism a threat "to transform 'the Great Republic of the West' into a 'European' country."[15] The labor unrest of the Gilded Age was, in part, fueled by the republican image of the United States and its declension from that vision. At least to some extent, labor militancy sought to protect values of equality and justice; it was, in that way, a defense of the republic.[16]

This tradition of producerist republicanism was deeply ingrained in the minds of native-born white workers. The meaning of independence and dignity was heightened in nineteenth-century America by reference to its opposite: African American slavery. The symbolic opposition was reaffirmed by imbecilic portraits of both free and en-slaved African Americans in literature, theater, and political dis-course. That organized workers frequently characterized their efforts to oppose their employers as battles against "wage slavery" only re-affirmed the connections between citizenship, independence, and whiteness on the one hand, and incompetency, dependency, and blackness on the other.[17] This opposition between the white citizen worker and the black slave instilled in the white mechanic a fear that entry by the African American into the wage labor market posed a degrading influence on the status of the white worker. If the republic was to be defended, that included its racial foundations.[18]

Together, producerism, arising out of conditions in the artisanal workshop, and republicanism, stemming from the world of politics, informed white native and assimilated immigrant workers as they experienced the destruction of the artisanal mode of production and became entwined in the less-personal relations of industrial capital-ism. Recent scholarship, which has emphasized working-class cul-ture, has enabled us to understand how workers could mount a chal-lenge to capitalists without opposing the private ownership of the means of production. As long as he was involved in the labor process to some extent, honored widely held values of justice, and respected the "independence" of his employees, the capitalist frequently found his position in the social hierarchy unchallenged. Only when he was perceived to ignore acceptable norms of behavior did workers ques-tion the justice of the system. Yet the intensification of competition in the expanding capitalist market throughout the nineteenth centu-ry continuously tempted capitalists to break with tradition.

These ideological strains were nurtured in the workplace, in neighborhoods, and in an associational matrix that included frater-nal orders, ethnic benevolent societies, fire companies, and temper-ance societies.[19] There workers congregated—often with small mas-ters, clerks, and the proprietors of modest retail establishments—and asserted their rights to self-activity without elite domination. Often, such voluntary associations were grounded in a preindustrial com-munity and a mutualistic ethic that opposed market ways of think-ing.[20] Dotted with such institutions, the plebeian community often remained a source of militant egalitarianism and opposition to "aris-tocratic" capital.

However, we know much less about how these cultural values op-erated within the sphere of electoral politics and this has by and large resulted from a bias of recent historians against the political system. John Cumbler sums up the reigning assumption about the meaning of electoral activity: "Political parties . . . had little effect on low-income groups" and participation in party politics "often failed to contribute to the workers daily struggle for dignity and bread. Their electoral success often meant their loss to the community. And their failure to deliver benefits observable to the workers frequently led to cynicism at the local level."[21] Here we have one of the lessons of the new labor history. If community institutions fanned the flames of labor militancy, kindled in the changing relations of production, then the political system put out the fire (or at least managed it, preventing it from spreading out of control). The temptations of the electoral process, in these accounts, lured workers into politics where their militancy was co-opted, drained of its radical content, and transformed into acquiescence. As Alan Dawley put it over a decade ago, "the ballot box was the coffin of class consciousness."[22]

Taken as a whole, the literature has made much of the hegemonic role that the political system has played in pacifying workers.[23] The guiding assumption is that parties obstructed the promotion of a class language while political campaigns unified communities across class lines, all the while sustaining the illusion of a fluid class system. For workers, then, the ballot alternately served as panacea and placebo. For labor historians politics fails to explain much about the real motives of classes and individuals; instead it serves as camouflage, covering the truly exploitative with an artificially democratic gloss.[24]

It is difficult to harmonize this understanding of the role of politics with the widespread fears of elite reformers about the dangers of working-class participation in the political process, and it forces us to ask why they were so unaware of this ongoing process of accommodation. The search for answers to this question has only begun; political scientists have led the way by taking seriously electoral appeals to workers and correlating them to class formation in attempts to explain the rise of the urban political machine as a relatively autonomous institution.[25] More recently, labor historians have found the Civil War to be fertile ground for the exploration of party politics as a means by which classes negotiate with each other.[26] This is a necessary project if we are to understand ideas that motivated the response of individuals and groups to industrialization. While a broad distinction between politics and culture may seem sensible in our century, when mass media and commercialized leisure have replaced politics as activities of popular choice, such a distinction made less sense in the nineteenth century when politics served as one of the most regularized and secularized rituals in the community. Then, workers flocked to the banners of their parties to fill ballot boxes with "unscratched" party tickets, voting at rates well above the twentieth-century experience. To comprehend the cultural response of the Gilded Age worker, we must grasp what it meant to participate in those parades and rallies. For it would be difficult to imagine a way that nineteenth-century males defined themselves more publicly than as a Democrat or a Whig or Republican.[27]

To accomplish this, we need to recast our understanding of producerism and republicanism by recognizing that their very flexibility allowed nonworkers to make use of them. Most important in this regard, we must recognize that by the mid-nineteenth century they had become broad public inheritances entrenched in the vocabulary of the party politician. We should not assume that their articulation was necessarily a direct reflection of transforming relations of production. As Gareth Stedman-Jones asserts in a recent study of Chartism, such languages need to be understood as linguistic orderings of experience that limit and guide interpretation and create recipes for action, and not as perfectly clear reflections of social forces.[28] While we need not argue like Stedman-Jones that working-class movements can be understood primarily as political phenomena, his analysis reminds us that the vitality of a political tradition might propel workers, hard-pressed by the exigencies of industrialization, to seek redress within the realm of party politics. For no less than in the English context, the radical articulations of American workers drew on an older republican language that reaffirmed the political nature of corruption and social inequality.

On this side of the Atlantic, that tradition retained a powerful hold on large segments of the American electorate through much of the nineteenth century. In the Jacksonian era it was most strongly maintained by the Democratic party, which rhetorically maintained a vigilant defense of an egalitarian republic. The recent work of John Ashworth emphasizes the ideological importance of beliefs about equality in the development of the second party system. Their Jeffersonian attachment to a natural social order that was both egalitarian and republican led Democrats to celebrate the virtue of the independent farmer and mechanic. In so doing, they questioned the source of wealth accrued by bankers, merchants, and manufacturers. Most saliently, they blamed growing inequality on the penchant of their Whig (and later Republican) opposition to enact "partial" or "class" legislation. By doing this, the opposition opened themselves to the republican charge that an unholy and corrupt alliance had been enjoined between the state and the money power.[29]

This language, so much a part of Jacksonian discourse, was hardly monopolized by the Democrats. From the beginning of the second party system Whigs had framed themselves as defenders of the people against a centralizing Presidency. As the party system unraveled, concerns about the corrupt nature of centralized power and its effects on liberty would fuel two new political movements. In the eyes of nativist Know Nothings, the massive infusions of German and Irish immigrant voters had allowed themselves to become the instruments of an entrenched corps of corrupt Democratic politicians, who were willing to destroy Protestant liberties to perpetuate their power. And it was particularly well suited to the emerging coalition of Whig businessmen and small producers that came together in the Republican party to keep the West free of slavery. Antislavery Republicans like Salmon Chase spread warnings about the dangers of an emerging "Slave Power" that was conspiring to snuff out liberty not only in the South but also throughout the land. It was their ability to cast Supreme Court decisions, executive actions, and legislative acts in this fashion that best explains the success of the Republican party in the late fifties.[30]

The emerging dominance of the old Whig elite within that party and its centralizing efforts during and after the Civil War revitalized the language of republican opposition as a tool for Democratic party politicians.[31] Beyond the extension of federal authority into the Southern states, Democrats assailed Republicans for enacting class legislation. This style of response had been developed during the war in the response to the draft and various orders by union generals.[32] After the war it settled into a critique of Republican monetary policy and the attempt to impose black suffrage on the nation. Now a new "monied aristocracy" of bondholders emerged whose interests were too closely identified with the Republican party, which attempted to bolster its power by reliance on the vote of ex-slaves. Again corruption threatened the republic.[33]

That these issues, along with land reform, were absorbed by many working-class activists suggests something more than the infusion of the values of middle-class reformers into worker organization. Instead it means that workers, schooled in a republican tradition, maintained a long-standing relationship with politicians of both parties. Yet if cross-class affiliation moderated the nature of working-class demands, it also heightened the tendencies of politicians to speak a language of class. In so doing, they often explicitly supported collective efforts by workers to oppose the will of men whom politicians termed "aristocratic" employers. The result was the perpetuation of a political language that legitimated trade-union activity. Far from being irrelevant to the concerns of workers, in some instances political life may have been formative.[34]

An emphasis on the capacity of political language to forge consent as well as sustain opposition, and the very public nature of its articulation, should alert us to the ambiguous uses that might be made of producerism and republicanism within the more private network of voluntary associations. While fire companies may have affirmed particular forms of "traditional" behavior, and fraternal associations may have celebrated and therefore retained a mutualistic approach to social relations, we should recognize that the plasticity of language affected both the public and the quasi-private realms of working-class culture. This leaves open the possibility that the voluntary cultural network as much as the political process might work to accommodate workers to industrial discipline.[35] At the same time, however, it suggests that both realms could nourish a spirit of opposition among workers. To find the changing terms under which accommodation and resistance proceeded we need to make stronger connections between politics and the more private associational networks.

In both realms in the smaller city it was rare that class-specific organization proceeded, for class conflict was waged in communities not composed merely of workers and capitalists. A large "petty bourgeoisie" or "middling sort" often provided leaders and members of plebeian associations that otherwise included workers. Comprised largely of individuals who owned a modest amount of wealth, were self-employed, or were employed as white-collar workers, the middling types often played a role in local affairs that was out of proportion to their small (relative to workers) numbers.[36] Of them Jonathan Wiener has written, "Their capacity for independent political action, including its most militant forms, makes the men of small property a crucial political force."[37] Frequently embodying both the producer ideal of manual involvement in productive labor and the entrepreneurial ideal of self-employment, the petty bourgeoisie at times allied with the working class in opposition to the pretensions of the rich, and at other times supported the capitalist elite in fits of anxiety concerning possible disruptions of order and local economic prosperity. In studies of French revolutionary politics and language, Albert Soboul and William Sewell have shown them to have played a critical role in the conflagrations of the 1790s and of 1848.[38] In the United States, political insurgencies like antislavery and greenbackism thrived in many communities with the support of the middling sort. It is important that we understand what it meant for them to associate with workers in both voluntary association and within political life.

The importance of both political life and of interclass association is explored in the following pages as they were manifest in two Ohio River cities, New Albany and Evansville, Indiana. As late as 1860, both were characterized by small-scale manufacturing: the former as a steamboat building town of about twelve thousand inhabitants; the latter as an iron, woodworking, and leather center of nearly the same size. It was not until the Civil War that their paths diverged, when almost immediately New Albany's shipbuilding industry failed and in its place were built two iron mills, a glass works, and a woolen mill—all extensive works that by the late 1870s came under the control of one man, Washington C. DePauw. In the meantime, Evansville iron, leather, and furniture manufacturers continued to expand the size of their firms, but at a more gradual pace. Evansville's diversified economy, as well as its superior commercial opportunities, fueled rapid population growth, and by 1890 it was a city of over fifty thousand, nearly 2½ times the size of New Albany.

During these years, class lines in both communities hardened, though by different degrees. In the years before the Civil War, class formation had proceeded to a point at which white workers appeared to have one foot in the world of the artisan and the other in that of the proletarian. Apprenticeship had largely disappeared, and journeymen increasingly found themselves working for wealthy master craftsmen who no longer spent time at the workbench and had increased the scale of production to warrant a division of the work process. In many trades the journeyman found himself destined to remain a wage worker, and would have to seek upward mobility, if that was his intention, outside his calling—perhaps as a grocer or a saloonkeeper. The proximity to the slave regime led some runaway slaves to cross the Ohio River and settle in these cities; during and after the Civil War the number of African Americans increased dramatically, and their growing presence and participation in the labor market served to symbolize the loss of power and prestige that many white workers would endure in the postwar era, and the first response of the latter would be violent and tragic. However, on the eve of the Civil War, the social difference between white workers and their employers remained relatively small as most manufacturers had been trained in their trade and frequently their sons still plied it, if they themselves did not. In addition, neighborhoods and voluntary associations brought workers and employers together and created a context in which artisanal republicanism and producerism still held some shared meanings.

The years of rapid industrial growth following the war had great consequences for class formation in these cities. In New Albany, a sizable industrial working class came to be employed in iron, glass, and iron factories by men whose previous experiences were in mercantile and banking enterprises. Despite significant disparities in earning potential, workers gathered in neighborhoods around the factories and developed forms of organization at the workplace and in the community that were working class in composition. Downriver, industrial development meant the rise of large-scale furniture, iron, and leather producers, and growing numbers of Evansville workers employed in these shops faced declining wages. However, they were not as socially isolated from the rest of the community as their New Albany counterparts due to the continued importance of small-scale manufacturing in these and other industries. In Evansville the pattern of interclass association remained vital, important links between the labor movement and party politicians were forged, and a greater degree of working-class assertiveness appeared than in its upstream neighbor. This is contrary to much of what the current literature would have us expect; a focus solely on the workplace or on worker associations might lead us to expect more militancy on the part of the more "proletarianized" workers in New Albany.

However, the cities offered widely divergent opportunities for party politicians. The Democrats of Evansville learned to rely on an an antiaristocratic rhetoric that was forged in the Jacksonian era. Increasing class conflict and the presence of a largely German working class provided them with the opportunity to strengthen their ties to their constituency by attacking antiunion employers. They did well to follow this strategy; it enabled them to capture important city offices and the council during the 1870s to the chagrin of the better classes. And instead of depleting worker militancy, participation in local Democratic campaigns often reaffirmed their working-class identity and loyalty.

In New Albany, class conflict posed little opportunity for politicians in the postwar era despite the militancy and political insurgency of local ship carpenters during the 1850s and 1860s within the Know-Nothing and Republican parties. The growing and exceptional economic power of W. C. DePauw forced local politicians (and shopkeepers as well) to think twice before they spoke in favor of strikes. Instead they remained silent, or they condemned militant workers, while they created special police forces and exempted the glass works from city taxation at DePauw's request. That workers did not force politicians to be more responsive to their needs is in part due to the ethnic divisions within the working class. While in

Evansville class and ethnicity reinforced each other, New Albany working-class organizations were repeatedly torn by ethnic and religious conflict.

Finally, this examination reveals the importance of the political arena for the formation of interclass alliances. In antebellum New Albany, fraternal orders like the Odd Fellows articulated a social vision that celebrated the industrious producer while casting doubt on the virtue of the wealthy. In addition significant ties were made between militant ship carpenters and the son of a master wagon maker in a fire company, ties that would lead the latter to articulate in the political realm the aspirations of his manualist neighbors in the years following the Civil War. In Evansville, this tradition remained vital well into the Gilded Age. The failure of class-specific neighborhoods to appear and the continuing importance of interclass association nourished a culture that allowed white collar workers and master craftsmen to articulate strongly socialistic appeals in defense of strike activities. Further, it is certainly of no small consequence that the man most clearly associated with the first working-class intrusion into electoral politics made his living by teaching the sons of workers the finer points of penmanship and bookkeeping that allowed a modicum of upward mobility. That the relationship was established largely within one of the established parties during the 1870s is noteworthy; it diminished the *political* impact of the Knights of Labor.[39] It is this set of relationships that this study explores.

Examination of politics and its relationship to other cultural forms offers the means to reconcile what T. J. Jackson Lears calls "the apparent contradiction between the power wielded by dominant groups and the relative cultural autonomy of subordinate groups whom they victimize."[40] Careful treatment of party and local politics, in all their intricacy, in conjunction with examinations of other forms of activity that are engaged in the public sphere, including strikes, temperance drives and local celebrations, can give us a fuller depiction of what is at stake in the political realm and the manner in which power is negotiated in industrializing communities. By enlarging the scope of the political to include these other public conflicts and celebrations, while treating party conflict in all its relevancy to class relations, we can begin to reconstruct what one historian has called a "public culture . . . a product of historical processes, one made and remade in time."[41] By doing so, we can move beyond studies of the working class toward more systematic analysis of class relations, looking for the complex sources of what David Montgomery has termed "the 'dominance' of the industrialists and the 'restraints' which they faced."[42]

PART ONE

New Albany, 1850–66: Society and Politics in the Shipbuilding Town

The town that chips,
from Hoosier trees,
Such steamboats as the *Shotwell* and *Eclipse*
Is bound to please—
Is bound to win. Her steamboats "run all night,"
And why not she,
Run through the night, and hail the morning light!
Say what lacks she?"

—From *The Commercial and Manufacturing
Advantages of New Albany, Ind.*, 1857

Last Days of the Mechanic: Patterns of Work and Association in the Shipbuilding Town

2   On the eve of the Civil War, New Albany was just the kind of place in which alliances between workers and the "middling sort" could be expected to develop and thrive. Highly skilled native-born mechanics employed in local shipyards were often prosperous and well integrated into the local associational network, and they frequently asserted themselves in the political arena to elect one of their own to office, or to defeat the public improvement schemes of the city's mercantile elite.

Their power in the community was rooted in the local pattern of industrialization. Uneven development bequeathed the city a large number of small shops and a few larger firms that employed between thirty and a hundred workers. Even within this more "modern" sector of the economy—marked by expanding firms in the shipbuilding, foundry, and furniture-making trades—there was much ambiguity. Though some manufacturers had grown wealthy enough to rival the merchant elite in economic power, most had been trained in their craft and many were still involved to some extent in the productive process. In the most important trades, skills retained sufficient salience to enable workers to acquire modest amounts of property. In this chapter, I explore class formation alongside the persistence of forms and appearances from the past. For despite increasing militancy among shipyard workers, as late as 1860 New Albany remained in many ways merely a larger and more prosperous version of the village on the Ohio River that began to build steamboats in 1818.

Founding and the Early Years

The city's origins go back to the departure of Abner, Joel, and Nathaniel Scribner from their home in Duchess County, New York, for business opportunities in the West. Struck by the potential water power of the falls of the Ohio, the brothers decided to buy a tract of land on the Indiana side of the river opposite Louisville, Kentucky. The only available parcel was a couple of miles beneath the falls, and after purchasing it for $8,000 they laid out lots for a town, naming it after the capital of their home state. Attending to the business of promotion, the Scribners sang the praises of New Albany in a real estate hand-bill. Possessing "spacious streets, public squares, markets, etc.," the proposed town boasted natural beauty "not surpassed by any in the western country." In a burst of optimistic hyperbole, they claimed the site offered unrivaled advantages as a center for trade. They were considerably more prescient when they added that "this will be one of the best ports in the United States for the building of vessels."[1]

The Scribners were interested in more than making a fortune; they were also looking for a new home. Hailing from small-town New York and Connecticut, their purchase of land by the falls put them face-to-face with the slave regime of Kentucky and the rowdy culture of the frontier. The Scribners took pains to make New Albany appealing to other Yankee Presbyterians like themselves. In their efforts to re-create a New England town on the Ohio, the Scribners gave 120 lots to the community, half for the church and half for social purposes. They also established a permanent fund of $5,000 for the maintenance of a system of public schools.[2]

Despite these efforts, New Albany was slow to live up to its billing. An early guidebook to the West noted in 1817 that the town "has been puffed throughout the Union; but has not yet realized the anticipations of its proprietors."[3] In some ways it never would, most notably in its failure to become a major port, due to its proximity to Louisville, which gathered in the bulk of regional trade. Likewise early attempts to re-create a cohesive Yankee town on the frontier failed as New Albany developed a reputation as a raw river village with crude housing and an irreligious populace. Isaac Reed, who assumed ministerial duties at the First Presbyterian Church in 1818, counted thirteen members, including the founders, out of a population of some 700. He described a town filled with poor, young, and single mechanics who had come to better their position. Of New Albany he wrote, "its morals were low; its general society was rude, and much of it profane."[4] The reverend Reed probably did not overstate the case; the only other religious institution was a small Methodist meeting house. The crudeness of the place led most passers-through to give but brief notice of it, one describing "a little village inhabited by tavern keepers and mechanics."[5]

It was with those very mechanics that New Albany's success was to lie, for it was as a center of steamboat building that it prospered. As the Scribners had hoped, proximity to timber and its position just below the falls of the Ohio made the site a convenient spot for captains to lay their boats up for repair during the low water summer months. Before long workmen in the shipyards were building steamboats as well, and between 1818 and 1820 local yards produced five for the southern trade.[6] Soon travelers were describing New Albany as a "thriving" or "business-doing" place filled with "industrious mechanics."[7]

New Albany became what it would remain throughout the nineteenth century—a manufacturing town. Unlike towns in the Northeast, where preindustrial relationships were disrupted by capitalist development, New Albany was created by it. Founded soon after the introduction of the western steamboat to the Ohio and Mississippi rivers, it was born of enterprise and the mechanical arts, building the steamboat that was so central to western commercial life. Here, the processes of capitalist development continuously transformed the character of work and of the town, sometimes in small increments, while at others in more abrupt and disruptive doses. Whatever sense of community that developed had to come second to the spirit of enterprise that so animated life in the river towns of the trans-Appalachian West.[8]

The town grew with the shipbuilding industry. In the 1820s, local shipyards produced ten steamboats; 47 and 88 were built in subsequent decades.[9] By the 1850s, New Albany was a leading construction site and the point of origin for about 8 percent of all antebellum steamboats that paddled western rivers. With time it gained a reputation for craftsmanship. As a newspaper located in downstream Evansville put it: "the glory of New Albany is in her construction of magnificent steamers. In this noble art her mechanics stand unrivaled. She is second only to Pittsburgh in the number of tons launched from her shores; but in the size of her boats, their models and strength, beauty and finish, she has no rival. The mechanics that have framed the Shotwell and Eclipse, and given them their grace, beauty, and speed, may challenge the world."[10]

With expansion of the industry came increasing numbers; by mid-century New Albany was the largest city in Indiana with 8,181 residents and ten years later more than 12,000 people made it home.[11] Growth filled local business houses with confidence. The board of trade, in an effort to attract capital, declared that New Albany offered commercial and manufacturing advantages that rivaled those of Pittsburgh, including better access to both shipping and raw materials.[12] The press concurred, adding "as a manufacturing point New Albany certainly has vastly superior *natural* advantages over Cincinnati" and forecast sanguinely that "we shall soon witness the dawn of the brightest day in our city's history."[13]

The Rise of an Elite

For some New Albanians the future looked especially bright. By midcentury local merchants had extended their commercial reach into the southern Indiana hinterland with the completion of the New Albany and Salem Railroad. Buoyed by success, a company formed to build another to Lake Erie, which its president told potential investors "must certainly become the great high road of trade and travel between the southern lines of communication concentrating at the head of river navigation below the falls, and . . . the north and east."[14] The result of rising prosperity was the consolidation of an economic elite. In 1860, when the majority of household estates amounted to less than $500, at least 117 individuals and families had accumulated over $10,000 in combined personal and real property. This group, amounting to less than 4 percent of the city's population, controlled 55 percent of locally owned wealth.[15]

Well over half were directly engaged in commerce. The largest single group were the forty-nine merchants carrying on various aspects of the wholesale and jobbing trade. These men had responded to the completion of the railroad by specializing by line of trade or by function. The editor of the New Albany *Ledger* noted the pattern in 1852, observing that "one year ago there was not an exclusive wholesale dry goods establishment in this city," whereas "now there are six." A year later he counted 34 exclusively wholesale and jobbing businesses, dealing in dry goods, groceries, hardware, queensware, notions, hats and caps, and boots and shoes. The significance of commercial enterprise in building wealth becomes more apparent on noting that every individual with an estate worth over $50,000 was either a merchant or a banker.[16]

Though the richest men in the city were merchants, the boom in steamboat building and trade opened up opportunities for some master craftsmen. This was demonstrated in newspaper articles listing the numerous firms that contributed to the completion of particularly lavish steamboats. In addition to the shipyard the building of a steamboat usually meant contracts for founders, blacksmiths, rope makers, furniture makers, and painters.[17] While many such firms were modest, some shipyards employed over thirty workers, and the largest foundry, specializing in steamboat engines, employed over a hundred.[18] Other manufacturers made their fortune by taking advantage of New Albany's newfound status as a minor trade center, expanding output of furniture, shoes, and clothing. Production in these industries at least doubled during the 1850s.[19] Just as they were for merchants, these were halcyon days for the manufacturers of New Albany; 23 boasted estates worth $10,000 or more in 1860.[20]

As fortunes accumulated, merchants, bankers, and some manufacturers began to build substantial houses on upper Main Street. In so doing, they removed their residences from the commercial hub of the city, which was undoubtedly made busier and less pleasant by the recent establishment of a railroad depot nearby. The extent to which Main Street had become an enclave of the rich is illustrated by the large number of servants, over one-third of the city total, who found employment there.[21]

In cultural association the elite reaffirmed their distance from the mass of citizens. Nowhere was this more apparent than in the membership of the First Presbyterian church. Called by one local historian "the church of the gentry," it gathered within its rather small fold many of the wealthiest men and women in New Albany. Census data reaffirm the homogeneous portrait.[22] All were native-born with the great majority hailing from the mid-Atlantic states as well as Indiana. And just under half of them were worth at least $10,000. Nearly half were directly engaged in trade—as wholesalers, retailers, steamboat captains, or bankers. A quarter were "mechanics"—except for one carpenter they were masters—and five of them owned property valued at well over $10,000. Only one master, a painter, owned an estate valued at less than $1,000.

While the city's Methodist churches were more diverse, elite Methodists were active in developing the institutions of their class. During the 1850s they established Asbury Female College, which prepared the daughters of the well-to-do for their future roles as wives and mothers.[23] The dedication of the latter was a particularly proud moment, during which one speaker praised the leadership "of this beautiful city" for showing "a deep interest in education" and for exceeding the efforts of other cities in creating "a thorough and extensive system of education for the daughters of the members and friends of that branch of the Christian church which in this State exceeds in numbers any other religious denomination."[24] The best men and women of New Albany took strides during these prosperous years to make the city something more than a midwestern backwater.

Diversity in Manufacturing

Despite the pretensions of the better sort, few residents ever lost sight of the nexus between the prosperity of the workshops and that of the city as a whole. It was the mechanics—"the bone and sinew of our city"—wrote the editor of the *Ledger*, who furnished "the strong arms and skillful hands to which New Albany is mainly indebted for her prosperity in the past, and upon whom rest her hopes for prosperity in the future."[25]

When the editor spoke of "bone and sinew," he meant both master and journeyman. Public discourse rarely recognized the existence of a working class that was in any significant way different from its employers. Most commonly masters and journeymen were spoken of as one, joined by the "interests of the trade." The editors, however, were not engaging in the obfuscation of social processes. Despite the growing size of workshops that came with the prosperity of these years, important vestiges of the artisanal mode of production remained, many of which helped to smooth ideological rough spots created by the unfolding logic of enterprise.

Employees in local workshops had some reasons to conceive of themselves and their employers as producers, instead of as proletarians and capitalists. Unlike many of their postwar successors, antebellum manufacturers were usually trained in the craft, and they often retained at least a supervisorial function over work. Commonly, these masters started out as journeymen who managed to set up their own shop. Many such concerns remained quite small, while a few grew as their owners took advantage of improving market conditions.

Both paths are illustrated by the cabinetmaking trade. At midcentury, it was made up of small shops, the largest employing nine workers and producing $8,000 in furniture.[26] The artisanal nature of the workplace is suggested by the large number of journeymen and apprentices who boarded with their bosses. In master George W. Porter's household, for example, resided his partner and two journeyman chair makers. Likewise, master John Brindley housed a journeyman and an apprentice. The pattern was a general one as at least two employees—all single and under the age of twenty-three—in each shop lived with their employer.[27]

It was in this trade that David Scott, who in 1848 worked as a journeyman chair maker, established himself as a master with cabinetmaker John Brindley.[28] By 1850, the new partnership was the largest cabinetmaking shop in New Albany, employing six men and three women who earned an average of $32 and $12 a month, respectively.

That year their sales exceeded that of the nearest local competitor by over 30 percent. Scott and Brindley assumed dominance by hiring female labor, paying it poorly, and dividing the labor process. After paying wages and settling debts incurred in the purchase of raw material, the firm's owners were left with $3,700 for rent and profit in 1850.[29] The partners reinvested capital and expanded production, and by 1854 they reportedly employed forty workers. Still they continued to "superintend the making of all their furniture themselves." Three years later, the firm physically separated distribution from production, moving its showroom to a building in the heart of the business district and moving its factory further west into the lower wards.[30] By decade's end, Scott and Brindley had increased production by more than 400 percent, and the two former journeymen had accumulated estates worth $6,500 and $10,000, respectively.[31]

Other master cabinetmakers of New Albany failed to keep up. Faced with stiff competition, they were forced to lower wages. In 1850, Scott and Brindley's male workers were paid the going rate; ten years later they were the highest paid cabinetmakers in the city.[32] Though other shops remained small, the more competitive nature of the industry undoubtedly strained relations between master and journeymen; by 1860 a master who boarded one of his workers was the exception, not the rule.[33]

The men's clothing and shoemaking industries were similarly dominated by one or two large shops that hired between seven and fourteen women. Merchant tailor John Gadient employed ten in addition to his thirty male workers, and produced pants, coats and vests worth $50,000 in 1860. The next largest shop made "all kinds of clothing" worth $12,000 while others produced less than $6,000. In like fashion, the boot and shoemaking shops of Joseph Terstegge and Jonathan Kimball employed twenty-seven and twenty-eight workers (among them seven and fourteen women), and produced shoes worth $22,000 and $15,000, respectively. Two other shops, hiring seven and ten men produced $9000 and $10,000 in boots and shoes. The rest of the industry, as in men's clothing, was conducted on a very small basis.[34]

These industries were comprised chiefly of small shops, and in that way were characteristic of local industry generally. In 1860 production in 74 of the city's 107 workshops amounted to less than $10,000.[35] As most were unmechanized, capital needs were low. Investment in only one such shop exceeded $6,000, while 41 proprietors had sunk no more than $1,000 into theirs. It was minimal capital requirements like these that enabled journeymen like David

Scott and John Brindley to open a shop, and it held out to others the possibility of achieving independence. Since 41 employed no more than three workers and 65 employed fewer than seven, work in this sector of the economy must have proceeded to some degree along traditional lines, with journeymen laboring closely under the supervision of master craftsmen.

George Hood's boot and shoe shop was probably not atypical. A currier employed in a tannery in 1848, Hood branched into shoemaking and by 1856 had opened a small shop in the Fourth Ward. In 1860 he employed three workers, to whom he paid $1,080. At $1,400, the acquisition of raw material, mostly leather, was his largest expense. The shop produced 360 pairs of boots and 728 pairs of shoes, grossing $3,078. And like other small masters, Hood did his share of repair work.[36] After paying his suppliers and workers, Hood was left with $598 with which to pay rent and support his family.[37] Certainly this was no mean figure—it was well over $200 more than what his workers averaged in wages. On the other hand, it would not support a significantly higher standard of living than that achieved by his workmen. Master Hood may have achieved independence, but not wealth.

In the production of steamboat engines and boilers, however, artisanal patterns were more clearly left behind. The largest producer of such goods, the Phoenix foundry, was owned by three partners—William Lent, Benjamin South, and W. C. Shipman—who were described by the *Ledger* as "mechanics" and "young men of energy." Hailing from Pennsylvania, they bought a small foundry in 1843. By 1860, they had substantially enlarged it so that it employed between 100 and 140 workers and consisted of foundry, fitting, boiling, finishing, pattern, and blacksmith shops, each separately supervised by a foreman.[38] Work was specialized; no worker followed the construction of an engine from beginning to end. And the owners were unable to personally supervise all aspects of the productive process.

The shipyards provide a less-dramatic departure from the artisanal workshop. Some were sizable, as the three largest employed between thirty-five and fifty workers.[39] Yet the proprietors, trained in ship carpentry, retained a significant role in the productive process, personally supervising work and often working alongside the journeymen they employed. Many of these men were long-time residents of New Albany whose skills were well known. One such master, just deceased, was remembered as meriting "approbation as a superior workman," and it was claimed that "there never worked a man for him but that honored him, and no apprentice but that loved him."[40]

The workshops of New Albany, then, were characterized by diversity. What they normally shared was that employers were skilled in the trade and took an active part in the productive process. While some masters left the physical operation of the workshop to foremen and supervisors, most did not. Though some may have accumulated substantial fortunes and in so doing may have introduced women and unskilled laborers into the workshop, some aspects of the artisanal workshop persisted, and masters as a group could still be spoken of as "mechanics."

The Skilled Work force

Diversity also marked the experience of journeymen. The prevalence of large firms in the foundry and shipbuilding trades, and the persistence of small workshops in most others created a class of skilled workers that shared little other than the experience of selling their labor to an employer. Shop size, however, reveals an important but limited amount of information about the work force. Other data, revealing the ethnic and sexual composition of the labor force, and the ability of working families to accumulate some property provide the historian with the tools to reconstruct some of the conditions under which journeymen in these trades lived and labored.[41]

A substantial minority (22.1 percent) of the manufacturing work force labored in the city's numerous small shops where no more than six workers were employed. Though small shops persisted in most trades, they were especially prevalent in the shoemaking and men's clothing industries. Here the work force underwent an ethnic transformation during the 1850s, as large numbers of Germans entered the shops. During this decade the percentage of shoemakers who were German increased from 29 to 52 percent; among tailors it grew from 44 to 63 percent. Conversely natives, the largest single ethnic group of journeymen in either trade in 1850, comprised only 31 percent of shoemakers and but 16 percent of tailors.[42] This was by no means typical, for in 1860 shoemaking and tailoring were the only manufacturing trades of any significance in which German workers numerically dominated (see table 1).

These were the trades that most extensively experienced sweated conditions, where wages were forced down and the workday was prolonged due to competition and an oversupply of labor.[43] The relatively large number of women employed in these firms—the manufacture of shoes and men's clothing were the only two industries in which both male and female workers were hired on anything ap-

Table 1. Ethnicity of Workers, New Albany, 1860

	No.	Native white	German	Irish	English	French	Scot
Building Trades	277	74.4	17.0	2.9	2.5	1.1	0.4
Shipbuilding	213	83.6	2.5	6.1	3.3	1.5	1.0
Machinists/							
Blacksmiths	139	66.9	10.1	4.3	6.5	2.9	5.0
Shoemakers	119	31.1	52.9	5.9	0.8	6.7	0.8
Painters	90	80.0	11.1	3.3	3.3	1.1	0.0
Engineers	89	87.6	5.6	3.4	2.2	0.0	0.0
Tailors	56	16.4	63.6	10.9	1.8	7.3	0.0
Leather Workers	54	55.5	35.2	3.7	3.7	0.0	0.0
Furniture Workers	51	60.8	31.4	3.7	3.7	0.0	0.0
Coopers	41	70.7	19.5	0.0	2.4	7.3	0.0
Other Metals	87	75.9	11.5	3.4	4.6	1.1	0.0
Coppersmiths/							
Tinners	38	76.3	18.4	2.6	2.6	0.0	0.0
Boilermakers	17	64.7	17.6	5.9	5.9	0.0	0.0
Moulders	16	68.8	0.0	6.3	12.5	6.3	0.0
Pattern Makers	8	100.0	0.0	0.0	0.0	0.0	0.0
Sheet Iron							
Workers	8	100.0	0.0	0.0	0.0	0.0	0.0

SOURCE: Eighth Census, population schedules, Floyd County.

proaching a regular basis—suggests that masters were using women to do the simpler, repetitive tasks of sewing and stitching to free journeymen to do more difficult chores.[44]

Shoemakers and tailors—native and immigrant—were not a prosperous group. Few accumulated as much as $500 in property; only 30 percent of tailors and 24 percent of shoemakers had achieved this modest pinnacle in 1860 (see table 2). Taking into account the large number of masters relative to workers in these trades, it is likely that no more than half of these successful mechanics were actually wage earners. While many were propertyless—52 percent of tailors and 45 percent of shoemakers—due to the structure of the industry and its low capital requirements, journeyman could still entertain hopes of achieving independence as a master, if not of great wealth.[45]

The equation was different in the shipyards. Here there was little immigrant presence, as all steamboat construction trades were dom-

Table 2. Wealth by Trade, New Albany, 1860

	Total No.	Percentage Propertyless	Percentage $1-499	Percentage $500+
Building Trades	285	38.9	21.4	39.6
Shipbuilding	213	28.6	29.6	41.8
Machinists/Blacksmiths	139	58.3	22.3	19.4
Shoemakers	119	44.5	31.1	24.4
Painters	90	57.8	21.1	21.1
Engineers	89	62.9	16.9	20.2
Tailors	56	51.8	17.9	30.4
Leather Workers	54	38.9	22.2	38.9
Cabinetmakers	51	56.9	13.7	29.4
Coopers	41	56.1	7.3	36.6
Other Metal Workers				
Coppersmiths/Tinners	38	60.1	10.5	28.9
Boilermakers	17	58.8	17.6	23.5
Moulders	16	50.0	25.0	25.0
Pattern Makers	8	25.0	37.5	37.5
Sheet Iron Workers	8	62.5	12.5	25.0

SOURCE: Eighth Census, population schedules, Floyd County.

inated by natives. While firms tended to be larger in shipbuilding, some having as many as fifty workers on the payroll, this did not have an impoverishing or degrading effect on skilled workers employed there.[46] Instead, ship carpenters and joiners commanded good wages, accumulated property at a rate higher than other workers, and successfully passed on their status to their children.

More than any other group of journeymen, ship carpenters had a high propensity toward the acquisition of property (table 2). Only 29 percent were propertyless in 1860, and most of these were young men. On settling into their middle years, they could expect to acquire enough property to buy a lot and house. A ship carpenter rarely reached his final years propertyless; in 1860, only 13 percent of all ship carpenters and joiners over the age of thirty-five were so situated.[47]

The relative prosperity of the men engaged in shipbuilding was tied to the retention of traditional work patterns. In his study of artisanal politics in London, Iorwerth Prothero describes shipwrights as "a highly skilled body of men who regarded themselves as superior to most artisans and entitled to a respectable position in life."[48] This was no less the case in the New World. Chronicling the "bastardization" of trades in New York City, Sean Wilentz asserts that maritime trades generally retained their artisanal character more than others and that none "required greater skill, commanded more respect, or held more tenaciously to established routines than did shipbuilding." As a rule, masters treated their workers with respect, each striving "to preserve his image . . . as 'a genuine mechanic.'" Though labor disputes were not unknown, they lacked the harsh rhetoric so common during strikes in other trades.[49] A similar portrait of the shipyard regime is provided by the reminiscences of Frank Harley, a ship carpenter who served an apprenticeship in New York in the 1830s. Harley depicted a trade in which highly skilled masters actively educated their apprentices in the secrets of the trade. Despite his support for unions, Harley recounted strikes for the ten-hour day with no malice toward masters; in fact, Harley had nothing but praise for the employer who took him on as an apprentice.[50]

The account books of Thomas Humphrey, a wealthy master ship carpenter who operated a shipyard together with Matthias Dowerman, suggest that similar conditions prevailed in New Albany.[51] Work groups consisted of between seven and ten skilled workmen, including a partner or two and a family member working as a journeyman. The one repairing the steamboat "Diana" during the summer and autumn of 1862 was fairly typical. For four weeks in September, six ship carpenters worked alongside Dowerman and Humphrey, each putting in five or six days of labor a week. For six days during the first half of the month they were joined by two sawyers. As work progressed on the deck and the hull, caulkers were hired to fill the seams between the planks with oakum to keep the steamboat watertight. Regardless of their trade these skilled workmen were paid about twice the daily wage that laborer Calvin Prime received for the five days he put into the project. Aside from Prime, repairs on the "Diana" were the domain of skilled workmen who were paid $2.50 a day. Work groups employed on other boats were similar in structure, though sometimes an apprentice—in one case a member of Dowerman's family—was included.[52]

The journeymen who worked on the "Diana" were a prosperous group. Four of the six have been identified in the census rolls; three of them were worth $1,500 or more, which was held almost exclusively in the form of real estate, while the total reported wealth of the other was nearly evenly divided between real and personal property and totaled $950.[53] The workers employed by Humphrey and Dowerman achieved, at least in economic terms, what Iorwerth Prothero called a "respectable position in life."[54]

Acquisition of property was eased by high wages and the structure of employment in the shipyards. Journeymen hired on with a master to complete a job, and when the work was finished they often moved on and found work in another shipyard. The Humphrey account books illustrate the matter. Between April and November of 1862, the firm repaired five steamboats. Of the six journeymen who worked on the "John Raine" in April and early May, only two continued to do so from May 26 until July 21, and they worked less than four days.[55] When work resumed on the "Autocrat," two of the six, John Poland and Sackett Cook, no longer appeared on the firm's payroll and were replaced by Isaac Cooper, Eli Holwell, and Robert King—all of whom would work on the "Diana" in the fall. By September George Lonnon left the firm's employ only to return in mid-November.[56] When times were good, as they often were during the 1850s, journeymen were able to move from shipyard to shipyard, looking for the best jobs and the best working conditions.

And they often supplemented their wages by subcontracting, usually on the building of new vessels. In the summer of 1860, 26 year old Isaac Bruce contracted with Humphrey and Dowerman to do the planking on a boat for $575.[57] Such agreements usually offered the workman more than the prevailing wage, and allowed him to work in a few yards at the same time.[58] Subcontracting also permitted former shipyard owner Sylvester Lee to ply his craft in a style somewhat commensurate with his status within the trade as a "master."[59] In some cases journeymen worked in both capacities, as subcontractor and wage laborer, at the same time in the same shipyard. Lexington Wolf, who earned $180 for "filling weels," also earned a daily wage of $2.50 for work on the same boat.[60]

High wages, plentiful work, and subcontracting made the ship carpenters a relatively secure lot, enabling them to establish a private family life that was consistent with the Victorian ideal usually associated with the middle class. Fewer than one in every five shipbuilding households included unrelated individuals.[61] In the vast majority of cases (more than 80 percent), the journeyman's wife took on no form of wage labor and spent her energies, presumably, raising children and maintaining a home. In the twenty-three instances (16.4 percent of households headed by ship carpenters) in which they worked for wages, all but two were engaged in some aspect of the needle trades, which did not necessitate leaving the home.[62] By and large it was married women in the poorer households that sought such work, but this was not always the case. In some instances it was related to the latter stages of family development and middle-class aspirations, as it was with Dummer and Annabella Hooper.

The family headed by Dummer M. Hooper, a fifty-seven-year-old ship carpenter of New England stock, owned real and personal property worth $2,700 in 1860.[63] Dummer had once owned a shipyard, but bad times had forced him out.[64] After a sojourn to California to seek his fortune, he returned to the New Albany shipyards a master in title but not in practice. Still, a journeyman's wages were considerable, and it was only when a brief depression in steamboat building put Dummer out of work in 1857 that the family was forced to seek other sources of income.[65] Annabella's wages as a seamstress, and those of her two oldest children, helped the family survive. Yet when prosperity resumed, she did not set her needle down. Eleven years Dummer's junior, Annabella had given birth to seven children between 1834 and 1848. By 1860, her youngest, Eleanor, was twelve years old and attending school.[66] No longer caring for small children, Annabella worked to supplement the income of her husband.

The combined exertions of Dummer and Annabella Hooper enabled them to maintain a relatively substantial family estate and to pass their status on to their children. In 1858, the family was largely dependent on the incomes of Susan, a teacher, and William, a bookkeeper and minister. Their climb to nonmanual occupations was no accident, for the Hoopers exemplified the virtuous, native-born artisanal family. All their children attended school until they were sixteen. At least three members of the family—Dummer, Susan, and Annabella—were active in temperance circles, and to that number Methodist minister William could probably be added.[67] Of the two remaining sons, David became a carpenter and Shadrach a blacksmith.[68] The Hoopers weathered Dummer's fall from master to journeymen quite well.

The experience of the Hoopers was not exceptional. As might be expected of a prosperous group of native-born workmen, ship carpenters sent their children to school at a high rate. Nearly 90 percent of their children between the ages of seven and fifteen attended school, a rate far higher than those for families headed by workers in other trades. Few sons of ship carpenters worked as common laborers in 1860, while 20 percent entered nonmanual occupations as ministers, teachers, clerks, or grocers. The rest followed their fathers into the skilled trades; the largest single group worked as ship carpenters.[69]

These skilled workers had carved out a comfortable niche for themselves. While masters accumulated wealth, journeymen shared in the prosperity of the trade, and there was little evidence of class tension in the wards where the shipyards were located. There, journeymen and their families managed to accumulate property, educate their children, and start them off on equal or improved career paths. Despite the growing numbers of journeymen relative to shipyards and the limited opportunities for occupational mobility that this implied, the ship carpenters of New Albany still seemed more like artisans than proletarians. Certainly they had much to protect.

Workers without a Trade

At the bottom of the social hierarchy were unskilled workers who comprised the largest occupational groups in the city. More than five hundred men alone made their living as day laborers. Lacking a marketable skill, the day laborer sold his time to his employer on the basis of brute strength. As their numbers were high wages remained low, usually about a dollar a day.[70] While some, like Calvin Prime, found sporadic employment in the shipyards, most sought work in the business district and along the wharf, transporting goods and materials. Others turned to the municipal government for work repairing the streets. In any case, work for the day laborer was unpredictable, dependent as he was on the flow of goods in and out of the city, and on the munificence of the city fathers. The bitter cold of winter that sometimes brought commerce on the river to a standstill was a frequent source of great suffering for them. Periodic calls for charity that appeared in the press every winter attest to the destitution that faced many impoverished families.[71]

A large majority of day laborers were propertyless, and less than one in seven owned as much as $500 worth of property, a rate that compares unfavorably with the experience of workers in even the poorest trades (see table 2). In part this poverty was a function of age, as a large minority of laborers with families to support accumulated some property by the time they entered their middle and declining years, and some even acquired enough to buy a fairly comfortable home. Nevertheless, over half (55.6 percent) of the heads of households over thirty-five remained propertyless.[72]

Even this modest attainment came at considerable cost. Only half of the children in such families attended school, a lower rate than that for those of most skilled workmen. The difference in experience was more striking for those between twelve and fifteen; they stayed away from the classroom at a rate of 3:1 (the ratio for the same age cohort in ship carpenter families was less than 1:4). Presumably these children were pulled out of school early so that they could work and help the family pay its bills. The numerical prominence of young German and Irish female servants in the households of the elite suggests as much.[73] The stress that this practice placed on the family was undoubtedly great, yet economic necessity demanded it be done.

It is doubtful that such girls happily worked as "help" in elite homes. An article in the press bemoaned a "shortage" of good servants. Most "girls," said the editor, were unskilled and those who were not "have no disposition to sling the pots and kettles." The crisis in domestic labor led a number of elite women to organize a meeting to seek a remedy for the situation. One woman who questioned the intentions of the "ladies," wrote that rather than find "good homes for poor girls at good living wages" as they had put it, their real motive was "to reduce the wages of those already employed." A solution, she offered, was to pay servants "a fair price for their labor" and to treat them with the respect normally accorded citizens. "There is perhaps no country in the world," she reminded her elite sisters, "where all persons feel such a repugnance to performing menial offices. Foreigners who have nothing else, soon feel it after landing on our shores. Respect that feeling ladies. It is the offspring of that glorious feeling which actuated our forefathers in their struggle for independence."[74]

Though white native-born Americans made up the single largest group of laborers (33.3 percent), the unskilled male worker, like the female servant, was commonly an immigrant and somewhat less typically a Catholic. German laborers comprised 25 percent of the total and the Irish made up 31 percent. More important, however, over 60 percent of Irish males with occupations were unskilled laborers.[75] This was due in part to the agrarian background of Irish immigrants, who unlike their German counterparts, brought little experience in the crafts as they emigrated. But this pattern was reinforced by prejudice and practice once the Irish arrived in America, much as it was for the substantially smaller black community, the only other local group concentrated so heavily in unskilled labor.[76] The Irish turned in large numbers to the only opportunity that was open to them—unskilled day labor.

Natives usually associated them with disorder. Irish laborers were largely portrayed as a criminal element, and the presumption of alcohol abuse followed all Irish. In 1854, the editor of the Democratic *Ledger* thought it remarkable that there were no reports of Irish intoxication on St. Patrick's Day. Reporting that a prosperous local car-

penter had stabbed six men on a steamboat near Evansville before
jumping overboard to his death, he assured readers that "he was an
Irishman by birth" and was drunk.[77] Many members of the Protestant churches associated Catholicism and alcohol with the ruin of
public education. Presbyterian Sunday School agent Joseph Gale de-
spaired that "Romanism prevails" in the schools and he blamed it on
the "influence of ignorant, intemperate Infidel teachers."[78] Many
New Albanians did not welcome the Irish immigrant.

The Structural Position of the Petty Bourgeoisie

Though they may not have abounded, opportunities for upward
mobility existed, even for immigrants. A number of interstitial social roles, in which individuals neither directed the economy nor
sold their labor, were open to men who aspired to escape manual labor and accumulate a modest amount of property. Within the confines of an ambiguous class structure, their position was ambiguity
itself. Many had accumulated enough property to assure a comfortable, if not luxurious, standard of living. Yet they came in daily contact with workers, either as a retailer with a working-class clientele
or as a master of a small workshop. Defined partly by wealth and
partly by status, the petty bourgeoisie included white-collar workers,
proprietors of modest retail establishments (including groceries and
saloons) and masters of small workshops.

The single largest group in 1860 were the over two hundred white-
collar workers, mostly bookkeepers and clerks employed in the commercial establishments of the city. The vast majority (88.1 percent)
were native, reflecting the dominance of the native population in the
commercial affairs of the city. For the most part, they were propertyless young men; two-thirds were under 25. Yet for the minority who
continued in these positions into their thirties, clerical work could
be financially rewarding. Of the 28 who were over the age of 35 in
1860, all but seven had property holdings worth over $500.[79]

For the sons of merchants and prosperous retailers, a job as a clerk
in the family firm served as an apprenticeship for the young aspiring
proprietor. A few white-collar workers who were employed by someone outside their family were able to use their tenure in clerical work
to gain the requisite skills and personal connections to become a proprietor in their own right. Of the 123 listed in the 1860 directory, 77
reappeared in later listings between the end of the war and the onset
of depression in 1873, and eight of them had become proprietors
without joining a family partnership.[80] This situation does not by any

means imply the existence of a well-worn path leading from rags to riches. Most came from families with commercial backgrounds or were sons of prosperous men. Such was the case of Osem Sackett, son of a wealthy master carpenter, who worked in 1860 in the wholesale drug establishment of W. J. Newkirk and who by the end of the war had set himself up as a wholesale druggist.[81] For sons of prosperous families, work as a clerk, whether for a relative or not, offered the possibility of replicating the economic success of the father.

None of the white-collar workers who came from working-class families became proprietors during these years. Those who can be traced remained clerks or salesmen.[82] This initial rise to white-collar status was the extent of occupational mobility that they experienced. And the meaning of that rise is difficult to assess. Clerical work was often unremunerative and clerks worked exceptionally long days.[83] In any case, it meant leaving the workbench behind and it represented an entry, if only a limited one, into the world of commerce.

Another upward path was the operation of a small grocery or saloon. Petty proprietorship offered aging workers a physically less-demanding work regimen as well as a measure of independence. Yet here too the experience is difficult to evaluate. Clyde and Sally Griffen emphasize the meager livelihood that many such ventures provided and suggest that their establishment was more the expression of a desire for independence than "any aspirations to success or gentility suggested by the honorific designation of white collar." Further, since they were usually patronized by a largely working-class clientele, the transition from journeymen to grocer or saloon-keeper, while occasioning a departure from the mechanic's workshop, did not remove the new proprietor from the working-class community.[84] The ease of entry into these business ventures explains, in part, the early development of a German petty bourgeoisie. By 1860, 14 percent of the local German adult male population were saloonkeepers, storekeepers or grocers. This figure was far higher than that of any other ethnic group—the percentage for native-born whites was 4.3, for the Irish it was 3.6—and in fact, Germans accounted for over 40 percent of these proprietors in the city.[85]

Rounding out the petty bourgeoisie was the small master craftsman. Distinct from workers by his position in the employment relation—he did not sell his labor time; instead he bought that of others—the small master was nonetheless distinct from more prosperous manufacturers. Employing a small number of workers, six or less for our purposes, and active in the productive process, he had not yet severed the bonds between labor and capital, still merging them within his own role in the workshop. A reminder of the days of artisanal production, the small master was not a disappearing species.[86] To the contrary, the expansion of New Albany's population and trade encouraged the growth in number of such workshops. Though over two-thirds of all workshops in New Albany were still small enough to fit the description, less than a quarter of its work force found employment there, and over 40 percent worked in establishments of thirty or more.[87] Less and less the experience of local journeymen was that of a young artisan who worked closely alongside a master. Despite this, the persistence of the small master pointed to the continuing existence of a path toward independence that was open to journeymen in some trades.

The small master played an ambiguous social role. Owning property, and employing possibly undisciplined workmen, he had an interest in social order and the subordination of workers to his authority. Social relations were not always harmonious between master and journeymen, and the need to compete with larger shops forced masters to push journeymen to produce more for less pay. And yet, still active in the practice of the craft, and with family members still working as journeymen, masters like shoemaker George Hood could hardly be lumped in the same class with wealthy shoemaker Joseph Terstegge or foundry owners William Lent or Benjamin South. Together, with the more modest retailers, grocers and saloonkeepers, small masters formed a stratum of modestly propertied and independent men who were in constant personal contact with the working class.

Yet these were men of property who, in many cases through their own sweat and aspirations, had left the workbench behind. In so doing, many may have internalized the ethos of thrift, hard work, and punctuality that promised success in a bourgeois world. And their own material success may have been translated into a general respect for the absolute rights of property. Their allegiances in the struggles of others could have great bearing in both political and industrial conflict. It was this ambiguous experience that the petty bourgeoisie brought to the fraternal associations, the fire companies, and the temperance societies of New Albany, where they discussed with workers the meaning of virtue and work in a republican society.

Social Character of the Wards

To understand precisely how people came into contact with each other, it is necessary to momentarily shift the focus from occupa-

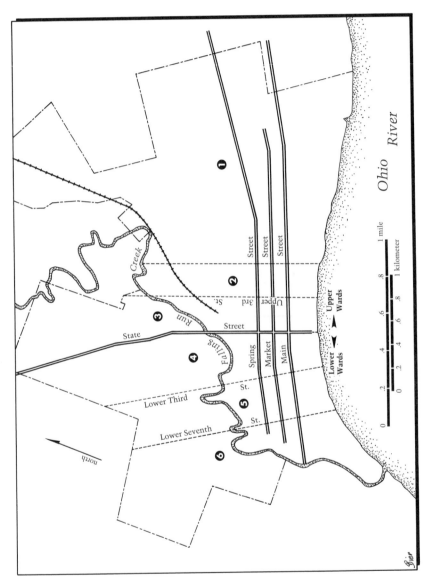

Map 1. New Albany, 1860

tional to geographic structure. Residency patterns give our under-standing of society a physical context, much as it was experienced sensibly by the historical actors.[88] It was in neighborhoods where men and women worked, lived and socialized, and it was there that responses to changing conditions would be formulated. Reconstruc-tion of residential patterns reveals that New Albany was two distinct communities, each with its own social structure and pattern of lead-ership (see map 1).[89]

The upper wards were characterized by occupational diversity. Clerks, businessmen, and professionals lived there in large numbers, taking advantage of the proximity to the business district, which was centered in the Second, Third, and Fourth wards. Considerable num-bers of German mechanics—particularly in the shoemaking and tai-loring trades, which depended on merchant-capitalists for supplying raw materials and marketing the finished product—also lived in the upper four wards. Finally, laborers of all ethnic backgrounds heavily concentrated there, particularly in the first where they made up near-ly a third of all males of working age.

While proximity to the commercial district was helpful for labor-ers looking for work, many lived on the far eastern side of the First Ward, up to fifteen blocks away from downtown. For many the sig-nificant factor was the centrality of the church for the Catholic worker. Both the German and Irish Catholic churches (they had di-vided in 1852 on ethnic lines[90]) were on the western end of the First Ward. As the churches served as social and educational institutions, as well as centers of worship, many Catholic workers settled within walking distance of them. Four of every five day laborers in the city lived in such proximity to the Catholic churches, making their homes in the upper three wards of the city.

Though the location of the church and the largely unskilled nature of the Irish immigrant created a tendency toward the creation of eth-nic neighborhoods, this was mitigated by the small size of the Irish community. Even in the First Ward there were nearly as many na-tive-born laborers as Irish. While pockets of German and Irish exist-ed, they were not extensive.[91] Often living nearby were equally im-poverished native-born laborers who found lower rents in these working-class immigrant bastions. The pattern of day laborer resi-dency suggests that class and culture in a short time had become in-extricably entangled as causes for the establishment of neighborhood patterns.

Despite the concentration of immigrants in the upper portion of the city, the native-born comprised a majority in each of the wards,

Table 3.   Wealth by Ward, New Albany, 1860

Ward	Total Wealth	Number of Wealthy	Percentage Controlled by Wealthy	Percentage Propertyless
1	$1,376,595	33	70	53.2
2	1,024,055	18	59	55.8
3	1,359,095	24	64	49.9
4	1,214,385	26	48	42.8
5	687,120	12	31	39.8
6	406,865	4	24	36.6

SOURCE: Eighth Census, population schedules, Floyd County.

even in the first. The diversity of the upper wards of the city worked against the development of a cohesive political movement of the lower orders except under the most drastic of conditions. As a result, the "best men"—bankers, merchants, and professionals—monopolized seats on the council representing the First, Second, and Third wards.[92]

Elite domination of council seats corresponded to their position atop the social structure. The wealthy controlled nearly two-thirds of the property owned by inhabitants of the upper three wards. Thirty-three individuals who lived in the First Ward alone owned estates worth at least $10,000, whereas the majority of men over the age of sixteen in the upper wards lived in families that owned no property, or they were propertyless boarders (see table 3).

If diversity and inequality were the hallmarks of the upper part of the city, the opposite characterized the lower. Location of the shipyards along the riverfront of the Fifth and Sixth wards led to the rise of a mechanic's community. There masters and journeymen who engaged in the steamboat trades made their homes. Ship carpenters and joiners alone constituted 27.9 percent of the adult male population of the Sixth Ward. Because these mechanics were largely native-born whites (76.5 percent), the lower wards acquired a distinct character from the rest of the city, lacking the small ethnic neighborhoods of the upper wards. Due to the predominance of skilled workers in well-paid trades, as well as the relative absence of the rich (only four families with over $10,000 in wealth made their homes in the Sixth Ward), the lower two wards were marked by a considerably more equitable division of wealth.[93] The mechanics there normally elected master craftsmen or journeymen to the city council. Here, the ethos of artisanal republicanism was most evident, and it was from these wards that the most significant challenges to elite control of the city would come.

Plebeian Culture: Vestiges of an Artisanal Past

In a city with so much ambiguity in its social structure, it is not surprising that cultural institutions continued to reflect artisanal patterns. As late as 1860, a truly "working-class" culture had yet to emerge in New Albany. Instead, skilled workers commonly joined in association with significant numbers of *petit bourgeois*—clerks, retail storekeepers, and masters of the more modest workshops. Persistent throughout the wide range of organizations for which data exist, the pattern suggests the existence of what Francis Couvares has called a "plebeian culture," which he describes as a "broad, public inheritance that included citizens of all kinds—save, perhaps, for a small elite too genteel or too scrupulous to indulge in common leisure."[94] Based in the neighborhoods of the "walking city," plebeian culture was fiercely localistic. Shopkeepers relied on a native, Irish, and German working-class clientele, and wage earners made their homes near the workshops that employed them. The close, personal nature of the walking city nurtured a culture common to the lower and middling orders of urban society, with its own amusements, symbols, and associations.

The lodges of the Odd Fellows, which attracted members from the lower and middle orders, best illustrates this pattern. Aside from its fraternal aspects, it was the order's function as an insurance benefit society that made it especially appealing to workers. As one member wrote, the role of the Odd Fellows was "to guard its members against what is most to be dread in these unavoidable ills of life; or rather to prevent their coming to such a condition by affording timely relief. It is not poverty, sickness and death which are so much to be dreaded; but the consequences to which they lead, either in our own case or that of our families, or both together."[95] Contributors to the *Western Odd Fellows' Magazine*, published in New Albany in 1852–53, distinguished the society's relief function from charity. Odd Fellows received aid whether rich or poor so that "when a poor man receives a benefit, the heart is not made sick and the feelings crushed and degraded by the thought that it is bestowed because he is poor." Writers emphasized that when an Odd Fellow received relief, he did so "as a man ... because he is a *man*, not because he is poor and needy." The goal was "to preserve the feeling of equality, and the dignity of a *man*."[96]

Through the benefit function and the rhetorical flourishes over independence and manly dignity, the Odd Fellows appealed to those men who had accumulated small amounts of property and whose families faced poverty in the event of death or injury. The leadership of local lodges bears this out. With the exception of two trustees of Hope Lodge No. 83, no merchant, professional, or wealthy manufacturer appeared in the published lists of officials. None owned over $5,000 in property. The Odd Fellows, unlike the elite-dominated Masons, were composed of men of limited means; indeed, 41 percent of the *leadership* owned less than $500 in property.[97]

Odd Fellowship was rooted in the self-help movement of English workingmen in the nineteenth century.[98] In part, its lodges were formed in imitation of the Freemasons who, as one observer noted, obtained "noblemen and gentlemen of the first rank" as members. Though the insurance aspect of the order eventually became dominant, from the start they emphasized brotherhood and conviviality. Similarities in ritual, meeting place, and membership with early trade unions suggest that the Odd Fellows arose out of the artisan community.[99] In New Albany the order retained some of its original social base. Journeymen accounted for a large share of the leaders, numbering about one-third of the total. This was particularly the case in New Albany Lodge No. 1, which elected a screwcutter, four printers and a small master boat builder to office in 1859. The next largest group were master craftsmen. Some like carpenter William Bane of Hope Lodge were propertyless, while a few others like pump and block maker John Roberts, who was worth $4,700, were considerably better off. All told, "mechanics" comprised 58 percent of the order's local leadership. Nearly all the rest were storekeepers and white collar workers. The Odd Fellows, then, united in association journeyman and master, as well as mechanics with clerks and retailers in cultural association.

This interclass pattern was reflected in the pages of the *Western Odd Fellows Magazine*, which read like a primer for "self-made men."[100] Liberally sprinkled through its pages were appeals to industry, honesty, temperance, thrift, and brotherly love. One quizzed the reader, "Did you ever see a man who was punctual, who did not prosper in the long run?[101] Writers offered admonitions against idleness urging readers not to be "too proud too work" or to be "ashamed of a hard fist or a sunburnt countenance." Most of all, they urged, "let no man be ashamed of poverty," for only "ignorance and sloth" as well as "dishonesty and idleness" were deemed truly shameful.[102]

Left at that, the journal hardly seems different from other guides to success in the bourgeois world. But that is not what the Odd Fellows were about; instead they were self-consciously *petit bourgeois* in outlook. In an exercise of self-definition, one leader wrote, "our rank have not contained those who are clothed in purple and fine linen, and who fare sumpuously [*sic*] every day, not those who could be esteemed the lords of creation, because of advantages which they themselves had little agency in procuring." Instead Odd Fellows were "engaged in the daily struggle for subsistence." Such men, "however humble their occupations, and lowly their pretensions," possessed qualities "on which the safety of the nation will at last be found to rest."[103]

Sometimes articles took a defensive posture. For instance, one writer attacked Henry Ward Beecher's suggestion that the "honor" accorded callings was in direct proportion to the intellect demanded for their proper exercise. In response the writer argued that social rank was rooted in profits, "hence, book publishers rate above authors, because publishing is more profitable than authorship; and merchants above mechanics, because the trade of the former makes men rich, while the toil of the latter merely gains them a livelihood."[104]

The critique of idle wealth and the anti-elite sentiment among the Odd Fellows frequently went hand-in-hand with Victorian ideas about gender. Like men, it was argued, women must work industriously, though the sphere for them to engage in their calling was in the home. However, the daughters and the wives of the rich were another matter entirely. One writer warned, "once you allow a girl's head to get full of finery and her heels full of waltzes, polkas and cotillons, you may as well throw her books into the fire, and marry her to the first simpleton who will take her off your hands—for her days of study and improvement are at an end."[105] Riches led to degradation and a loss of purpose. A short witticism defined "somewhere else" as "a place that a rich man's wife always wants to go to." The author tartly prescribed a remedy "to cure this species of ennui" by recommending she take "a short course in poverty and a scrubbing brush."[106]

Both in social composition and ideology, the Odd Fellows suggest an earlier stage of historical development when craft workers considered themselves—along with farmers—the virtuous portion of society. Though industrialization had forged two distinct classes out of the artisanal workshop, significant ideological vestiges persisted. One such remain was the notion of the virtuous middling orders of society "on which the safety of the nation will at last be found to rest."[107] The Odd Fellows remained true to this heritage. Here are the

roots of their concerns about the respective "intellects" of the merchant and the mechanic, and their obsession with industry and the
equation of the rich with idleness. Implicit in the pages of the journal is an agreement with one of the general tenets of producerism—
that dignity derives from one's industry and direct involvement in
labor, not in the mere accumulation of wealth.

Despite this and the collective self-help nature of the Odd Fellows,
the overall tone of the *Western Odd Fellows Magazine* was individualistic and bourgeois, praising such values while condemning the
bourgeoisie.[108] Ideas that once more or less expressed the joint interests of master and journeyman in the artisanal workplace, by the
1850s, seemed to legitimate social relations between classes. Be
punctual and honest, so the Odd Fellows read, and a man cannot help
but prosper. The constant repetition of the optimistic cant of bourgeois individualism suggests that associations like the Odd Fellows
played a role in the legitimation of capitalist dominance.

Of course, we might expect this of an association that was led
largely by the petty bourgeoisie. But the interclass nature of the Odd
Fellows and their continued adherence to producerism makes them
important in defining the roots of community support for labor. The
defense of the dignity of the laborer and the critique of the idle rich
were essential elements of the culture that the Odd Fellows borrowed from and sustained. In such language lay much of the foundation for working-class radicalism.

The fire companies were a more publicly visible part of the plebeian network. Recent historians have focused on antebellum fire companies as working-class institutions. Bruce Laurie, for example, describes them as bastions of "traditionalists"—journeymen who
worked in small workshops where traditional rhythms of work and
leisure prevailed. Laurie points out that while they provided a necessary service to property owners, the firemen also used fire companies
as social institutions. Competitions between companies were common while businessmen condemned their rowdiness and their tendency to abandon work at the first sound of an alarm.[109]

In New Albany, fire companies similarly played a dual role, regularly mixing fire fighting with competition. Notice of a fire occasioned a
race to the burning edifice, followed by efforts to squirt the largest
stream of water and best impress onlookers. At less-urgent times companies gathered in front of tall buildings to hold stream-throwing du-
els. By the end of the 1850s this had become a popular sport and companies traveled as far as Indianapolis to challenge others.[110] On
holidays and at public celebrations, like the one in honor of the laying

of the Trans Atlantic cable, fire companies paraded in full regalia. On that occasion the *Ledger* praised them as "the most active" participants, and noted "they form the principal attraction of every procession, except those composed entirely of the secret fraternities."[111]

Like other organizations, the fire companies elected men from both the working class and the middling sort to positions of leadership. As with the Odd Fellows, mechanics filled most of the positions, though in this case journeymen held over 50 percent of them. The rest were mostly master craftsmen, retailers, and white-collar workers. But unlike the Odd Fellows, the fire companies included an occasional merchant, professional or manufacturer. Otherwise, the companies seem to have been, like the Odd Fellows, the domain of men of limited means.[112]

Two companies were particularly dominated by mechanics. Leadership of the Franklin company in the First Ward was the province of journeymen and small masters in the building trades. But only in the Sixth Ward did a fire company elect an overwhelming majority of journeymen to positions of leadership. Nine of the eleven officers there were wage earners involved in the building of steamboats.[113] The only master, Josiah McLain, was a thirty-three-year old cordwainer who had managed to save $100, and the only "nonproducer" was a young teacher, James V. Kelso, who was worth $200.

Relief Company No. 5, in the heart of the shipbuilding Sixth Ward, most closely approximated a working-class organization in antebellum New Albany. Class, however, was not the only measure that characterized this company; its leaders were all native-born. This was not the case in other companies, especially those in the upper three wards that elected some Germans to office. The fire companies of New Albany, more than being intrinsically working class, reflected the social composition of the neighborhoods in which they were located. In most cases this led to the inclusion of a considerable number of petty bourgeois.

The domination of petty bourgeois leadership within a fire company could affect the nature of social intercourse within them, as is evident from the by-laws of the Hook and Ladder company of the Third Ward. Journeymen filled but 31 percent of the Hook and Ladder's official positions; the rest fell to retailers, master craftsmen, and white-collar workers. The results were rules against disorderly conduct or intoxication, and the discussion of political or religious topics. Appearance at meetings and fires was enforced by a system of fines.[114] Far from the model of traditionalist behavior, the Hook and Ladder company, at least in intent, was an orderly company of temperate men. The extent that intention was parlayed into practice is unknown; so is the degree to which other companies incorporated similar guidelines into their by-laws. It is clear, however, that local fire companies were not unqualified bastions of working-class traditionalism.

Hostility to drink was also manifest in plebeian temperance associations that had their origins in the Washingtonian movement of the 1840s. Before the Civil War, New Albany boasted five of these, four of which were led by men of small means engaged in mechanical occupations. None of these leaders had amassed an estate worth more than $4,000, and slightly less than half were journeymen. The rest were a cross section of petty bourgeois New Albany.[115]

In some cases, like that of the family of ship carpenter Dummer Hooper and his wife, Annabella, enthusiasm for temperance went hand-in-hand with involvement in the Methodist church. Wesley and Roberts chapels were located in the lower wards and their strong ties to the mechanics' community are suggested by their respective nicknames, "old ship" and "yawl."[116] Methodism was attractive to many workers due to its egalitarian views regarding sin and the dispensation of grace. The strong strain of perfectionism in John Wesley's theology remained both an inducement toward discipline and a potent source of reforming zeal, and the mechanics' temperance societies were one of its manifestations.[117]

Since the Odd Fellows also worked to promote temperance, their writings on the subject provide an opening into the spirit of plebeian temperance. For them drinking was a destructive act that destroyed a man's dignity. Consequently, the editors of the *Western Odd Fellows' Magazine* warned young women: "never marry a man who is addicted to the use of ardent spirits. Depend upon it, you are better off alone, than you would be if you were tied to a man whose breath is polluted and vitals are being gnawed out by alcohol."[118] The intemperate, they sermonized, were "a burden to themselves, a disgrace to the community, and a curse to their families." In response to charges that the order countenanced intemperance by not excommunicating drunkards, the editors responded, "as Odd Fellows we strive to reclaim the erring, to sustain the falling, to raise and redeem the fallen. This cannot be done by expulsion, or by any other mark of disgrace, which a lodge can affix."[119] Readers were reminded that the alcoholic "is a man, and as such a brother" and that his death demands "our grief for him and our sympathy for his family" for "our laws require of us to do all for him and for his family that we could do for the most worthy and most consistent member."[120]

Absent from their discourse was a compulsion to purify the order of evil. Intemperance was treated as an illness; the drinker was to be cured and strengthened, not shunned, and his family was to be sustained. The workers and petty bourgeois of the Odd Fellows were too close to the deprivations of want themselves to withdraw aid from a brother, though an intemperate one, and his family in need. In any case, it is clear that if plebeian culture sustained the drunkard in taverns, it also was capable of sustaining the teetotaler.

It is probably the size of New Albany that explains the associational pattern elaborated here. As opposed to the large metropolis where large neighborhoods defined by ethnicity and class kept different groups apart, the small city was marked by more personal relations.[121] The paucity of meeting halls and theaters on the outskirts of town, as well as the continued importance of the central marketplace lured all classes to the center of town on a regular basis. Celebrations and political rallies frequently were communitywide affairs. It is likely that the highly visible nature of organizations like the fire companies, which played a role in most local parades, motivated small businessmen to participate in an urban institution that in larger places had been abandoned to workers.

The associations of plebeian New Albany and the ideas that can be ascribed to them suggest an ambiguous cultural landscape, not unlike the nature of its social structure. The presence of "middling" types in association with journeymen opens numerous possibilities. For one, it suggests that languages like republicanism and producerism were open to interpretation and were probably filtered through the experience of these modestly propertied men. Values of punctuality and the dignity of manual labor existed side by side. While this pattern may have served to defuse class tensions at times, at others it might have had opposite effects. When industrial strife came to New Albany, these "older community ties" that the middling sort had established with workers led some to overcome their class position in supporting striking workers against the industrial employer.

The Ambiguity of Economic Development

Economic growth left New Albany with an ambiguous legacy on the eve of the Civil War. Joining a predominantly commercial elite were successful masters like foundryman Peter Tellon, shoemaker Joseph Terstegge, cabinetmaker John Brindley, and ship carpenter Thomas Humphrey. Of this group, only Humphrey is known to have been closely involved in the work process in 1860. Despite this growth of a manufacturing elite, artisanal practices persisted. Certainly this was true in the shipyards. But even in other industries employers were skilled in the trade, and though at the moment appeared as capital personified, distinct from labor, their personal histories and their understandings of their trades that they had gathered from their own experience at the mechanic's workbench suggested otherwise. As of 1860, a class of capitalists untrained in the mechanical arts had not yet appeared. Monied men still sought to gain their fortunes in commerce and real estate, not in manufacturing.[122]

Alongside the larger establishments, a considerable number of modest workshops, characterized by small capital investment and a handful of employees, continued in more traditional ways. Shop size prevented the application of much of a division of labor, and masters commonly joined journeymen in the production of goods. Here ambiguity was most apparent, for while production seemed to proceed along traditional lines, the growth of larger shops locally, in Louisville, and throughout the West, had transformed the nature of the market. To compete with these more efficient producers, small masters either turned to the custom trade or sweated their workers, lowering wages and increasing the work load. In most of these trades, masters were aided by the increase of skilled labor that came with German immigration. What at first glance seemed artisanal in nature, truly was something different.[123]

Though its ideological manifestations had yet to emerge, a diverse working class—divided by skill, wealth, and ethnicity, but nonetheless a class—was in the process of "being made." Sharing the experience of being on the same end of the wage labor contract, the city's wage earners, nearly half of whom were propertyless, lived a precarious economic existence. An important exception were the ship carpenters, joiners, and caulkers, who were able to augment their daily wage by engaging in subcontracting, and who tended to accumulate more property than other workmen. Yet due to the concentration of ownership of the shipyards in the hands of a few mostly wealthy masters, the continued prosperity of journeymen in the shipbuilding trades could easily be placed in jeopardy. It was only slightly ironic that the journeymen best able to preserve the status of the skilled artisan were the ones who would in the years to come signal the emerging rupture within the mechanics' community.

From "Mechanic" to "Worker": The Emergence of Class Politics, 1854–66

3 The evening of July 21, 1860, was an uncomfortably hot one; despite the stifling heat, some six thousand men jammed the public square for a Democratic party ratification meeting. To view the proceedings, women crowded the yards and doorways of adjacent residences as well as the balcony of the Tabler House. Balloons and rockets were sent to the heavens while the Cornet Band played. The scene approached, thought the editor of the *Ledger*, "a splendor rarely achieved." After seventy-six officers were selected, Col. W. W. Tuley, a scion of a wealthy family, addressed the assembled and offered a resolution ratifying the nomination of Stephen Douglas for the presidency and endorsing "the principle of non-intervention by Congress in the domestic affairs of the people of the Territories, as the only true and solid basis of national concord and peace." Then E. A. Maginess, a druggist of more modest means, inveighed mightily against both "northern and southern sectionalism."[1]

The concern with peace and unity expressed by the speakers at this meeting of the local Democracy paralleled the unstated but symbolic role that the ritual itself played for the participants. For there in the town square, all strata of the local social structure congregated in an impressive display of political unity and purpose. It was the dynamics of party politics that led elites to associate with workers whose normal association pattern rarely extended beyond the reach of plebeian New Albany. The seventy-six officers selected underscores this break in the pattern. Seventeen of those identified (30 percent) were from elite families. Among them were publishers, manufacturers, merchants, bankers, lawyers, and farmers. On the other hand, the property holdings of fifteen others (26.8 percent) amounted to less than $2,000, and journeymen like steamboat engineer J. W. Swift, an officer of the local engineer's union, boat joiner David Harbison, and ship carpenter Thompson Jones joined the elite in political battle.

For the wealthy, the political arena offered prestige and power. Organizing the local party machinery was a necessary prerequisite to rising in the state and national party apparatus. But local politics offered more. Control of the council could assure support for plans of improvement like the construction of railroads that might improve local business. For plebeian New Albany political life promised an opportunity to assert citizenship in a political democracy on an equal basis with their social betters, offering as Michael McGerr argues, a forum "to declare their worth and to diminish, symbolically, the social distance between" the classes.[2] What is more, it allowed them to express approval or disdain for the schemes of the rich.

No matter the goal, success usually demanded that appeals be made to the large numbers of laborers and journeymen who filled out the bottom of the social structure. Failure to do so by one party risked the mass movement of workers into the other, a certain formula for continual defeat. Workingmen were actively involved in the political culture of nineteenth-century America. It was hardly strange or foreign to them. Though they often made racial and ethnic appeals, the instinct for survival led many politicians to cast their arguments in a way that reaffirmed class ways of thinking. Generally they referred to all those involved in manufacturing as "mechanics," regardless of wealth or relation to manual work, rather than to a wage-laboring class of workers. This broadest form of producerism retained its explanatory power up to the outbreak of the war. Though strikes were not unknown in the antebellum era, they rarely occasioned much excitement and they had minimal impact upon political discussion.

Still, economic issues did come between businessmen and the mechanics (in the broad sense) of the shipbuilding trades. This political division was reinforced by residency patterns and ethnic hostility exacerbated by the rise of the nativist Know-Nothing party. However, it was the experience of war—including the draft, the failure of wages to keep up with prices, and the debate over black equality that led to riot among the poor of the upper wards and to the permanent organization of workers in the shipyards—that was instrumental in the emergence of a clear and distinct working-class presence in politics.

Episodes of Unrest

In spite of the overall harmonious melody of the 1850s, dissonant notes were occasionally heard, the loudest coming from the employees of the sole local corporation—the New Albany and Salem Railroad. Employing about 125 workers, the company experienced trouble with its labor force both in the train yards and in its machine shops. Problems first arose when the company attempted to force employees to sign a waiver absolving it from financial responsibility in case of accident. While most complied, a majority of engineers refused and were fired. When the explosion of a locomotive boiler resulted in the death of an engineer and a fireman and the injuring of a brakeman, the Louisville *Courier* blamed the company. The new men, charged the editor, were "incompetent for the duties of the position" and culpability was attributed "to the dismissal of the experienced engineers." The New Albany *Ledger*, however, stood by the local corporation, denying both that the engineer was new and that the company was responsible.[3] Mostly, it ignored the conflict, mentioning only the end of the "difficulty" four months later, noting that "hereafter the freight and passenger trains will make their regular trips."[4]

Another "misunderstanding" arose the following spring over nonpayment of wages to workers in the company's machine shop. Financial difficulties led railroad president James Brooks, a local merchant, to order the superintendent to pay only half the wages due, and this in devalued company paper. In a meeting at the courthouse, the workers resolved not "to strike another blow for the New Albany and Salem Railroad Company" until they received their pay. A committee of three was appointed to discuss the matter with Brooks, who promptly discharged them. The next day Brooks met the workmen in the shop and blamed the unrest on "a few dissatisfied spirits." He warned that he could "obtain five hundred men in one day to go to work for half pay, even if they never get the balance." The unhappy men resolved to continue their strike, though there is no further record of it.[5]

Discontent over the matter lingered a couple of years. Two ex-machine shop employees unsuccessfully tried to convince the local Know-Nothing organ, the *Tribune*, to condemn company policy. The editor recognized one of them as an "instigator" of the strike and accused him of "striving to sow the seeds of discontent among the other hands now at work, out of sheer revenge for his own dismissal."[6] Seeking to discredit them, the editor wrote that on a visit to the shops there were no signs of dissatisfaction among the workmen and that relations between employer and workers were never better.

There may have been an element of truth in the editor's words. Dissatisfaction over irregular payment of wages did not stop workmen in September 1857 from presenting the resigning master mechanic with a gold watch, seal, and chain worth $317.[7] The discharging of a number of workers in the shop the following month due to "the pressure of the times" underscored the weak position unorganized workers held vis à vis corporations like the New Albany and Salem Railroad.[8] The dependency of workmen on the company was never clearer than it was the following spring after a destructive fire had reduced the shops to ashes. Suspecting arson, the *Ledger* estimated that five hundred persons who were dependent on the machine shops "for their bread" would suffer as a consequence. As the shops were under-insured, it became apparent that rebuilding would proceed only with local support.[9] Taking the lead of the master machinist, workers met to raise funds for the company. Over 90 percent of the employees subscribed, mostly in increments between $5 and $25, though some highly paid workers—fitters, blacksmiths and engineers—subscribed $50 or more.[10] Despite ill feelings caused by the irregular payment of wages, workers in the shops preferred it to unemployment.

Though ship carpenters were better off than the employees of the railroad, the shipyards experienced a strike in the summer of 1856. Taking advantage of one of the busiest years at local dry docks, the mechanics demanded a raise of 25 cents a day for unskilled labor, and an increase from $2.00 to $2.50 for skilled work. With the great amount of work waiting to be done in New Albany and elsewhere, ship carpenters were "in demand at very high wages," and it is likely that the strike was quickly settled.[11] No permanent organization resulted as the strike was less a protest against employers than the collective effort of highly skilled workers to improve their market value.

Only two groups of local workers took steps to establish organizations before the war. The first were the journeymen stonecutters, who in 1854 adopted a set of "bye-laws" while engaged in a strike to obtain a higher "bill of prices."[12] A few years later the journeymen steamboat engineers seceded from the New Albany Beneficial Association, whose constitution forbade the discussion of wage rates.[13] By 1857, they affiliated with the Grand Union Association of Steamboat Engineers, which required locals to adopt a standard of wages no lower than that adopted by the general association. In addition, the union regulated apprenticeship, restricting it to men who were "practical blacksmiths or machinists of at least three years standing."[14]

In smaller workshops where collective action was more difficult, the divergent interests of journeyman and master were still liable to erupt into conflict, as they did in the shoemaking shop of George and

John Trinler. The incident resulted from the decision of journeyman Milo Turner to leave their employ to "tramp." A bloody brawl ensued, after which the Trinlers rushed to the local justice of the peace and had Turner arrested for assault and battery. The justice proved less obliging than the masters had hoped, however, discharging Turner and convicting the Trinlers for assault on the basis of testimony from another employee—which nearly led to yet another brawl between the Trinlers and the witness.[15]

Apart from the state of affairs existing between the New Albany and Salem Railroad and its employees, local workplaces were marked by an absence of sustained working-class discontent and organization. Like the withholding of highly needed skills by the ship carpenters during a prosperous building season, or the decision of journeyman shoemaker Milo Turner to "tramp" against the will of his masters, protest tended to be spasmodic, reflex responses to events or situations. The events chronicled here fail to indicate an awareness of an essential and permanent chasm dividing the workplace.

Mechanics, Producerism, and Politics

Strong class sentiments rarely made their way into local political discourse in the fifties. Though politicians appealed to workers, their interests were rarely described as being opposed to those of another class, or even individuals of another class. Instead a more abstract and generalized discourse fueled by producerism prevailed, which allowed politicians to argue that the interests of "mechanics' and "workingmen" would best be served by any of the following remedies: the defense of free public schools, immigration reform, the continued subjugation of blacks and the nonextension of slavery into western territories. At the same time, this discourse allowed workers to press their own demands in the political arena.

Until 1854, New Albany was, like the rest of southern Indiana, Democratic in its politics. Floyd County was a stronghold of the Democracy, largely due to the southern origin of many of the inhabitants, and Democrats were particularly dominant in the rural townships. Political conflict was more competitive in New Albany, where manufacturing and commerce created more interest in a strong central government that would have the power to improve the region's transportation network.

The basis of political division in New Albany was most visibly a geographical one, as the lower two ship-building wards—and particularly the sixth—consistently voted at odds with the rest of the city.

The spring election of 1854 was an especially strong example of this kind of political behavior on the part of the voters of the Sixth Ward. The ship carpenters there threw their support to mechanics, be they master or journeyman. For the office of City Clerk, banker and Democrat Elijah Sabin won a plurality in every ward, except the sixth, where he came in third with 14 percent of the vote. Similarly, treasurer-elect Samuel M. Dorsey, a grocer and a Democrat, won a majority in the upper three wards, a solid plurality in the fourth and a bare plurality in the fifth. In the Sixth Ward Dorsey came in last in a field of five, appearing on a mere 11.4 percent of the ballots. In both cases, the mechanics of the sixth supported a ship carpenter in a losing effort. Journeyman Thomas Ellis (a resident of the first ward) won 57.8 percent of their votes in his losing candidacy for city clerk, while master yawl builder Henry T. Wible won a plurality in the ward with 30 percent of the vote in his unsuccessful bid for the office of treasurer. Neither Ellis nor Wible received over 21 percent of the city-wide total. When given a choice between two mechanics, Sixth Ward voters opted for the native son. Jonathan Kelso, a Whig, received 77 percent of the mayoral vote in the sixth, where he had operated a wagon-making shop. In the other five wards, however, Kelso gathered between 25 and 37 percent, losing the election to master blacksmith Joseph A. Moffett, a Democrat.[16]

It might appear that the Sixth Ward electorate was resolutely Whig in a city where the Democrats normally prevailed in political contests, but this clearly was not so. When no mechanic was running, the shipbuilding community could strongly support a Democrat, as it did when it gave Michael C. Kerr 82.1 percent in his successful bid for the office of city attorney. No other ward named Kerr on more than 67 percent of its ballots. However, subsequent events would make the Sixth Ward voter more partisan.

Soon after the spring election, cryptic notices appeared in the *Tribune*, up to then a Whig organ, detailing meeting places and times for the secret lodges of the Know-Nothing movement.[17] By the end of the summer, Know-Nothing lodges were strong enough to dominate the local "People's" convention that nominated an anti-Democratic slates.[18] The success of the "People's" ticket that swept the county election, largely on the basis of capturing 61.9 percent of the vote within the city of New Albany, signaled the end of Democratic dominance of local politics.[19]

Know-Nothingism proved a powerful political force in other manufacturing cities, feeding on heightened concern over the danger to republican institutions posed by growing numbers of mostly Catholic German and Irish immigrants. Calling for an extended period of naturalization, Know-Nothing leaders accused Democrats of buying elections with the aid of these newcomers.[20] Accordingly, New Albany Know-Nothings resolved just before the congressional election of 1854 "to guard the purity of the ballot box at all hazards."[21] On election day, a number of Irish were beaten at the polls as they attempted to vote, and gangs of young native-born males roamed the Irish neighborhoods of the upper wards, hurling stones through the windows of the city's Catholic churches and a number of Irish homes.[22] What began as an attempt to defend against electoral fraud—and it was defended as such[23]—was transformed into a general attack on the local Irish community.

Hostility to the Irish ran high in some quarters. Most Irish were poor unskilled laborers who rarely fraternized with the rest of New Albany society.[24] The only contact that many New Albanians had with them was what they read in the press, and on nearly a daily basis that meant reports of drunkenness and criminality.[25] When the Democratic State Convention in May 1854 adopted a plank opposing a proscriptive temperance law, it appeared that Democrats and German and Irish immigrants had struck an unholy alliance to keep republican society mired in sin.[26] For many the Irish, and in many cases the Germans too, were nothing but a baneful influence upon American social and political life.[27]

In defense of its immigrant constituency the editor of the *Ledger* applied the tenets of producerism. It was true that the Irish were largely poor laborers. Yet he reminded his readers that "labor is the great original source of all wealth" adding that "the capitalist may speculate and make money but let him examine closely and he will find it is the laborer's toil that lies at the foundation of his wealth." Failure to "protect the laborer" and efforts to drive him out of the city, he warned, would lead to "decay and retrogression." Three days after the violence the *Ledger* ran a short article defending laborers as "the palace builders of the world" and queried "who dares to cast odium on such an eminent and patriotic race?"[28]

Local political life of the mid-1850s revolved around more than ethnic and religious antagonisms. Know-Nothing victory was closely tied to the political turmoil unleashed by the Kansas-Nebraska Act, which created great difficulties for northern Democrats who had long portrayed themselves as the party of white workingmen. Now they appeared to have traded the interests of free white mechanics in exchange for the political favors of Democratic slaveowners.[29] These problems are illuminated in the response to the bill by the editors of the *Ledger*, who first opposed it, swearing allegiance to the Missouri Compromise. Arguing that Nebraska should be organized as a free territory if at all, they cast the scheme in ignoble light, declaring it an "attempt to force the administration and its friends into a measure that violates twice-plighted faith, for the benefit of a presidential aspirant."[30]

Over a month later, the *Ledger* accepted the inevitability of the measure's ultimate passage, speaking of it as a concession to the South. To make it more palatable, the editors urged adoption of a Homestead Act, which would compensate northerners by giving "the poor men of the North an opportunity to settle in the new territory before the slavery question is finally decided."[31] But reasons for doubt abounded. Only a few days before, the *Ledger* had responded to a sectional vote in the Senate that had excluded foreigners from the processes of popular sovereignty, charging that the South was not "satisfied with the repeal of the Missouri Compromise" but was now determined to disfranchise men eligible to vote in Indiana.[32]

By the end of May, however, the *Ledger* had dutifully lined up behind the party. Popular sovereignty was the proper policy, declared the editors who argued that if it was not, "then Republicanism is wrong, and Democracy has no basis upon which to rest." They tried to convince their readers that the issue was not sectional, but rather the old contest between "Aristocracy and Democracy."[33] For many of the rank and file, however, these arguments were unconvincing. The Democratic party had always drawn considerable support from the South, and in the days, months, and years after the passage of the Kansas-Nebraska Act, its subservience to the interests of southern slaveowners became increasingly difficult to tolerate for northerners imbued with a belief in equality and a vision of a producer's republic. In response to Senator Douglas's bill, a number of local Democrats turned to the Know-Nothing movement as the vehicle in which to distance themselves from the increasingly proslavery Democracy.

The issue that excited the most interest, however, was a local one. In early 1855, a movement arose to prevent the city council from ratifying a decision to subscribe to $400,000 in stock of the New Albany and Sandusky City Railroad.[34] On March 3, at a well-attended citywide meeting chaired by ship carpenter Dummer Hooper, the assembled warned the council not to do so until after the upcoming local elections, threatening to "employ all legal means to rescind" such a decision.[35] The council ignored this threat, voting seven to four to ratify, both members from the Sixth Ward—one a Whig, the other a Democrat—voting against the measure.[36] Ratification and the tax it necessitated caused a furor, especially among "small property-holders, mechanics, and laboring men" of the lower wards.[37] Though the press of both parties continued to support the railroad, the debate crystallized the division between parties and established the ship-building community of the lower wards as the bulwark of the local Know-Nothing party.

The municipal election in May 1855 was swept by the Know-Nothings, who ran unopposed, as Democrats had withdrawn in protest of the violence against the Irish during the previous campaign.[38] Having gained control of the council the Know-Nothing majority raised a substantial tax, nominally for railroad purposes, but widely understood to be earmarked for the support of the public schools.[39] However, as the tax bill came due, dissatisfaction again mounted as mechanics from the lower wards urged the council to out and out repudiate the city's relationship with the railroad. In early November more than one hundred taxpayers gathered at Woodward Hall to determine "the best method of resisting the railroad tax." The result was a petition asking the council to post a bond for their railroad taxes that would not be sold by the city treasurer until the courts had determined the legality of the tax.[40] The signers were largely from the lower wards (65 percent) and a substantial number *worked* in the shipyards (26 percent). The Know-Nothing council acceded to their wishes, voting nine to two to sign the agreement.[41] A few weeks later the council further repudiated its predecessor's work by forbidding payment of city taxes with Sandusky City railroad bonds issued by the city.[42] These events branded the Know-Nothing council and party as antirailroad, and it was on this issue that the election the following spring would turn.[43]

Though opposition to the railroad tax was not limited to "workingmen,"—merchants J. K. Woodward and E. R. Day, foundry proprietor Peter Tellon, and shipyard owner William Jones were prominent in the movement[44]—the base of opposition was firmly rooted in the mechanic's community of the lower wards. This geographical division was recognized by the *Ledger*, which noted "there is no use any longer to disguise the fact, that a struggle is going on mainly between the lower, on the one hand and the business, and upper parts of the city on the other." For skilled workmen in the lower wards, opposition to the railroad expressed a desire to protect the mechanic's community. It was not uncommon for workmen in the shipyards to have acquired a modest amount of property, and fewer persons in the lower wards were propertyless than elsewhere in the city. These mechanics, termed by the *Ledger* "simon pure, national Know Nothings," feared that taxes and increased railroad connections would "dry up the boat-building business" and place an unfair burden of taxation on the rewards of their labor.[45]

As the local campaign of 1856 heated up, Dummer Hooper stated their case. Rather than serve all equally, he argued, higher property values brought by railroads worked only to the "benefit of a few speculators." For the workingman "who owns a small residence for his family" it was another story, for he could not sell it without having to buy another that had similarly accrued in value. Hooper reminded his readers that the poor man paid taxes at a greatly increased rate and paid double what he had ten years before for provisions while "his wages remain at about the same price, or at the most [have] not increased more than fifteen per cent." To those who claimed that mechanics had benefited from railroad construction in the past, Hooper suggested "it will take a magnificent pair of spectacles to show it to the hard working men of this city."[46] And when prorailroad writers defended the stockholders, calling them "industrious" as opposed to men they deemed "too lazy" to work and succeed, Hooper made rhetorical use of producerism by questioning the source of their wealth: "Now if either of these many citizens can or will show that he ever earned a dollar by work, we shall be much surprised. We think they have acquired their property by a more objectionable way than daily labor."[47]

Though the railroad remained the salient issue of the campaign, briefly in late winter the dispute threatened to turn into a confrontation over the public school tax. Prorailroad men, angered at the council's use of monies collected under the railroad assessment for the support of the public schools, turned to the courts to resist payment of the school tax.[48] This turn of events briefly fanned the flames on a smoldering debate over control of the public schools. A correspondent to the *Ledger* argued it was foolish to expect citizens to support the schools when they, "like everything else connected with the city, have been brought into disrepute by the ignorance and miserably proscriptive policy of our present Know-Nothing rulers."[49] The following day, the editor of the *Ledger* complained that the school board fired Catholic teachers and hired only Know-Nothings to replace them, though the former charge was later rescinded. In defense of the school board the editor of the *Tribune* claimed that no city had "twelve more liberal-minded, better educated, disinterested, and practical business men . . . selected as a Board of School Trustees."[50]

Much of the long-standing controversy over the schools, as in other places, emanated from the use of the Protestant King James version of the Bible, a practice objectionable to Catholic parents and clergymen.[51] In response to Democratic critics, the *Tribune* maintained that the "only *grave charge*" that could be justly brought against the school board was that "the Bible has been read in them [the schools] 'without note or comment.'"[52] The issue dissolved soon after Judge Bicknell of the local circuit court sustained the legality of the school tax. However its brief appearance into political debate suggests that politics in New Albany and presumably elsewhere can rarely be adequately discussed solely in terms of class or ethnicity, and how dormant underlying issues can influence elections that seem on the surface to be one-issue affairs.

When the votes for council were counted it became clear that New Albany was politically divided along ethnic and occupational lines. In the upper wards—with large numbers of unskilled laborers and well-to-do merchants, and the vast majority of the local Irish and German population—Democrats won handily, gaining up to 79 percent of the vote. Downriver in the predominantly native-born shipbuilding Fifth and Sixth wards the Know-Nothings had a similarly easy time of it. Only in the Fourth Ward, which divided its vote, was there any semblance of competition between the parties.[53]

Debate over the railroad was renewed briefly in June 1857, when the company announced it would be unable to complete the project. With dreams of a connection to Lake Erie dead, the mercantile interests successfully engaged in battle with councilmen from the shipbuilding wards, who unanimously favored repudiation of the debt, and the railroad subsequently disappeared as an issue. Apart from its role in solidifying party lines, the chief significance of the battle over the railroad was the ideological plane on which it was fought. With little variance, the railroad debate was termed a battle of "poor men" or "working men" against the "speculators." Both local newspapers supported the railroad project, though the *Tribune* succumbed to pressure within Know-Nothing ranks by the spring of 1856 and assumed a neutral posture, and consequently most correspondence and editorials that appeared in them fought to remove the stigma of "speculation" from the railroad. For example, the editor of the *Tribune* took on the charge that the railroad company was "a *speculating association* formed expressly *for their own benefit, and without regard to the city generally,*" by arguing that the stockholders included "all classes of the community" including "the mechanic, the trader, the boatman, the day laborer—the bone and sinew of the country."[54] In response to Hooper's defense of small men of property, a correspondent mocked his belief that the railroad "would only tend to enrich speculators, and those whose interests are antagonistic to the interests of the People," and sarcastically defined "the People" as "that class of citizens which has so often been spoken of, as being the owners of little homes worth about nine hundred dollars, which they do not want to sell, and which these wicked speculators are willing should be taxed year after year for their own personal aggrandizement."[55]

Though the ideas expressed by the opposition to the railroad fall short of a class analysis, they reveal a sense of identity—as mechanics, as workingmen, as common men—that legitimized political activity in their own interests and opposed to those of the rich. The arguments made by ship carpenter Hooper defending the small propertied workingman were strongly reminiscent of the language used in the *Western Odd Fellows Magazine*. The similarity suggests that the tradition of producerism, of the artisanate as the virtuous hardworking middle order of society, retained salience. While this artisanal inheritance propelled workers into cross-class alliances, it also legitimated the expression of their own interests. If and when those interests were perceived as being in opposition to a class of employers, producerism would ease the transition toward a class politics.

Participation by mechanics in politics was not limited to local elections. During the three-way presidential contest of 1856, Republicans and Know-Nothings alike sized upon Buchanan's subtreasury speech, delivered to the U.S. Senate in 1840, in which he was alleged to have argued that wages in the United States were too high and should be brought down to the level of the hard money countries of Europe.[56] When Know-Nothing mechanics arrived at a Fillmore demonstration atop a wagon with a blacksmith's furnace and anvil, the *Tribune* interpreted the display as the response of "sturdy workmen" to the notion that their labor was worth but "ten cents per day." The *Tribune* claimed workers employed in the railroad machine shops were solid Fillmore men and that "out of hundreds of ship-carpenters, in this city, there are not *ten* who will vote for either BUCHANAN or FREMONT. All are for FILLMORE."[57]

Know-Nothingism was strong in New Albany, and this strength was in no small part due to its image as a nonsectional party. The city's dependence on the South—nearly all steamboats built there were engaged in the southern river trade—and the sense of community that many southern Indianans felt with Kentuckians prevented Republicans from winning elections in New Albany.[58] The many themes of local Know-Nothingism were enumerated and symbolized by the speech of a daughter of a steamboat captain at a Fillmore flag presentation and pole-raising. Hailing the efforts of the men in defense of "American Nationality and Protestant civilization" from "foreign influence and Jesuit tyranny," she also warned of "the grim demon of Sectionalism . . . [who] threatens to crush our cherished institutions in his relentless grasp."[59] The Know-Nothing party enabled voters to express their opposition to what they perceived as a proslavery and pro-immigrant Democratic party, without the stain of "abolitionism."

In 1856, rank-and-file Know-Nothings opposed fusion with the Republicans. At a joint meeting of the parties, several Fillmore men brought a cannon and fired it during pro-Fremont speeches. Others were heard to shout "we want a straight out Fillmore ticket, and no amalgamation with the nigger candidate."[60] Despite their opposition, a fusion ticket was organized for the October state and congressional election, and Democrats once again were soundly defeated in the lower wards. A few weeks later Buchanan won a slight plurality in the city, attracting 46 percent of the vote to Fillmore's 44.9 and Fremont's 9.1.[61]

With the collapse of the national Know-Nothing movement, nativism locally lost much of its primacy as well. In its place exploded the debate over the extension of slavery into the territories, and while local divisions were rarely discussed, the nature of the audience led politicians to frame matters in class terms. The Democrats framed the debate in terms of abolition and raised the specter of racial equality during the campaign of 1860, arguing that Republicans cared only about the black slave and not a whit for free white workers. Abolition, the *Ledger* warned, would lead to the migration of millions of blacks into the cities of border states where they would "be thrown into immediate competition with the free white laborers . . . cutting down wages to a nominal sum or compelling the white laborer to abandon the field entirely."[62]

Such sentiments uttered in the heat of a presidential campaign, reflected the relationship between Democrats and their poorest constituents. For they appeared amid a breakdown of social order. A week earlier the small black community had gathered for a picnic where a minister spoke disparagingly of Democrats who, he was quoted as saying, "will permit every ignorant Irish and Dutchman to vote." Afterward another speaker was said to have denounced "poor insignificant white trash," while advising the black community to stand up for its rights. Here Democratic political discourse nearly reaped a violent harvest. The following evening a mob of young whites chased a hundred black men and women who had gathered for a dance in the upper wards to the small black district in the Third and Fourth wards north of the railroad station. Barber-shop owner, G. W. Carter, the wealthiest man in the black community, tried to pacify emotions in a letter to the *Ledger* distancing himself and others from the proceedings at the picnic.[63]

Passions were not easily calmed, and after a black man fired an errant shot at a German in a dispute over the use of a well, a mob of two hundred young white men gathered in the marketplace. There they determined to visit the black neighborhood, in the words of the *Ledger*, "to make an example of a few of the free negroes in our midst who have been seen with arms and heard to threaten the lives of white men." Violence was prevented only when the city marshall promised to warn out those blacks who had migrated to Indiana in violation of the 1851 constitution.[64] The warning was issued, blaming trouble on "recent imprudent conduct" of "many persons of color," and the city council appropriated fifty dollars for their removal.[65] This unhappy incident reveals the close relationship between the rhetoric of politicians and the aspirations and fears of their followers.

The Republicans, too, frequently framed their discussion of slavery in context of its effect on free white labor, and in so doing they were better able to tap into the reservoir of understanding about virtue and independence that was so widespread among artisans. Noting that a Democratic vice-presidential candidate had once said that capital should own labor and that the Democratic governor of South Carolina had called northern workingmen "the mudsills of society," the editor of the *Tribune* asked how long it would be before the South attempted to enslave white men. For that reason, he said, the Republican party fought the extension of slavery into the territories "not for the freedom of the negro" but "for our own race."[66]

New Albany's reliance on and proximity to the slaveholding South, however, led its citizenry to fear the consequences of war above all. Large numbers of previously Know-Nothing mechanics flocked to the banner of the Constitutional Union party and its candidate John Bell of Tennessee. Three of the five members of the executive committee of the Bell and Everett Union Club were journeymen, as was the corresponding secretary and two members of a so-called "committee of five."[67] Enthusiasm for this middle course was particularly high in the lower wards. As a result Know-Nothing strength was not translated into a Republican victory, and Douglas handily defeated Lincoln—49.7 to 38.1 percent—within the city. Even in the lower wards, Lincoln did poorly, appearing on only 42.9 percent of the ballots cast. There, in the shipbuilding community, a significant percentage of the electorate (21.1) voted quixotically for

Bell, despite a call from wealthy leaders of the Union party to throw their votes to Douglas.[68]

Within three weeks of the election merchants, bankers, and manufacturers who feared the disruption of commerce that war promised issued a call for a "Union Meeting."[69] The theme was compromise as the assembled called for repeal of the "personal liberty" laws enacted by several of the northern states (Indiana was not among them) to retard the efficiency of the Fugitive Slave Law, chastised hasty action by southerners that might lead to disunion, and resolved to remain neutral in case of war since they had "no cause of quarrel with our immediate neighbors."[70]

A month later and a few miles upriver, the workingmen of Louisville assembled and called for workers across the country to "unite in one solid column for a single purpose—the preservation of the Federal Union." Workers were urged to demand the resignation of congressmen who worked against compromise.[71] The call was taken up by those engaged in the mechanical arts in New Albany. In this instance, however, the mass meeting was not an example of self-directed activity by workers; instead it was a carefully staged pageant of interclass harmony and the broadest meanings of producerism. Peter Tellon, the wealthy proprietor of the American Foundry, chaired the meeting. Among the six vice-presidents elected by the "bone and sinew" of New Albany were a prosperous master carpenter, a similarly well-to-do master cabinetmaker, a wealthy planing mill owner, a grocer, an engineer and a molder. Two other manufacturers, John S. Cash and Benjamin South, each worth at least $20,000, served as secretaries. The meeting issued a set of resolutions that in nearly all respects were the same as those issued five weeks before by the elite "union meeting." After the resolutions were adopted, a curtain was raised and revealed the stage dressed with an American flag and with the figure of George Washington in the center. In front stood apart two "beautiful young misses" representing North and South, who were united by a "sturdy mechanic."[72]

The intent of the meeting was announced by a committee of seven that included three skilled workers, Dummer Hooper among them. Workingmen should support peace, they wrote, for "it is the industrial classes—those who live by the sweat of their brow—who are the greatest sufferers in times of panic and distrust, to say nothing of war." In a similar vein, the *Ledger* described the assembled as "emphatically the bone and sinew of our day" and concluded, "it is upon the strong shoulders, the brawny arms, the stout hearts of the Working Men of the land, that the hopes of the Union now depend."[73]

The apparent disjuncture between a discourse addressing mechanics who "live by the sweat of their brow" and the selection of wealthy manufacturers as officers of the meeting was possible because of the lack of ideological distinction between worker and employer that was inscribed in American political language. Though the meeting called for an end to party conflict, it was in other ways a continuation of the patterns of the previous decade. While workers expressed their interests from time to time, it was never per se as wage earners involved in a wage contract with an employer. That was a more private affair, to be worked out between capitalist and worker or a group of workers in some instances. Such disputes simply did not enter the realm of political discussion. However, workers did engage regularly in politics and politicians who sought their votes spoke of "sturdy mechanics" or "the bone and sinew of our country" and flattered them by calling them the "source of all wealth." And workers used this language in political struggle, identifying themselves as the virtuous, hard working, small propertyholder. Though Hooper had spoken of "wages" and not "prices" that failed to keep up with taxes and provisions, his adversary was not the employer but the "speculator." Seen in this way, the "workingmen's" union meeting was in step with a tradition of interclass politics in New Albany, and in some ways, was its culmination.

War and the End of Harmony

The contingencies of war, however, strained the unity of producerism nearly to the breaking point and revealed in more transparent form the widening gap between classes. As structural change proceeded and tensions at the workplace increased, workers began to press their own class interests in political battle. Though these tensions were, in some respects, fueled by contradictions within producerism, it did not entirely lose its vitality as a unifying force that could promote peace between the classes at the workplace and at the ballot box.

At first the outbreak of hostilities in 1861 seemed to unify the community. While most supported the Union in patriotic outrage, other factors reinforced local commitment to the cause. Support for enlistment was strengthened by the fear that Kentucky might secede, exposing New Albany to the frontlines of battle. Political distinctions dissolved overnight, as the *Ledger* quickly threw its support behind the war effort and soon became the chief organ for Indiana's "War Democrats," in part due to the fear that Confederate control of the Mississippi would strangle commerce, a prevalent concern in southern Indiana.[74]

Republicans, Know-Nothings, and Democrats alike volunteered for the army or for one of the numerous local militia groups that were organized to protect local lives and property.[75] However, they joined militias in much the same pattern that they joined other associations; consequently, workers and elites rarely belonged to the same company. Many of New Albany's best men joined "Home Guards No. 1" or the "Independent Home Guards."[76] As patriotic as others, the elite were also concerned with order and the protection of property. The Independent Home Guards agreed that their purpose was to protect "our families, ourselves, and our homes" from "reckless men" who might take advantage of the confusion of war "to disturb the public peace, depredate upon property, public or private, and in all respects to protect each other as members of a legal and peaceable community."[77]

Others were similar in leadership and membership to plebeian associations. The "Franklin Home Guards," composed chiefly of journeymen from the First Ward, were led by master edge toolmaker George W. Beck, master carpenter Daniel E. Sittason, grocer Jacob Heyd, and journeymen Joseph Crandell, Fred Ailer, and J. C. Gibson.[78] Likewise the "Lower Albany and Plank Road Citizen Rifle Guards" selected small farmers John Cleland and Smith Reasor, grocer Charles Eisman, and journeymen ship carpenters James Nicholson and Robert King as officers.[79] The social composition of the various militias offered a warning that the war would not be experienced by all in the same way.

The economic stagnation that had stifled business on the river since Lincoln's election began to show signs of easing in the fall of 1861.[80] In September Joseph Terstegge, proprietor of the largest shoe manufacturing firm in the city, delivered 1,010 pairs of shoes to the 38th Regiment and then set to work fulfilling contracts to supply two others. In a more irregular fashion, shoe manufacturer John Kimball and merchant tailors Conrad Nunemacher and William Shaw received orders for boots and uniforms from various officers that they gladly filled. By February of the following year the newly established woolen mills of John T. Creed and Company were filling an "extensive" contract with the government for wool socks. By May prosperity reached the shipyards when Peter Tellon received a contract to build "a large, first class iron-clad gunboat."[81] To some extent, workers shared in this prosperity as wages rose due to the increased de-

mand for labor. In June draymen were said to be "reaping a rich harvest," due to "the immense quantities of tobacco, grain, flour, and
other produce and merchandise" that traveled through the port of
New Albany. By the following winter, ship carpenters were in short
supply, commanding $2.50 a day in cash wages.[82]

Prosperity was not an unqualified blessing for workers. Though
wages were high, prices rose higher still, due in part to the flood of
paper money printed by the federal government and in part to the
actions of speculators who supplied quartermasters with overpriced
goods. By the spring of 1863 the *Ledger* noted a shortage of dwellings,
"especially small ones suitable for mechanics," and suggested that
"capitalists . . . put some of their surplus greenbacks into small tenements."[83] A few months later, complaints from tenants over exorbitant rents were heard, and the inability to pay $200 or $250 rent a
year threatened to drive many out of the city.[84] While the wealthy
indulged in extravagance like never before, spending greenbacks before they lost their value, the "laboring population" was said to "find
it difficult to make the two ends meet, although they never toiled as
hard or received so high nominal pay as at present." In response,
workers cut back on consumption, no longer buying butter and reducing their purchases of eggs, milk, and beef.[85]

To many it was evident that workers were bearing more than their
share of the hardships of war. It was widely believed that they filled
the ranks of the Union Army with greater regularity than businessmen, a sentiment adroitly exploited by Democratic politicians. At a
meeting called to meet the threat of invasion by confederate raiders,
local militia commander W. W. Tuley, a Democratic party regular,
accused the elite of holding back in its support of the militia and the
army, expecting "the laboring, the poor men, to do the fighting." To
the cheers of the crowd, he charged that the rich were unwilling "to
use the money and means they possessed for the aid of the brave men
who were willing to volunteer or for the support of the wives and little ones they must leave behind." He concluded by charging that it
was "moneyed men, the property holders of the city" who had the
greatest interest in a secure border. In like fashion, the *Ledger*
charged that some businessmen deemed it "almost a capital crime if
poor men, the laboring classes of the community, do not enlist and
leave their families unprovided for."[86]

Efforts were made to ameliorate the hardships felt by the poor.
Local fund-raising efforts successfully raised enough money to exempt New Albany Township from the draft. Throughout the course
of the war, the money raised was used to increase the bounty offered

to volunteers by the federal government.[87] This practice worked to the benefit of many for only the rich could afford to hire a substitute. And it encouraged poor young men to enlist, since the combined federal, county, and city bounties by the end of 1863 totaled $200, which was a significant percentage of what an unskilled laborer could make in a year. By January 1865, local government increased its bounty to $250 "to all persons volunteering . . . who may be credited upon the quota of New Albany township."[88]

Again the issue of class inequities was raised. Amid a subscription drive for money with which to buy substitutes, the *Ledger* claimed that it was "the poor men of the township, the laborers and mechanics," who have raised the bulk of the money by borrowing money, selling furniture, or denying themselves "of their ordinary food" to save the necessary $25. The *Ledger* suggested that "the businessmen of the city," whose "trade is made up from these poor mechanics and laboring men," should subscribe generously to help New Albany avoid the draft.[89] Certainly the editor was aware of the political capital that could be made on this score, and eight months later on the day of a county election he attempted to cash in, suggesting that "our poor people will remember that not a single Democrat in New Albany refused to make such a sacrifice. The only persons who refused were Republicans."[90]

During the war, New Albany's bifurcated working-class community registered its discontent, though in widely divergent ways. For those in the upper wards, where ethnic and racial divisions were common, the response was violent. Here resided many Irish, German, and Native white workers employed in the sweated trades or as casual laborers who bore the burden of much of the fighting and who felt the pinch of wartime inflation, paying increasingly high rents and prices for provisions. Such men were strongly influenced by Democrats who warned that the war was being fought to emancipate the slaves.[91] In the midst of a campaign to fill the city's quota of volunteers, the white workers of the upper wards again turned toward the black community to express their rage.

Four young white men—Charles Lansford, John Locke, Charles Bishop, and Robert Kemp—were standing on a corner in the Second Ward on the evening of July 21, 1862, when two black men, smoking cigars, turned the corner. When one of the whites offered the opinion that "them niggers are putting on a good deal of style," a gunfight ensued, and Lansford and Locke were shot, the latter fatally.[92] News of the shooting spread rapidly and the next morning a crowd of whites attacked three blacks with gunfire, perhaps fatally wounding one while severely beating the other two who eventually escaped.[93] At least six other violent confrontations occurred that day, and by afternoon the mob, composed mostly of young men, was two hundred strong. As darkness descended upon the city, the mob turned its attention to the destruction of black property, including the vineyards and gardens of G. W. Carter who had tried to calm passions during the previous moment of white rage in 1860. Undaunted by the presence of soldiers in the city, the mob mounted an unsuccessful attempt at lynching the black prisoners held in the city jail. Again, the *Ledger* blamed the violence on "the immigration of negroes unlawfully."[94] Thirty black families, and a number of young men employed on the river left the town as a result of the riot.[95]

Though the *Ledger* condemned the riot, many believed that the Democrats in control of the city government could have done more to suppress it.[96] In a sermon delivered to the elite and largely Republican congregation of the First Presbyterian Church, the reverend John Atterbury linked Democratic reluctance to support the war with their failure to control the mob. Calling the rebellion of the South a "crime against God," Atterbury argued that "the enforcement of law and the suppression of rebellion is a sacred duty," demanded by God upon the rulers of the people. He then turned his attention to affairs more local.

> All hesitation or neglect . . . to repress and punish by all available means, riot, rowdyism, violence . . . is a gross violation of official trust. It is infidelity to God whose authority they represent as well as injurious to the community. Whether they are restrained by fear or a still baser motive in the hope of future elections, they are deserving of reprobation. They should abandon their stations to men who have courage enough and honesty enough to do their duty. Such an instance of unrepressed riot, and unpunished rioters, as our own city witnessed this past summer, to its wide-spread infamy, does a terrible work of depravation of the minds of our youth all too prone to lawlessness and crime.[97]

Fifteen of the wealthier congregants of the church applauded the sentiments expressed and had the sermon published.

A final incident occurred the following spring. Three Irish laborers, conversing near the spot where John Locke was killed the previous summer, spied black steamboat fireman Thomas Cordel standing in the yard in front of his house. Believing that Cordel was eavesdropping on them, the Irishmen ordered him to retreat to his house. A fight broke out and after two of the white laborers were stabbed, one fatally, Cordel ran to the safety of the city jail. Again a mob of Irish men organized, and talk of ridding the city of blacks filled the air, but occasion to riot and lynch was prevented this time by the intervention of army troops.[98]

Division in the Shipbuilding Community

In the lower wards the changes wrought by war manifested a new spirit among the men employed in the shipyards. Responding to the failure of wages to keep up with prices as well as to the attempt by employers to dictate changes in the nature of work groups, the journeymen ship carpenters, caulkers, painters, and joiners of New Albany unionized during the last two years of the war. In doing so they came into contact with ideas of militant and unionized workers elsewhere; the result was their energetic involvement in the eight-hour day movement and motivation to press their own class demands in the political arena. This terrain was hardly unknown to them, for a decade of experience in the Know-Nothing, Constitutional Union, and Republican parties had prepared them well.

The first sign of working-class self-activity in the lower wards came in the May 1863 city election. In a four-way race for the mayor's office, Republican ship carpenter Dummer Hooper won with only one-third of the vote on the strength of his support in the Fifth and Sixth wards, where he received 57 and 51.4 percent of the vote, respectively. The mechanics of the lower wards were even more enthusiastic in their support for fellow ship carpenter Thomas Ellis in his unsuccessful bid to become city clerk, casting 64 percent of the ballots in the Fifth Ward with his name on them, and 53.9 percent in the sixth.[99] Though the issues on which the election turned are unknown, and despite the placid nature of council debate in the latter stages of the war, Hooper's election and Ellis's strong bid for office suggests that the journeymen of the shipyards were flexing their muscles and preparing to stretch the parameters of producerism.

That burst of self-activity appeared in the fall of the same year when the "Ship Carpenter and Caulkers' Protective Union" organized in response to the employment by shipyard owners of unskilled workers. Such men, said union president Jonathan W. Derrimore, "allowed themselves to be used as tools in the hands of the employers to crush us" and in response the ship carpenters "claim the right to band ourselves together for our self protection." The union struck against the shipyard of D. C. Hill and W. C. D. Payne, which had discharged ten union carpenters and in their place "hired men that are not mechanics at all." Confident of the value of their skills and the strength of their union—they claimed that "all of the good workmen in New Albany are members of the Ship Carpenters' Union"—they offered to "give their employers their choice" to hire whom they desired.[100]

Defending their almost exclusive role in the shipyard work group and aided by the large number of contracts waiting to be filled, the union men prevailed over the opposition of the masters. In the following year and a half, the union raised the daily wage from its pre-war high of $2.50 up to $4.00 on new work and $5.00 on repairs. Certainly, the ability of the union to acquire a near monopoly of skilled labor contributed to their success. However, Derrimore also attributed it to the friendship of merchant-manufacturer John B. Ford, who by the end of the war owned the largest local shipyard, which in a little over a year constructed ten steamboats. To demands for the three-dollar day Ford was said to have responded, "your labor is worth that to me, your demand is just, and you must have the money." In the eyes of the union men of New Albany, Ford, despite his inexperience in the shipyards, was a beneficent capitalist, and the ship carpenters "stuck to Captain Ford" in appreciation of his patronage. "If all the capitalists were such men as Captain J. B. Ford," Derrimore admiringly reported, "we would have but little trouble in getting employment."[101]

The ship carpenters who took an active role in the labor movement were representative of the men practicing their trade in New Albany. All (fourteen have been identified) had worked in local shipyards before the war and many, like Dummer Hooper, for much longer. Men like Jacob Alford, Isaac Bruce, and Hooper had been active in the fire companies and in local politics. Most were in their thirties and forties and headed nuclear families. (Only one did not.) Uniformly they sent their children to school; all eleven, between the ages of seven and fifteen in 1860, attended. In economic station they reflected the prosperity that journeymen in the shipbuilding trades so often enjoyed. Two activists, Alford and Hooper, had once owned a shipyard, while others like Isaac Bruce are known to have subcontracted on occasion. While three owned less than $300 worth of personal goods in 1860, most owned some real estate and total property holdings worth more than $1,000. The ship carpenters who disturbed the unity of the mechanic's community were stable and well-integrated citizens who responded to the changes wrought by the war with a class fervor previously unseen in New Albany.[102]

For some the burgeoning labor movement took on the character of a crusade. James Nicholson explained the effort to unionize other workers as a means of accomplishing "that great work which is laid out for us; and we can, if they will only unite."[103] The cause transcended parochial concerns for Nicholson, who continued to spread the labor gospel while serving as a lieutenant in the 144th regiment. Desiring "to do some good for my fellow workmen," he requested his copy of *Finchers' Trades' Review* be forwarded to him since the army was filled with mechanics and "a great many of them do not know anything about what their fellow men are doing at home for their benefit."[104]

Having successfully organized ship carpenters and caulkers, the leaders of the union worked to organize others who lived and worked around the shipyards. To that end the union invited Detroit ship carpenter and union activist Richard Trevellick to speak in New Albany "to arouse the workingmen of this place to come out like men and help us in the labor reform movement which is going on."[105] Trevellick did just that, and by early April 1865 the "Journeymen Painters' Protective Union" and the "Joiners' Union" had been organized.[106]

Organization at the workplace provided the momentum for broader community efforts. News of the Union Army victory at Richmond was greeted by a celebration organized by the ship carpenters' union.[107] Three months later they organized a picnic to celebrate the Fourth of July. The following year local unions combined efforts to put on a similar celebration that attracted over five thousand people. These festivities included "fine music, dancing and general enjoyment," while the temperance and Know-Nothing background of the mechanics of the lower wards was evident in their prohibition of the use of "liquors of any kind."[108]

The most important result of the working-class mobilization of the lower wards, however, was the movement for the eight-hour day, called by one historian "the peculiar issue of the wage earner."[109] While the eight-hour day was first instituted in the shipyards of Charlestown, Massachusetts, in 1842, after the war it became a widespread demand of journeymen. At the Buffalo convention of the Ship Carpenters' and Caulkers' International Union, attended by James Nicholson, the union agreed to make a concerted effort to gain the eight-hour day on May 10, 1866.[110] As the demand expressed the particular class interests of trade unionists and other workers, it created a host of problems and opportunities for local politicians.

Republicans perceived the greater danger in this political environment. Their local dominance had been based on an alliance between important segments of the elite and the mechanic's community in opposition to an expanding "slave power." The raising of class issues far closer to home by an emerging cadre of unionized workers threatened the viability of this coalition. To reinforce loyalty among the shipyard men, who had consistently voted against the Democrats since 1855, Republicans labeled their slate in the spring of 1865 the "Working Men's Union Ticket," though the only journeyman on it was the council candidate from the fifth ward.[111] More telling of Republican reluctance to absorb working-class discontent at home was their unceremonious deposing of Mayor Hooper at the head of the ticket in favor of merchant John McCulloch. Claiming that the local convention was packed with his enemies, Hooper vowed to run as an independent. Hooper mocked the convention's nominee and suggested to the voter that "if his wealth gives him more claims on you, vote for him. If his inexperience makes him better qualified, vote for him."[112] Facing certain defeat from the popular Democratic nominee, master cabinetmaker and Union Army officer William Sanderson, Hooper eventually withdrew and the Republicans lost the election without him.[113]

By the end of the year, Hooper reemerged in the public eye as the leader of the local eight-hour day movement. In November he was elected First Vice-President of the Indiana Workingmen's Convention in Indianapolis. His name appeared atop a committee of three that issued an address to their "fellow workingmen of the state of Indiana" that called for the organization of eight-hour leagues.[114] The document's fluency in producerist republicanism was evident when the committee lamented what it perceived as greater privileges for the wealthy that was "inconsistent with the spirit of our American institutions, being based on false and pernicious distinctions calculated to elevate wealth above labor in the social and political scale of life, and degrade the producers so low that wealth and honor will never reach them." United action, the committee urged, promised that labor would be "elevated to the standard that the Divine Creator intended it should be held at." Only then would workingmen attain the position "God designed for you and our National Institutions entitle you to hold."[115]

Almost immediately the workers of New Albany, led by ship carpenters and boat painters, set to work to organize an eight-hour league.[116] On the first of December, an overflowing crowd filled Cannon's Hall. Those gathered came "to assert the dignity of labor" which they agreed was "the foundation of government credit, as well as [being] productive of the substantial wealth of the country." Declaring that their own "physical and mental condition" and their "obligations" to their families demanded shorter hours, the assembled workers resolved that "eight hours should constitute a day's work" and served notice that they would give their political support only to candidates who agreed.[117]

A week later, the "Workingmen's Unions" met again, and were addressed by Robert Gilchrist, president of the Louisville Trades Assembly, and William Horan, Treasurer of the International Molders' Union. The meeting sparked an ideological explosion, shattering whatever remained of the unity of the mechanic's community. In familiar terms Gilchrist began, using biblical allusion to defend the honor and dignity of labor. Since the creation of the world was an instance of divine labor, and as Mary's husband was "a laborer-a carpenter," Gilchrist argued it was clear that labor was meant to be a dignified undertaking.[118]

From there, however, Gilchrist took a line of argument that led beyond the confines of producerism. The problem was that between work and the laborer appeared parasitic capital that "sits like an incubus upon the living breast of labor, stifling it if possible." Contending that this was a systematic problem and not the work of a few greedy individuals, Gilchrist offered that "there has ever been a conflict between labor and capital, and ever will be." The solution would necessitate a prolonged struggle. Though he supported organization to shorten the workday and to raise wages, he told his audience that the capitalist would merely pass on the increased cost to the consumer rather than bear it himself. The real solution was to dispose of the capitalist and restore labor to its traditionally honored position through the creation of a cooperative economy. Upon concluding his remarks, the workingmen of New Albany demonstrated their appreciation with "the most enthusiastic applause."[119]

The radical nature of Gilchrist's speech, posing an essential rift between capital and labor, and its positive reception by local workers presented Republicans with a dilemma—how to maintain support among the skilled workers of the lower wards without catering to the spirit of class conflict. Less than two months before, the newly established Republican organ, the New Albany *Commercial*, had touched some nerves in a dispute over the eight-hour day with a writer using the sobriquet of "mechanic." The editor acknowledged that many were overworked and suggested that this was the cause of much working-class drunkenness. However, he warned that without taking pains "to elevate the moral character of our people" a shortened workday could only mean "two hours more to spend in the grog shop, or some worse place."[120]

The response of "mechanic," appearing three days later in the *Led-*

ger, merged the ideas of the eight-hour movement with Democratic party rhetoric. Doubting the sincerity of the *Commercial's* sympathy for working people, he asked "if being overworked is the cause of so many of the laboring men being drunkards, why in his sympathy, is he unwilling to remove the cause?" Two extra hours of leisure time posed few problems for "mechanic" who asserted that it would allow workingmen to "bestow a little more care upon" their wives, to teach their children to become "useful members of society," and to mentally improve themselves.[121]

The political explosiveness of the movement was revealed when "mechanic" accused the *Commercial* of callous indifference to white workingmen. "If the laboring men throughout were black," he suggested, "the gentlemen would be horrorstruck at the idea of opposing the movement, and would remind us of the man who was unwilling to go into the water until he could swim." To the white worker's ability "to wash off the black occasionally," he attributed Republican opposition to a shorter workday.[122] In response the editor of the *Commercial* criticized the "partizan rancor" of "mechanic," accusing him of demagoguery. It was "childish" to speak generally of employers as "oppressors," he argued, for the interests of capital and labor "are mutual."[123]

As the eight-hour movement began to attract large numbers of workers, William Curry of the *Commercial* attempted to guide it in a more moderate direction. A week after Gilchrist's fiery speech, Curry addressed a smaller than usual turnout and spoke of interclass harmony. Beginning with the tenets of producerism, he flattered his audience in much the way that politicians of the fifties had. Capital is transitory, he said, requiring labor "to renew and preserve it." Without it, social life was impossible, for labor "is the Lord of Wealth, the Master of Civilization, the Minister of Virtue." As the possessor of labor, the workingman was assured that he "may feel that he is as true a teacher of civilization and virtue as the most learned collegian." While Curry expressed sympathy for the goal of shorter hours, the gist of his speech was an appeal for class harmony. Despite all its dignity, he lectured that "labor cannot subsist without capital" and that cooperation between the two was necessary for the improvement of workingmen.[124] The following week, in another appearance before the League, Curry argued that "capitalists and laborers were not fixed classes of men" and that "it was a mistake to suppose that they had conflicting interests."[125]

Workers continued to agitate the issue into the new year, meeting weekly and circulating a petition to Congress calling for enactment of a national eight-hour law.[126] However, enthusiasm was soon dampened by two unrelated events. The first occurred at the annual convention of the ship carpenters' international union, held in January at New Albany. Other locals had not been as successful in organizing as the New Albany men, and the assembled ship carpenters concluded that it was "inexpedient and impolitic" to try to establish a uniform workday by March as they had hoped.[127] The second came a few weeks later at the Republican County Convention, when James V. Kelso introduced a resolution calling for the party to take a stand in favor of the shortened workday. In the words of the *Ledger*, it "fell like a thunderclap upon the Convention."[128] These two setbacks demoralized the movement, and it receded from the public eye.[129]

The politicians spent the rest of the year preparing for the midterm congressional elections. While the Republican campaign focused almost entirely on the treacherous behavior of the Democratic party during the war, leaving discussions of class iniquities far behind, the Democrats made a two-faced appeal to white workingmen. First, they continued the white supremacist tradition and argued that Republicans were more concerned with the ex-slaves than they were with white workingmen. But they expanded the argument, arguing that the Republicans had engaged in class legislation at the expense of the working classes.

This line of argument was most eloquently presented by former Republican, James V. Kelso.[130] Conceding that the federal debt was amassed in a "just" cause, Kelso railed against the exemption of bonded wealth from taxation. By taxing only the property of the common man, the debt threatened to become a "chain by which labor is to be bound to the car of capital." The war, he declared, was waged "to protect all the property in the Union, and *all* the property in the Union should be pledged for its payment." But the Republicans, Kelso warned, expected the debt to be shouldered by the mechanics and farmers of the country, and administered in their hands the debt would become a "lien upon the toiling masses of the country for the payment of the debt." In response to the argument that the men who loaned the government acted patriotically and should therefore be exempt from taxation, Kelso asked his audience whether "the men who loaned to government their services, their blood, their lives" were any less patriotic.[131]

Following Kelso's lead, the *Ledger* emphasized the class nature of Republican legislation. At Democratic meetings, "mechanics and laboring men" were said to have attended in unprecedented numbers, while the "nabobs of shoddy aristocracy" were noticeable only by their absence.[132] The workingman, said the *Ledger*, feared Republican policy would reduce him "to the condition of a hewer of wood and carrier of water . . . and that he has to hammer and plough, toil and dig, labor and sweat, and give to the tax gatherer the profits of his toil, while the rich bondholder rolls in his wealth."[133]

While the Democrats won in both the city and the county, the voters of the lower wards maintained their allegiance to the Republican party. However, in subsequent elections, beginning the following spring, the mechanics' community, and especially the Sixth Ward, began to vote solidly Democratic for the first time in over a decade.[134] It is likely that this change in voting signaled growing disenchantment among workers with the Republicans, who opposed the eight-hour day while remaining silent on the question of bondholder exemption from taxation.

A Legacy for the Future?

The story related here is a multilayered one. On the surface it appears that prosperous and self-reliant skilled workers, confronted with higher food and housing costs in the marketplace and a challenge from master craftsmen to their monopoly over work in the shipyards, organized a trade union. By stopping the use of unskilled men and raising the prevailing wage rate, these mechanics enjoyed a brief period of success in controlling their working lives. And there was more to it. Not content with control over aspects of work in their trade, the ship carpenters' union became infused with a kind of class consciousness that led them to work to organize workers in other trades. And they entered the political arena where they struggled in vain for a shortened workday for all workers.

However, the ship carpenters of New Albany did not act in isolation. By no means was the organization of the union their introduction to public and associational life; skilled workers had been in close contact with the middling orders of the city in an extensive web of plebeian associations. It is notable that James Kelso, who raised the troublesome eight-hour issue at the Republican County Convention, had been a member of the Relief No. 5 fire company, located in the Sixth Ward. There Kelso, then a teacher, associated with journeymen ship carpenters and other mechanics. By war's end, Kelso had opened a law practice, but he still remained in close contact with his working-class neighbors. After delivering a speech at the mechanics' picnic on July 4, 1866, E. C. Duncan, a member of the ship carpenters' union, labeled Kelso "the working man's friend," and publicly thanked him for his "able and eloquent defence of the working man."[135] In the postwar period, James Kelso would make a habit of speaking on behalf of workingmen.

That ship carpenters had been involved, as had other skilled workers, in local political life adds more texture to the tale. At times, workers sought the fulfillment of their own economic interests within the political arena, as they did in opposing the New Albany and Sandusky City Railroad. Though in that instance they did not express their interests as wage earners, they did seek a settlement of the problem that would favorably affect the modestly propertied workingmen of the shipbuilding community. At other times workers participated in politics when the issues were not clearly economic. They were not strangers to the political process, and as a result, politicians framed arguments that appealed to working-class voters. Though the exact role of the political arena in class formation is unclear, it is certain that politicians at times had to placate working-class aspirations.

Politics was largely a game of give and take, between classes on the one hand and politicians and constituents on the other. No one completely controlled the flow of events. It is unlikely that local Democrats offered racist rhetoric so that workers of the upper wards would riot and pillage the black community. Undoubtedly the editor of the *Ledger* spoke frankly when he deplored the violence, yet the perpetrators of these crimes went unpunished by the Democrats in control of the city, much to the displeasure of the Republicans who listened to the Reverend Atterbury's sermon. The Democrats gave the rioters room in exchange for political support, breathing space that the unskilled had demanded.

In the shipbuilding wards a similar confrontation developed. Only the decision by the international ship carpenters' union to postpone its demands for the eight-hour day prevented Kelso's resolution from being a test of Republican responsiveness to its working-class constituency. By abdicating the road of class politics, the Republicans left it to the Democrats who had been developing a politics of division during the war. It was the flexibility of political discourse, which allowed for most expressions of class tension, that eased the incorporation of workers into politics. Producerism not only provided a language that could be used by politicians to rally working-class voters behind their party, it also allowed workers to express their own concerns within the political arena. And by the end of the war, the republican fear of corrupt bargains between rulers and monied interests served the Democrats in their efforts to solidify an increasingly radicalized constituency. In the political marketplace, the buying and selling of ideas, was a two-way street. In these years, political life was an important element of an emerging working-class culture.

Considering the events recounted here, one might expect New Albany to have become a locus for radical protest and worker organization in the postwar period. Abrupt economic change negated such possibilities, however. Soon after the war, the local shipbuilding industry collapsed, in part a casualty of railroad competition.[136] It was not long before John Ford quit the business and put his capital into his latest entrepreneurial venture—the manufacture of plate glass. Ship carpenters either worked locally as house carpenters, commuted to the thriving Howard shipyard in neighboring Jeffersonville, or moved on entirely. Built on the ruins of the shipbuilding community arose a new community of workers, dependent on the recently constructed iron mills of the lower wards. This new community would be more heterogeneous and it would have fewer ties to the rest of the social structure. As a result of these and other changes, local working-class protest in the 1870s and 1880s remained largely confined to the individual trades in the workplace.

Before examining the new social and economic landscape of Gilded Age New Albany, a detour downriver to Evansville, Indiana, offers an environment where the kind of class politics discussed here developed into a fairly permanent, if tenuous, alliance between the city's unionized workers and the Democratic party. There class and ethnicity repeatedly reinforced each other, and the result was a strong German working-class constituency that at times led Democratic politicians further down the road of class conflict than they probably wanted to go.

Part Two

Evansville: Skilled Workers and Politicians in the Gilded Age

Pa, what place is that?
That is a brickyard, my son.
Whose brickyard is it, pa?
It belongs to me, my son.
Do all those big piles of brick belong to you?
Yes, my son, every brick of them.
My! . . . Did you make them all alone by yourself?
No, my son; these men you see working there made them for
    me.
Do these men belong to you, pa?
No, my son; these men are free men. No man can own another.
    If he could the other would be a slave.
What is a slave, pa?
A slave is a man who has to work for another all his life, for
    only his board and clothes.
If a slave gets sick who pays for the doctor, pa?
Well, his owner does. He can't afford to lose his property.
Why do these men work so hard, pa? Do they like it?
Well, no, I don't suppose they do; but they must work or
    starve.
Are these men rich, pa?
Not to any great extent, my son.
Do they own any houses, pa?
I rather guess not, my son.
Have they any horses and nice clothes, and do they go to the

seaside when it's warm, like we do, pa?

Well, hardly. It takes them all their time to earn a living.

What is a living, pa?

Why, a living—well, for them a living is what they eat and wear.

Isn't that board and clothes, pa?

I suppose it is. . . .

If they get sick, do you pay the doctor, pa?

Catch me! What have I got to do with it? They must pay for their own doctor.

Can you afford to lose one of the men who work for you, pa?

Of course I can; it don't make any difference to me. I can hire another whenever I like.

Then you aren't as particular about them as if they were your slaves, are you, pa?

> —Excerpted from "A Small Boy Asks His Father Some Pertinent Questions." Reprinted from *Inland Printer* in the Evansville *Trades and Labor Directory*, 1895–6

Continuity and Transformation: The Diversified Economy of Evansville, 1850–80

4 The Ohio River offered diverse opportunities, and while the prosperity of New Albany ebbed and flowed with the shipyards, that of Evansville was more closely tied to commerce. This situation was largely a simple result of geography. So close to Louisville, New Albany's share of trade was bound to be limited. Evansville was more fortunate. Nine miles downstream from the mouth of the Green River and within easy access of the Wabash, Tennessee, and Cumberland, Evansville seemed destined for commercial success, to which the comments of early visitors attest. In 1817, William Cobbett wrote that it looked "to be a town of considerable trade," and a guidebook to the west described it as having "among the best natural situations for mercantile business in the state."[1]

Access to markets and the discovery of coal in the 1850s made Evansville increasingly attractive to manufacturers. By 1860 substantial saw mills as well as agricultural implement and furniture factories had been established. They were soon joined by stove foundries and textile mills. Alongside the factories survived smaller shops that employed between fifteen and thirty workers, producing bricks, leather, saddles, wagons, beer, and barrels. Consequently, the three decades after midcentury witnessed the transformation of Evansville from a small commercial settlement of 3,325 residents into a diverse manufacturing city of nearly 30,000.[2] To the young Theodore Dreiser, raised in a small town to the north—and undoubtedly to other rural migrants—Evansville in 1882 offered "great crowds and countless lights and vehicles and streetcars and brightly-lighted shops."[3]

A large flow of German immigrants, particularly in the late 1840s and early 1850s, provided much of the labor and skill for this expan-

sion. By 1860, Evansville was a largely German city; 45 percent of its
work force had been born in Germany, and in manufacturing the proportion was considerably higher.[4] Though the local German population was by no means homogeneous, shared traditions and political
battles with nativists created a sense of community among immigrants from the various German states that minimized divisiveness
among the city's workers. This relative lack of ethnic fragmentation,
so common among workers in Gilded Age cities, encouraged Democratic politicians to support efforts at workplace organization.

Equally important was the pattern of economic growth. Since
many factories grew out of smaller workshops, and the latter continued to persist in many trades, a not insignificant degree of continuity existed. Evansville workers did not experience the wholesale dislocations that lay in store for New Albany workers after the closing
of the shipyards. Whole communities were not forced to relocate,
though they did have to adapt to a changing social and work environment, one that was less artisanal in character.

And perhaps most important, the diverse nature of industry in
Evansville meant that the prosperity of the city was not tied to any
one industry as New Albany had been in the antebellum period, or
to any one industrialist as it would be in the postwar era. The lack of
common cause opened the door for public disputes between the city's
wealthiest men, and the shrillness of their disagreements reinforced
a tendency of local Democratic leaders to speak a highly charged
class rhetoric, especially when antiunion employers were active in
Republican party politics. Consequently, a political culture of class
antagonism, similar to that which developed in New Albany during
the Civil War, arose during the war and persisted through the Gilded
Age in Evansville. This chapter examines the changing social context
in which these political and cultural forces operated.

A Commercial Importance Not Possessed by Any Other

At midcentury Evansville was a small place. A mere village of
1,228 in 1838, it experienced the beginnings of a boom in the late
1840s with the general revival of commerce along the river, and in
1850 its population reached 3,325, and that of neighboring Lamasco
added another 1,441.[5] The results were visible in 1852, when a correspondent to the New Albany–based *Western Odd Fellows' Magazine*
traveled downstream to Evansville and marveled at the changes that
had occurred there in the five years since his last visit. Fine business
houses and residences had been built, giving the city a stately appearance from the river. Reflecting on its domination of the Wabash and

Green River trades, the reporter thought Evansville now ranked "a commercial importance . . . not possessed by any other city of southern Indiana." And he remarked that the vigorous prosecution of the final leg of the Wabash and Erie Canal and the extension of the Evansville and Princeton Railroad to Terre Haute—both of which had Evansville as their southern terminus—were evidence of the "energy and capital of her citizens."[6]

These enterprising men were the heart of a relatively homogeneous elite. Of the wealthiest sixty-eight individuals in town, half were directly engaged in commerce, and most lived along the waterfront just south of the business district. Natives were overrepresented among the wealthy—67.6 percent as compared to less than a third of the total adult male population—and they were joined by equal numbers of Germans, English, and Irish.[7] The rise to wealth by a handful of immigrants only slightly diminished the homogeneity of the commercial elite at midcentury. Most were active in the Protestant churches of the city. Irish merchants, like John Shanklin, emigrated in search of improved business opportunities. After serving an apprenticeship in a general store, Shanklin left Donegal County in 1815 and proceeded to work in a few mercantile establishments in New York and Kentucky. In 1823 he came to Evansville and started a wholesale business. Shipping produce to New Orleans, Shanklin accumulated a substantial fortune. For the remainder of their lives, he and his wife, a native of Vermont, were intimately involved in the affairs of the Walnut Street Presbyterian Church, to which many elite families were connected.[8]

The elite supplied much of the "energy and capital" that led Evansville to commercial prosperity in the years to come. In 1847 the merchant-dominated city government contracted to build a wharf suitable for an important river port. Two years later both the city and Vanderburgh County issued $100,000 in bonds toward the completion of the Evansville and Crawfordsville Railroad, which promised to bring the products of farmland to the north to local commercial houses. Merchants and steamboatmen organized packets connecting Evansville with the Green River as far south as Bowling Green, Kentucky, and to the north up the Wabash.[9] Collectively they established a board of trade in 1857 to expedite the expansion of local commerce.[10] Individually merchants specialized to take advantage of increasing opportunities, establishing distinct wholesaling and commission houses after midcentury. By 1870 there were 150 of them.[11]

The active stance of the commercial community toward improvements was most clearly articulated in its united defense of the Wabash and Erie Canal in the summer of 1855. The inciting deed was perpetrated by a group of "regulators" in Clay County—a hundred miles to the north—who cut the levees of the Birch Creek Reservoir, which fed the canal, draining it of water. The act was a response to negligent contractors who failed to remove felled and living trees in the reservoir before filling it, creating swamp conditions. Fearing the outbreak of disease, a not unknown occurrence along the canal, and facing an unresponsive group of canal trustees, the "regulators" took the law into their own hands and destroyed private property.[12] In so doing they rendered the portion of the canal south of Terre Haute useless.

News of the depredations to the north led Evansville businessmen to organize a meeting to condemn the mob spirit fostered by "irresponsible desperados." But it was the closing of an artery of trade more than any breakdown of order that galvanized them. Local merchants had long awaited the opening of the canal—work had stopped for many years after the panic of 1837. In resolutions to the governor, they portrayed Evansville as the center of a vast transportation network linking the Mississippi and Ohio rivers with the Great Lakes. "Looking to the future," they agreed, "we scarcely can calculate the golden showers it will scatter in our midst." Loss of the canal, they feared, would have a deleterious effect: "The warehouses built with reference to it, would be useless—lots purchased on account of it sink to nominal value—the commerce and trade which she [Evansville] already began largely to enjoy by means of it, will cease and be diverted to other channels."[13] In another set of resolutions, the assembled offered their services as a militia to restore order in Clay County.

When the governor accepted, another meeting was held, and about fifty young men—"merchants, clerks, lawyers &c., armed with rifles and pistols"—formed the Evansville Guards.[14] Letters from the "front" to local newspapers further establish the commercial credentials of the troop. One described a routine of carrying a "heavy rifle four or five miles" in the heat of the day, and patrolling at night for three hours at a time, a regimen the author thought "rather severe to those accustomed to sit at a desk."[15] And so the bourgeoisie of Evansville went to war in defense of social order, progress, commerce, and real estate speculation. The interrelationship of these causes was clear to the editor of the Evansville *Journal*, who waxed indignant on learning that the Evansville Guards stood alone against a hostile population. Even nearby Terre Haute failed to find evidence of mob rule compelling cause to assemble a militia.[16]

In Clay County the militiamen wrote of threats from the "regulators," but for the most part the men passed time hunting, fishing and playing cards.[17] A few arrests were made, but the defendants were found innocent by a sympathetic Terre Haute jury. A correspondent to the Evansville *Journal* wrote despondently that "there is no security for life or property there so long as a band of reckless and unprincipled men control public opinion."[18] This proved prophetic and the southern section of the canal remained largely unusable.[19]

The failure of the canal to meet expectations, however, hardly slowed merchants in their drive to increase Evansville's share of commerce. Packets up the Wabash and Green rivers and the Evansville and Terre Haute Railroad brought local warehouses an expanding regional produce. Most of this antebellum wholesale trade was bound for the South. In 1857, over 200,000 bushels of corn—and smaller quantities of wheat, oats, and tobacco—were shipped down the Mississippi. Similarly, sizable quantities of boots and shoes, leather, saddlery, and clothing—some of it produced locally—were shipped southward. At the same time, Evansville merchants imported salt, groceries, and queensware from New Orleans to be sold locally or reshipped northward.[20]

Though the Civil War briefly deprived them of markets, the 1860s brought greater riches. Prosperity returned with the fall of Vicksburg and the full reopening of river traffic. Traders realized profits due to a general rise in prices, and those dealing in corn made fortunes supplying the army when the city was made a quartermaster's depot.[21] After the war, local merchants penetrated the cotton and tobacco growing regions of the South by means of twice-weekly packets on the Cumberland and Tennessee rivers.[22] These efforts were richly rewarded. Between 1857 and 1867, exports of corn grew nearly nine-fold to just under 2 million bushels; tobacco sales increased by 365 percent; and a minor cotton market emerged. Markets for other goods increased as well. In 1867, dry goods sales were three times higher than a decade before. Wholesalers also moved more manufactured goods. Sales of boots and shoes increased more than nine-fold, and large jumps were registered for drug, iron, hardware, and queensware dealers.[23]

Fortunes accumulated with the expansion of trade. Whereas only 111 residents possessed personal and real estate holdings totaling $10,000 or more on the eve of war, 270 owned at least double that sum ten years later.[24] Men of commerce continued to dominate the elite, accounting for 54.4 percent of the total, and they continued to concentrate in a small area south of the business district, away from the city's growing workshops.[25] The greatest change was in the numbers of Germans. As late as 1860, only four German merchants held as much as $10,000 in property. Ten years later, twenty-one owned estates worth at least $20,000. Another two German bankers and twelve retailers also were counted among the economic elite in 1870.[26] And through the 1870s, Germans solidified their position in the commercial community. In 1880, first- and second-generation German immigrants comprised 41.7 percent of the local merchant population, and 45.1 percent of retail storekeepers.[27] Thus, as Evansville entered the Gilded Age, its men of commerce were increasingly a diverse lot.

But at the very highest ranks of the elite much of the old homogeneity was preserved. Here commercial interests were most eminent; of the fourteen individuals with at least $50,000 in 1860, all but two were merchants. Ten years later, thirty-four owned $100,000 or more. With the exception of two lawyers and four German-born iron manufacturers, they were uniformly engaged in the exchange, rather than the production, of value—as bankers, merchants, and real estate brokers. Furthermore, only two of these twenty-eight were German.[28]

Individuals long engaged in trade and commodity speculation, like New Englanders Marcus Sherwood and Willard Carpenter, invested their profits in the local real estate market, which if tax assessments can be used as a guide, rarely declined, and periodically demonstrated huge increases in value. Such men symbolized the connection between riches and local prospects. The wealthy, as did others, invested most of their money in land, and much of it was in the county. The constant rise in real estate values suggested an air of confidence in Evansville's future.[29]

It also reflected a rising population. Though it was about the same size as New Albany in 1860, Evansville subsequently grew at a rate double that of its upstream rival. By 1870, over 21,000 people made their home in Evansville. Growing numbers of residents required housing, and in 1867 alone 274 dwellings were constructed. Few were built of brick; the vast majority were frame dwellings, the kind appropriate for increasing numbers of workers employed in manufacturing establishments.[30] As it happened, the promise and realization of commercial prosperity created attractive conditions for prospective manufacturers.

From Master to Manufacturer: Forces of Transformation

As much as the area just south of the business district was commercial, the area to its north, known as Lamasco, was marked by

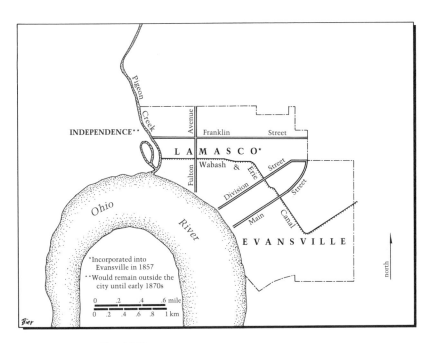

Map 2. Evansville, 1860

workshops, though the beginnings of local manufacturing were modest (see map 2).[31] At midcentury few industries were important. Only
shoemaking, tailoring and brick making engaged as many as twenty-
five workers, which reinforces the commercial picture as shoemakers and tailors were tied closely to merchants, who sent low-quality
goods to the South, while brick makers provided the raw material for
the construction of the growing number of business houses that im-
pressed the correspondent from New Albany. Midcentury workshops
were almost uniformly small. Nearly nine of ten employed fewer
than seven workers, and nearly two-thirds of the manufacturing labor force worked in such shops. Only one, a foundry, employed more
than fifteen. That firm further set itself apart by using a steam engine; all others relied solely on muscle or water power. Output levels, as a consequence, were low. Only one shop produced as much as
$20,000, and just six others managed to reach the $10,000 level.[32]

The men who ran these modest workshops were similar in ethnic
background to the workers they hired. Germans made up the largest
single group, accounting for 44.8 percent of the masters, and 47.8 of

all men engaged in manufacturing trades. Native-born whites comprised the next largest group with 40.8 and 33.4 percent, respectively. The rest were primarily English and Irish.[33] Considering the close quarters in which masters and journeymen worked, their shared ethnic backgrounds, and the low production levels that were so common, the social distance between employer and employee was small. Certainly the physical distance was, for most masters took in journeymen as boarders and in a significantly high number of cases (37.8 percent), it was more than one.[34]

The households of the three master carriage makers reveal how closely tied work and home were at midcentury. New Yorker Varner Satterlee and his wife Julia came to Indiana no later than 1831 when their first child, Newton, was born. In 1850 Newton, still living with his family, worked as a carriage maker. Boarding with the family was Noah Pritchett, an eighteen-year-old Indiana native who followed the blacksmith's trade, George Cummings, an eighteen-year-old English wheelwright, and George Gable, a twenty-six-year-old carriage painter from Pennsylvania. In the household of native-born E. H. and Mildred DeGarmo, two carriage makers—Indianian Oron Clark, and Irish-born Peter McDavitt—took their board. Living with the German family of Christian and Ann Decker was twenty-three-year-old French-born wheelwright, Andrew Myer. In 1850 these shops combined to produce $9,290 in carriages and wagons. The capital requirements to undertake the business were light—investment totaled $4,000. The shops employed between four and six workers each and paid wages that averaged about $18 a month, which in many cases were supplemented with room and board.[35]

The artisanal character of local manufacturing, depending on the industry, would persist into the last half of the century. But over the course of the next thirty years, most trades became dominated by larger firms as many masters took advantage of the greater opportunities offered by Evansville's improved status as a wholesale distribution center. The growth of railroads and steamboat packets that so enriched local merchants encouraged manufacturers to increase production levels.

The opening of the Bodiam Coal mine just outside the city provided a further inducement toward local manufacturing. It had long been suspected that Vanderburgh County lay atop a thick seam of coal, so when William Kersteman began to sink a shaft, the importance of the project was quickly grasped by businessmen. The city council granted Kersteman the right to tunnel beneath the city streets, and they exempted his property from taxation for a five-year period. The success of the venture was celebrated with an auction held by the miners who sold the first cart of Evansville coal for over $40 to foundrymen William Heilman and Christian Kratz.[36]

By 1874, most coal used in the city was mined locally or in the surrounding countryside.[37] The cheapness of this new supply of coal proved an asset to manufacturers and production levels soared. In 1860 twenty-two firms produced goods worth over $20,000, and the output of the foundry and machine shop of Kratz and Heilman alone reached $200,000. Twenty years later, the number of firms producing at least $20,000 in goods climbed to seventy-four, and sixteen exceeded $100,000.[38] This rise in productivity reflected increased mechanization. One of the first responses by masters was to install steam engines; by 1860 about fifty shops operated no fewer than seventy-five of them.[39] Accordingly, capital investment grew. In the ten years between 1850 and 1860 the number of firms with more than $10,000 invested in them climbed from two to seventeen, and seven exceeded $25,000. In 1880 capital investment for forty-seven firms exceeded $25,000.[40]

This continuous expansion of capacity required a larger labor force and the number of workers in manufacturing grew 220 percent during the 1850s alone—from 290 to 927. By 1880 over 3,000 found employment in local workshops and factories. Increasingly they worked in larger shops; the number of wage earners employed in the shops employing no more than six workers declined during the 1850s from 183 to 175, and as early as 1860 they were outnumbered by those in the largest. This trend continued into the Gilded Age, and by 1880 more than 40 percent worked for the fourteen firms that employed at least fifty workers, and a large majority (64.8) worked in shops employing at least twenty-five.[41]

The sources for this transformation were diverse. In many cases masters like Christian Kratz and William Heilman steadily expanded their businesses into large concerns. These two German immigrants started in 1847 with a capital stock of less than $2,000, which included two blind horses for motive power.[42] Within three years they employed fifteen men and produced castings and tinware worth $11,500.[43] In 1852, they erected a brick machine shop in Lamasco and two years later a three-story brick sales outlet on Main Street. Three years later, the original foundry was replaced by a three-story brick edifice that was divided into pattern making, foundry, and finishing shops, where 100 workers found employment.[44] By 1860 Kratz and Heilman had become the largest industrial firm in the city, building engines, steamboat and mill machinery, boilers, and threshing machines while employing 111 workers.[45]

In the postwar years, other iron firms experienced growth, particularly stove and plow manufacturers. By 1870, the plow factory of H. T. Blount housed a twenty-four horsepower engine and hired 34 workers, whose combined exertions produced 6,000 plows worth $54,000. Ten years later Blount employed 44 workers and output rose to 12,000 plows worth $92,981. For stove manufacturers, the 1860s were even more profitable. John H. Roelker, master of a small foundry in the 1850s, increased his shop's capacity during the following decade and became the leading local producer in a prospering industry. By 1870, his Eagle Foundry employed twenty-seven workers who produced $110,000 worth of stoves and other goods. Though the dollar value of sales did not improve during the deflationary 1870s, business must have warranted expansion, for his payroll increased to sixty workmen. Other shops in the industry experienced a similar pattern.[46]

The appeal of expanding southern and western markets encouraged masters outside of the iron industry to respond in similar ways. Master saddlers, coopers, tanners, as well as the carpenters who established planing mills, responded by mechanizing and increasing the size of the workshops, so that by 1880 firms employing over forty workers prospered in each of these industries.[47]

Other manufacturers were lured to Evansville by reports of cheap fuel and accessible markets. This and Evansville's status as an important lumber market probably explain the relocation of furniture manufacturer Cyrus Armstrong from Lawrenceburg, Indiana, in 1854.[48] Enjoying considerable growth during the war decade, the factory in 1870 employed 155 workers (including 50 children and 5 women) and produced $205,000 worth of furniture. When the proprietors incorporated in 1874 as a regular stock company with $200,000 in capital, the firm immediately enlarged its capacity. Situated on a 5 1/2-acre parcel of land, the new factory was a six-story brick structure with dimensions of 150 by 60 feet. Soon these accommodations proved inadequate to the tasks of the rising firm and a three-story addition was built. Two engines, with a capacity of 150 horsepower, and new machinery were added.[49] The factory was divided into separate saw and planing mills, as well as distinct machine, cabinet, carving, and varnishing shops.[50] The labor force grew to 240, one-third of whom were children. Production increased as well, reaching the quarter million mark.[51]

Manufacturers of wood products replaced the iron masters as the leading employers of labor. By 1880 nearly six hundred men, women, and children worked for one of nine furniture companies. In that year six of the more modest firms sold between $30,000 and $75,000 worth of furniture; each also employed between thirty-eight and a hundred workers.[52] With the growth of furniture factories came the even greater expansion of the saw mill business. Though small mills operated as early as 1850, expansion in the industry came after 1860. In some cases, proprietors reinvested earnings and turned small mills into large operations. Others like former saw mill hand, Henry Rietman, who formed a partnership with merchants Ben Nurrie and Charles Schulte, drew on outside sources of capital. In the two decades to follow, mill production rose from $27,500 to $958,405 while the labor force increased fifteen-fold, from 25 to 401. In 1880 three mills each employed at least 80 workers.[53]

And still in other cases, the local industrial revolution was effected by merchants who entered the manufacturing sector. They did this in two ways. Some did so directly, like dry goods wholesaler James Oakley, who opened a steam powered barrel factory that employed twenty-five workers and that began mechanization of the cooperage industry.[54] Others invested as silent partners in works run by master mechanics. In this way, Willard Carpenter supplied some of the capital for the foundry business of Reitz and Haney, which in 1860 sold $50,000 in iron products.[55]

The largest factory in Evansville resulted from such a union of manufacturer and merchant. Responding to the rise of a local wholesale cotton market, William Heilman and a group of wealthy merchants, notably Charles Viele and D. J. Mackey, founded the Evansville Cotton Manufacturing Company. Capitalized at $100,000 and starting up with just forty workers, the firm's business grew rapidly. By the early 1870s the mill employed ninety hands and produced nearly $200,000 worth of sheeting and yarn. Success led to the erection of a new and larger mill on the western edge of the city. The new structure housed 400 looms, 14,000 spindles, 110 cards, and "a full complement of drawing frames, lappens and coarse and fine speeders." To run this collection of machinery the firm employed some three hundred workers, the vast majority of whom were women and children.[56]

Thirty years of industrial growth widened the social distance between employer and wage earner. These years witnessed a steady rise in the property holdings of manufacturers. While only twenty-eight were worth at least $10,000 in 1860, fifty owned twice that amount or more just ten years later.[57] Some experienced more dramatic accumulations of wealth. In ten years William Heilman increased his property holdings from $59,000 to $550,000, a figure that placed him among the wealthiest individuals in the city. During these years he moved out of the manufacturing district and built an imposing brick house on a large parcel of land along the northern portion of First Avenue, which was becoming a small enclave of the rich. On the other hand, John Reitz, who accumulated a similar fortune, moved to the waterfront of the upper wards, settling in with the commercial elite. Most, however, chose not to leave the mechanical community behind. Instead they continued to live predominantly in the manufacturing wards (what had once been the city of Lamasco) near their workers.[58]

Neighborhoods were one thing; households were another. Growing divisions between workers and employers were evident in the declining practice of boarding employees. Increasingly manufacturers opted to include, aside from servants, only kin in their households. The percentage of employer households without unrelated wage-earning boarders increased from 42.2 at midcentury, to 68.6 ten years later, and to 84.0 in 1880.[59] This trend suggests a desire to develop a more private family life, a pattern that appealed to broad segments of society able to dispense with the income generated by boarders. While so doing, masters relinquished some authority over the personal lives of their employees, and it may have lessened the sense of community among those engaged in the mechanical arts. In any case, it strengthened the primacy of the cash nexus between employer and employee at the expense of others.

Changes in Work and the Work Force

Journeymen and less-skilled workers in the workshops of Evansville shared the same side of a growing social chasm between themselves and their employers. While some workers in the iron industry were able to maintain high wages and levels of skill retention, most were not. As improving transportation opened new markets to local businessmen, it also brought increased competition with producers elsewhere. Efforts to keep or expand their share of the market in the competitive environment often necessitated efforts to cheapen production costs. One way of doing this was to divide skilled and complex trades into repetitive and more easily learned processes. As more work could be done by workers who had not undergone long apprenticeships, and as competitive pressures mounted, employers were increasingly tempted to reduce wages, while others increased the pace of work. This was felt not only by employees of the largest firms, however; such patterns were becoming increasingly manifest even in some of the medium-size shops.

The perception of growing class distinctions was viewed by workers through a relatively homogeneous cultural background. Most workers in nearly all manual trades were either first- or second-generation German immigrants. Though they brought diverse traditions with them in the trans-Atlantic migration, a sense of Germanness pervaded much of Evansville society. As a result, both working-class neighborhoods *and* workshops lacked the ethnic diversity that so frequently frustrated the growth of class solidarity in other cities.

The Decline of Craft

The fall of the artisanal regime was felt first and foremost at work. In large factories the breakdown of the work process into its constituent parts was incorporated into the very edifice itself, as different floors and wings housed particular branches of the trade. In smaller shops the introduction of one device like the sewing machine could revolutionize production. In nearly all cases, masters responded to the innovations of their local competitors, as well as to those in other cities, with changes of their own. The result was an overall cheapening of labor that adversely affected skilled workers in most trades.

The effect on work is best illustrated by changes in cabinetmaking. At midcentury the trade proceeded along artisanal lines much as it did in New Albany. Motive power was supplied entirely by hand. No shop hired more than five workers, so it is doubtful that any significant division of labor was attempted. Master and journeyman worked on a product from beginning to end—sawing, planing, assembling, carving, and finishing.[60] Thirty years later the trade had been transformed nearly beyond recognition. Following the lead of the Armstrong Company, manufacturers instituted steam-driven machinery and an extensive division of labor. Under the new regime, production at the Armstrong factory was a collective process involving many departments, each in one repetitive aspect of the whole. Hands in the firm's saw mill cut rough wood and put it on a conveyor that brought it either to the drying house, or to the workmen in the planing mill, who cut the lumber into the requisite shapes. The wood was then sanded, and in simple cases, carved in the machine shops before it was brought to the cabinetmaking shops for assembly. The nearly completed item was then taken to the varnishing department.[61] What had once been the work of the cabinetmaker was now divided among sawyers, planers, machine-hands, cabinetmakers and varnishers. And where once adult males monopolized work, now children—fully one-third of the work force at Armstrong—played a substantial role.[62]

The benefits to proprietors were immense. A report by the U.S. Commissioner of Labor suggested that mechanization and the division of the work process reduced labor costs substantially. For example, the amount of labor time required to build twelve oak bookcases, three by five feet, by hand was four hundred hours. Under factory conditions, comparable bookcases were produced in just over forty-one hours. The cost in wages declined in similar proportions.[63]

The effect on furniture workers was appreciable; they did not share in the city's growing prosperity. Between 1860 and 1870 the percentage of cabinetmakers without property climbed from 33.9 to 57.7. Chair makers too increasingly found themselves among the propertyless, as their numbers rose from 57.1 percent to 66.7 percent. Among those working in the new subtrade of "varnisher," more than 80 percent were without any estate.[64] And the deterioration of the furniture worker's condition continued. By 1886 an old artisanal practice had become too burdensome, and the Furniture Workers' International Union (in convention at Evansville) resolved that employers should provide "all necessary tools."[65] Five years later, responding to questionnaires from the Indiana Department of Statistics, 68 cabinetmakers claimed daily wages ranging from $1.00 to $2.25, with an average of $1.52. Average wages for fifty-two machine-hands were less, at $1.40, and those for thirty-two varnishers were lower still—$1.33 (see table 4). Average annual earnings ranged from $350 for varnishers to $401 for cabinetmakers, totals barely sufficient, if that, to support a family.[66]

The extensive introduction of machinery led to lower wages and speedups in other industries. The proprietors of the cotton mill increased an already heavy reliance on female labor in 1875 when they equipped their new building with looms that allowed them to dispense with high-priced male weavers. The young women who replaced them received between 75 and 90 cents a day. The following year they were forced to accept a 5 percent reduction. Male workers too experienced downward pressure on wages as mule spinners received repeated wage reductions.[67] The small woolen mill run by J. A. Lemcke also used technology in response to declining prices during the depression. First, new carding machines were introduced, which increased the output of each worker by 33 percent. Then, in 1875 "self-operating" spinning mules were adopted, which led to a 50 percent reduction in the cost of labor. This innovation was followed by a speedup among the female weavers.[68]

Workers employed outside the large factories also faced deteriorating conditions. This was particularly the case for workers plying the

Table 4.   Wages in Selected Industries and Trades, Evansville, 1891

Trade	Number	Average Age	Average Day Wage	Average Annual Income
Furniture				
Cabinetmakers	68	40	$1.52	$401
Machine-hands	52	32	1.40	368
Varnishers	32	32	1.33	350
Apprentices	17	18	.93	257
Cooperage				
Coopers	14	40	1.32	279
Flour Barrel Makers	5	47	1.19	259
Slack Barrel Makers	6	33	1.16	291
Tight Barrel Makers	6	39	1.41	372
Iron				
Machinists	10	31	1.70	496
Molders	10	34	2.17	611
Pattern Makers	17	35	2.07	589
Plow Stokers	15	28	1.86	556
Blacksmiths	10	31	2.08	588
Finishers	9	30	1.84	431
Stove Mounters	7	31	2.02	590
Engineers	6	34	2.02	521
Apprentices	29	18	.83	218
Laborers				
Furniture	23	30	1.09	294
Cooperage	3	21	1.23	286
Planing Mills	16	30	1.26	227
Iron	28	18	1.05	242

SOURCE: Indiana, *Fourth Biennial Report of the Department of Statistics for 1891-92*, pp. 63, 99, 116, 129.

cooper's trade. Cooperages began to mechanize before the war, and by 1880 the industry was marked by two heavily mechanized shops employing about forty workers, two others that depended less on machinery while employing sixteen and twenty-eight workers, and six small shops that relied on human power. But even in these shops masters felt the competitive pressure of more efficient producers, and in turn responded by cutting wages. As a result, the percentage of propertyless coopers rose from 42.9 to 51.2 during the 1860s.[69] And wage rates continued to fall. To speed up production and ensure that machinery was being used to its fullest, masters typically imposed a piece rate, which fell as low at 10 cents a barrel in the midst of the depression of the 1870s. By 1880 the rate had been forced up by the coopers' union to 12 cents, which enabled workers to earn between $1.75 and 2.00 a day. Still many coopers labored for as little as $1.50.[70] With the collapse of the union, the trend resumed. In 1891 coopers earned an average of $1.32 an hour and $279 a year, an annual total lower than that of any of the furniture trades.[71]

One more example, that of harness makers, illustrates how the introduction of one simple technological innovation—the sewing machine in this case—could hasten the degradation of a trade. Under artisanal methods harness makers cut leather, treated it in water to make it pliable, and fitted the pieces together. Then, with needle and awl in hand, the worker stitched the parts of the harness. The single process of stitching consumed about 55 percent of the total labor time required by the entire productive process.[72] Masters often had apprentices do this slow and monotonous task, but until this process could be shortened, production remained stuck in traditional methods as there was little incentive to transform other processes.

The introduction of the sewing machine changed all that by substantially reducing the time necessary for stitching. Where once it had taken thirty-six hours to stitch six sets of blinders with needle and awl, a sewing machine operator could accomplish the task in twenty-four minutes.[73] This encouraged masters to hire unskilled labor. Where it was once necessary for stitchers to deftly handle a needle and awl, now retailers and sales agents boasted that sewing machines were "equal to hand sewing" though there was "no special knowledge required to operate successfully."[74] As early as 1870, five of the six harness shops in Evansville housed two sewing machines.[75] Masters increased their reliance on apprentices, and by 1870 the census lists one for every three journeymen. The rising employment of apprentices and other unskilled workers and the breakdown of the work process into its constituent parts had a malignant effect on journeymen in the trade. Though the ranks of propertyless workers swelled only slightly during the 1860s from 54.1 to 59.6 percent, later developments suggest that this increase was a long-term trend. In 1871 journeymen saddlers and harness makers resisted a reduction in wages they claimed would "reduce them to a starvation point." In 1880, employers paid their skilled men between $1.25 and $2.00; most paid $1.50, a wage comparable to that earned by both furniture workers and coopers.[76]

There were exceptions to the downward portrait drawn here, the most notable being workers in the burgeoning iron industry. While most others found that lower-paying wages and speedups followed the onset of mechanization, metal workers found expanding opportunity building those very engines and machines. Generally, this was the case for machinists; as David Montgomery has put it, "modern technology was the machinist's natural habitat, and technological improvements were as often as not their own inventions."[77]

Indeed the growth of machine shops and foundries was a boon for machinists, as they were the only local group of workers to rise in significant numbers from the ranks of the propertyless, the proportion falling from 59.3 in 1860, to 31.8 a decade later. As late as 1880 machinists commonly earned $2.00 a day, the same as molders and blacksmiths.[78] Yet, machinists usually worked in shops where they were a minority of the skilled work force, and in these workplaces their exclusive craft orientation remained a weakness. They rarely displayed a militancy capable of defending established wage rates before the late 1880s, when the International Association of Machinists was founded.[79] As a result, machinists earned less than some other iron workers. In 1891, respondents to the Department of Statistics reported an average income of $496 which, while higher than that earned in the debased crafts discussed above, fell well below the $611 earned by molders.[80]

It was the molder who most clearly reaped the benefits of industrialization in Evansville. Due to the growth of stove foundries, the number of molders increased from 39 in 1860 to 149 in 1880. Molding was hard and exacting work, and the molder played an indispensable role in production, one that defied mechanization well into the 1880s.[81] Employers commonly tried to cheapen labor costs by hiring greater numbers of apprentices. Molders everywhere adamantly opposed this and it was policy of the Iron Molders' International Union to insist that employers bind themselves contractually to apprentices in the traditional manner, and when this was not done to limit their employment to one for every eight journeymen. In Evansville, as elsewhere, this was a constant source of tension and conflict between molder and employer. However, through unceasing militancy and the support of a strong international union, local molders retained their lofty position throughout this period. Clearly, then, not all workers in Evansville's manufacturing sector suffered impoverishment as a result of industrialization.

The experience of molders and machinists were exceptions. More commonly, as a result of mechanization and the competition-in-

duced restructuring of the work process, skilled workers in the manufacturing trades suffered a series of wage reductions that in many
cases left them earning hardly more than unskilled laborers. And in
some cases, like that of the cooperage industry, the work load was
structured such that laborers earned more in a year than the more
highly skilled coopers.[82]

The Burden at Home

How workers coped with reduced wages was determined by multiple decisions within individual families. Consumption levels had
to be agreed upon with opportunities for alternate sources of income
in mind. While available evidence—primarily annual budgets for
twenty Evansville working-class families gathered by the Indiana
Bureau of Statistics—is sometimes inconclusive and reveals much
idiosyncrasy, some patterns emerge. The most important is that by
1890 a roughly equal standard of living seems to have been shared by
many working-class families headed by adult males, regardless of
their occupation. It was the size of the family that was crucial in
determining expenses. Spending ranged from $334 by a varnisher's
family of two, to $810 by an engineer's family of eight. Perhaps un-
expectedly, the third largest budget came from a family of nine that
was headed by a common laborer.[83]

Workers in Evansville spent the largest share on food, which accounted for about half of expenditures.[84] Prosperous families spent
more than a third of the food budget on meat, poultry and fish, while
poorer ones spent less than a fifth. On an average adults probably
consumed between three and four pounds of meat a week.[85] In families of five or more, per capita meat spending was highest in three
headed by a teamster, a molder, and a machinist—ranging from
$20.80 down to $14.38—while others headed by a laborer, a sawyer
and a fireman spent as little as $7.80. Yet the evidence suggests no
simple rule. The largest family, headed by a laborer, consumed
$11.67 worth of meat a person, which is noteworthy since expendi-
ture per person generally declined with increases in family size. Of
equal note was the purchase of meat costing $52 by a family of two,
again headed by a laborer, which was substantially more than the
amount bought by other small families.

Rents also seem to have been determined by family size. Workers
often lived near their place of employment, paying more than if they
resided in less-convenient areas. It was common only for families of
five or less to find accommodations costing less than $100 a year.
Larger households spent between $96 and $168, the highest figure

having been paid by the laborer's family of nine. Typically what workers received for their rent were single-unit detached cottages. Wooden structures of 1 or 1 1/2 stories, they followed the contours of city lots, which were long and narrow. Most had their own outbuilding along the alley, some of which must have been storage sheds or toilet facilities, though the larger two-story buildings may have housed boarders. On many lots, buildings took up little more than half the ground, leaving ample space for a small garden.

But the fundamental aspect of working-class housing was its tight quarters. Most units—not counting attics or cellars—were about eight hundred square feet. In some cases larger structures were divided into two smaller domiciles, either side-by-side, or by floor. Probably the most cramped conditions were experienced by workers who lived in the brick row houses scattered throughout the western part of the city. Some one-story, others two, they were all tiny—about six hundred square feet.[86] Such housing was provided for some cotton worker families by the mill owners, which they claimed rented at half the ordinary rate for houses.[87]

Small houses and tenements required little furniture; consequently the homes of workers were furnished with only the most necessary items. Twelve of the budgets reveal no expenditures on furniture, and three others spent $10 or less.[88] Probate inventories of worker estates corroborate the limited expenditures of furniture; none mentioned parlor furniture of any kind, the lack of which distinguished the working-class home from those of the petty bourgeoisie.[89]

Only in the purchase of shoes and clothing was consumption strongly correlated with occupational status. The purchase of these items amounted to between 10 and 20 percent of the budget in skilled worker households. Less-skilled workers and their families spent considerably less. Two households headed by varnishers, two by laborers, and one by a sawyer spent between 7.0 and 8.4 percent of their budget on clothing and footware. Yet again, the boundaries were not hard and fast, as the above mentioned laborer household of nine spent 15.1 percent.[90]

From the budgets prepared by these twenty women emerges a tentative picture of the vagaries of working-class life. Even lowly paid workers like varnishers maintained a comfortable standard of living before the arrival of children. Each birth, however, brought increasing hardship, and such families experienced long periods of relative deprivation throughout the childbearing years. Housewives in the poorer families spent considerably more on flour, sugar, and bakery products than they did on meat, substituting bread and other starches for the higher protein foods. Despite the presumed presence of small children, these families spent a tiny amount on clothing, suggesting that housewives sewed their own, or that the children walked around in tatters. Not until their children reached working age, would they live more comfortably.[91]

Yet families were often resourceful, and limited purchases at the grocers and tailors could be supplemented by alternatives. The probate inventory of laborer William Tieman, who had at least five children, reveals the possession by the family of a brown cow and calf that undoubtedly supplied the family with dairy products in good times as well as bad. Similarly, the family of laborer Philip Woehler, and perhaps that of his iron molder son Simon who lived next door, benefited from the eggs laid by their eight chickens. Others, like cabinetmaker Christian Hobell, whose estate included a sewing machine, probably spent less on clothing due to his wife's labor.[92]

Survival often necessitated the reliance upon more than one income, and this tendency seems to have increased with the growth of manufacturing. In 1860 working-class households rarely included more than one wage earner—in households headed by married males, the head of household was the sole income provider in 70.9 percent of the cases—and few children were employed.[93] An examination of the structure of molder, cabinetmaker, cooper, and harness maker households twenty years later suggests that two decades of industrial growth had some transforming effects.[94]

Though the practice remained relatively uncommon, some took in boarders, which netted families as much as $100 a year.[95] Consequently, it was households headed by low paid harness makers (10.7) and cabinetmakeis (7.9) that most frequently resorted to this strategy. While the added income supplied by boarders often helped families survive critical periods, it meant added work for the housewife, cramped conditions, and a general loss of privacy. The reliance of harness maker families on this strategy probably reflected the youth of their children; to a far greater extent than with coopers and cabinetmakers, married harness makers were thirty-five years of age or younger. That molders who were equally young took in boarders least often was a manifestation of the high wages that they commanded.

More commonly, supplementary income was provided by other family members, including siblings and in-laws. Most families, however, relied on the employment of unmarried children whose cumulative earnings could be substantial. The reliance on child labor was not limited by trade, though the practice was most common in households headed by coopers. Nearly half (48.3) relied on this resource, which was 20 percent more than the next trade. If only those

with children over the age of twelve are counted, 84.4 percent of cooper households included working children. As children grew older
this was not an uncommon practice. Seven of ten molder families
with older children did similarly, as did 64.3 percent of cabinetmaker families. If fewer total molder, cabinetmaker, and harness maker
households relied on their children's labor, this fact probably reflected their youth, not their attitudes toward their children.

This did not always work to the disadvantage of the child; most of
these working children were over the age of fifteen, and entry into
the labor force could prove beneficial to teen-age boys. An early entrance into the workshop could provide a skill that would soon enable the young worker to provide for a family. In such cases, then, the
practice of putting children to work transmitted the father's status
as a skilled worker to his male progeny without weakening the bonds
of the nuclear family while perhaps strengthening the authority of
the father. It will be remembered that in 1850 master craftsmen typically took in one or two of their journeymen as boarders. During the
intervening thirty years masters had ceased this practice and young
workers now continued to reside with their families until marriage.

Yet, some families were forced to put younger children to work.
In households headed by cabinetmakers, one-third of the children
between the ages of thirteen and fifteen earned wages. The rate for
cooper and molder households was lower, about one in five, though
in the former case it was the frequent and multiple employment of
their oldest offspring that allowed coopers to dispense with the labor
of their younger children.

Though molders relied less on boarders or young children to supplement their earnings than did workers in the debased crafts, the
evidence suggests that these were differences of degree, not kind.
However, regardless of the age of entry into the workshop, employment proved more stable for molders than other workers.[96] In 1890
more than six of ten molders who headed households ten years before continued to ply their trade locally or work as foremen in molding departments, while no more than 45 percent of the workers in the
other three trades did. For younger workers who lived with their parents or boarded in 1880, the divergence was just as great. These less-
rooted molders experienced a 45.1 percent rate of persistence, while
cabinetmakers, harness makers, and coopers stayed on at rates of
35.4, 33.3, and 20.5 percent, respectively. It is probable that despite
the expansion of production in their industries, these young workers
found that they could not hope to support a family on the reduced
wages that the decade brought.

Yet these figures must be read with care. Though younger harness makers seem to have persisted at a relatively high rate, that six were listed as "collar makers" and one as a "collar cutter" in 1890 means that they had either specialized in collar production during the 1880s, or had originally been trained only in that aspect of the trade. In the cabinetmaking trade, six older workers who headed households—all in their thirties or forties in 1880—were employed outside the furniture industry as carpenters, suggesting that their training in wood working was broad enough to find work outside the factories. Not so with younger cabinetmakers, who frequently left the city. Those that remained in the industry, found work in 1890 as machine-hands, again suggesting that early employment in the factories was more limited than the label "cabinetmaker" might have suggested.[97]

Working-class families then adapted to low wages in traditional ways, as in the household production of food and clothing, and in others that emphasized multiple incomes. This was particularly evident among workers in the debased trades, though it was not completely foreign to better paid workers like iron molders. Despite the diversity of trades and the relative lack of powerful industrialists, a working-class standard of living was emerging that journeymen of an earlier day, like the ship carpenters of New Albany, would have found quite foreign. Yet to many German immigrants it was a standard that probably looked too familiar.

Ethnicity, Race, and Working-Class Communities

Evansville lured a large number of German immigrants at midcentury. In the early nineteenth century, German society was poised at an awkward stage between feudalism and industrial capitalism, and the results were a limiting of opportunity for some and the threat of starvation for many others. Due to rapid population growth, as well as land speculation fueled by bourgeois investment, many farmers found they were unable to buy enough land to support a family on farms already subdivided to the subsistence point. Artisans, who contributed a greater than proportional share to the migration, were also bound by social forces. Competition from new factories in some trades, oversaturation of the labor supply in others, the loss of tariff protection that allowed British goods easy access to German markets, and masters who responded to the competitive environment by debasing trades, requiring longer hours and reducing wages, threatened German artisans with impoverishment. Yet the weak German bourgeoisie was slow to respond with the expansion of productive capacity. Out of the displaced peasantry, the impoverished craftsmen, and women and children entering the labor force for the first

time arose a German proletariat, for which there was little employment. German workers in 1845 were faced with what looked like a
grim future.[98]

A series of crop failures, particularly of the potato, which had been
instrumental in permitting peasant families to survive on small
farms, led to soaring food prices and unleashed a torrent of unrest.
The year 1847 witnessed violent strikes and food riots. The discontent reached the political arena, fueling working-class support for the
unsuccessful liberal revolution of 1848. In its wake, immigration to
the United States rose to unprecedented levels as farmers and workers were lured by the prospect of acquiring cheap land or better wages.[99] It was from this social material out of which the working class
of Evansville was cut.

From 1850 until at least 1880 German immigrants and their progeny comprised the largest single component of the Evansville population. At midcentury, 43.3 percent of those who listed an occupation
in the census were born in Germany.[100] During the 1850s, the years
of greatest immigration, the percentage of Germans rose slightly to
45.2 percent.[101] By 1880 the German community, including a large
second generation, comprised 43.0 percent of the city's work force,
and an additional 4.3 percent were native-born with one German
parent. Germans were the most significant ethnic bloc throughout
the occupational structure of the city—after whites with native-born
parents, who accounted for 21.2 percent of the work force, and blacks
who comprised 12.8 percent, the next highest group was English
immigrants and their children at 4.4 percent.[102] As one historian has
observed for Milwaukee, the Germans in Evansville were the only
group to be well represented throughout the urban class structure.[103]

But it was in manufacturing that the German presence was most
evident. As local factories and workshops expanded in the second
half of the century, German immigrants continued to fill the bulk of
the jobs created there (see table 5) This was particularly true in the
more highly skilled positions. By 1880 only a handful of skilled
trades employed a majority of workers from outside the German
community.

Immigrants and their children, however, tended to fill different
jobs. Those born in Germany were most likely to be employed in the
older skilled trades. In 1880, twenty-two of the twenty-three German
brewers in the city were immigrants, and among the thirty blacksmiths of German background, again twenty-two were born in Germany. These numbers were reflected in the construction industry as
well, where immigrant brickmasons outnumbered their children by

Table 5.   Proportion of Germans in Leading Skilled Trades, Evansville, 1850–80

Trade	1850	1860	1880
Manufacturing: metals			
Blacksmith	55.0	50.7	59.0
Boilermaker	—	54.5	60.7
Engineer	11.1	10.4	18.0
Finisher	—	48.4	60.0
Machinist	—	7.4	36.4
Molder	—	43.6	79.4
Pattern Maker	—	44.4	45.5
Tinner	34.8	46.3	58.6
Manufacturing: wood			
Cabinetmaker	87.0	78.0	78.2
Chair maker	—	57.1	67.4
Cooper	57.9	53.8	67.4
Sawyer	—	60.0	29.3
Turner	—	86.7	76.7
Manufacturing: leather			
Collarmaker	—	—	65.4
Saddler	31.3	54.1	70.0
Shoemaker	73.3	65.0	75.8
Tanner	—	80.0	61.5
Manufacturing: other			
Brewer	—	88.9	82.1
Brick Maker	—	91.3	66.7
Cigar Maker	83.3	54.3	72.8
Potter	70.0	66.7	85.7
Printer	10.5	17.5	16.5
Stone Cutter	12.5	65.2	76.9
Tailor	71.4	81.0	77.1
Wagon Maker	30.8	59.5	70.7
Wheelwright	33.3	—	—
Construction			
Brickmason	47.4	68.8	54.0
Carpenter	38.0	44.8	45.0
Painter	5.3	26.5	32.4
Plasterer	38.1	48.4	50.0

Note: Trades with no figures in a given year numbered less than six practicioners.

SOURCE: Seventh Census, Eighth Census, and Tenth Census, manufacturing schedule, Vanderburgh County.

more than four to one; the ratio for carpenters was nearly two to one. But the difference was most pronounced in manufacturing trades that proceeded under sweated conditions like tailoring or shoemaking, or that had experienced extensive mechanization and the debasement of skill like cabinetmaking and tanning. In these trades immigrants outnumbered the second generation by between 3.65 to 1 to well over 9 to 1.

The second generation followed their elders into the workshops and factories, though when they did it was usually in the new and plentiful low-status jobs in industries making broad use of a division of labor, or in expanding skilled trades like iron molding or cigar making. In the furniture factories machine-hands, varnishers, upholsters, chair caners and those that were listed merely by their employment there were most likely to be the children of immigrants. This situation was due in part to the younger generation's youth; however, it also reflected the changing structure of work that was discussed above. The division of labor and the mechanization of productive processes created a large number of semiskilled jobs in the growing factories of the city. It was here that the younger generations were most likely to find work, and unlike earlier forms of apprenticeship, such forms of employment were unlikely to train the young worker for considerably higher skilled jobs.

Throughout the period, the geographical center of both the German community and manufacturing was in the lower part of the city, in what continued to be known as Lamasco, even though the district had been incorporated into Evansville in 1857. That all but one of the numerous German churches were located north of Main Street solidifies the impression. The oldest churches, established in the forties and fifties, were concentrated in the Third, Fourth, and Fifth wards (as constituted in 1880), while newer ones were built during the eighties on the outskirts of Lamasco. While the largest were Catholic, smaller Lutheran and Reformed churches prospered in the same neighborhoods. More than religious centers, the churches reaffirmed a German identity by worshipping in the German language into the twentieth century; this was also the case for instruction in many Lutheran and Catholic schools.[104]

The occupational structure of the wards in 1880 affirms the relationship between manufacturing and the German community. Comprising less than a third of the work force in the first two wards, the percentage of Germans in wards three, four, and six was between 42.6 and 48.6, and they dominated the Fifth Ward with 65.4 percent.[105] It was precisely these wards that were home to most work-

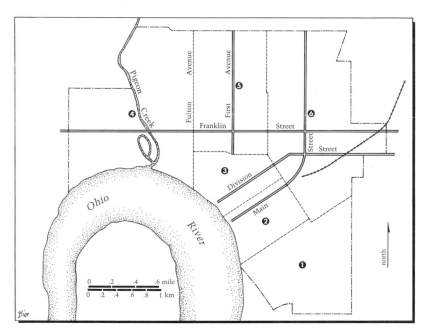

Map 3. Evansville, 1880

ers engaged in manufacturing. In 1880, between 25 and 46 percent of
the work force in these wards was comprised of workers in leading
manufacturing industries, while in the elite-dominated First and Second wards the figures were 14.6 and 11.4 percent, respectively. The
Fifth and Sixth wards especially were bastions of skilled workers,
where they comprised more than a third of the work force. Most
workers in the manufacturing sector of the economy resided in a
broad area that was bounded on the west by Pigeon Creek and on the
south by Main Street (see map 3). Marked by its plebeian character,
this area was not characterized by industry-specific residential patterns.

Nor was it entirely demarcated by class, as journeymen and laborers lived next door to petty producers. The 100 block of Delaware
Street, a few blocks northeast of the intersection of Fulton Avenue
and Franklin Street in the Fifth Ward, illustrates the pattern. Walking east, the census enumerator in 1880 came across families headed
by a bricklayer, a cabinetmaker, a master shoemaker, a fireman, a
carpenter, a molder, a janitor, a molder, a brickmason, a journeyman

shoemaker, a laborer, and a machinist. Returning on the south side of the street, he encountered two families headed by brickmasons, a master blacksmith, a former woolen cloth finisher who recently received a promotion to bookkeeper, and a chair maker.[106]

Here, away from the high priced and congested downtown and waterfront areas, working-class families were able to build a mechanics' neighborhood that shared more than a little with other postartisanal communities like that of the New Albany ship carpenters of the 1860s. Nearly all households on the street were simple nuclear families, more than half with at least three children. Some evidence suggests that these were geographically stable households; with only one exception the children were born in Indiana. Male heads of households provided the sole support for their families except in a couple of cases where a member of his spouse's family resided with them—one seamstress and one cabinetmaker—and when children entered their late teens.[107]

Yet there were differences that were specific to the particular time and place. For one, this was not a group of native artisans long schooled in American republicanism. Still it was an ethnically homogeneous group. Fifteen of the seventeen households on the block were headed by a German immigrant or the son of one. Of the two that were not, one was English and the other was the son of English parents. Second, the diverse occupational nature of the block precluded the development of the kind of uniform experience that united workplace and neighborhood in the shipbuilding wards of New Albany. However, the uniformly mechanical background of the male residents suggests conditions that would nurture a similar kind of plebeian political culture. These German workers came from an environment that had grown hostile to the independent producer and the journeyman. For them, the United States offered a more egalitarian environment in which skilled workers could maintain living conditions that were somewhat commensurate with artisanal standards. Threats to their ability to achieve this were often seen in light of earlier experience in Germany and were denounced as attempts to impose a European-style class tyranny. In the years following the Civil War, this social context gave rise to a militant form of republicanism and producerism that eased the development of trade unions as well as coalitions with the Democrats.

A different type of working-class community was arising in the western half of the Fourth Ward, across Pigeon Creek in the factory suburb of Independence. Incorporated into the city in the early 1870s, the area was less diverse occupationally, dominated as it was by a few

large-scale firms, and the artisan past was less evident. Here resided
the laborers in the saw mills, the planing mills, and the cotton mill,
as well as the coal miners who worked in mines just west of the city.
The extent that this was, indeed, a different kind of community is
revealed by the collective decision of furniture workers to live elsewhere, despite the Armstrong Company's location just across the
creek. And though Germans comprised the largest group of wage
earners in Independence, they were a smaller portion of the work
force than in the rest of Lamasco, where the crafts, if in diluted form,
were more prevalent.

On the western edge of Independence stood the cotton mill, the
city's single largest employer. Competing in a low-wage industry, the
mill from the beginning recruited its largely female labor force from
the least stable and most desperate portions of the white population.
At first the mill drew from war refugees from the South. Twenty-
eight workers from eleven families were found in the 1870 census
schedule, and none of these families had a child over the age of four
that was born in Indiana. Most workers were teenage boys and girls
born in Tennessee, Georgia, or Alabama, who moved with widowed
mothers to Evansville during or after the war.[108]

Ten years later the mill increased its dependence on low-wage labor, employing nearly three hundred workers, a third of whom were
under the age of sixteen. A fifth of the 1880 work force continued to
come from families headed by widowed females. While only 12.5
percent lived in those headed by day laborers, the age of these workers suggests that their family circumstances may have been dire.
Such families supplied the mills with 34 percent of its youngest
workers—those under fourteen—as they were unable to wait until
their children reached the latter teen years to exploit their earning
power.[109] Another 18 percent of the work force came from families
headed by skilled workers, who supplemented their own earnings as
well as those of their sons by sending their daughters into the mill.

Nearly a fifth of this work force lived apart from their parents,
boarding with one of the families that lived near the mill. On the
north side of Pennsylvania Street, for example, in a row of particularly long narrow houses, families headed by a cigar maker, a janitor,
and a river pilot gave room and board to between two and five female
employees of the cotton mill. In this way, families supplemented
their incomes while providing a convenient source of housing, and
perhaps a good deal of freedom from paternal authority, for single
women workers.

In the ten years after 1870, the ethnic composition of the cotton mill labor force changed considerably, as second-generation German immigrants (34.5 percent) replaced Southerners as the largest group. The next largest group continued to be daughters of native parents, many born in the south, who comprised a quarter of the work force. The saw mills drew similarly on the German population to meet its labor needs, employing a work force that was 40 percent German. Mine owners too, depended on a multiethnic work force in which the German element, at 35 percent, was the largest component, while natives and the English added 16.5 and 13.4 percent, respectively. It was this influx of the second generation into these workplaces, and the increasingly German nature of Independence that led saw mill proprietors like Charles Schulte, Henry Rietman, and Adam Helfrich to work for the establishment of a new Catholic parish, St. Boniface, in Independence in the late seventies.[110]

The result is that a slightly less German work force, employed primarily by large firms, arose on the western edge of the city, separated by Pigeon Creek from the more occupationally diverse working-class community with its artisan origins. Though at times joining the rest of the working population in politics and organization building, the workers of Independence rarely took the lead in city-wide labor efforts until the appearance of the Knights of Labor. Instead, leadership generally came from skilled German workers who lived east of the creek.

In debasing many skills, the processes of industrialization created a growing demand for less-skilled labor in the factories. As we have seen, this was largely met by the children of German immigrants, who followed their fathers into the manufacturing sector of the economy. As a consequence, Germans provided a shrinking percentage of the day-laboring population, decreasing from 53.3 to 29.9 in the twenty years after 1860, a decline that was not equaled in any other occupation. Among those that continued to work as laborers, immigrants outnumbered the younger generation by a two to one ratio. Clearly then, the second generation chose to exchange the vagaries of casual labor for the relative regularity of factory work.

The movement of young Germans into the factories left the least remunerative and most irregular work of common labor to the rapidly growing black population. Largely due to the migration of ex-slaves, the local black community grew from just 96 on the eve of war to 2,686 in 1880, when black workers comprised 12.8 percent of the labor force. Aside from the local tobacco factory, which almost exclusively hired them, blacks were largely excluded from the manufacturing sector. As a result, most black men were confined to back-breaking work unloading goods at the wharf and transporting them on the city streets, and 35 percent of the city's day laborers were black.[111] The irregularity of work for these men made it a necessity for their wives to work for wages. As it did for men, a racial division of labor precluded the entrance of black women into manufacturing establishments like the cotton mill, and almost four hundred black women worked as domestic servants, washerwomen or in similar capacities.[112]

Blacks concentrated in a growing ghetto in the eastern portion of the First and Second wards, and the southern part of the Sixth. Close to the railroad yards, the wharf, and the elite neighborhoods along the waterfront that provided employment for black women, they found themselves isolated both at work and at home from the rest of the working-class population. To some extent residential segregation reflected a desire to live near their workplace. However, the hostility of whites, including that of the Germans who in one instance warned blacks out of a neighborhood, and in another threatened to burn down a home that was rented to a black family, strengthened the tendency. The hostility between races encouraged mine operators to use black workers as strikebreakers in the late 1890s.[113]

Growth of the Middle

A picture that reveals only the emergence of a working-class employed by wealthy merchants and manufacturers misses the complexity of local social and economic development. The processes of industrialization did not reduce Evansville society to opposing classes of employers and workers. Many of the developments described above actually led to growth among the "virtuous middle," a trend most evident in the rising numbers of white-collar workers, storekeepers and master craftsmen.

Despite the changes wrought by leading manufacturers, all was not transformed and the small producer retained a significant role in economic life. The large number of immigrant craftsmen in the city provided a surplus of skill that could do the kind of custom work on which small shops thrived, and for which the rising wealth of the proprietary class provided a market. While a shrinking percentage of the labor force was employed in such places (63.1 percent in 1850, 12.6 in 1880), in absolute terms this sector experienced growth as small shops more than doubled the number of workers they employed to 429 in 1880. And the number of small shops more than tripled, reaching 172 by 1880.

These workshops were directly operated by a master who retained an active role in the work process. The small number of workers he employed precluded much in the way of a division of labor and the social divide between master and employee must have resembled that of the midcentury workshop. Such masters lived in predominantly working-class neighborhoods and at a level that was hardly bourgeois. While self-employment was often a goal, it was in some industries like tailoring and shoemaking the only way to survive. Aside from these trades, the small workshop survived most commonly among bakers, butchers, blacksmiths, cigar makers, tinners, and wagon makers. Even a few cooperages, machine shops, and harness shops continued to work on a small scale, often the result of years of savings on the part of a journeyman.[114]

The rise of Evansville as a wholesale market, bringing farmers and country merchants to the city, as well as the growth of population, also increased the vitality of local retailing. Large outlets for eastern manufacturers, like the clothing house of Strouse & Brothers, appeared in the postwar era.[115] And successful retail operations expanded out from Evansville into the surrounding countryside. In opening outlets in Rockport and Vincennes, Vickery Brothers & Company ignored the displeasure of grocers in those towns unable to buy as competitively or stock as wide a selection as the more prosperous Evansville firm.[116] The growing firm employed thirty-five workers in Evansville alone in 1880.[117]

The expansion of wholesale and retail businesses, in addition to the growth of factories, created jobs for a host of white-collar workers. In the twenty years after 1860, the number of clerks in the city more than tripled, reaching 629, while the demand for bookkeepers increased by a factor of 9. Further, new white-collar positions, like those of salesman and commercial traveler, appeared in the postwar environment. Combined, in 1880, more than 1000 white-collar workers eased the exchange of value in Evansville.[118]

With the exception of commercial travelers, whose dealings were with merchants outside the city, white collar workers—particularly salesmen and clerks who dealt primarily with the Evansville public—increasingly hailed from the German community. While just under a third of the clerks in 1860 were German, they accounted for 43.7 percent in 1880. Though the rise corresponds to an increase in German proprietorship, it also reflected the calculated desires of native merchants to appeal to a largely German clientele. It was this strategy that led a Republican politician, hoping to gain Governor Conrad Baker's aid in securing a local real estate and insurance agency, to assure him of his intention "to have a German help me when I get fairly started, which you know will be an advantage in our community."[119] Most of these German clerks were born in the United States, and many were the sons of petty proprietors and skilled workers.[120] A considerable number were trained for clerical positions by John J. Kleiner, the proprietor of the Evansville Commercial college. Teaching basic bookkeeping and penmanship, Kleiner parlayed a growing popularity into a seat on the city council, and later into a successful mayoral candidacy.[121]

The growth of population and the physical expansion of the city away from the waterfront also created more opportunities for the opening of groceries and saloons. Increasingly spread out over the city, their numbers more than doubled in the twenty years after 1860, until the city boasted 164 grocers and 68 saloonkeepers in 1880. And Germans, particularly immigrants, continued to dominate these occupations, accounting for 72 percent of the grocers and 76.5 percent of the saloonkeepers.[122]

The climb out of the working class could bring material rewards, for some of the petty bourgeoisie lived in a style different from that of their working-class neighbors. Though often living in the same neighborhoods, their homes were usually larger and sometimes made of brick. The size of the homes is reflected in probate inventories that include parlor furniture. Though not in the quantity held by the rich, homes of the middling sort housed books, parlor- and sitting-room furniture, and mirrors. For example, foundry foreman George Nolte, who rose from the position of stove mounter, owned a "parlor table," and the home of Peter Blend, a moderately successful cigar manufacturer, boasted a piano.[123]

While many small proprietors and white collar workers struggled to distinguish themselves from the working masses, evidence suggests that the pattern of interclass association uncovered in antebellum New Albany persisted well into the Gilded Age in Evansville. Continuity is most clear in the leadership of the Odd Fellows, which in the early 1870s was still comprised of small proprietors, white collar employees, and skilled workers. Nearly a third of the elected officers in Morning Star Lodge were skilled manualists, primarily construction workers, machinists, and molders, while the remainder were chiefly small masters, bookkeepers, and insurance agents. A similar pattern marked the German Schiller Lodge.[124]

Rather than a mere residue of artisanal life, the pattern of plebeian association grew more prominent with industrialization. As the depression of the 1870s came to an end a number of fraternal orders appeared that stressed the provision of death benefits as their chief function. Locally the most successful were the four lodges of the Knights of Honor, which claimed 600 members in 1889, and the six lodges of the Ancient Order of United Workmen (AOUW), which could name 1,350 members in 1894. Though it stressed the importance of brotherhood and the significance of ritual, the AOUW was particularly oriented around death benefits. This was evident not only in the way it sold itself but also in the great amount of attention insurance was given at meetings of the national Supreme Lodge.[125]

While the leadership pattern for both orders reveals a continuation of the plebeian pattern,[126] it is the complete roster of AOUW membership that allows the most detailed observation. In each lodge manual workers equaled or outnumbered proprietors (most of whom were farmers, saloonkeepers, and small masters), professionals, and white collar workers combined; in Humboldt lodge, in which all affairs were conducted in German, the ratio was two to one. Among the best-represented occupations were those of day laborer and machine-hand, though the skilled trades were not unrepresented. Carpenters, machinists, cigar makers, and iron molders joined the AOUW, and among them were trade-union leaders like Emil Levy and Fred Brennecke.[127] For workers who experienced declining opportunity to gain an "independence" in the Gilded Age, the AOUW and other fraternal and benevolent associations offered a means of providing for one's family after death. The importance of this function is suggested in the probate inventory of cooper John Bobinger whose $2,000 AOUW benefit and another $1,000 policy accounted for all but $18 of the estate that he left behind for his four children.[128]

The insecurity of the industrial regime and the decline in the rate of property ownership revealed in the eighth and ninth censuses suggest that workers retained a powerful incentive to join interclass fraternal associations. Organizations like the AOUW were absorbed with questions of financial solvency, and a rising membership constituted in part of the petty bourgeoisie was perceived as a strength. While saloonkeepers, drunkards, and those engaged in particularly dangerous occupations—railroad workers for instance—were perceived as poor candidates for membership, this was solely for medical and financial reasons.[129]

The continued strength of such associations, along with the nature of the manufacturing districts of Evansville, suggests that a plebeian community continued to be vital. At times, it may have served to limit worker demands, imbuing them with the outlook of the middle class.[130] However, that this could be a source of strength for workers was evident in political activity in Evansville during the 1870s and 1880s, when some small masters publicly articulated socialist principles, when the most radical statement about municipal spending came from a clerk in a foundry, and when the labor movement rallied to the support of a mayoral candidate who taught plebeian sons the art of penmanship.[131] The evidence suggests that the Gilded Age labor movement in Evansville had many sources of community strength.

Diversity and Conflict

With a different set of players—the German artisan instead of the native-born ship carpenter—development in Evansville in the second-half of the nineteenth century continues the trends uncovered in wartime New Albany. Industrial capitalism did not always overwhelm older communities, immediately transforming all in its path. Frequently changes were more piecemeal, as forms from the past existed at various levels of tension with those of the future. This is most clearly seen in the still-vital middle that thrived in New Albany in the antebellum period and in Evansville into the Gilded Age. Their vitality offered the skilled worker an ally in battles against overly assertive manufacturers. They also reminded the skilled worker of what he once was and tempted him with what he could still be.

If the Gilded Age skilled workers of Evansville were "less artisanal" than the shipyard workers of Civil War New Albany (and they were), there are two explanations. First, they worked in a period of general transformation. Larger and more mechanized firms, relying on a subdivided labor process, were increasingly the rule of the day in the postwar environment. Second, many of the industries of Evansville—like cabinetmaking, coopering, and harness making—were particularly susceptible to such changes in ways that ship carpentry was not.

But the particular pattern of economic development affected the monied class too. A consequence of the uneven transformation of society was the lack of a unified elite. The diversity of economic enterprise in the city left its wealthy rudderless, without a course well set. No industrial interest stood paramount above all others. The kind of unity that was displayed in response to the "regulators" of Clay County in defense of the Wabash and Erie Canal would not be repeated in the postwar years. Instead attempts to gain advantage over each other led to long-term feuds, which were intensified by political combat.

At the same time, the working class was becoming relatively homogeneous. Many skilled trades had declined to the point that wage earners practicing them hardly earned more than common laborers. Despite its artisanal origins, the working class of Evansville had traveled long on the road to proletarianization. And the overwhelming domination of manufacturing occupations, in particular the skilled trades, by Germans created a working class that possessed fewer of the structural divisions that so commonly divided American workers, though by no means did it maintain a constantly unified bloc. Yet at times of stress and agitation, divisions within the local elite allowed militant workers a voice that rang louder and longer in Evansville than it did in many other places. Because it was in the arena of electoral politics that these divisions were articulated in their most public fashion, we turn to the changing relationship between party politicians and Evansville's working class.

The Search for a Majority:
Class, Culture, and the
Democratic Party of Evansville

5 Beginning with the Civil War, and then to a greater extent during the 1870s and 1880s, workers in Evansville publicly mounted a challenge to the increasing power of their employers. Changes at the workplace and downward pressure on wages led workers in many trades to establish unions to protect what remained of their ability to provide for their families. Collective activity, however, was not limited to the trade union as workers organized consumers' and producers' cooperatives, eight-hour leagues and—on one occasion—a general strike. This process is, by now, a familiar story.[1]

Yet equally important and less well documented is the political context in which this process developed. Efforts to form and maintain coalitions by politicians took into account class as well as ethnic constituencies in the promulgation of appeals and platforms. In the mid-1850s political conflict revolved first around ethnic antagonisms, and then around the extension of slavery. However, as the energy of the Know-Nothing party peaked, as the South was vanquished in war, as workshops were transformed into factories, and as the German community settled in, politics increasingly focused on local class divisions. Though cultural differences continued to retain salience, party competition evolved by the 1870s to the point where electoral campaigns reinforced the tendency of workers to think in class ways and to perceive interests that were opposed to those of their employers. In Gilded Age Evansville, then, the relationship between workers and politicians extended the pattern uncovered in New Albany into a later period and onto new terrain.

This chapter uncovers the changing political coalitions that competed for control of local government in the years just before and after the Civil War. Struggles for ascendancy are discussed in the context of national developments, local ethnic tensions, the organization of workers during the latter stages of the war, and raging divisions within the local elite as capitalists vied for municipal contracts and railroad subscriptions. By 1868, as a result of these diverse forces, the Democratic party recovered from years of ineffectiveness to compete evenly for city offices by regaining its hold on German workers. The improving fortunes of the party of Jackson was not a mere reflection of working-class power, for it is clear that workers, both native and immigrant, in New Albany as well as Evansville, could find a home in the Know-Nothing and Republican parties. This was evident in the late 1850s when the Democrats of Evansville came out in open support of landed propertyowners, a posture that weakened their hold on workers. It was only in the postwar years, after a long absence from power, that Democrats began to experience success wielding a politics of class division.

Politicians and the Forging of Coalitions

The absorption of a great number of German immigrants into the social structure had considerable effect on local political life. Long a stronghold of the Whig party, Evansville and the surrounding Pigeon Township had given Democrat Franklin Pierce 54.9 percent of the vote in 1852.[2] However, as in New Albany, subsequent years were marked by shifting alliances as issues of slavery and nativism achieved and lost salience, and the languages of producerism and republicanism played a vital role in the construction of new coalitions. Introduction into Congress of the Kansas-Nebraska bill in the winter of 1854 brought this process into motion, sparking many local elites to call for a meeting. The large gathering that resulted adopted resolutions declaring "to open the door to slavery in the Territories . . . is to close it upon the free labor and free laborers of the Northern States and of the old world."[3]

The threat of slavery's expansion into Kansas was the kind of issue around which a broad interethnic coalition could be formed. This was especially true in cities like Evansville, where an energetic elite was advancing the cause of commerce and manufacturing. Menacing as it did the westward growth of this free-labor capitalist society, the Kansas-Nebraska Act rallied its vanguard—merchants, manufacturers, and lawyers—in opposition.[4] Acting to defend a vision of society and a way of life, their involvement in some cases reflected a deep hatred of slavery and the fettered feudal past that it represented. For men like Theodor Dietsch, a member of the Frankfurt Parliament who in Evansville edited the short-lived *Die Reform*, abrogation of the Missouri Compromise must have appeared as an American manifestation of the reaction that snuffed out the life of nascent liberalism in Germany.[5]

Former Whig politicians harnessed this passion into attacks on Democrats. Dissatisfaction with the party of Jackson grew with Pierce's veto of a homestead bill, which the editors of the Whig Evansville *Journal* connected to the Kansas-Nebraska Act and reminded its readers that their Congressman, Smith Miller, was on the wrong side of both.[6] These efforts only slightly weakened recently established Democratic dominance as voters cast a split ballot, supporting Democrats for state and local office while voting against Miller, who was reelected only due to his strength in rural portions of the district.[7]

Antislavery zeal was soon eclipsed by nativism, though the political effect was far different than it was upstream. While the rise of the American party in New Albany united shipyard workers against a railroad scheme of the wealthy, here it further strengthened the hand of the Democrats, unifying Germans under their banner. Even the independently minded Dietsch cast aside his hatred of slavery to work with the "hunker sheet" forces against those who "proscribe a whole religion, a whole sect and thereby abolish the truly republican principle of religious freedom."[8]

During the spring municipal campaign of 1856, the editors of the *Journal* tried to exacerbate divisions among the Democrats, charging that Sheriff John Gavitt and the small Irish wing of the party controlled the nominating convention to the disadvantage of the German faithful. They were given an opening when the Irish retaliated against Peter Kempf for bolting the party the previous fall and running an independent campaign for justice of the peace that had led to a Know-Nothing victory, by defeating his bid to gain the nomination for City Recorder. Noting that Kempf was the only German up for office, the *Journal* asked if "our Democratic friends are going to try to get along without the Germans—or do they think the Germans have already had their full share of offices, and are now only to be used as *voting* tools?"[9] To assure their loyalty Democrats urged Germans to consider the xenophobic nature of the opposition; a correspondent to the *Enquirer* asked "did the Democrats murder you, Germans? Did they destroy your ballot boxes?"[10] The Germans stayed true, helping the Democrats survive a divisive convention with a near sweep of city offices.[11]

Undiscouraged, Know-Nothing leaders renewed these tactics in the fall. In August, the Fillmore Club offered a dollar "reward" for the name of each native-born Democrat not already on a list of twenty-six, all of whom were said to be perpetual officeholders.[12] There was some truth in this. The native-born accounted for less than a third of Democratic activists while Germans comprised 40 percent of the total, figures that conformed to the ethnic breakdown of the community; yet, natives did gain more than their share of nominations.[13] The implications were two-fold. Like sheep the Germans allowed themselves to be herded into supporting demagogues. The *Journal* pointedly remarked that four of the eight nominees up for election were from this group. Immigrants, who "comprise the whole Democratic party here, excepting twenty-six" were "deluded" into accepting an equal number of nominations as the much smaller native wing of the party. The list was also calculated to reinforce the tendency of native voters to line up against the Democrats, since the use of immigrants to keep a small group of officeholders in power conformed to Know-Nothing beliefs about the corrupt nature of the Democratic party.[14]

Again, the use of nativism failed to result in political ascendancy for the anti-Democratic forces. Largely on the strength of the immigrant vote, Democrats swept the county. In a three-way race, Buchanan outpolled Fillmore by a 35 percent margin, and Fremont came in a distant third.[15] The Know-Nothing movement served to solidify local Democratic domination of the ballot box. However, with the subsiding of nativist political strength, the Democrats would once again find themselves in the position of a minority party.

Railroads, Schools, and Landed Wealth

The fall of the Democrats resulted from a dispute over the funding of a railroad that engaged competing elite factions and hardly involved local plebes. As the animosity generated in debate spilled over into conflict over taxation, rival elites argued the merits of speculation and industry. Out of the fray emerged a clear articulation of a harmonious form of producerism that was representative of the young capitalist order of the North. Similarities to working-class producerism and the opaque meanings of terms like "labor" allowed workers and employers to unite in defense of free productive labor against the forces of reaction—slaveowners, landlords, and the Democratic party.

The dispute revolved around Willard Carpenter, an enigmatic and wealthy speculator, and his efforts to build a direct rail line to Indianapolis commonly known as the Straight Line.[16] Even his critics conceded that he was tireless in his efforts to build the road, and his exertions netted a subscription to $200,000 in stock by the city of Evansville and another $50,000 from Lamasco. As the project bogged down, Carpenter resigned the vice-presidency of the company and assumed the contract to build the road at double the original price. That he continued as the financial agent of the company suggested a conflict of interest. Moreover, the weak financial condition of the company and his extensive speculation in land along the Southern portion of the route, particularly at the proposed crossing with the Mississippi and Ohio, suggested a disinclination to complete the road to Indianapolis. If so, Evansville stood to gain a relatively worthless fifty-five-mile trunk line for its investment.

In part these fears moved the city council to refuse the company's request for the second of two equal installments of the city's subscription. Led by M. W. Foster, a director of the rival Evansville and Terre Haute railroad (E&TH), the council demanded an accounting of company affairs. When Straight Line president Oliver H. Smith refused, the council unanimously voted not to issue the bonds. It was not a popular decision and the press scoured the city fathers. "There can be no more mortal or wicked stab at the welfare of a community," challenged the *Journal*, "than to have all the efforts and labors of its public spirited citizens . . . paralyzed and thwarted by false charges and slander." The editor likened Foster and others to "midnight incendiaries" because their action would lower property values. Calling on the city to fulfill its obligation to the road, the *Enquirer* blamed the impasse on "two or three selfish dolts in the City Council" who sacrificed local interests "to gratify their avarice, ignorance and stupidity."[17] Such personal attacks on members of the elite were bound to stir passions. The first result of this incendiary rhetoric came a month later with the formation of a "desperate opposition" to the election of editors F. Y. Carlile of the *Journal* and Charles Denby of the *Enquirer* to the board of directors of the elite Library Association.[18] This was only the beginning.

Passions ignited again in March when a long "expose" of the company's affairs, penned by the hardly disinterested John Ingle, Jr., president of the E&TH, appeared in the *Journal*.[19] Ingle charged Carpenter with malfeasance and ineptitude. The road, he warned, would not reach Indianapolis due to the costly contract with Carpenter and the decision to build the road by sections. Noting that company reports portrayed this plan as a means of quickly making the road profitable to its stockholders, Ingle countered, "if 'Willard Carpenter & Co.,' are to be considered as the stockholders, and certainly they appear to be so at this date, [they] may not have been very wrong."[20]

If Ingle failed to prove fraudulent intent on the part of Carpenter, he raised difficult questions concerning the company's ability to reach Indianapolis. When he challenged Smith and Carpenter to publicly debate the issue, the former stood on his honor and refused while the latter found it necessary to be out of town.[21] As the Straight Line lay moribund, Ingle moved in for the kill. Printing handbills and pamphlets of the "expose," he played an active role in the spring city election, spreading what the *Journal* termed "injudicious assaults upon the advocates of the Straight Line Road."[22] His efforts were rewarded when the new council likewise refused to issue the bonds.[23]

Carpenter took the defeat badly. Friends and associates later recalled that he "always complained that he had been robbed in the building of the Straight Line" and that Ingle and Foster had "wronged his character."[24] And Willard Carpenter was not one to forgive and forget; he had other grievances to air. The tax to pay the first issue of Straight Line bonds had been assessed solely on real estate; moreover, the council was in the practice of appraising land at what seemed arbitrarily high levels. As the city's most prominent landowner, Carpenter had reasons to seek a remedy. Letters critical of the tax policy appeared in the press, one claiming it was "unjust and oppressive in the extreme, to discriminate between citizens by exempting productive, and imposing the heaviest burthens of taxation upon vacant and unproductive property."[25]

Such views went against the grain of the entrepreneurial order, and both dailies responded with defenses of productive labor. The *Journal* denounced landlords who believe they "hold the only substantial interests in the community, and that they ought to govern it, or at least decide all questions of taxation; as if property had inherent values, and was not wholly dependent upon the labor, the skill, and enterprise around it to give it any worth—or in fact to make it property at all." The *Enquirer* copied the editorial, endorsing its sentiments.[26] When another letter urged a more "democratic" policy marked by "equality of rights and privileges, equality in public benefits and burthens, and equal justice to all, rich and poor," the *Journal* replied "it is the spirit of Feudalism, not democracy, to tax labor and not the monopolizers of real estate."[27]

The dispute became more politicized in the fall of 1857 when the *Enquirer* joined Carpenter in an attack on the council. To the dismay and embarrassment of some members, it was revealed that their own appraisals were far too low. While J. P. Elliot, corrected his from $350 to $3,350, others stood their ground.[28] Straight Line opponent M. W. Foster defended low assessments on productive property, arguing that manufacturers and merchants create value by investing "money where the community needs the improvement." Responding to arguments that appraisals should be based on the income generated by the property, Foster argued that though the rich man's mansion failed to turn a profit, "his taste for splendor ought not to exempt him from taxation." Appealing to the labor theory of value, he justified council policy with a distinction between "ideal" and "intrinsic" value. The former was "the work of the Almighty, and depends for its value on accidental location or the general opinion of men," while the latter "attaches to improvements and depends on the amount and cost of labor it takes to construct them."[29]

The dispute proved an illusory opportunity for Democrats who hoped to weaken the political position of men like Foster and Ingle by supporting the cantankerous Carpenter. However, besides mounting a challenge to leading manufacturers and merchants, they assumed a position hostile to the aspirations of common people. An early sign that they might lose a grip on the plebeian vote appeared when Democratic councilmembers voted to defer acceptance of city orders in payment of taxes for a few months. The *Journal* pointed out that this caused laborers to sell them at a discount to "large property holders" who could afford to wait, and asked whether the Democratic party's "regard for the interests of labor and the masses," was less important than "the personal quarrels of large property holders about their assessments."[30]

The dispute between elite factions fully imposed itself on electoral politics when Carpenter tried to get the city to adopt a new charter that would equalize taxation on real and personal property. But his timing was unfortunate. Only weeks before the Indiana State Supreme Court had ruled against a law providing for the enactment of school taxes by cities.[31] Opponents like Foster and Ingle warned that surrender of the old charter, by virtue of its precedence over the state constitution, would destroy the local system of public education. They spoke of the democratic advantages that schools offered children of laboring families.[32] The attempt to equalize taxation was thus turned into a referendum on the public schools.

The *Enquirer* denied the schools were at risk and declared that increased revenues and equal taxation were the real issues. "If the houses in this city were set down at their fair value for taxation," the editor suggested, "that item alone would add to the taxables of the city $800,000." Under the new charter, "all kinds of taxables will share equally," and Democrats promoted the new document as the "equal rights charter."[33] Yet, increasing the tax on improvements on land did not appeal to German workers, the party's strongest base of support, who would pay that tax as homeowners or indirectly in the form of higher rents. The *Journal*, defending productive labor, held the stronger position. The editors, on the day of the election, praised the old charter for allowing the council "to discriminate in favor of improvements erected by enterprising residents, and the dwelling house, or shop, or factory of the laboring man, and against the vacant unused lots of the resident and non-resident speculator."[34]

Voters rallied to the defense of the schools. Noting that the charter was defeated by Democratic voters, the *Enquirer* blamed a "mistaken zeal in behalf of the city schools."[35] The *Journal* attributed the victory to "the enlightened and public-spirited exertions of our German fellow citizens." Voting results support these interpretations, as opposition to the new charter was *greatest* in the German worker district of Lamasco, where it reached 78.7 percent. Most importantly, it shook loose the Democratic hold on the German electorate. With the spring elections in sight, the *Journal* urged voters to remember that out of "avarice and selfishness" heavy tax-payers and politicians "plotted . . . to overthrow the schools, and colluded to sell the birth-right of every child in the city for a mess of treasury pap for themselves."[36] When they accused Democrats of conspiring against the public interest for the benefit of a landed elite, their arguments resonated louder in the winter of 1858 than they might have in preceding years.

For the introduction of the new charter was doubly ill-timed. Just days before, President Buchanan had submitted to Congress the highly suspect Lecompton constitution, which would have admitted Kansas to the Union as a slave state. The document was widely associated with electoral fraud and along with other events helped cast the Democratic party as a central player in what many Northerners saw as a conspiracy to pervert free institutions by the "slave power."[37] In case the connection was not clear, the *Journal* hammered it home during the campaign, referring to Democrats interchangeably as "Lecomptonites" or "new charterites."[38] They also played up the Democratic mayor's alleged vow to oppose municipal appropriations for the schools.[39]

The election was a huge victory for the Republicans. "Every New Charter man and opponent of the Free Schools was condemned and repudiated," applauded the *Journal*.[40] Most importantly, it suggests widespread German disenchantment with the Democrats. Largely on the strength of his support in Lamasco, German-born Augustus Lemcke defeated popular Democrat Well H. Walker for city clerk. Active defender of the old charter, H. Q. Wheeler, defeated Democrat Thomas McAvoy in the race for school trustee. While Wheeler appeared on only 46.1 percent of the ballots cast in Lamasco—his association with the "aristocratic" high school probably weakened his hold on the German vote[41]—even this level of support for someone so tied to the Protestant elite would have been unthinkable two years before. Finally, in a contest of Germans for city collector, George Wolfin, a consistent opponent of the extension of slavery, handily defeated Peter Schmuck, an articulate German supporter of the new charter. Wolfin's margin of victory was particularly large in Lamasco where he gathered 80.2 percent of the vote.[42]

Arising out of conflict between rival sets of entrepreneurs, the charter issue reordered local political life. By identifying itself too closely with Willard Carpenter, Democrats supported the efforts of a landed elite in opposition to the productive sectors of Northern society. Thus, local politics reproduced the terms of national conflict. It was in this spirit that the *Journal* warned that attacks on the schools "will be held to be worse than Lecompton treason to the Sovereignty of the people."[43] The Democrats could no longer count on the support of the German community; the result was again evident in October 1858 when Evansville voters opposed Democratic candidates for Congress and the state legislature by nearly a two-to-one margin.[44]

This period of intense local conflict bequeathed Evansville another legacy—one of intense interelite conflict. The dispute between Ingle and Carpenter would continue into the postwar era as the E&TH took shape as the most prominent "ring" or monopoly in the city. New men would take part in the dispute—James Shanklin on one side and William Heilman on the other—but animosity persisted. And Willard Carpenter, a long-time Whig and a fierce opponent of slavery, would emerge in the mid-1860s as an active Democrat.[45]

Aristocrats, Demagogues, and Class Formation

Their position weakened, local Democrats attempted to regain the German vote with broad class appeals. This forced an about face on the part of the *Enquirer*, which before the Straight Line imbroglio had termed such efforts "humbugs of the meanest and most contemptible sort." Using language reminiscent of George Henry Evans and the Jacksonian labor movement, but turning it on its head, the *Enquirer* declared: "it may do in English and French elections to make great show and pretense of sympathy and love for the laboring classes; but those classes are too intelligent and well informed in this country to be 'caught' by such fulsome and insulting appeals."[46]

In the summer of 1860 Democrats reached into the Jacksonian rhetorical tradition of "antiaristocracy" and took a less respectable path. The *Enquirer* tried to spark the fires of class resentment in its description of a Republican "standing shirt affair" in which participants allegedly "moved through the streets with all the dignity of an Autocrat" presuming "common people should look up to them." Further, the editors claimed that all "thirty-three young ladies" representing the states were from "the upper tendon and not a single one of them was a mechanic's daughter." The haughtiness of the elite was the issue, as they attempted to translate style into substance. Republicans, they charged, wanted "exclusive powers and privileges—because some of them happened to be born rich—over the poor man that tills the soil or works in the shops."[47]

The *Journal* condemned such "panderings" to "the envy and jealousy of one portion of [the] community against another." Though Republicans appealed directly to workers, especially when they charged that Democrats and southerners believed slavery an appropriate status for all laborers, there was a difference. Republicans envisioned a united political bloc of "hard-fisted laborers of the country, and men of business who earn an honest living by hard hand and head work."[48] There were no aristocrats in Evansville, no oppressors of white workingmen; they were all to the South. The threat to local harmony, Republicans argued, came not from workingmen or capitalists, but from an unprincipled Democratic leadership.

Rhetorical appeals were ineffective in retarding the growth of the Republican party. Pigeon Township supported Lincoln, giving him nearly 50 percent of the vote in a four-way race.[49] Unlike their party brethren in New Albany, Evansville Democrats found that commercial ties to the South were not enough to perpetuate their dominance. Burdened with unpopular positions locally and nationally, the Democrats lost control of the German electorate. In the late 1850s, Democrats were hardly credible as an antiaristocracy party; they were too closely tied to Southern slaveowners and local landlords.

The attempt by Democrats to rally plebeian Evansville in political battle suffered from a transparent message and it was out of step with economic development. By and large workshops remained small, and while conflict was not unknown, overall these were years of unity and confidence for mechanics. When councilmember Foster declared that productive labor in all its forms (bourgeois among them) was the basis of a progressive community, he articulated this sensibility. It was this confidence in the city's future, and in the viability of a free capitalist order, that the Republican party rode to local power.

When discord in the workplace arose, Republicans attempted to make political capital out of it. They got a chance during the fall 1858 campaign when journeymen coopers accused merchant James Oakley of following a "dishonorable, unjust and uncalled for" course when he mechanized his shop and lowered the piece-rate.[50] Recognizing the transforming effect that machinery would have on the trade, the journeymen struggled to stem the tide by urging all coopers employed by Oakley to quit, and agreeing to try to sustain the "regular price of cooperage" and to "put down any attempt at monopoly." The issue was tailor-made for Republicans who agreed that workers were in danger of degradation. The *Journal* urged them to free themselves from the control of "Southern Lecompton Democrats and their Northern abettors" whose free-trade policy threatened to reduce American wages to that "of the abject labor of Europe." The editors added that the Oakleys were "not grasping, avaricious men"; their decision to mechanize was an "inevitable" result of Democratic free trade.[51]

Such appeals for harmony between employers and employees resonated deeply for the workers who gathered for a "mechanic's" celebration of the Fourth of July in 1860. The idea came from local manufacturers and merchants who encouraged "each Trade and Craft to turn out in full force . . . with such emblems of their profession as may seem to them proper or appropriate."[52] Trade after trade organized to prepare for the event, usually with the guidance of master craftsmen.[53] The editors of the *Enquirer* speculated that these efforts would bring "employer and the employees on a more mutual and lasting friendship."[54]

For the moment, there was cause to suggest such a thing.[55] Over two thousand "mechanics and workingmen" marched together in no fewer than twenty trades behind a banner reading "Mechanics' and Workingmen's Union of Evansville—1776–1860." Trades typically presented a horse-drawn wagon carrying products as well as workers busily engaged in the productive process. Banners bearing mottos, like "Industry" in the case of the blacksmiths, were suspended alongside the wagons. Behind them marched other journeymen who proudly wore the leather apron of the craftsman.

After wending their way through the city streets, the mechanics were joined by some 10,000 others in a nearby grove. There they were addressed by prominent Republican Conrad Baker, who linked Victorian virtues of self-discipline and industry to patriotism in his praises of the "hard working" mechanic. The man who learns to "watch over his own spirit, restrain his own passion, preserve his own self-respect and personal integrity, and develop his own manhood," Baker affirmed, was well on his way toward proving his virtue as a husband, father, and citizen. Incorporating working people into Victorian notions of hearth and domesticity, Baker asserted that "any woman with the soul of a true woman within her" would forego affluence for "the protection of the brawniest arms of the brawniest laborer of all the land, and with him share a life of toil."[56] Afterward, master tanner Victor Bisch read the Declaration of Independence, and praised the local community for its "generous support lent to mechanical enterprise" especially those who "felt it their duty to patronize Home Manufacturers."[57]

Thus the celebration was doubly patriotic. Brass bands triumphantly played "Hail Columbia" and "Yankee Doodle," celebrating the success of the republican experiment, while the Liederkranz and Maennerchor societies sang the Germanic "Freedom Song" and "War Song for Freedom."[58] But as Bisch's speech made clear, and which the procession made manifest—with its masters and journeymen, its native and German mechanics—the gathering celebrated local patriotism and the unity of the city itself. At once it reaffirmed the marginality of nativism as a political vehicle while suggesting that tensions in the workshops were not yet salient enough to serve as the basis for a successful electoral strategy. For Democrats it posed minority status.

The Civil War and Political Discourse

As it did in New Albany, the war brought increasing tension and strife to Evansville. Local political conflict intensified as Democrats attacked the war as an abolitionist conspiracy. In this regard they took a far more belligerent position than their party brethren upriver, and the shrillness of political debate was a bellwether of increasing divisiveness in the city. This partisan rancor became evident in early 1862 after the Indiana Democratic Convention denounced both Northern and Southern extremism.[59] The Weekly *Gazette*, the first of three wartime successors to the *Enquirer*, extended the point, denouncing abolitionists as "the blackest traitors and the most unscrupulous enemies of the Republic" and arguing that these "secessionists of the north—should be imprisoned and made war upon equally with their co-workers, the secessionists of the South."[60]

As the Congressional campaign heated up, Democrats stoked the fires of racial fear, denouncing Republican emancipation for putting "the interests of the negro paramount to the interests of white men" by "taxing the white laborers of the North for the purpose of paying uncounted millions of money for Southern slaves."[61] When Democrats claimed to be in "favor of the 'Constitution as it is, and the Union as it was,'" their followers understood the message as an appeal to maintain a white man's republic.[62] The efficacy of the race issue was revealed by the *Journal*'s efforts to distance itself from calls for black equality, despite the sympathy many Republicans had for the black population.[63] Even in an 1864 editorial that declared "no man is a true, reliable friend of the Union . . . unless he desires to see human slavery wiped out" they found it necessary to counter Democratic arguments that emancipation would unleash a flood of black migrants northward to compete with white workers for jobs and housing. Freedmen, the editors asserted, would remain in the South because "the climate there is more congenial for them than that of the North."[64]

More commonly, Republicans took the offensive by questioning the loyalty of Democrats who were accused of "doing all they can to inaugurate civil war in our midst and at our doors."[65] In the fall of 1864, the *Journal* denounced the Democratic "McClellan Club" as a "treasonable organization" with ties to the Copperhead "Knights of the Golden Circle."[66] When Democrats on the council unwisely resurrected the new charter in March 1862, Republicans called them traitors to local interests and made the reelection of Mayor William Baker a crusade to save public education.[67] Again the *Journal* warned that Democrats were out to sabotage the schools and would impose the new charter on the city if given half a chance, a charge Democrats struggled to deny. The *Gazette* recognized the political inefficacy of the charter issue and encouraged the council to drop it.[68] The next year Republicans again linked Democrats with the new charter and opposition to the schools, a charge the latter had trouble escaping. Democrats, their opponents charged, opposed the schools "for they 'love darkness rather than light, for their deeds are evil.'"[69]

The results of the municipal election of 1863, however, were mixed. Though Republicans won a majority of council seats and most citywide offices, cracks appeared in the coalition. Wards with high concentrations of Catholics, Germans, and workers gave Baker, a prominent banker, distinctly lower levels of support than did strongholds of the elite, where he received nearly two-thirds of the vote (see map 4). Wards near the E&TH shops and the older areas of Lamasco voted for Democrat Morris Johnson.[70]

This limited weakening of Republican domination was based in part on cultural rivalry. Both the Catholic German Trinity Church and the Irish Church of the Assumption were located in the Third

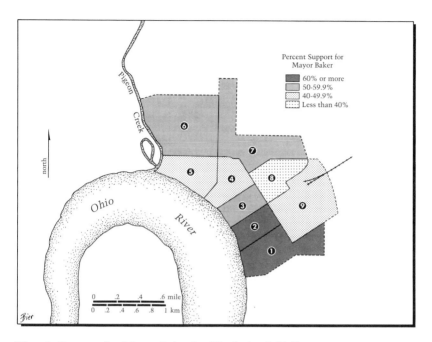

Map 4. Support for Mayor Baker by Ward, April 1862

Ward, and the area surrounding it was an enclave of German and Irish workers. The greater distance from these churches may also explain higher levels of support for Baker in the German Sixth and Seventh wards, where some of the German reformed and Lutheran churches were located. Clearly the *Journal* attributed the Democratic revival to the Catholics and by the spring of 1864 had written them off, indulging in a full-scale assault on Rome. Focusing on the Papacy's support for French intrigues in Mexico, the editors constructed a broad conspiracy against free institutions that included foreign despots, the Catholic church, the slaveholding aristocracy and Northern Democrats.[71] When the *Times*, the successor to the *Gazette*, denied the existence of such a cabal, the Republican editors denounced it as "a champion of the Roman Propaganda and the Roman Catholic hierarchy," as well as a supporter of slavery and treason.[72]

The War and Working-Class Organization

Yet, Catholics were but a minority of voters, and it is not unlikely that many had always supported the Democrats, even in the late 1850s. A fuller understanding of local politics is revealed by an examination of working-class organization in response to changing economic conditions and policies during the war, which at times led workers to oppose Republican leadership.

The first year of the war was marked by a severe trade depression, a result of the secession crisis and the subsequent embargo on river traffic imposed by the federal government. Merchandise remained in warehouses while workers experienced widespread unemployment. A year after the outbreak of war, Mayor Baker recalled that "every department of enterprise and industry was temporarily stricken down, and gloom and despondency were almost universally prevalent."[73] It was not until 1863 that full prosperity returned to the city, and when it did it came in unequal doses. Wealthy merchants and manufacturers, taking advantage of the opening of river ports by Union forces, amassed huge profits in the latter years of the war. The prosperity of this class was observed by attorney Charles Denby, who noted: "the City is rather gay. Dresses are most extravagant among the fair. Money is abundant and real estate goes off like hot cakes. There is very little said about the war. People are content to leave that to the Army and to make money for themselves."[74]

For the city's workers rising prices meant hardship. The same real estate speculation that filled the pockets of the monied, plus competition from growing numbers of black and white refugees from the South, made housing increasingly unaffordable. Rents rose faster than either the price of labor or building materials, and it was said that some mechanics were forced to move elsewhere for want of a dwelling.[75] At the same time the cost of many commodities doubled, while cloth jumped by more than 500 percent.[76] To help make ends meet, growing numbers of poor women applied for work to the Township Trustee, who farmed them out to work as domestics in the homes of affluent citizens.[77]

Wartime experience was distinguished by class in other ways. The draft weighed most heavily on the poor, a fact noted by the press of both parties. The *Journal* enthusiastically reported a war meeting held to pressure the city council to raise higher bounties, paraphrasing master saddler Joseph P. Elliot who said "he did not blame poor men for not wanting to go . . . while rich men were staying at home crying patriotism," which, he added to "furious" applause, "would not feed a man's family when sugar was 30 cents a pound, bacon 20c and coffee 50c." Yet the editors aimed to fill the ranks of the Union Army, not to excite class tensions; earlier in the conflict they had urged the city council to ignore a petition of the unemployed for work and instead directed the idle to the recruitment office.[78]

Workers recognized the baneful effects of war-generated inflation and made efforts to remedy the situation *outside* the political arena. The spring of 1863 witnessed strikes by the bricklayers' and carpenters' unions for $2.50 a day.[79] Later in the year, the miners at the Bodiam mines struck for an increase from 4 to 5 cents a bushel of coal, arguing that the effect of inflation on their ability to support their families required it.[80] The new year brought union organizing into workshops in the metal trades. Iron molders revived their organization and successfully struck for an increase of 40 percent over 1862 wages.[81] At the same time, machinists and blacksmiths organized and waged a strike against Kratz and Heilman.[82] Tinners and coppersmiths also effected an organization, demanding a wage hike of 25 percent, which was acceded to by two of the larger shops but resisted by the others. Union leader David Cooper described the steadfast adherence to the union by the men—"some going in the army rather than yield."[83]

Like the ship carpenters in New Albany, Evansville workers were connected to a larger movement by *Finchers' Trades' Review*, which reached a substantial cross-section of plebeian Evansville by virtue of efforts by a small cadre of trade-union leaders. Of the seven subscription agents, only one was not an officer of a union.[84] *Finchers'* was well served; its agents were successful selling subscriptions to a journal that was often short of operating expenses.[85] Traveling activist Richard Trevellick wrote to Jonathan Fincher, "I find the true spirit of Unionism here," explaining "more copies of the REVIEW are taken here than in any other place according to the number of inhabitants."[86]

At least 114 residents of Evansville subscribed and were thus placed in touch with national developments, as were others who borrowed the paper.[87] Most who took it were manual workers (70.8 percent), with the greatest frequency among those in trades that had recently organized—carpenters, machinists, and molders. Eleven worked in the wood, machine, and blacksmith shops of the E&TH. Ten percent were small masters, or the sons of such men, while two were clerks employed by the railroad. That many subscribers resided in the area around the railroad depot that had opposed Mayor Baker's reelection suggests that the nascent labor movement and the Democratic party thrived under similar conditions.

The list of subscribers also suggests the rise of a plebeian cultural network that included German and native-born workers. The presence of German saloonkeepers Charles Habbe, George Schulz, and Christian Weisheimer (also a member of the Carpenters' Union) among them reveals that the labor reform message reached beyond

the native Protestant community. German-born workers like molders Henry Webber and Conrad Muth and chair maker Fred Guth also
subscribed, and at least in the case of Muth spread the vision of working-class solidarity to their fellow workers.[88]

The vision of solidarity led trade unionists to identify with unorganized workers in Evansville and elsewhere, and when they did they
often became immersed in politics. This tendency was first evident
in their response to the orders of Union Army Generals William
Rosecrans in St. Louis and Stephen Burbridge in Louisville prohibit-
ing the organization of workers engaged in war production while
guaranteeing protection for strikebreakers.[89] Trade unionists organized a mass meeting in Crescent City Hall on June 25, 1864. A large
crowd adopted resolutions condemning the generals for having "been
duped or bribed to do the dirty work of contemptible capitalists and
scheming contractors." They suggested that loyal workers deserved
better from the government, noting that "over a quarter of a million
of our fellow laborers have sealed their devotion to their country
with their life's blood."[90]

The assembled did more than denounce acts of Union officers;
they also laid the groundwork for a citywide association. The committee spoke of the need for a body "to protect ourselves from any
unwarrantable decrease of wages, and to elevate our position in society and educate our families."[91] The result was the Evansville Workingmen's Association, open to "any man, in good standing, who
works." Organizers recognized that many workers were unable to
develop strong unions, and as one activist put it, "the most expedi-
ent way for the producing classes to have justice done them, is for all
producers to unite in one brotherhood for the benefit of *all*."[92]

Though they professed no interest in politics, workingmen could
not steer clear of it. That their protests were compatible with Democratic positions and their meeting was held in a "copperhead" hall
did not escape the eye of the watchful *Journal* editor, always wary of
attacks on any part of the war effort.[93] And despite the assembly's
nonpartisan status, Democrats viewed it as a stick with which to
beat Republicans. After the *Journal* urged workers to moderate their
resolutions and criticized them for ignoring Confederate treatment
of workers, the *Times* accused the *Journal* of working "in the interests of the capitalists."[94] Three weeks later, a Democratic district
convention called for "the protection of the workingmen of this
country against tyrannical military orders similar to those recently
issued by General Rosecrans and Burbridge."[95] Republicans responded as they did before the war, locating the threat to a just society in a

class outside the North. They argued that the war was a battle against aristocracy, and they cited Lincoln's common origins as evidence of the virtue of Northern society, where "the poor man is by law the equal of the rich."[96]

The Democratic press continued to focus on class divisions in the North. The German-language *Demokrat* asserted that many staunch Republicans and defenders of the draft bought substitutes for their sons, who the editors assumed were "too good for cannon fodder." They also related how a Republican quartermaster fired workers opposed to Lincoln.[97] On the eve of the election, the *Journal* again felt compelled to respond to "a villainous attempt to incite the laboring men against the property-holders, and to stir up a mob."[98]

Despite efforts by Democrats, local workers remained loyal to the Lincoln administration. The citizens of Pigeon Township voted to reelect controversial Governor Oliver P. Morton by a 13 percent margin, and a month later they cast 60 percent of their ballots for Lincoln.[99] Despite grievances with military orders, most workers agreed that the immediate enemy was the slaveholding aristocracy. As David Montgomery has observed, wartime working-class protest "did not signal the accession of labor to the old-line Democrats, but rather the vitalization of an entirely new political force—the labor-reform movement."[100]

The Aftermath of War: Disorder, Self-Improvement, and the Lure of Politics

With the Confederate foe vanquished, various tendencies unleashed by the conflict intensified. The war broke down the relative harmony between classes evident in the late 1850s. In addition, wartime brought to Evansville waves of black and white refugees from the South who competed with German laborers for employment and housing. At the same time, saloons became increasingly visible in the later years of the war, when their numbers more than doubled.[101] Postwar Evansville posed a new environment for many local residents, and many probably observed a breakdown in the local order.

Order did break down in the summer of 1865 as racial antipathies, long encouraged by political debate, resulted in a lynching. To some extent, the incident arose out of economic and demographic changes. The opening of the Tennessee and Cumberland rivers by 1863 encouraged the building of two tobacco stemmeries in the city. Originally employing white men, women, and children, the owners hired black labor soon after the war, and for the rest of the nineteenth century, tobacco stemming remained one of the few manufacturing jobs open to black workers.[102] To some white workers this must have confirmed Democratic warnings about the results of abolition. Seething resentments were given expression when a fifty-year-old German Catholic woman on her way to church was raped and nearly murdered by two assailants in August. Two black men were quickly rounded up and arrested and even the *Journal* urged severe punishment for the alleged perpetrators.[103] Before justice could be meted out, however, over 100 persons pledged an oath of mutual support and proceeded to the jail where they broke down the doors with sledge hammers. The mob dragged the accused, at least one of whom was probably innocent, into the street where they were beaten, shot, and hung from a lamppost. Rioters then randomly assaulted blacks on the street, set fire to their houses, and threatened to burn down the tobacco stemmeries unless the owners fired their black labor force.[104]

Local Republicans wrote Governor Morton, urging him to send the state militia. One, noting the broad support of the German community for the violence, claimed that the murderers "feel so well assured of protection by the mob that by their conduct they seem to dare the civil authority to arrest them." Lieutenant Governor Conrad Baker added that the mob was swelled by "well armed" war veterans and warned that without the militia "more discharged soldiers will be enlisted to prevent the arrests."[105] Before order was restored, many recent black immigrants had left the city.[106]

Disorder was felt in less dramatic ways. The elders of the local Presbyterian churches encountered the postwar years with a growing concern with the behavior of members when a relatively large number were brought before them on charges of intoxication. Individuals were suspended from full membership for failing to answer accusations of neglecting church attendance, attending the theater, and "hanging around places of evil resort, as billiard saloons . . . [and] restaurants."[107] Others admitted to their guilt. The response of a young clerk accused of "drunkenness and profanity" reveals the anguish felt by those who failed to control themselves in this new cultural context: "I have fallen before the tempter and have been shamefully intoxicated, and now I am ready to cry out 'O wretched man that I am' who shall deliver me from this fearful bondage. As officers of the church you must do your duty, and it seems but folly for me to make promises. Pray for me dear friends that I may not go to the pit of destruction."[108]

Church members not only took care of their own, but in some instances their concern with the apparent decline in public morality led them to reach outside the church community. This was particularly true for women who believed that the amoral environment of the industrial city posed dangers for single women, who apart from church, family, and friends might fall prey to the machinations of evil males. Female concern with the malevolent effects of male passion was hardly new or limited to Evansville.[109] However, changes brought by the war led women like Eleanor Johnson, a Presbyterian missionary and teacher in a local school for black children, to work for the establishment of the Home for the Friendless, which due to the financial largesse of Willard Carpenter, became a reality in 1869.[110]

The institution was established as a refuge for prostitutes and "ruined" young women. In her report of 1872, Johnson wrote of women who had been lured to the city by men with promises of marriage, and then found themselves "ruined," penniless, and abandoned. For cases in which pregnancy was the result, the Home provided a refuge where the child could be born and put up for adoption before the woman returned to her family. For others, who as a result of their seduction "drifted into the whirlpool of vice" and became themselves a "power for evil in the community," the Home offered a cure of cleanliness and religiosity.[111]

It was in this climate that the Workingmen's Assembly began to agitate for reforms that focused as much on self-improvement as conflict with employers. Early in the summer of 1865, the assembly succeeded in opening a cooperative store. A few months later, it held a fund-raising picnic for the establishment of a mechanic's reading room and lyceum, which trade-union leader John Taylor hoped would serve as an alternative to "Gaming Houses and Lager Beer Saloons, and many other dens of pollution." The intention to acquire both English and German works reflected a desire that "all mechanics" be "elevated, no matter whether they be English, German or what."[112]

However, most energy went toward building the eight-hour day movement. Early in the summer, the Workingmen's Assembly sent a subscription to *Fincher's* and petitions calling for a federal law to Congressman William Niblack.[113] In July, workingmen and their wives who crowded the county courthouse were held "spellbound, as if listening to the words of inspiration," by eight-hour day advocate Richard Trevellick. The correspondent to *Fincher's* opined that if Trevellick had the strength "all, male and female, would have remained all night in their places." In the glow of success, a trade-union committee was organized to raise funds for the procurement of additional speakers.[114]

A month later, workingmen and "their wives and sweethearts"

heard John Swinton preach the labor gospel of cooperation and self-improvement. Speaking to the fears of cabinetmakers, coopers, and other journeymen whose skills were being degraded, Swinton advocated an apprenticeship law that would provide a boy with "a fair opportunity to make himself master of all the several branches of the trade . . . and not be confined to a single specialty." Yet, Swinton did not romanticize the days of the artisanal workshop; instead, he tied together themes of mechanization, cooperation and the eight-hour day as heralding a new era. "Labor-saving machines had lessened the demand for laborers," he reminded his audience, "hence the necessity of reducing the hours of labor, that all may have work."[115] Swinton told his listeners that agitation would give the matter political salience, for the press, which was "controlled by capital," would ignore the issue until workers forced them to take sides. Finally, he urged mechanics to vote only for candidates who supported the shorter workday.[116]

It could hardly have been any other way, as the eight-hour day movement quickly was absorbed into local political debate and soon became associated with the Democratic party. In December, an eight-hour advocate from St. Louis was chastened by the *Journal* when he described Republican tax policy as benefiting blacks at the expense of white men.[117] Similarly, Jonathan Fincher received criticism a week later when he addressed local workers and advocated taxing federal bonds, which the editors thought sounded suspiciously "like a Copperhead stump-speech injected into a labor address."[118]

As it did in New Albany, the very idea of the reform made many Evansville Republicans uncomfortable, and some were moved to assail the assumptions of the movement. One denied there was anything unfair about the operation of the labor market and argued that "as a rule, every man finds his level." This writer presented the self-improvement aspect of the movement in more respectable dressing: "The proper way to elevate the laborer's mind is by education rather than by legislation, and to make that labor honorable and respectable depends on the laborer himself. He must educate, also, his children as well, and not only give them the advantages of our Free School system but also train them up in the ways of virtue and religion. Let him spend his leisure at home and patronize the street corners and beer saloons less."[119]

The activity of eight-hour advocates became politicized as well. In the fall of 1865, war veteran Noyes White, a master carpenter, assumed leadership over the local movement. White had been elected President of the Indiana Workingmen's Convention, and on his return he organized a local eight-hour league of which he was elected president. In that capacity he penned a tribute to Democratic Congressman Niblack for introducing federal eight-hour day legislation. White then asked workers "now that we have drew [sic] the sword for freedom, shall it be sheathed again while slavery exists in its present forms?" Continuing, he called for laws protecting workers from "purse-proud corporations and individuals who consider that everything is right as matters now stand, and who think to make a bare existence men, women and children should work from before daylight till after dark the year round to gain a miserable living, they in the meantime pocketing the proceeds of the industry of their operatives."[120]

Noting that the Democratic press was carrying "demagogical articles in favor of eight hours," the *Journal* criticized White for his inflammatory rhetoric. "Who—when—what—where are these white slaves? Are they in Evansville?" queried the editors.[121] They then waged a campaign to convince workers that a plot was underfoot to "prostitute their organizations to strengthen and build up a rebel sympathizing party."[122] Letters from John Taylor and John Hutchens, officers of the carpenters' union, denied the existence of any ties between the movement and the Democrats. Endorsements, Taylor insisted, hinged on the eight-hour question and were not subject to the interests of party "for the subject of our political rights is a point that is too tender for outsiders to meddle with." Hutchens went further and denounced the *Courier* as a "Jeff Davis–loving sheet."[123]

Fears that the labor men would ally themselves with the Democrats were warranted. On March 17, a workingmen's meeting with a strong machinists' union presence agreed to support a "workingmen's eight hour" ticket headed by city clerk candidate Noyes White. Revealing a partisan spirit, White delivered a speech that enumerated the local enemies of reform, including "Lord Mayor" William Baker.[124] However, aside from White and machinist John Torrence, who was the nominee for the Ninth Ward council seat, the ticket was little different from others. The nominee for treasurer was wholesale grocer Frank P. Carson. Among council hopefuls were three manufacturers, the son of a wealthy merchant/manufacturer, a grocer, a real estate agent and a physician. Aside from Torrence, workers were nominated only for constable. Noting that the ticket "had on it but four or five workingmen out of twenty-one candidates," the *Journal* concluded it "was Copperhead by a large majority, and with not a true representative of the workingmen."[125]

Yet its support of the eight-hour day forced a response by Republicans who two days later stole their thunder when they passed a council resolution calling for an eight-hour day for city employees.[126] The *Journal* then denounced the nominees as "tools of the Catholic Church," and the ticket as a "Copperhead trick" organized "to strike down our public schools, the great arsenal from which the children of workingmen draw knowledge and power." Should they be elected, the "schools of our city will be at the mercy of Jesuits for the ensuing year."[127]

The Republicans ran a successful campaign, winning six of nine council races and sweeping the city offices. The results were consistent with previous trends. The Workingmen did poorest in solidly Republican areas such as the mercantile and native upper two wards, which went more than three to one against White. The only wards that went Democratic were the Sixth and Ninth, where prominent manufacturer J. J. Reitz and machinist John Torrence won their respective council seats. Still, only the Ninth Ward—which surrounded the shops and yards of the E&TH and was home to much of the trade-union leadership—thoroughly supported the ticket, giving White 55.1 percent of the vote. For the moment Republican dominance held, as they swept the Congressional and state election of 1866, and had similar success in the spring election of 1867.[128]

The eight-hour movement only briefly survived the electoral debacle. A week after the election, White chaired a large meeting gathered to hear William Sylvis of the International Molders' Union speak about the virtues of cooperation as a means of harmonizing capital and labor. The *Journal* noted the absence of "political demagogues, who were so loud-mouthed about the interests of the workingmen a few weeks ago."[129] Without the aid of politicians, workingmen continued their organizing through the month of May.[130] Yet this burst of activity, begun in the throes of war soon began to lose steam, and for the next few years there is little notice of "workingmen's meetings" or strikes. The movement was a casualty of an economic downturn that began in the summer of 1866 and that soon resulted in wage cuts of 12 to 15 percent for many workers.[131] An independent working-class movement would not reappear until the 1870s.

Greenbacks and the Revitalization of Democratic Fortunes

The downturn in business coincided with a change in the fortunes of local Democrats who began to campaign against Republican monetary policy as well as Radical Reconstruction. In the fall of 1867, they adopted the "soft-money" position of Ohioan George Pendleton, which called for the retiring of the war debt by paying off the principle in greenbacks. The bonds had been issued as a war measure, and while the legislation had specified payment of the interest in specie it was silent on the retiring of the principle.[132] Early in the 1868 campaign, local Democrats seized the issue. Republicans, they said, were not only the party of black equality but also of bonded aristocrats to whom they granted a tax exemption and now promised repayment in gold, all in the name of patriotism. Further, they had little use for the poor white man, one speaker suggested when he asked "did they pay the soldiers in gold?"[133]

It was the combination of disenchantment with Radical Reconstruction and a militant rhetoric regarding the bonds that led to Democratic revival in 1868. Their nominee for Mayor, William H. Walker, ran a campaign that stressed class legislation and local Republican corruption. The *Demokrat* asked voters if "a booty-hungry contractor and speculator clique" should continue "to be fed at the cost of the city and the general welfare."[134] The editors charged that land owned by wealthy Republicans like William Heilman was kept out of the city merely to exempt it from municipal taxation.[135] And Democrats supported an investigation into alleged improprieties by Republican county auditor Victor Bisch, sustaining an indictment.[136] As the election neared, Democrats warned that reelection of Mayor Baker would make him an "unlimited autocrat."[137] Finally, Walker charged that Baker ignored the needs of German and working-class neighborhoods, citing the expenditure by the Republican council of up to $40,000 on a school building in the upper end of the city.[138]

Republicans countered again by appealing to the virtues of a progressive free society. Bakery owner William Troup addressed a Ninth Ward audience and spoke in defense of the free schools "by which the child of the poor man, the laborer and the mechanic can obtain an education equal to that of the rich man and millionaire." When the *Courier* offered the slogan "light taxes and free schools," the *Journal* reminded readers that "during the past twelve years the Democratic leaders have done all they dare to injure the efficiency and retard the progress of the noble system of public schools."[139] In addition, Republicans attempted to link the Democrats to the rise in disorder and vice in the city. The audience of one Democratic meeting was described by the *Journal* as "inebriated," and on the day before the election it implied that since Republican council members had cast votes for the "suppression of houses of ill fame," the Democrats had become the choice of the keepers of such institutions.[140]

However, the Democratic strategy of highlighting class divisions and Republican corruption paid off this time as they won a majority of council seats and city offices. In the mayor's race, Walker narrowly defeated Baker, largely on the strength of support for the Democratic ticket in the heavily German Third, Fourth, Fifth and Sixth wards, and the industrial Ninth. The Republican editors attributed the loss to the appearance of impropriety, remarking that "long and continuous control of the City, with its improvements, its taxes, appraisements, &c., have occasioned a very considerable amount of dissatisfaction."[141] But it also reflected a loss of Republican hegemony over local politics. In the fall, Democrats were aided by speakers like Richard Trevellick, who encouraged workers at the moment to vote the Democratic ticket because of its greenback position.[142] The strategy succeeded as Democratic gubernatorial candidate Thomas Hendricks evenly contested native-son Conrad Baker due to strong support in the working-class areas of the city.[143]

For years to come, the parties competed evenly for local office. Though the Democrats lost the municipal election of 1869 despite charges that Republicans intended to racially integrate the schools— a charge they denied—they rebounded in 1870, and again the use of broad class appeals proved the key to success. The effective issue was the building of a water works. The need for such an improvement had been discussed for a number of years. In 1866, a nonpartisan group of wealthy men joined together to construct such a works, but nothing came of it. At a meeting of Fifth Ward Republicans the following spring, manufacturer Cyrus Armstrong asked the councilmembers to "do all in their power for the erection of water works."[144] A destructive fire in December 1868 revived interest.[145] However, not until the spring of 1870 were concrete proposals made. These were quickly politicized. At a meeting to support the construction of the works by a private company chartered by the city, Democrats John Reitz and Mathew Bray warned it was a ploy of speculators who wanted the city to invest in it while they retained majority control over the completed water system.[146] The next day the Democratic city convention assumed a position in favor of municipal ownership of the water works.

While only splitting the citywide offices with the Republicans, the Democrats emerged with a clear majority on the council by winning seven of nine council races.[147] A month later the council submitted a plan to contract for the building of a municipally owned water works to a referendum. When the *Journal* warned against putting such a lucrative contract in the hands of an unreliable Democratic council, the *Demokrat* attributed this opposition to a desire to have the works "built by its friends, the capitalists and monopolists."[148] After the voters approved the plan, the editor of the *Courier* praised the results and charged the editors of the *Journal* were dismayed that "Radical *speculators* and *vultures* did not succeed in imposing another "ring" of monopolists upon the people of Evansville."[149]

When Democrats spoke of the "ring" it was clearly identified with the Republican party and the E&TH. In the summer of 1865, John Ingle, Jr., and James Jones had renewed the battle over the building of the Straight Line Railroad. Jones not only accused Ingle of protecting a railroad monopoly but also suggested that Ingle was concerned that the "Straight Line road will . . . reduce the profits of the Bodiam Mining Company."[150] At the same time, Willard Carpenter was frequently observed working behind the scenes at Democratic ward meetings, attempting to rally support for the Straight Line while accusing "the merchants of First Street" of lacking public spirit and preferring to hold tax-exempt government bonds rather than stock in a railroad that would improve the city's interests.[151] In the spring of 1868, the *Journal* warned that a Walker administration would result in Carpenter's control of local improvements, a sure prescription for "catastrophe."[152]

The story recounted here is one of trial and error. For over a decade after the demise of Know-Nothingism, Democrats attempted to put together a victorious coalition. It was not a simple process. After losing their grip on the German plebeian community, they struggled to regain it by speaking a loose class discourse. Much of this effort was ineffective since Democratic ties to the South and local landlords placed them in opposition to the material interests of workers and their employers. Only when the "slaveocracy" had been vanquished and the issue of disloyalty was behind them would Democratic anti-aristocratic rhetoric garner a sufficient number of working-class votes. The use of radical greenbackism in the following years would continue to work to their benefit.

However, the class language indulged in by the Democrats remained vague, mired in the ambiguities of American political language. Instead of workers and capitalists, the Democratic press continued to speak of the rich and the poor. And they would continue to do so until the rise of powerful local unions would force them to do otherwise. That time was not far off.

Class Conflict as Political Opportunity: Labor Activists and Politicians

Blessed are the parasites, for theirs are the palaces.
Cursed are the producers, and they shall rot in hovels.
Bless the rich robbers.
Damn the poor victims.
Bless the crafty usurer who wants more bonds, more interest,
more gold, and more blood money.

—*Trades and Labor Directory*, 1895–96

6 The 1870s brought decided change to the nature of political debate in Evansville. Competing evenly for power on the basis of support in the German and working-class wards of the city, Democrats adopted a less-ambiguous language in response to the growing strength of the local labor movement. In one respect, this represented considerable continuity, for Democrats in Evansville had long succeeded or failed depending on their ability to keep a strong hold on this sector of the electorate.

In other ways it marked a departure. By 1870, over half of the manufacturing work force worked in shops employing at least twenty-five workers, and this figure would reach 64.8 percent a decade later. With the growth of units of production came increased divisions between employer and employee. During the Gilded Age, increasing numbers of manufacturers achieved great wealth while many workers faced an increasingly mechanized workplace and downward pressures on wages. The possibility emerged that a political language filled with vague references to the "poor" and "rich" could be transformed into a discussion of inequities at the workplace. Under the developing industrial regime it became tempting for Democrats to do just that—to speak of the divisions between capitalist and worker.

Democrats did not merely respond to a new social landscape; they were led by the labor movement. Workers in numerous trades established unions—many strong enough to survive the periodic depressions that rocked the American economy during these years—while forming citywide labor assemblies. Frequently these union workers overcame the parochial tendency to ignore the unskilled, most notably when trade-union leaders led efforts to organize assemblies of the Knights of Labor. Workers merged concerns for "justice" and the dignity of labor with bread and butter issues. They also engaged in other forms of organizing, and in politics. It was to this growing working-class presence in various aspects of public life that Democrats in the Gilded Age responded. Yet it was a single iron molder's strike that set in motion this new relationship between Democrats and workers.

Mobilization

The late 1860s were quiet years in local workplaces; strikes rarely occurred and workers in few trades successfully organized. In 1870 this period of acquiescence came to an end when wood turners opposed an attempt by furniture manufacturers to reduce wages. Shortly thereafter members of the chair makers' union went on strike. These efforts came to little; within five weeks they dropped their demands in the face of an influx of strikebreakers. Similarly, when the printers tried to enforce union rules at the *Courier* and the *Journal* to remove "the screw of oppression [that] has been turned down upon us," employers turned out editions with nonunion labor. Despite a strike fund of $150 with which they hoped to send scabs back home, the strike was broken.[1]

Though these strikes failed, the labor movement soon gained in strength. In May 1872, the coopers in Wiltshire and Kreipke's shop forced wages upward.[2] Newly founded unions of chair makers, coopers, harness makers, machinists and blacksmiths swelled the ranks of organized labor.[3] With the growth of organization came a rebirth of a community of labor. Workers filled halls to hear activists like Martin Foran, president of the International Coopers' Union, speak for shorter hours and against the technological displacement of skilled labor.[4] Unions held balls to mix fund-raising and socializing, and their popularity is attested to by a press report of a molders' ball that remarked it was "so largely attended that when the supper tables were filled there was still a large company left in the dancing room."[5]

It was in this context of labor activity at the workplace and in the community that the iron molders' union battled a Republican employer and redirected the tone and to some extent the substance of local politics. Founded during the war, the molders' local made quick inroads among skilled workers in the stove foundries and by 1870 over fifty of the city's eighty-four molders belonged.[6] Through adherence to the union, molders continued to command high wages while many other workers experienced decline. Union rules were restrictive and in the winter of 1873 efforts by foundry proprietor John Roelker to free himself of them exacerbated class tensions in Evansville.

When Roelker broke with established practice and hired an additional apprentice, his workers informed him that it violated a union law restricting the employment of apprentices to one for every eight journeymen.[7] Roelker responded by locking the union men out and refusing to submit the problem to arbitration. As other local employers had done, Roelker advertised outside the city for strikebreakers. A business partner in Cincinnati placed an ad in the *Commercial* and within two weeks the Eagle Foundry was back in operation, working thirteen apprentices alongside twenty-one molders.[8]

Replacement of the union molders was not a peaceful process; they were determined to defeat this tactic and the following weeks were marked by threats and fights. Union man Joe Kleiner was arrested for attacking "independent" molder William Alberts with "metal knuckles."[9] In response, the strikebreakers publicly warned "if we are molested by any of the Union moulders we will try and protect ourselves."[10] Roelker himself took steps. Using his seat on the City Council, he introduced a resolution that conferred the title of "special policeman" on his watchman. More quietly, Roelker armed his employees. It is not hard to understand why rumors of impending riot appeared in the press.[11]

These tensions exploded on March 17 when strikebreaker Louis Buzan shot union molder Conrad Hartman dead in an alley outside the Orchestrion Saloon.[12] Hartman had been followed there by Buzan, fellow strikebreaker James Wiley, and John Roelker. (His testimony states that he "reluctantly" joined his employees.[13]) The brawny Hartman confronted Buzan at the bar and may have threatened him with a beer glass, after which the strikebreaker pulled out a pistol. At this point Roelker departed and the barkeeper showed Buzan and his companion the door to the alley. Hartman and fellow union molders Conrad Muth, Fred Brennecke, and Jacob Jourdan, and cigar maker Anton Sehnle, followed. Threats were exchanged and when Hartman attempted to wrestle the gun out of Buzan's hand, it fired and sent a bullet into the union man's skull. After freeing himself of the fallen Hartman, Buzan and two of his companions turned and fired on the other union men, wounding both Muth and Jourdan.

In many small industrial cities, attempts by workers to intimidate strikebreakers received broad community sanction. In Braidwood, Illinois, Buena Vista, Pennsylvania, and Newport, Kentucky, acts of violence between union men and strikebreakers resulted in strong support for the union, much to the frustration of the manufacturer. In Evansville the strike did not unite the community; instead it focused attention on some important differences. For two months, the trial of Louis Buzan kept the strike in the public eye. The *Journal* seized the moment to condemn attempts to intimidate strikebreakers. The right to unionize was "fully conceded" by the editors, but they continued: "When they begin to annoy a proprietor for disregarding their rules, and attempt to intimidate fellow-workmen who do not choose to comply with the regulations of a Union of which they are not members, the Union men cannot hope to meet with the approval of law-abiding and order-loving citizens."[14]

When the editors spoke of intimidation, they addressed a point of contention between workers and employers. Faced with unions with strong support in the community, employers turned elsewhere for labor. The editors, in speaking of intimidation, defended this strategy and linked unions to disorder. The point was strengthened by the coincidental opening of the trial of cooper J. B. Simpson for setting a fire in Wiltshire and Kreipke's shop. A member of the firm claimed that Simpson was angry due to his failure to get enough work—a problem that faced many coopers in the era of mechanization—while another testified that Simpson had intended to go to the railroad depot "with clubs and beat the coopers who were coming from Terre Haute."[15]

Intimidation was the theme of the Buzan trial. Roelker described Hartman as "dangerous" and inclined toward drunkenness, and he accused the union of conspiring to force the "independent moulders out of town." More specific charges were levied by the "independents" themselves. William Alberts claimed Hartman had tried to force him to join the union.[16] James Wiley accused union leader Fred Brennecke of boasting that "there were sixty-nine of them who would run us out of town." Brennecke was also said to have proposed a wager of five dollars that "he could whip any G—— d—— Independent moulder."[17]

Ultimately the trial turned on the defendant's testimony. Out of work in Cincinnati, Buzan answered the advertisement in the *Com-*

mercial and came to Evansville where Roelker put him to work. He made it a practice to carry a gun, as he put it, "to defend myself against the Moulder's Union." Never a member of a union himself, he blamed union belligerence for the tragedy at the Orchestrion. Hartman allegedly had called Buzan a "damned liar" and attempted to strike him. Buzan described how he backed out of the saloon with the union men closely following—Hartman calling him a "damned coward," Muth boasting "he could whip any damned scab," and Brennecke urging Muth to knock Buzan down from behind.[18] The defense portrayed a lawless cadre of union leaders who conspired to intimidate their replacements.

A different interpretation emerged from the testimony of the union men and their friends. Stable owner Thomas Bullen, who was with Muth and Brennecke at the saloon, described an aggressive Buzan who on taking out his gun told Hartman, "I'll give it to you." Brennecke told the court that Buzan walked out of the saloon boasting that "he could whip any one who interfered with him." It was Hartman's efforts to have a fair fight that led to the battle for the gun, but the gun went off intentionally, Buzan again crying out "I'll give it to you." And molder Henry Schnake described how Buzan, after emptying his pistol, asked a fellow "scab" for another gun, while yet another had already pulled out his and started firing.[19] For them it was a case of cold-blooded murder. Roelker, they believed, ordered his scabs to "shoot any union man who would come around the place." The events of March 17 were set in motion by this fear—Hartman entered the saloon concerned that "Roelker's scabs were following him." As far as the union was concerned, the ensuing violence was perpetrated by a group of lawless nonunion workers encouraged by their employer to assume a belligerent posture. The sense that ultimate responsibility lay with the employer was revealed when a union corespondent reported that "Roelker has not as yet been arrested" for "this premeditated butchery."[20]

However, the antiunion interpretation convinced the jurors—only two of whom were workers—to acquit Buzan. The *Journal* applauded while noting that there was great disagreement on this subject. Buzan was then tried for shooting Muth and Jourdan. This trial was speedier, and the jury ruled Buzan guilty of attempted murder, and he was sentenced to two years imprisonment. In response, Roelker circulated a petition in the business community requesting the Governor to commute the sentence.[21]

Buzan's trial hardly ended the matter as strong feelings persisted and the strike continued. In June, four union men destroyed a mold at Roelker's; one was fined twelve dollars for disorderly conduct.[22] While reports of intimidation persisted, in some cases like that of James Wiley, strikebreakers were converted to unionism.[23] Still the Eagle Foundry continued to operate as a nonunion shop for a number of years, and a few of Roelker's former employees like Conrad Muth established the cooperative Evansville Foundry Association.[24]

The murder of Hartman strengthened bonds among workers. Friends and relatives of the deceased were joined by three hundred members of the bricklayers', carpenters', chair makers', coopers', and molders' unions, as well as the Crescent City Band in a funeral procession from St. Emanuel's Lutheran Evangelical Church to the cemetery.[25] Two months later, the first mention of a labor assembly was made in the *Journal,* the formation of which was an important step in the re-creation of a community of labor as interunion activity became increasingly prevalent. In the summer of 1873, the labor assembly sent Muth, Brennecke, and cigar maker Fred Blend to the Industrial Congress in Cleveland.[26] In the fall, workers attended the Trades' Assembly Ball and danced to the music of the Germanis Orchestra.[27] In the coming year, the assembly would impose itself on the body politic.

Political Allies and Opportunities

The first foray of the Labor Assembly into politics came in the winter of 1873–74 as the economic depression was unfolding. A committee petitioned the council to relieve the "sufferings of such as may be in a destitute condition" by establishing a soup house and shelter and by increasing street work, a source of employment for the poor.[28] In response, council member John J. Kleiner proposed the city open a fire house as a shelter and provide food for a soup house. He also called on the city to give work to the unemployed by extending the water works.[29] The *Journal* was vociferous in its opposition. Its editors claimed the petition was not "the legitimate outgrowth of American conditions" where "political and legal equality" prevail, but was the result of "passion long kindled and nurtured in a society molded and pervaded by the spirit of feudalism." In America, they argued, "if the laborer does not, in a few years, become an employer of labor, the failure is generally his own fault."[30]

It is little wonder that workingmen turned to the Democrats as they pondered the viability of an electoral campaign. For more than relief was on their minds. Hartman's murder, Buzan's acquittal, and the use of the city machinery to protect strikebreakers remained significant grievances. Through the winter, committees of labor activists met with Democrats to discuss a joint campaign. The *Courier*, the Democratic daily, courted them, calling itself the "workingman's friend," and denouncing the *Journal* for having "made a direct and open attack upon the laboring classes of the country. Its hostility is especially manifested against 'Unions' and those organizations by which workingmen seek to advance their own interests and better their condition."[31]

The prospect of a unified working-class presence appealed to many Democrats. The party had long struggled to gain parity in local elections, largely by appealing to inchoate class sentiments. Nevertheless, Democrats again found themselves a minority party in the wake of revelations of corruption by a scandalous Democratic council, headed by Eccles Van Riper.[32] Republican charges of fraud led to the defeat of Democratic incumbents in 1871, and for two years after the Democrats failed to run a local ticket.[33]

In January 1874, the first steps by the labor assembly toward electoral activity were taken when the "bone and muscle of the population" turned out to hear Richard Trevellick preach the canon of working-class republicanism. Though workers benefited from a political system "where the safeguard of the citizen was at the ballot box," Trevellick warned that the rise of powerful monied interests threatened its stability. Like corrupt feudal tyrannies in Europe that were being overthrown because they had "oppressed their workingmen," the American republic would fail unless it protected "all in the exercise of their natural rights and gives artificial rights to none." The equitable solution, Trevellick concluded, was an expansion of greenbacks and an end to the preferential treatment of bondholders, for "the rights of labor must be as well protected as the rights of money."[34]

A committee of union leaders drew up a list of resolutions decrying the "alarming development of aggregated wealth, on the one side, and pauperism and hopeless degradation on the other." Continued enjoyment of the blessings of republican government, they agreed, required that "a check must be placed upon . . . unjust accumulation, and a system adopted which will secure to the laborer the fruits of his toil." The committee urged the preservation of western lands for "actual settlers" rather than railroads, the establishment of producers' and consumers' cooperatives, the substitution of arbitration for strikes, and the creation of a national paper currency. These were to become staples of working-class radicalism in the 1870s.

Though local issues were not discussed, the selection of John

Kleiner as chair was of some significance. A native of Pennsylvania, Kleiner came in 1867 to Evansville and soon became the sole proprietor of the Evansville Commercial College, where he taught young men the requisite skills for white-collar employment. The popular Kleiner, not yet twenty-nine and inexperienced in politics, ran for council in the spring of 1873 in a nonpartisan election and handily won a council seat.[35] Kleiner had reported favorably on the petition for relief a month before, and was quickly becoming identified with working-class politics.

That spring, his popularity with workers made Kleiner an attractive candidate to the Democratic Convention, which nominated him for mayor. Democrats strengthened their ties to labor by nominating Conrad Muth as their candidate for the Fourth Ward council seat. Otherwise, union men did not fare so well. They failed to prevent the nomination of Sam Jones, an insurance agent who had signed the petition for Louis Buzan's pardon. Cigar maker Union officer Emil Levy ran a poor third in the nominations for clerk, and Fred Brennecke fell ten votes shy of taking the nomination for marshall away from party regular John Gavitt.[36]

Not everyone was pleased. The *Journal* condemned Kleiner's candidacy as a "stupendous joke," and warned "tax-payers" to consider the "consequences" of his election. Terming his relief report a "souphouse and bunks for loafers proposition," the editors charged that his supporters were "communistic in their tendencies . . . and dangerous to the prosperity of the city and the contentment of the population."[37] Two days later, the editor expanded their analysis, claiming that such men "look upon taxes as so much tribute levied upon the rich for the benefit of the poor."[38] The *Courier* also expressed reservations. The editors spoke of Kleiner's newness to the city and argued that his brief tenure on the council had demonstrated "no ability to warrant such official advancement."[39] Only the *Demokrat*, which portrayed Kleiner as "a deadly enemy to monopoly and ring rule," applauded the choice. Reminding the *Courier* that Kleiner had been easily nominated on the first ballot, the editor argued that his ethnic heritage would gain support from German Republicans mindful of mounting pressure to enforce a statewide temperance law, to which Kleiner had voiced a clear opposition.[40]

No firm alliance had yet been made. The following evening, the Labor Assembly met to map out a strategy. The members easily agreed to a pledge not to support any candidate who had signed the petition for Buzan's pardon. To maintain their independence, they supported a bi-partisan ticket, endorsing Republicans for treasurer (rather than vote for the offensive Sam Jones), collector, assessor, and for council seats in the First and Third wards. For other offices, they pledged to support Democrats.[41]

The campaign heated up when Richard Trevellick returned to address an audience so large that "hundreds were turned away." Trevellick held their attention for hours and delivered what the *Demokrat* deemed "a masterpiece."[42] To Republican charges against Kleiner he asked, "is it true, that because an Alderman advocates free soup houses and bunks for the hungry and homeless poor, he is a communist?" If that was so, he answered, "Christ was a Communist." He lectured workers on the need to use the ballot box to oppose class legislation favoring capitalists. The proper course, he argued, was to support the party that was willing to befriend them, but to remain attached only to their interests as workers. In Evansville, at the moment, that meant supporting the Democrats.[43]

Workers took this advice to heart. In a hard fought battle, Kleiner narrowly defeated the well-respected Republican incumbent, Charles Butterfield. Results for the other offices were more striking. Every citywide office was filled by a Labor Assembly sponsored candidate, regardless of ethnicity or party. In the race for marshal, Democrat John Gavitt beat Republican Henry Huber by nearly a 6 percent margin, and Republican Benjamin Sansom was the clear choice for collector over Democrat William Maynard. Signers of the Buzan petitions were resoundingly defeated. Offending German Republican August Pfafflin was punished as Democratic rival James D. Saunders received 60 percent of the vote. Ethnicity and "blacklisting" together proved an especially potent force. This was most evident in the contest for treasurer, where Republican Charles Ohning trounced Sam Jones by a 3.5 to 1 margin. Jones's firmest rejection came in the German working-class wards of Lamasco (the Fourth, Fifth and Sixth), where he garnered only 16.4 percent of the vote.[44]

Once again, Republican supremacy had been destroyed. Cigar maker Fred Blend boasted that workers "wiped out the dominant party who generally carried [sic] the city by about 600 majority." Many celebrated while bands triumphantly played rousing victory melodies.[45] Again a crowd of workers flocked to the court house to hear Trevellick (now characterized by the *Journal* as an "imported demagogue") encourage them to mobilize for the battle to come—to elect a Congressman that was "sound on the money question."[46]

The meaning of the election was clear. The *Journal* ascribed Republican losses to working-class resentment, noting that the "strength of the labor associations and their discipline were altogether underestimated." The editors found in this strength a dangerous "proscriptive spirit." Labor Assembly leaders, they asserted, do "not tolerate the right of individual judgment" and instead use "black lists" to "intimidate and domineer over all." The editors quickly assumed a threatening posture. They pointed out that labor activists "depend for employment upon men whom they post as enemies of the workingmen, and against whom they are continually declaiming in their secret meetings." Also prominent on the labor "black list" were wealthy men on whom the city had traditionally relied for "their counsel, credit and money." The editors warned that such men might withdraw credit in response to the blacklist. Further, they warned that "capital is proverbially timid" and suggested that the election of Kleiner would result in the removal of investment capital from the local economy.[47]

Such threats did not dissuade the laborites from following the political path. In May, they convened to develop a program for the fall. In voicing concern that the rise of "aggregated wealth, which unless checked will lead to pauperization and hopeless degradation of the toiling masses, and which will finally destroy the Republic," they echoed Trevellick. In the interests of "equality, justice and humanity," they articulated a broad reform platform that included an eight-hour day, strong apprentice laws, compulsory education, public markets that would "do away with middle men and speculators," nationalization of the railroads, civil service reform, and the direct election of all national officers. Most important were the call for the national government to print more greenbacks that would be "legal tender in the payment of all debts, public and private," and the demand that laws exempting government bonds from taxation be repealed. No doubt, Richard Trevellick would have been pleased. And local Democrats had reason to be pleased as well, as the greenback planks of the platform put the laborites on similar ground.[48]

Forging an Alliance

The labor activists had not been absorbed into the Democratic party; instead they sent Mayor Kleiner to head their delegation to the statewide Independent Convention.[49] The Independent movement arose in response to President Grant's veto of a Congressional measure that would have inflated the country's money supply. Aside from a few trade unionists and currency reformers, it was mostly farmers who gathered in Indianapolis that June. There, they agreed that the tariff and black civil rights in the South were antiquated questions, and that on the vital question of currency there was no real difference between Republicans and Democrats.[50]

At the end of August, Vanderburgh County Independents convened and selected a full ticket. As the *Journal* charged, the nominees were almost all Democrats. Yet there were some union men among them, including machinist William H. Miller for state representative and Fred Blend for township trustee.[51] Two weeks later, the Democrats put forth a nearly identical ticket. The two forces had yet to merge, however; the Labor Assembly retained its independence by endorsing the candidacy of Republican manufacturer William Heilman, who had publicly taken an inflationary position.[52] Election day gave Democrats and union men cause for celebration, as between them they shared all but three offices; among the victors were assembly members Blend and Miller. Yet workers had remained truly independent, helping William Heilman, who narrowly lost in his race for Congress, rout his Democratic opponent within the city of Evansville.[53]

Overall it was the Democrats who benefited most from the Labor Assembly's entry into electoral politics. Emboldened by success, the Democrats offered a full ticket of party regulars in the spring of 1875. Well-to-do businessmen and professionals like physician Matthew Mulhausen, saw mill proprietor Adam Helfrich, and wholesale liquor dealer Henry Gumberts were offered to the voters. An important exception was made in the unanimous nomination of molder Fred Brennecke for city marshall.[54]

Political enthusiasm by the city's workers, however, was already in decline. This was evident earlier in the year; when Trevellick again spoke in Evansville, only forty of the devout attended.[55] Now, two months later, fewer than eighty attended the Independent convention, which nominated a distinct slate of council candidates that shared only carpenter Alfred White with the Republicans. Yet when it came time to discuss citywide offices, mention of Brennecke's name led to great excitement and a nomination. The Independents also endorsed Charles Ohning, the Republican candidate for treasurer, and James Saunders, the Democratic nominee for surveyor.[56]

For citywide office, endorsement by the Independents in a two-way race translated to easy victories. The support given Brennecke was particularly noteworthy as he defeated Henry Huber by nearly a two-to-one margin. But Democrats won every three-way race, though by narrower margins. And they took every contested council seat except the one representing the strongly Republican First Ward.[57] Now the Democrats controlled not only the mayor's office but also the council. To Republicans, suspicious of Democratic scruples in the handling of contracts, and fearful of their ties to working-men, this did not bode well.

Concern from the business community quickly emerged when prominent bankers pressured Kleiner to retain Republican city auditor Henry C. Gwathmey. To the better sort, handing over the city books to a Kleiner appointee seemed like trusting the chicken coop to the fox, and men like Samuel Bayard of the Evansville National Bank tried to prevent it by threatening to withdraw credit from the city. The editors of the *Journal* backed this course, asserting that "the bank has great confidence in . . . [Gwathmey's] financial shrewdness and very little in either the Mayor or a majority of the newly elected Council."[58] They damned Kleiner with faint praise when they spoke of his courage in defying party dictates and retaining Gwathmey, which they thought proved he lacked administrative talent. On the other hand, the *Courier* responded to this move by Republican bankers with a call for the mayor and council to "look these money bullies fairly in the face and defy them."[59] Gwathmey remained in office until June when Kleiner, with the aid of leading Democrats, procured funds from outside sources.[60]

The battle to dislodge Gwathmey led the *Courier* to resume a divisive political style. In response to calls for the election of businessmen to prevent the misappropriation of public funds, the editors linked the Republican party to the rich and to corruption. Denying that raids on public funds resulted from the election of common men to office, they argued that "every job by which our people have been robbed . . . has been conceived, planned and executed by a Ring of rich plunderers." The wealthy, they went on, amassed fortunes "by the building of sewers and bridges, the opening of streets and filling in of marshes at public expense." In addition, they accused "rich" council members of regularly voting to grant "chartered rights to corporations in which they were among the largest stockholders." Such abuses, the editors remarked, would have continued had not the "people at last shaken off these respectable plunderers and placed the Democratic party in power."[61]

There was some personal animus behind this attack. The editors of the *Courier* were John and George Shanklin, scions of an elite local family, who had accused William Heilman of bribing voters during the previous Congressional election and then dared him to bring a libel suit against them. Heilman did just that, and when the Shanklins were found innocent they responded by publishing the entire trial transcript which was filled with allegations of Heilman directly, or through his friends, treating voters to a drink.[62] At best the depiction was unseemly; at worst it suggested the extent to which wealthy manufacturers might use their influence to sway the outcome of elections.

In the spring of 1876, voters were unmoved by the radical language of the Democratic press as Republican candidates for clerk and treasurer prevailed. The Democrats succeeded in holding on to the surveyor's office, but only Fred Brennecke retained a strong hold on the citywide electorate, besting cooperage manufacturer, Philip Klein. And only the Fourth Ward, by reelecting molder Conrad Muth, returned a Democrat to council.[63] Democratic fortunes would continue to depend on their willingness to meet the needs of labor activists.

Unemployment, Relief, and Political Inertia

Frequently, however, the Democratic leadership failed to do this. Declining activity by labor activists suggests that the political fervor unleashed by the Buzan trial had been largely spent. Democrats in turn nominated conservative businessmen to office and the party grew less responsive to working-class aspirations. The decline in political activity paralleled the rise of acquiescence in the workshops, where years of depression had led to lower expectations. The few strikes that were waged, like that of the cabinetmakers employed by the Armstrong company, suggest desperation more than militancy. In response to a 15 to 40 percent wage cut, the latest in a series, they declared it "better to starve at once, than to faint away at the workbench with a but hardly half stilled hunger."[64]

Many workers experienced deprivation during the depression. "Tramps"—unemployed single men from other places—descended upon the city, gaining only sympathy from Kleiner who worried that Evansville attracted too many such men.[65] Residents too turned to local government for aid. That workers had gained some political influence, particularly by electing cigar maker Fred Blend township trustee, created a more sympathetic if still inadequate response to their appeals. Speaking before the council in January 1876, Blend claimed that more than five hundred local residents were in dire need of work. Blend offered to loan the city $3,000 from an unused special township school fund to finance a work-relief program.[66]

Out of this and other proposals for relief arose a debate over the nature of the poor. Elite charity workers and employers had long argued that unemployment was not a legitimate cause for relief. Any able-bodied man, they believed, who failed to find work was not "truly needy." The deserving poor, then, were mostly women and children who suffered due to male indolence, and not infrequently, alcoholism. These attitudes were strengthened by the frequent practice of using church women to seek out the poor in a given district.[67]

Though unemployment during the depression was too widespread for workers to accept this, they too made distinctions. Blend agreed that nothing could be done for tramps, and he renounced his efforts to run a soup house as an inducement to "idleness and depravity."[68] But in presenting his proposal, Blend spoke not of paupers or tramps but of "fathers and husbands," all "worthy citizens . . . who had lived here for many years, and whom the hard times and scarcity of work has driven to poverty." Such men, he told the council, refuse charity as beneath their manly dignity and ask only for work.[69] It was the taking on of family responsibility that made the worker deserving of relief; in a city where so many German workers had settled and established families, Blend's distinction was a defense of the working-class community.

The divergent approaches to relief became more evident the following winter when 42 laborers petitioned the county Board of Commissioners to create work for the unemployed "to keep the hunger from our children, and prevent the divorces of so many wives and husbands."[70] A similar petition was presented to the city council. The response to the deepening crisis revealed not only the differences between elite and plebeian visions of relief but also the limitations of political alliance with the Democrats. A combination of class and political affiliation set the terms of council debate. Democratic molder Conrad Muth moved to grant the petition, and fellow Democrat William Rahm, a grocer, seconded the motion. Kleiner gave his support and spoke of "great suffering and distress among our own citizens, heads of families, women and children."[71] Yet, he was unwilling to force the largely Republican council to a vote, and instead proposed a public meeting to express opinion on the matter.

Considerable public debate ensued. Most Republicans and not a few Democrats, who opposed adding to the city debt to do less than urgent improvements, believed the petitions were mere calls for charity. Frank Thayer, editor of the *Journal*, thought there "should be discrimination between the worthy and unworthy poor," and that each applicant should be subjected to "a rigid scrutiny" by visitors. He endorsed the efforts of the Indianapolis Benevolent Society to have volunteers "call at unseasonable hours . . . to ascertain whether there are any men about the premises, and if so to learn their character and occupation, if any." Council member John S. Hopkins, a banker, agreed and suggested that the churches could take the lead.[72]

Workers and their allies disagreed. Blend, no longer township trustee, told a meeting that they "would starve almost before they would receive charity." The new Republican Trustee, boss steam pipe fitter Ronald Fisher, thought leaving relief to the churches offered little hope to the poor. Kleiner insisted it was "not a question of charitable relief, but a question of the employment of laboring men out of work." He spoke of men "who wanted work and could not procure it," and of families that "were absolutely suffering for the necessaries of life." Yet he denied that the city could do anything without a tax levy.[73]

The debate over relief was closely tied to views about labor and capital. Wealthy Democratic manufacturer John A. Reitz, who backed Thayer's proposal, denied there was any lack of employment opportunities. He pointed out that workers in the rolling mill had just struck in protest of a wage reduction and was adamant that "such men should not be helped." Banker Hopkins then spoke of employers unable to get workers to chop wood at 75 cents a cord. A group of "leading men" presented a petition protesting any improvements or relief while demanding a reduction of taxes and assessments for the following year.[74]

In the midst of the controversy a more radical voice emerged that demanded a distinctly stronger role for local government. Ben Jewett, a bookkeeper at Reitz and Haney's iron foundry, wrote two letters to the *Courier* chastising Kleiner, "the purported 'friend of Evansville's poor,'" for his inaction. Jewett proposed a property tax to create a work fund for "honest and needy" workers who are "discharged through the greed or poverty of employer." Such a plan, he suggested, would defend "the manhood and spirit of American labor." For Jewett, this was not charity, but "justice." A tax on the rich, he averred, was a fair price to pay for those who exploited labor. "The surplus wealth of the rich is nothing but the accumulation of poor men's surplus earnings, and the rich had better now (than later) learn the righteousness of returning to labor in time of need that which in time of plenty is extracted (this with permission) from them."[75]

Now that the terms of the debate had more clearly been spelled out, the *Courier* came out against relief. Regarding the rolling mill strike, the Shanklins echoed Reitz, arguing "surely work can not be so scarce, when laborers feel independent enough to dictate, or attempt to dictate, terms to their employers." They suggested an industrious man could support a family with food for 25 cents a day. The problem was that low wages would not "supply the husband with his three glasses of beer and his half a dozen pipes of tobacco besides." The Shanklins concluded that Hopkins, Reitz, and Thayer were right; the proper course was to leave it to church committees "to hunt up the worthy poor and aid them according to their necessities."[76]

However, the strength of popular sentiment made it, as John Hopkins put it, "not a matter of policy but one of necessity."[77] The council authorized a citizen's committee to supervise the extension of a sewer. All were not satisfied, however, and the council was soon besieged with a dispute over wages. Willard Carpenter, who headed the committee, challenged the reading of the minutes because they included a wage scale that he argued was the proper domain of his committee. Conrad Muth responded that he had voted for the project assuming that workers would receive at least a dollar a day. William Rahm then moved that the daily wage for common labor be increased to a dollar. Fred Blend, also on the committee, added fuel to the fire when he questioned the motives of some committee members. Blend told the council that "it was a shame that the city should permit such a degradation of labor as to force men to work for the paltry sum of 85 cents per day" and he called for an investigation. That was not something the Republican dominated council was inclined to do, and businessmen like Thomas Kerth, Samuel Orr, and John Reitz agreed that the matter was settled, and they convinced Rahm to withdraw his motion.[78]

The debate over relief suggests the difficulties of maintaining a political alliance. In debate it became clear that staunch Democrats like John Reitz opposed work-relief with as much vigor as any Republican. Fearful that higher taxes would alienate the Democratic elite, and operating within a republican political tradition that emphasized the desirability of a neutral state, Kleiner was reluctant to support bold initiatives. The kind of program that Jewett proposed remained outside mainstream political debate, and small expansions in the municipal work force remained the primary response to unemployment.

While politicians confronted the demands of the unemployed, many workers put their hopes in the development of a cooperative economy at the urging of Thomas D. Worrall. Soon after his arrival in the city, Worral was invited to speak by the Molders' Union after which they formed Evansville Foundrymen's Guild No. 57, which boasted a membership of about a hundred. Matilda Muth, wife of the molder and council member, was elected president of the Ladies Guild, whose 89 members aimed to establish a cooperative dressmaking shop. Smaller guilds were founded by carpenters and cabinetmakers. The optimism of the movement was expressed by molder F. M. Mercer, who in a public lecture proclaimed their goal to make Evansville the "Rochdale of America."[79]

Evansville proved fertile ground. Workers had found unions incapable of resisting wage cuts and government unwilling to address adequately the problem of unemployment. Worrall offered an alternative they had seen work. The first local cooperative, a furniture factory, had been established in 1870, and three years later a foundry had been put into operation by former employees of John Roelker. Both enjoyed early success and by 1880 each was producing near $70,000 a year in goods, though it is unclear that they were still operating as cooperatives.[80] Worrall offered the vision of transforming a few experiments into a cooperative economy that would fully employ all workers.

Worrall and his following established the basis for a movement culture.[81] The guilds rented a meeting hall, where lectures were given on the virtues of cooperation. Members also gathered for lighter entertainment as they did to hear the singing of Ida Akers, the five-year-old daughter of a Prussian-born cabinetmaker, or when the Cooperative Dramatic Club offered a rendition of the temperance classic, "Ten Nights in a Barroom." Members also came to use the library and reading room, and plans were made to open a cooperative grocery on the first floor.[82]

Though the movement was short-lived—by July 1877 reports of the closure of cooperatives appeared[83]—it further weakened ties between workers and the Democratic party. At the local Greenback party convention, Worrall claimed that guild men would vote for the "party which offered the most employment to the poor."[84] In light of the positions taken by the *Courier* and by Democratic councilman John Reitz on the question of relief, it was by no means clear that this would work to the benefit of the Democrats. And it did not. The decline in Democratic fortunes continued in the spring election, when only two of the six wards elected Democratic councilmen, and though Kleiner was reelected, it was by less than 150 votes, and he barely carried the Sixth Ward and lost the Fourth.[85] Not only had Democrats been relegated to minority status on the council but also their strongholds, the working-class Fourth and Sixth wards had proved unreliable.

Crisis

The *Courier* responded to defeat with a divisive posture. In early June 1877, the editors again spoke of rich Republicans milking the city treasury for their own gain. Their plunder "was so much money stolen from the pockets of the taxpayers, from the laboring man who has accumulated enough in the best years of his life to have secured him a little home."[86] A few weeks later, the *Courier* intensified its language, sparking the embers of class resentment by arguing that the exploitation of labor was the source of wealth. "The shrewd businessman who amasses a great fortune in a score or more of years," the editors charged, does so only by overcharging his customers or by "underpaying the laborer who made the goods he sells." They continued: "No man ever becomes very wealthy who depends solely upon his own labor for increase. It is the tradesman, the shopkeeper, the banker, the boss manufacturer who 'makes a fortune,' and the greater the number of men he employs, the more he accumulates."[87]

Such radical posturing was soon tested by the great railroad strike of 1877. The uprising began on the Baltimore and Ohio Railroad when workers at Martinsburg, West Virginia, protested against the last in a series of wage cuts. The strike spread to other lines and railroad companies prevailed on governors to call up the militia, and on President Rutherford Hayes to send the army to break it. In some places, most notably Pittsburgh, violent confrontations between workers and the armed emissaries of the state expanded the conflict beyond the confines of the railroads, and in cities like Chicago, Louisville, St. Louis, and Evansville other workers began to press their own demands.[88]

The *Journal* condemned the strike and the destruction of property that ensued and counseled workers to exercise caution. "It is the old story," the editors wrote, "of the characterless, shifting, lazy and discontented leading the honest, hard worker into trouble."[89] The *Courier*, on the other hand, responded by intensifying its radical language, for its editors perceived another opportunity to lash out at Republicans. Their language was reminiscent of the labor defense of work-relief as they portrayed strikers as "sober, steady, industrious and courageous" men who "had already been compelled to work for less than a living for their families." The companies were interested only in satisfying the demands of "bondholders," and they treated their workmen like "slaves who should esteem it a high privilege to be permitted to live at all." Justice demanded a workman's wage be "ample to support and educate his children, even though the bondholder be compelled to have his interest on his bond passed occasionally."

The Democratic editors condemned the violence and reminded readers that the ballot was the proper tool with which to express discontent—but not without an opinion on how it should be used. The "only hope for relief from the grinding curse of hard times," they insisted, "is to vote solidly against the party whose Fraudulent President is but the servile tool of the bondholders and money-mongers, who are growing richer as the poor grow poorer."[90] The editors called for an alliance of the "laboring and middle classes" against the bondholders. They urged voters to support the abolition of banks and the payment of the government debt in greenbacks. And if the bondholders refused to accept them, the editors called for repudiation of the bonds.[91]

More than the ballot box was on the minds of workers. On July 23 two thousand crowded the courthouse to express solidarity with the railroad strikers. Resolutions supported their efforts to "secure just and equitable rewards for their labor" and termed their revolt a "most righteous struggle of labor against robbery and oppression." Speakers who wholeheartedly endorsed the strike, like socialist woodcarver George Thobe, received the cheers of the assembled, while lawyer S. R. Hornbrook who counseled moderation and spoke of class harmony was booed off the platform. Most addressed problems of poverty and deprivation. A letter from Benjamin Jewett was read, which asked why railroad magnate Tom Scott should be able "to keep up his prostitutes in luxury while the laborer's family nearly starves." Hoping to benefit from this renewal of working-class protest, the *Courier* was unsparing in its praise for the meeting, warning "money mongers" that "the 'Patient Ass' has begun to kick.[92]

For the next week between four hundred and fifteen hundred workers met nightly. Quickly the tone changed as speakers addressed questions closer to home. Martin Coniff denounced the replacement of male weavers by women in the cotton mill two years before "because they could be had to work for two dollars a week, thus forcing men to become tramps." Coniff claimed that workingmen merely wanted a living wage and to be "treated like men," and as a step toward that end he called for men to replace boys under the age of fourteen employed in local workshops.[93] The prevalence of such sentiments led workers to petition the council to adopt an eight-hour day and Congress to enact a bill abolishing child labor.[94]

Protest was given organizational form with the founding of the Workingmen's Protective Union (WPU). The constitution of the WPU welcomed "all laboring men and mechanics," while reflecting the political experience of the previous four years. It blamed the pauperization of labor on the "ruinous financial policy now fostered and upheld by our government for the interest of banks and bondholders and heartless monied corporations," and warned that workers were threatened with "a slavery far more humiliating than any that ever existed." Members of the WPU pledged to vote only for candidates who vowed to work to repeal the government's currency contraction policy. To this extent, the WPU seemed to renew the political efforts of the now-defunct Labor Assembly.

Yet there were departures, not the least of which was the inclusion of black workers. Bushrod Taylor spoke for himself and other black steamboatmen who worked for just 66 cents a day in expressing a desire to join the movement. Little fuss was made over the contingent of blacks, and socialist Thobe spoke of the uniting of white and black workers as a beneficial result of the depression.[95] In addition, while much attention was placed on the political sources of poverty, portions of the document reoriented attention toward the workplace. In an important section, it focused on the failure of local employers to pay a just wage and it called on workers to unite in a "general call upon our employers to advance all labor to that standard which will insure to us sufficient means to educate our children, nurse our sick, to live, feed, and clothe our families in accordance with the laws of humanity."

The WPU declared the right to "strike and withhold our labor" until employers raised wages. George Thobe—who declared that local workers experienced "poorer wages and worse grub than any of them"—urged each trade to set up committees to meet with employers and make demands.[96] Opposition to the proposal soon arose as some complained of a lack of volunteers, while others expressed a distrust of a small committee to handle the details of negotiation.[97] In a meeting of over fifteen hundred, it was agreed to enroll over a hundred to march in a procession from workshop to workshop.[98]

With this change toward direct local action, the *Courier* experienced sober second thoughts. Immediately a city ravaged by exploiting capitalists and "ring rule" disappeared and in its place appeared a more harmonious community. Struggling to make up for past indiscretions, the editors claimed: "Here in Evansville, thanks to the mutual confidence between employers and employes, there is not likely to be any disturbance. All are suffering alike in the city. . . . We do not believe that there are a score of employers in a thousand in Evansville who will not cheerfully advance wages whenever they find it possible . . . *Let us exercise charity, one towards the other.*"[99]

The mayor himself walked a fine line. Kleiner assured the members of the WPU of "the hearty sympathy" of local citizens in their "efforts to elevate the real laborer's position to that which God intended it should have." He urged them to cooperate with city authorities in maintaining order, which the labor men agreed to do.[100] To this end, Kleiner ordered the closing of saloons on the day of the procession.[101] This was consistent with his handling of the strike in the train yards of the St. Louis and Southeastern Railroad. On July 26, J. H. Wilson, the receiver of the road, telegraphed Judge Walter Q. Gresham for protection and was told to turn to the mayor. However, "for fear of adding to the excitement," Kleiner refused. Only when Gresham threatened to send in federal troops did Kleiner dispatch a few police to the yard.[102]

Despite the opposition of the press and the ambivalence of the mayor, Fred Blend and others reaffirmed the need for workers to confront employers.[103] Some fifteen hundred gathered at the courthouse on the morning of July 30.[104] Two hundred became official participants in the procession and were sworn in by Kleiner as a special police force. A few hundred more accompanied them as they set off to visit the city's workshops to talk to workers to see if they were satisfied with their wages. In a few cases, like that of furniture manufacturer Frank Blomer, employers resisted, claiming their workers were content, and in these instance tensions rose. When Emil Levy told Blomer that they had come with peaceful intentions and suggested a committee of two, the proprietor relented. The committee findings contradicted his claims; most of the men, who made as little as five dollars a week, were dissatisfied, and a few said they were only waiting for their paychecks to go on strike. Most, however, remained on the job, fearful of losing precious wages and of being replaced. Their reticence led those in the procession to be placated by employer statements of a willingness to increase wages if only other manufacturers would do the same.

For others, the procession allowed an opportunity to express grievances. One workman at Christian Kratz's foundry took off his apron, while two at the Evansville Furniture Company did the same. In anticipation of the general strike, twenty-five employees at Wiltshire and Kreipke's cooper shop, where skilled men earned between seven and nine dollars a week, joined the procession at the courthouse. Similarly, twenty-two of twenty-five varnishers at the Armstrong factory, who averaged about seven dollars a week, went on strike the previous Saturday night. And a few black roustabouts on one of the steamboats struck on the day of the procession, but their places were quickly filled by white stevedores.

Varieties of Political Discourse in the Aftermath

One result of the burst of organizing that accompanied the railroad strikes was the increasing public presence of socialists in Evansville. Almost immediately after the general strike, letters appeared in the

Courier that challenged the ability of the Democrats to respond to the interests of workers. The first, from "many workers," denied that workers would benefit from an inflated currency if "the machinery for distribution" remains in the hands of the rich.[105] Later on they termed the *Courier's* call for a movement of workers and debtors a "specious sophistic plea that has let into the labor associations, throughout the world, a lot of impecunious dead-heads . . . and this county and city will furnish ample evidences of the fact." Only a new social ethic offered hope and they called for "less of mammon, more of justice; less of pulpit talk, more of downright practice; less of selfishness, more of self-denial." A few weeks later, a letter signed "Labor" denied that class oppression was grounded in taxation or hard money, arguing that economic woes were caused by the exploitation of the worker who "has been defrauded of the result of his labor" by profit-hoarding employers. Since the employing class could spend a limited amount, while the masses of workers were too impoverished to do so, the return of good times required that "the rich . . . make restitution of the stolen tools" that they had taken from workers.[106] A month later, "Socialists" added that wages were kept to the subsistence point not only by the luxurious habits of employers but also by the need for firms "to 'meet the market' and 'secure the trade.'"[107]

The communications to the Democratic organ reflected the institutional development of the socialist left in Evansville. In the fall of 1877, socialists formed a militia, the "Liberty Guards," that by May 1878 numbered eighty members.[108] According to one member, the Guards organized in response to the appearance of the "Evansville Rifles" after the railroad strike. It was believed that the Rifles, comprised of "rich men's sons or 'toney' fellows about town," was organized to put down labor activity.[109]

By the spring of 1878, some five hundred socialists had organized English and German speaking organizations.[110] In May, Germans gathered to hear Gustav Luebkert of the Socialist Labor party present the party platform and defend the arming of workers as necessary "to protect the republic and to maintain it."[111] English-speaking workers heard German-born cigar maker Emil Levy introduce George McNeill, a widely respected labor leader from Massachusetts, who encouraged workers to support both economic and political organization. He, too, spoke of preserving republican institutions. He asked his audience: "is it right that those who produce should live in hovels? That those who make furniture should have none? That those who make shoes should see their children go barefooted? If it is right, then there is no God; then all hope is fled, and there is no need for a Republic."[112]

The socialist presence offered workers a political alternative to the established parties, and it forced Democrats to respond with greater attention to the aspirations of workers. Letters were sometimes criticized by the editors of the *Courier* for their sentimentalism, but never for extremism, and they urged workers to join them on a greenback platform as the proper remedy of class iniquities.[113] For instance, in a response to socialist charges that poverty was the result of capitalist exploitation, the editors (normally prone to discuss the inevitability of self-interested behavior) for the moment asserted that "the only just principle of trade" was one that set prices by the cost of production plus a "living profit." They added "let the laws of supply and demand go to the Devil from whence they sprang. There wouldn't be many millionaires under such a system, but there would be very few *l'miserables*."[114] And when a letter to the *Journal* denounced the Liberty Guards as a "menace" to property, the *Courier* seized another opportunity to lambaste the "money-mongers" who "are demanding the increase of the regular army to 100,000 men." Far from being a "menace," they argued, a worker's militia would safeguard democracy from the "despotism" of bondholder military rule.[115] The openness of the *Courier* was acknowledged implicitly by the number of letters sent for publication, and in one instance a writer commended the editors for their "semi-occasional fight for human happiness."[116]

The Democratic party was hardly taken over by socialist principles, yet the relationship between them and the socialists was a complex one. While the Democrats depended on German workers for electoral success, periodic lack of responsiveness to their constituency's interests weakened the bonds between party and voters. The very uncertainty of political dominance forced Democrats not to take their strongest constituency completely for granted, and the presence of an articulate socialist leadership ready to serve as an alternative helped keep them faithful. To assure that German workers would continue to turn out to fill the box with the correct ballots, Democrats took steps. The *Courier* provided radical workers a forum to engage its readers, and the editors frequently articulated agreement. By doing this, they legitimated class ways of thinking that helped develop a strong labor movement through the 1880s and beyond.

Within the electoral arena, Democrats directly responded to socialist influence and working-class frustration in the months following the general strike. Many workers saw reasons to respond. In the fall, forty female weavers at the cotton mill refused to accept the latest wage reduction and they were able to convince most of the work force, some three hundred women and ten men, to follow them out. The strike was widely supported in the west end where a ball was held to raise a strike fund. While community harassment of scabs with "abusive epithets" led management to seek protection from the city, Kleiner refused to send the police as the mill lay just across the city limits. Mill owner William Heilman then turned to Republican chief of police Philip Klein, who, less troubled by the matter of boundaries, sent the police outside the city to protect strikebreakers.

Democrats seized the opportunity to align themselves with the striking workers. The *Demokrat* thought the latest reduction "somewhat surprising" and the strike understandable. Democratic police officer Robert Hyde also believed the "hands had justly struck," and he condemned Chief Klein's abuse of the police "to intimidate the poor wage slave from remonstrating against a reduction of the miserable pittance paid for eleven to eleven and a half hours work." The use of the police was particularly grievous since the cotton mill did not "pay a cent of tax for the maintenance of said force."[117]

In the winter of 1877–78, Democrats took further measures to ingratiate themselves with working-class voters by adopting an unambiguous greenback platform and sending labor activists Fred Blend, George Thobe, Emil Levy, Mike Minnehan, and Nicolas Mace in its delegation to the state Democratic convention.[118] As local elections approached, the alliance between this working-class cadre and the Democrats was solidified. In response to a Republican resolution that city "work involving any considerable outlay of money should be let to the lowest responsible bidder," the Democratic convention distinguished between wages and other municipal expenses, declaring that the council "should not discriminate against the day laborer for the benefit of *corporations* and *monopolists*, and reduce the poor man's wages to starvation prices that the city may remit taxes to these unscrupulous and grasping capitalists and large property holders."[119] Democrats took special aim at the "gas ring," terming the company's contract as "an exorbitant oppression and an outrage upon our people."[120] In the days just before the election, the *Courier* tied these issues together, charging that the rich wanted to keep wages paid by the city low so the rings could extort more money. The editors argued that this was bad social policy and that "the growth and prosperity of a community depend largely upon the happiness and thrift of the middle and laboring classes."[121]

In part, this argument was smart politics as it again identified the

Republican party with monopoly. But it also reflected bad blood between elites. Only a few weeks before, John Reitz and William Heilman had nearly come to blows at a County Commissioner's meeting held to discuss whether the county should buy a tract of land for a poor house. Reitz opposed the project and suggested that Heilman supported it because he smelled a "job" in it, likening it to his position as president of the Gas Company. Heilman responded that if Reitz wanted cheaper gas he was welcome to build his own works. The meeting degenerated as the two men and a few others began to hurl insults at each other, and order was only restored with the efforts of the deputy marshal.[122]

Rancor between elites carried over into the autumn campaigns of 1878 and 1880, when Heilman ran for Congress on the Republican ticket. As Evansville's most prominent employer, Heilman offered a tempting target, one the *Courier* rarely missed an opportunity to hit. In 1878, the editors charged that the reduction of wages in the cotton mill to "starvation figures" enabled Heilman to donate $500 "to one of our fashionable churches." When Republicans boasted of his beneficence in supporting over a thousand workers, the *Courier* countered that workers *earned* their wages, and that Heilman enjoyed huge profits from their underpaid labor.[123]

In the spring, when Democrats promised workers control over the police, the result was that all township offices, four of six council seats, and three of four citywide offices were filled by Democrats who won by substantial margins. Victory in the Second Ward, and the narrow margin of defeat in the traditionally solid Republican First may have resulted from increased black support, perhaps nurtured in the WPU, and Bushrod Taylor and two others were rewarded for their efforts at organizing black voters with a place on the police force.[124] In addition, the Fourth and Fifth wards, with their large numbers of German workers, gave 55.1 and 62.3 percent of the vote, respectively, to Democratic council candidates.[125]

Efforts in the fall to portray Heilman as an avaricious employer were less successful. Heilman outpolled Democrat Thomas Garvin in all but one city precinct, garnering 60.6 percent of the vote. Two years later he carried all six precincts and 55.7 percent of the vote against John Kleiner.[126] Clearly, workers as a whole did not take on the Shanklin's dislike for Heilman as their own. That Heilman's foundry experienced few episodes of unrest suggests why he may have been perceived as a benevolent employer. Certainly his quick concession to the demand of the machinists' union for a substantial wage increase in the fall of 1879 contributed to that view.[127]

Heilman's success reveals further aspects of the relationship between party and constituency. Democratic success depended on the party's ability to attract German working-class voters. This had been the case since the 1850s. To do this, they nominated trade-union leaders Fred Blend, Fred Brennecke, and Conrad Muth; and they tended, especially in the case of William Rahm and John Kleiner, to respond more favorably to calls for relief than their Republican counterparts. Moreover, the *Courier* often made comments likely to reaffirm working-class distrust of employers. What led them to discard the vaguer notion of the "poor" was worker organization in trade unions *and* in politics. The rise of militant trade unionism and the appearance of a socialist left required an adjustment of political language. For the Democrats, this rhetorical shift proved beneficial.

However, Democratic victory did not always result. Their failure to respond decisively enough to the interests of workers could dampen enthusiasm for the party of Jackson. And while charges of extortion and monopoly often proved effective generally, the stigma did not necessarily hurt the political prospects of the "monopolist" himself. Labor may have shopped most frequently at the Democratic store, but it only chose the goods it found appealing. This independence further encouraged Democrats to appeal to working-class interests. Consequently, the *Courier,* in the years to come, supported the efforts of local Knights of Labor and trade unionists against their employers. In effect, political rhetoric came to reaffirm the legitimacy of unions, and the result was that a relatively friendly environment was created in which organization could proceed.

Unions, Strikes, and Politicians

And it did. Improving business conditions led to new initiatives by the city's work force in the autumn of 1879.[128] Long years of deprivation generated interest in a general strike, but leaders like Fred Blend prevailed in channeling worker energy into the formation and perfection of trade unions. Blend spoke from experience; the cigar makers' union had taken the lead by reorganizing as a local of the International and by selecting Blend as its first president. A few unions experienced success. The newly organized cooper's union raised wages by 20 percent, while 125 local carpenters founded a union and successfully fought to raise wages from $1.50 to 2.25 a day. Similarly, the plasterers took advantage of the boom in the construction trades and struck for an increase from $1.75 to 2.50.[129]

The struggle of the molders to raise wages did the most to revive intertrade activity. On the night of October 20, some four hundred workers demanded labor get "its just share of the revival" and promised financial assistance to the molders. Fred Brennecke presented the molders' case, claiming that they averaged $12 a week while "working so d——d hard . . . that we would sweat off half a dozen shirts if we only had 'em to wear." Fred Blend added that the worker's costs had risen as much as 80 percent while founders kept prices to depression levels. Shoemaker John J. Smith urged other workers to organize, and warned employers that the workingman "would never let his family starve in a land of plenty—money or no money."[130] Iron founders soon agreed to send a committee to Cincinnati to ascertain the wage rate there, and the molders returned to the shops.[131]

The meeting revealed collaboration between union leaders and socialists. George Thobe presided, and the resolution committee included Emil Levy, Fred Brennecke, printer James Huckeby, John Smith, and socialist wagon maker Andrew Ritz.[132] The meeting also revealed continuity in working-class leadership, which gave the local movement a considerable degree of strength and stability. Aside from shoemaker Smith, who had moved to the city only three years before, every one of the speakers and committee members had played a prominent role in the agitations of the summer of 1877. Further, Brennecke, Blend, and Levy had long merged trade-union interests with activism in the Democratic party, an alliance that evidently did not preclude cooperation with socialists like Thobe and Ritz.

Within this more active trade-union environment, parties redoubled their efforts to woo working-class voters. While Democrats attempted to link the Republican ticket to monopolists like William Heilman and avaricious employers like John Roelker, their adversaries praised the tariff as the guardian of American jobs.[133] The *Journal* told workers that German laborers earned 40 to 57 cents a day and that German molders worked for $4.64 a week. Free trade, they argued, would reduce wages and living conditions to the standard of the "pauper laborers of Europe."[134] Democrats responded with distortion and racism. Denying that Republicans had any intention to enact a protective tariff, Democrats blamed them for the "two great dangers to Evansville working men . . . cheap negro and Chinese laborers."[135] The *Courier* played up a forged letter that smeared James Garfield as a supporter of Chinese immigration, and drayman Mike Minnehan warned that the GOP was the party of capital and that "capital wants cheap labor and don't you forget it."[136]

The tariff issue worked for the Republicans, and Garfield defeated

Hancock in Evansville by nearly four hundred votes.[137] Protection of American industry allowed politicians to make economic appeals to workers without fanning the flames of class conflict. Here the factory owner was not portrayed as a despot but as a victim, like his workers, of foreign competition. After 1880, Democrats put more emphasis on free trade, while continuing to espouse a divisive politics. In the fall of 1884, in the midst of a downturn in business, this proved to be the path to a narrow victory.[138] The *Courier* published a letter from "Workingman" asking if wages had been raised "proportionate to the proprietor's income, secured by the tariff," and arguing that the Republican tariff "protects the manufacturer and leaves the mechanic and laborer to compete with the cheap labor of the world."[139]

Municipal politics continued to be the more divisive arena as the Shanklins once more battled William Heilman in the spring of 1882. This time the *Courier* charged that Heilman and a number of associates had diverted bonds issued by the city for the support of the Local Trade Railway to another road in which they had an interest, thus impoverishing the Local Trade. Moreover, the editors claimed that the council reversed its intention to file suit after Heilman had visited and bought off a number of members.[140] This time the bitterness of the Shanklins toward Heilman paid political dividends. The party took their lead and mounted a campaign that focused on Heilman. Ward meetings resolved to oppose "all rings and monopolies, especially the railroad and gas rings."[141] In citywide convention, Democrats demanded that "public servants . . . not prostitute their official position to aid jobbers and rings in plundering the community."[142] Voters apparently agreed, and five Democrats and an independent Republican, A. L. Robinson were elected to council.[143] Six months later, the new council brought suit against the Local Trade in Vanderburgh Circuit Court.[144]

At the same time, the city's finances had become so troubled that it was unable to meet interest payments on municipal bonds. When Democrats raised the possibility of not making one unless the debt was refinanced, Republicans charged repudiation, and it was on this ground that politicos battled in 1883. The *Journal* argued "an obligation is an obligation" and claimed that the only solution was for the city to reduce "extravagances."[145] This dispute between taxpayers and bondholders quickly was fused with class. Writing from Washington to the *Journal*, John W. Foster warned that repudiation would depress industry and that "the heaviest sufferers would be the *laboring men and their families, the element in the community from which the demagogue and repudiator would expect the greatest sup-*

port."[146] Indeed, Emil Levy and Conrad Muth were prominent at the Democratic convention that agreed to demand a restructuring of the debt, and called on bankers to pay their fair share of taxes. And Democrats resolved that laborers employed by the city be paid in cash, denouncing "the practice of compelling them to discount city orders at a sacrifice to themselves and family."[147] The lines were drawn; bankers or workers would have to sacrifice. The *Courier* drilled in the point, asking if workers are "not as worthy of their hire as the bondholder is of his interest."[148] Again the politics of class proved successful for the Democrats who swept city offices and won five of seven council seats, losing only the two open seats in the First Ward.[149]

The Knights of Labor and Working-Class Unity

While politics reinforced the tendency to think in class ways, new forms of working-class organization were emerging on the far west side of town known as Independence. There forty miners founded "Guiding Star Lodge" of the Knights of Labor in 1880.[150] Local miners complained that they suffered from the lack of a check-weighman and company insistence that workers buy powder from them at high prices.[151] In November 1880 these grievances led to a brief strike.[152] A year later, cotton weavers went on strike for higher wages.[153] Like the miner's strike, it received little coverage in the press and the outcome is unknown. In any case, a mixed assembly of miners and cotton mill workers was founded the following September. The link between miners and mill workers was manifest in the family of Scottish miner Robert D. Ramsey, secretary of "Thistle Assembly." The Ramseys lived in cotton mill housing; Robert's two eldest daughters supplemented his income by working as weavers.[154] The impetus for establishment of the Knights of Labor in Evansville, then, came from workers outside the German community and outside the old artisanal trades. Indeed, none of the earliest leaders appear to have been of German descent. Isolated from the rest of the labor community by Pigeon Creek, these miners and mill hands laid the basis for a larger movement.

Founded in 1869, the Noble Order of the Knights of Labor experienced a meteoric rise in membership and influence in the mid-1880s. Skilled workers in industrial communities across North America found in the Knights a means of uniting local workers, including the unskilled, as a political and economic force.[155] Similarly in Evansville, the rapid ascendancy of the Knights led to concerted efforts by skilled workers to organize the unskilled. The result was an increase in working-class economic and political power, manifested in boycotts, strikes, and electoral activity.

The Knights were involved in politics early on. In August 1882 they met at the courthouse to protest the enactment by the legislature of a "threat and intimidation law" that imposed a $20 fine on workers who tried to prevent strikebreakers from working, agreeing to support only those candidates who pledged to work to repeal the law.[156] The meeting brought together diverse groups in the plebeian community, including retailers, master craftsmen, farmers, and skilled wage earners.[157] Bridges were built between the mostly native Knights and the German community. Socialist Enoch Lutz, a master wagon maker who ran a marginal shop, spoke of the German's escape from an oppressive "step-mother government" in Europe and his desire to prevent it from being established in America.[158] Socialist influence would remain strong in the Knights; in 1886 District Assembly 58 recommended long-time socialist retailer August Illing as an organizer.[159] By January 1883, the movement to repeal the law had united the Noble Order with unions of cigar makers, molders, bricklayers, and printers.[160]

Philip Foner notes that many "non-working class elements" joined the Knights of Labor and sees in this a fundamental weakness.[161] By the end of 1883, this pattern of membership was already apparent in Evansville. Guiding Star Lodge, once a miners' trade assembly, was now led by Master Workman Emil Levy. Other positions went to men like master tailor Henry Dickman and agent Moses Smith, along with miner William Daum.[162] Yet it is not clear that the openness of the Evansville Knights was a weakness. If nothing else, it strengthened ties between workers and self-employed socialists like August Illing and Enoch Lutz.

And events soon transformed the Knights into the tool by which the local working class was to be united. In September 1885, the Knights were instrumental in helping railroad workers defeat capitalist Jay Gould and defend a previous union victory by the workers on the Wabash railroad. The press circulated reports exaggerating the power of the Knights, and workers across the country flocked to their standard.[163] In Evansville this was no less the case, and the Knights' brief ascendency brought forth the largest mobilization of workers yet seen as the rise of the Knights was closely tied to a revival of trade unionism. The first sign of the coming wave of organization came when existent unions joined to establish a Central Labor Union in November 1885. Officers for the CLU were selected from the city's three longest organized trades: molder Nicolas Mace as treasurer, printer H. B. Steward as secretary, and cigar maker Emil Levy, previously the Master Workman of Knights Assembly 1547, as president.[164]

A small cadre of trade-union men, most notably cigar makers Emil Levy and Charles Spalding, spent the next six months building a powerful labor movement. They were instrumental in organizing unions of bakers, brick makers, furniture workers, harness makers, machinists and blacksmiths, musicians, painters, plasterers, shoemakers, stonecutters, and tailors.[165] At the same time, Levy and Spalding played prominent roles in the growth of the Knights, addressing white workers in the collarmaking and tinning trades as well as black hod-carriers. They spread the gospel of organization to workmen of varying skill levels employed on the railroads, in the saw mills, and in the mines, each of whom formed local assemblies of the Knights.[166] By April 1886, Evansville workers had achieved an unprecedented level of organization.

The blurred line between the Knights and the trade unions in the first half of 1886 was manifest in the furniture workers' union, to which two hundred workers at the Armstrong factory belonged. Armstrong had led the transformation of local cabinetmaking into a highly mechanized process, dividing his factory into a number of departments where but one aspect of production proceeded. The newly formed union welcomed not only the cabinetmaker but also the more numerous machine hands and varnishers. Only those in the saw department remained outside; they had joined saw mill employees in Knights assembly 6589. In March, the furniture workers' union demanded that machine department foreman Henry Laswell be fired after he discharged two machine hands. When the company refused, the union men walked out and a day later workers in the saw mill department revealed their solidarity by joining the strike. The strike committee, which included a cabinetmaker, a carpenter and a machine hand, reflected the inclusive nature of the union.[167]

From the start the furniture workers received support from the CLU as President Emil Levy tried to arbitrate the dispute. Failing that, the CLU denounced the company and offered moral support and money "if it becomes necessary."[168] It never was, as the workers turned to other resources. Aid came from members of the community like Mr. Bushnell who opened up his theater for fund-raising productions like "Only a Miner's Wife"—something he commonly did for the Knights.[169] After rumors of a boycott began to circulate, Armstrong fired Laswell and agreed to reinstate all union workers.[170] On returning to work, the furniture workers expressed their gratitude to Levy and Spalding "for their assistance and support."[171]

Knights assemblies also struck for higher wages. Switchmen and brakemen on the E&TH demanded a raise of 35 cents a day, and when the company responded in "very insulting" fashion the workers quit. When management tried to secure strikebreakers the *Courier* reported they received replies like "no, sir, we work for no company who starve their men and make them keep up the rolling stock of the company." As the superintendent attempted to move trains linch-pins "mysteriously disappeared." When a train was prepared to leave the yard the switch was "turned in the twinkling of an eye." As the superintendent tried to move the switch the strikers slipped a padlock on it. The company called for the police, but the chief determined that persons or property were not endangered and left. The rest of the evening was spent with management breaking padlocks and strikers slipping new ones on. Before midnight, President Mackey of the E&TH agreed to the strikers' demands.[172]

The railroad men too found strength in the citywide labor movement. The switchmen and brakemen had secured the backing of the CLU before making their demands. And they too found an ally in the *Courier*. The E&TH had long been identified by Democrats with "ring rule." Two days later the paper gleefully reported the verdict in an industrial accident case handed down against the E&TH in Gibson Circuit Court—the company had asked for a change of venue believing it could not receive an impartial trial in Vanderburgh County. The railroad, the *Courier* claimed, was "a heartless as well as a soulless corporation, deserving the thorough detestation which it has earned under its present management."[173] Again, with pro-union coverage of the strike, Democrats attempted to seize an opportunity offered by the growth of the labor movement. The confluence of union and Democratic language appeared in the parting words of a labor activist's account of the strike: "Down with monopoly!"[174]

Trade unionists benefited from the ranks of newly organized workers and used the newfound unity to impose boycotts against recalcitrant employers. In February the CLU resolved to smoke "none but union-made cigars."[175] Two months later the cigar makers' local declared war against "rat shops, prison and filthy tenement house made cigars" and called on workers and others "friendly to the progress of labor" to boycott dealers of nonunion cigars.[176] At the same time the molders again took aim at John Roelker, threatening to impose a boycott unless he operated as a union shop and ceased carrying prison-made goods. When Roelker refused, calling the demands "unreasonable and unjust," the CLU levied a boycott.[177]

The CLU also led the effort to shorten the workday to eight hours. Across the country workers affiliated with the trade unions or the

Knights united to bring about the eight-hour day on May 1, 1886. Locally they won a victory when the council unanimously supported an ordinance submitted by the CLU making eight hours a legal day's work for municipal employees.[178] The CLU then turned its attention to private enterprise and called on unions to reduce their hours of labor to eight without a reduction in wages.[179] A number, including the bricklayers, the furniture workers and the carpenters, responded with declarations that eight hours would be considered a day's work.[180] The CLU also organized an eight-hour day procession on May 1, inviting the mayor and council to participate.[181] The result was a stunning display of class unity—the *Courier* called it the "largest labor demonstration ever witnessed in Evansville."[182]

Workers carried on the effort at work. They struck for an eight-hour day with no reduction of pay at Buehner's chair factory, at the Mechanic's Foundry, and at McFerson and Foster's box factory. Most accepted a 20 percent reduction to gain the principle of the shorter day. Armstrong complied with the demands of the furniture workers' union, and a 7:30 A.M. to 4:30 P.M. workday was promptly instituted. Box factory employees agreed to accept their boss's offer of shorter hours and less pay. In Heilman's machine works, a similar arrangement was made.[183]

Workers on the far west end, long a Knights stronghold, joined the movement for shorter hours.[184] There machine hands and sawyers employed in the saw mills, who earned a daily wage between $1.25 and 1.50, demanded a shortening of the workday from 11.5 to ten hours without a reduction in wages. After the procession, they notified their employers of their demands. On May 6 the refusal of proprietor Charles Schulte occasioned a walkout, and the men marched from mill to mill gathering strength from employees of other recalcitrant employers. After dinner a mass meeting of 1,000 workers was held on Coal Mine Hill where grievances were aired and a committee of Knights was appointed to negotiate with the mill owners. The results of the negotiations exemplify what Selig Perlman perceived as a tendency of the Knights to subordinate the interests of skilled workers to "lift up the unskilled and semi-skilled."[185] The agreement established a uniform ten-hour workday and an equalized wage-scale. Wages of saw mill workers earning 1.50 a day were reduced by 10 percent, while those paid less than $1.35 were raised to that level.[186]

For another week, workers continued to press demands. Those in the construction trades attempted to enforce a closed shop. The strike wave culminated when the Knights assembly of coopers demanded a raise in the piece-rate, which when refused, led to a walk-

out of 125 workmen.[187] While the results of these efforts remain unknown, the evidence is compelling that the burst of activity in the
city's workshops should be attributed to the unity of trade unions
and Knights of Labor in the CLU.

The Knights and Politics

It was the boycott against John Roelker that led the *Journal* to attack the CLU. Before this final act, the editors had restrained themselves, but the announcement of the boycott, they asserted, had
caused many to ask whether "such an injustice is to be permitted to
prevail." They told of a "heavy capitalist and property owner" who
resolved not to invest "another dollar" in the city "so long as the idea
of charging ten hours pay of eight hours work or this causeless striking and boycotting mania continues." The editors denounced "this
striking and boycotting business" as "un-American and inhumane"
and they urged workers to "put on their thinking caps" and consider
"whether they can afford to be used by professional agitators to give
the latter notoriety and to bolster up their communistic schemes."[188]

The local manifestation of the Great Upheaval received no such
condemnation from the *Courier*, for rather than a threat the editors
perceived in it another opportunity to prove itself the "workingman's
friend." The editors ran articles praising the Knights and General
Master Workman Terence Powderly while they condemned capitalists like Jay Gould for their "greed and arrogant caprices."[189] Though
they noted that the boycott was "an extreme measure," they argued
that the CLU used the tool only to make legitimate and legal demands.[190] When the *Journal* objected to the participation of city officials in the eight-hour demonstration, the *Courier* urged the Republican organ to "try and maintain its composure in discussing the
labor organizations. They are not composed of socialists, communists and anarchists, as its foolish correspondent assumes, but of law-
abiding and intelligent citizens and taxpayers."[191]

At another time the disparity in language between the political
organs might have been enough to ensure Democratic victory, but in
1886 the Democrats lost the mayor's office and four of six council
seats. Workers, now engaged in building workplace and community
organizations, remained aloof from the electoral process. In reports
of Democratic ward meetings, only Fred Blend among labor activists
appeared on a list of delegates to the city convention.[192] Distance was
reaffirmed by the CLU, when long-time Democrat Emil Levy urged
workers to "refrain from any political activity for the present."[193]

Democratic support was further weakened when the *Journal* informed voters that their mayoral candidate, William Rahm, had failed to speak out or vote against a "threat and intimidation" bill when a member of the state legislature.[194] This revelation placed the Democrats in a position they could not defend; as a result they won only the seats from the Second and Fourth wards, and Rahm ran well only in the Third, where he defeated Republican candidate John Dannetell by two votes. Citywide, Rahm lost by over seven hundred votes. While ethnicity may have played a part—Dannetell was a native of Hanover—both the *Journal* and the *Courier* attributed the outcome to the vote of workers.[195] The Democratic organ noted that it was the "hostility" of the working class "from which the Democracy has heretofore drawn its chief support" that condemned the ticket to failure.[196]

Democrats may have also been weakened by emerging divisions within the labor movement. A split between Levy and Spalding and miner William Daum appeared early in 1886 when the latter charged that the two cigar makers were ineligible for membership in the Knights because they were professional politicians.[197] Trouble continued into the summer when Daum was accused of embezzling "all the money and property, owned . . . by L. A. 1547."[198] Though the cause of the rupture between the assembly and Daum is uncertain, rivalry with Levy looms large. As Master Workman of District Assembly 58 Levy may have been instrumental in getting that body to endorse the blue label of the Cigar makers' International Union.[199] Three months later, the D. A. secretary protested to Powderly "against the Knights of Labor Label being placed on cigars that ar[e] manufactured for less than Six Dollars per thousand."[200] Elsewhere, the International and the Progressive Cigar makers' Union, which was closely associated with the Knights, were engaged in a bitter struggle, and though there was no rivalry in Evansville, the endorsement benefited the International.[201] Powderly noted that the Evansville letter was "exactly like the protests that come from the Cigar makers' I.U."[202] Though the relationship between trade unionists and others within the Knights in Evansville is unclear, that cigar makers were in this instance able to use the Knights specifically for trade-union purposes is not.

Had the labor movement remained united, a commitment to the electoral process might once again have aided the Democrats in their attempt to regain control of local government. Certainly they needed the help. The bond issue continued to dominate Evansville politics and the Democrats had proved unable to put the issue to rest.

The victory of the Republicans the previous spring may have reflect-ed some disenchantment with the Democratic refusal to either pay the bonds or repudiate them.

As it was, the entry of the Knights into local politics did not serve to unite workers. As in cities across the county, the Evansville Knights formed a Union Labor party, but its efforts lacked support from the well-entrenched unions. Activists tended to come from trades that had only recently organized.[203] Some trade unionists—mostly machinists, blacksmiths, carpenters, and miners—participated but none worked in trades that had organized before the rise of the Knights. Nonworkers also played a prominent role as attorney Charles Gould and dealer Moses Smith entered the party through the Knights of Labor. This was also the case with four clerical workers.[204]

These men, although new to politics, articulated positions that were more than vaguely consistent with a long-term Democratic posture. Like the *Courier,* they spoke of "exposing and breaking up the rings and cliques now existing in the manipulation of our present city affairs."[205] And they renewed the effort to resist full payment of the bonds, and to pay no more than 4 percent interest on them if the courts found them to be valid.[206] Yet a departure was made in the divisive but successful effort of lawyer C. H. Wessler to attach the single-tax idea of Henry George to the party platform by demanding that "all taxes for city purposes be levied on land value ... improved or unimproved, according to its rental value, and that all improve-ments and personal property be exempt from taxation."[207] There was little inherently radical about the proposal. In years past similar ideas had been expressed by businessmen in their critique of landed wealth and slaveowners; M. W. Foster had made such arguments to justify a high tax on real estate in the late 1850s in the dispute with Willard Carpenter. It had radical potential, however, which has been noted by Steven Ross who suggests that by imposing a tax equivalent to the rental value of the land, the benefit from rising land values would go to the community instead of the land speculator; in effect it would socialize land.[208] Yet in Gilded Age Evansville, where many workers had saved just enough money to purchase a lot and build a cottage on it, a policy that promised to tax real estate and not personal prop-erty went against the grain of working-class rhetoric, which since Richard Trevellick's visit in 1874 had demanded that bondholders pay their fair share of taxes.

Thus, these resolutions spoke no more, and perhaps less, to the working-class voter than the Democratic party had over the past de-cade. Aside from an expression of sympathy "with labor in its efforts

to make industrial and moral worth, and not wealth the true standard of individual and national greatness" and a resolution assuring
the electorate "that from the work shops and forges we have material for legislation," work was not discussed at all.

Nevertheless, assertions that those engaged in manufacturing
were suitable "material" were not fluff. The Union Labor party offered the first ticket in Evansville to be almost exclusively constituted of candidates from the city's workshops. However, the nominations bypassed those at the forefront of workplace centered
movements—men like molders Conrad Muth and Fred Brennecke or
cigar maker Fred Blend—in favor of individual workmen who had
proved their mettle. Of the six council candidates, three were foremen—two in leather shops and one in a pants factory—while another had once been a superintendent in the railroad machine shops and
now worked as a machinist at the Novelty Machine Works, which
also supplied the party's candidates for treasurer (the firm's manager) and township trustee (a foreman). The two other council candidates were an engineer in a saw mill and a manufacturer who employed six men. The absence of trade-union leaders from the ticket
suggests further that by 1887 the Knights of Labor had been seriously weakened by internal divisions.

The contrary position regarding taxation taken by the Union Labor party did not bother the Democrats who were more interested in
a constituency than a principle, and in city convention they agreed
to support the labor candidates.[209] The *Demokrat* and the *Courier*
continued to depict Republican hopefuls as "tools of the Railroad
monopolists" and Democrats as "avowed opponents of the monopoly."[210] The *Demokrat* asserted that a labor ticket was perfectly just
in a city where "the worker element makes up such a large percentage of the total population.[211] Fearful that the Democrats would again
gain control of the city through the vote of workers, the *Journal*
charged that certain leaders, "promised fat situations as the price of
their treachery," had sold the party out.[212] They need not have worried. The election was a landslide and the Republicans swept the
council and the offices except for that of city clerk, which they lost
narrowly.[213] The *Courier* blamed the defeat squarely on the Union
Labor men who had imposed candidates on the Democrats "whose
lives have been spent in manual pursuits" and "are not adapted to
office holding."[214] Thus the mobilization of the Knights in Evansville
did not lead to political victory; if anything it proved less successful
than previous efforts to effect local political life.

Class, Parties, and Alliances

There is, of course, something obscenely disingenuous about the *Courier*'s analysis. The trade-union men who gained election on the Democratic ticket in the 1870s had been equally trained in manual pursuits. That they may have been better candidates was due less to a proclivity toward policy-making than an ability to draw votes from the plebeian community. These men had been part of a growing trade-union movement that had considerable support in the manufacturing sections of town.

The efforts of the Democratic editors to appeal to this support suggest ways of understanding the relationship between Gilded Age politicians, labor leaders and plebeian electorates. For trade-union men like Fred Blend, Conrad Muth, Emil Levy, and Fred Brennecke, all of whom became a part of the local Democratic machinery in these years, politics offered a rise in status. This was not exceptional; labor leaders elsewhere found the path to office to be a tempting one to follow. To some extent this may have had a conciliatory effect on trade-union leadership. In this light, David Montgomery has argued that "the capacity of America's political structure to absorb talent from the working classes was perhaps the most effective deterrent to the maturing of a revolutionary class consciousness among the nation's workers." The exigencies of political life brought the trade-union activist into contact with liberal reformers who educated the worker in the ideas of middle-class reform.[215]

Though this is all true, it is important to note the kind of negotiations that occurred between workers and political parties. As in New Albany, the transmission of ideas often went both ways, and through their participation these leaders led some Evansville Democrats to speak a more radical language that more clearly addressed the concerns of workers. The issue of unemployment relief is instructive. As in other cities the debate was forced by workers. However, in Evansville they had advocates inside city hall who maintained a view of the unemployed worker as a virtuous citizen unwilling to take charity and in need only of work. In articulating this, they offered an alternative to elite view of relief as charity. Further, workers like Blend and Muth were not content to merely gain a work project; they followed their success with an agitation, albeit an unsuccessful one, to raise the wages of the laborers hired by the city.

By proving that they represented a potent force, trade-union politicians identified a working-class constituency for Democrats, which led them to speak of the exploitation of labor by employers, a far cry from the vague use of the "rich" and the "poor" of the predepression years. This tendency was reinforced by the relative independence of the working-class electorate and by the rise of a socialist movement in the wake of the railroad strikes. As a result, the pages of the *Courier* were opened to voices like those of the socialists. And in a less radical but perhaps more important vein, the *Courier* began to systematically defend the right of unions to act against local employers. Thus by the 1880s, a segment of the mainstream press was reaffirming the right to organize trade unions. Clearly, the activists of the 1870s in Evansville accomplished something by entering the political realm in the spring of 1874. They created a more open environment in which worker organization could proceed.

This process was aided by the evolutionary development of the local economy. The transition from the artisanal workshop to the small factory gave workers a degree of continuity. From 1873 to 1886 a cadre of skilled workers—many of German descent—dominated organizing efforts. Some, like cigar makers Fred Blend and Emil Levy who worked in a small shop industry, passed through stages of self-employment and wage work. So did others who were not so prominent like ex-union molders Fred Kiechle and Michael Gorman who became partners in foundries in these years.[216]

This winding path toward industrial development did not translate to higher wages as many masters struggled to compete with more efficient producers elsewhere; as a result workers suffered lower wages despite the local absence of large factories in their trade.[217] It is likely that the persistence of small workshops, where artisanal expectations remained, served as a source of radicalism; the presence of Enoch Lutz and Andrew Ritz, both master wagon makers, among the socialists culled from the press suggests that this was the case. The vitality of the plebeian German community explains a good part of the success that the Democrats enjoyed after uniting with the trade-union men.

The failure of the Knights of Labor to mobilize this community in electoral contest reveals the significance of long-term political analysis. Alone, the experience of the Evansville Union Labor party might reveal the dangers of political activity for working-class organization. However, for plebeian Evansville the rise of the Knights did not signal the first significant political challenge to capitalist domination; this had already been accomplished as early as 1874, and worker demands had long been a part of party politics. That the ULP failed to gain electoral success in the spring of 1887 was less due to the problems of electoral life than already emerging divisions within the Noble Order itself.

Just before the summer of 1886, the Knights helped revitalize the local labor movement, and persons long identified with the trade unions played a prominent role in its growth. That divisiveness emerged is certain; whether it was caused by an inherent conflict between the Knights and the trade unions is unclear. Still a place in the CLU was retained for the Knights well into the 1890s as an assembly of coal miners and mixed assembly Guiding Star Lodge continued to function. An 1895 CLU directory spoke kindly of the latter, reminding its readers that "many of the trades Unions now in healthy existence owe their initial step toward unionism to the spartan and untiring allegiance of the leaders of old 5233."[218]

The directory is itself testimony to the vitality of the local labor movement and its refusal to adopt pure bread-and-butter unionism. To the contrary it reveals a degree of ideological continuity and suggests a strong socialist influence in the CLU. Articles, mostly reprinted from other sources, spoke the language of radical producerism and republicanism. One divided society between producers and idlers, the former who supplied the soldiers for the Civil War, and the latter who "want the government to support them by paying interest on bonds that should never have been issued." Another condemned the "aristocratic, plutocratic and autocratic money power" that had "decreed the degradation and enslavement of labor in every department of the industrial affairs of the country." Yet here the solution lay in more active efforts than purging the state of entanglements with the money power. One writer called for the state to take over industry so that production would proceed "for use alone, instead of for profit."[219]

Though both parties were now condemned as capitalist, the continuity of language suggests the significance of political involvement in the Gilded Age. That publication of the directory was coincident with the break of Eugene Debs with the Democratic party suggests other parallels. Like the trade unionists of Evansville, Debs had identified with the left wing of the party of Jackson, which was strongly influenced by greenbackism. And perhaps for Debs, as well as for the workers in Evansville, the experience of engagement in that political culture did more than reinforce harmony between classes; in addition it may have reaffirmed a language of class.[220]

Political life, however, was closely related to a city's social structure. The formation of alliances was in the hands of local politicians, who were aware of power relationships and ethnic cleavages, and were not mandated by state central committees. Certainly the hostility of the *Enquirer* toward John Ingle, and later that of the *Courier* toward William Heilman, exacerbated the shrillness of political discourse. But while the Democratic party spoke a language of class in Evansville, other Indiana Democrats were hardly obliged to do the same. Even when a factory work force existed, other obstacles could arise to prevent an alliance between trade unions and one of the major political parties. For what if the factory owner was, indeed, a monopolist and held extraordinary economic power? Would the politician be tempted to wield radical forms of producerism for his own, and his party's, political advantage? An answer can be found by returning upstream to New Albany in the years after the Civil War.

PART THREE

New Albany, 1866–87: The Small Industrial City

The Poor Man's Woes
What tongue can recount the poor man's woes,
As on through the world of strife he goes,
Toiling his way through sorrow and pain,
Not for his own but for other men's gain,
Spending his strength and the sweat of his brow,
For the bare pittance wealth will allow,
Plodding his weary way to the grave,
Feeling he's branded the rich man's slave?

There is no place on earth where they greet him with cheer
No, not even home, while the wolf hovers near,
Who can tell of the want and distress where he goes?
Ask not the rich, the poor only knows.
That joyless existence eked out with ill fare,
That dearth of all comforts, that woe and despair—
All this while thy brothers with plenty overflows,
And turns a deaf ear to the poor man's woes.

Nay we can not deign to yield up our sway,
For surely we're molded of finer clay;
 We'll drain out your life-blood our coffers to fill,
While in humble subjection you bend to our will.
Why not be resigned, and bow to your fate,
Content to be Lazarus at the rich man's gate,
With the crumbs we will cast you your hunger appease,
We'll grow fat on your earnings and live at our ease.

Oh man! thou noblest work of God,
How galling the chains, how heavy the rod;
To be thus by thy brother man oppressed,
And of every joy of earth distressed;
O'er the land where full and plenty abound,
The cries of thy poor in pity resound,
And the gifts of God so lavishly strewn,
Are meted out to the grappling few.

> —Anonymous, from New Albany, published in
> the *Iron Molders' Journal* on May 31, 1880,
> soon after the glassworkers' strike

The Industrial Barony
of W. C. DePauw

7 Working-class politics and mass actions of the kind so
prevalent in postbellum Evansville were largely absent
from New Albany despite fervent organizing among ship
carpenters during the war. Rapid decline of the shipyards and their
replacement by glass, iron, and woolen mills led to the rise of a new
community of workers, heavily dependent on factory owners for
employment. Though structural development bestowed upon them
a more common, or class, experience by virtue of the appearance of
working-class neighborhoods, similar housing, and patterns of teenage employment, differences of ethnicity and skill level continued to
divide this new working class.

Transformed by large infusions of capital from bankers and merchants, New Albany followed another path to industrialization.
Unlike their counterparts in Evansville, where master craftsmen
gradually and persistently enlarged their workshops and expanded
production by subdividing and mechanizing the work process, the
industrialists of New Albany built large plants where none had existed before, in trades in which they had no prior experience. It was
not mechanics, then, but monied men, like John Ford and Washington C. DePauw, who initiated and guided New Albany's postwar industrial expansion. And it was constant infusions of capital that allowed DePauw to gain sole control of most of these industries by
the late 1870s, which granted him a position of power previously
unseen in the city's history.

As a result of this industrial metamorphosis, New Albany came to
be marked by a highly visible class structure in which most workers
had little in common with their employers. The old ambiguities of
producerism and the opaque meaning of the term *workingman* fell

away amidst the transparent nature of the new order. Though some remnants of an earlier plebeian culture persisted, local workers were rarely supported by the modestly propertied and by politicians who chose not to challenge the power of the industrialist. During the Gilded Age, New Albany was first and foremost the industrial barony of W. C. DePauw.

Decline and Persistence of the Old Economy

The growth of new industry came abruptly on the heels of the quick decline of local shipbuilding. The immediate aftermath of the war brought prosperity to New Albany boat builders. Fourteen boats were built in 1865, as were eight more in 1866, including the famous "Robert E. Lee." However, only four were built in the next two years. By 1870 the trade had been thoroughly decimated; none of the local shipyards were engaged in new construction. Only one was listed by the census as a steamboat repairing and jobbing shop; it employed but one worker.[1]

The reasons for this decline are many. The heyday of the riverboat was coming to an end as the rise of a regional railroad network provided traders and travelers with quicker and more reliable transportation. More specifically, the severing of sectional ties left local shipyards without a market, since northern river captains had normally contracted with builders situated above the falls. New Albany's location just below them now became a liability.[2] Full-scale decline had been delayed only by John Ford's entry into the industry. Along with his two sons, Ford ran a line of thirty-eight steamboats and flatboats during the war; it is likely that he provided his own market.[3] Ford's decision to reorient his energies and capital away from the river and toward iron and glass production signaled the end of the industry in New Albany.

The failure of the shipyards led to the dismantling of the shipbuilding community. Where two hundred ship carpenters and joiners lived and worked before the war, less than half remained in 1870 and their numbers further dwindled to fifty-five by 1880.[4] Those who persisted were married, older workmen with roots in the city. Few were propertyless. It was those who had the fewest ties—the young, the single, and the poor—who left.[5] Few of those who remained were able to ply their trade locally. Some traveled daily or weekly to Jeffersonville to work in the growing Howard Shipyards, while others found employment in other trades, most frequently in other branches of carpentry.[6]

Other industries with ties to the river declined as well, though in more incremental stages. The output of tin, copper, and sheet-iron shops, which were heavily dependent on the shipyards, declined between 1870 and 1880 by 42 percent. New Albany's decreasing share of the wholesale trade during the 1870s probably explains the decline in output by local shoemakers of 47 percent, and by tailors of 17 percent.[7] The number of shoemakers employed in local shops also fell from 114 in 1860 to 43 in 1880; for tailors the decrease in positions was nearly as precipitous, falling from 95 to 48.[8]

Traditional firms did persist, though they remained less important to the local economy than in Evansville. Built up by men skilled in their respective trades, many such businesses in the furniture, foundry, and tanning trades prospered throughout the late nineteenth century, employing between 30 and 125 workers. The owners of these shops were mechanics themselves—and in not a few cases, so were their sons—who either slowly increased the size of the firm, or accepted financial backing from outsiders. The former path was taken by cabinetmakers John Shrader and Henry Klerner who operated the two largest furniture factories in New Albany, while machinist Charles Hegewald went into partnership with DePauw, and molder Frank Gohmann expanded his National Stove Foundry by taking wealthy shoe dealer Joseph Terstegge on as a partner.[9]

These master mechanics shared more than an understanding of manual processes with their employees, for each was a German immigrant. Like their counterparts downriver, these shops relied on immigrant, chiefly German, labor. In 1880, nearly six of ten molders in the city were first- or second-generation German immigrants, and they likewise made up significant percentages of the blacksmith (40.8), cabinetmaker (38.1), boilermaker (37.9) and machinist (23.1) populations. In the foundry and machine shop trades, Irish immigrants as well made successful incursions, comprising nearly 20 percent of the city's molders and more than 10 percent of machinists. Workmen in these trades commanded high wages. Like it did for their bosses, the old economy of New Albany represented the greatest local opportunities for the non-Anglo immigrant workman.

Capitalists and the Growth of Industry

However, the most vital sectors of the local economy were merchant directed in the postwar era. Despite the disruption of trade, the years during and immediately after the Civil War were not idle ones for New Albany's elite. Many had profited greatly by supplying the

Union army or by investing in government securities; so much so that seven local bankers and merchants reported annual *incomes* in excess of $20,000, and three earned over $50,000.[10] Raging inflation threatened to decrease the value of idle cash while it promised profits for manufactured goods. Consequently, all seven invested capital in manufacturing establishments that were built between 1864 and 1870.[11]

The most active was John Ford, who operated the American Foundry while running a shipyard and steamboat packets during the war. In 1864, he was instrumental in the founding of a rolling mill, the first such establishment to be built in New Albany. Of Ford's efforts, the New Albany *Ledger* had nothing but praise, claiming that the city "never had a more energetic, enterprising citizen" and wishing "his capital was five millions that he might show our people what a wide-awake spirit of enterprise does toward building up a city."[12]

However, Ford's greatest impact on the local economy was a result of his vigilant efforts to open a glassworks. Convincing other capitalists that the sand bed along a nearby tributary of the Ohio River made New Albany an ideal site for the production of glass, he was able to organize the New Albany Glass Works in 1865. To free his capital for this new venture, Ford first sold the shipyard and foundry, and then his interest in the rolling mill.[13] Producing exclusively window glass at first, the new works were housed in a pair of two story buildings, each 85 feet by 65 feet, connected by a raised platform, while employing 45 men. Another sixty men were soon employed when Ford decided to add a bottle house.[14]

The works was an immediate success, and Ford soon turned his entrepreneurial energies to the production of polished plate glass, a product that had yet to be produced profitably in the United States. To raise the extensive capital required, Ford sold half his interest in the firm to three local bankers, one of whom took over the financial direction of the firm, leaving Ford and his two sons free to superintend production.[15] The plate department went into operation in the fall of 1869 and the renamed Star Glass Works then covered seven acres of riverfront in the eastern end of the city.

By 1870 New Albany had been transformed into a factory town, largely through Ford's efforts. The two substantial enterprises that he established—the rolling mill and the glassworks—were the largest in the city, putting out a combined product worth over a million dollars in 1870. These works were also the two largest employers, each with at least 175 workers.[16] Ford's influence was broader than these two factories, however. His success motivated other merchants and bankers to venture capital into iron and glassworks. Soon after the rolling mill of Bragdon, Ford & Co. started production, that of S. S. Marsh & Co. established the Hoosier Rolling Mill.[17] Similarly, Ford's success in the manufacture of window and bottle glass prompted a group of monied men in 1868 to establish the New Albany Glass Works across the street from Ford's own Star Glass Works.[18] Combined, these four firms in which merchants and bankers had invested almost $900,000, employed 678 workers in 1870, amounting to 40 percent of the local labor force.[19] Much as the prosperity of the city previously depended on the shipyards, it now became closely tied to these new industries. The dependency increased dramatically in the years to follow as large infusions of capital from W. C. DePauw brought forth an extensive expansion of productive capability.

Washington Charles DePauw was born in Salem, Indiana, in a neighboring county. His father had been a prominent man who had served as a member of the Indiana constitutional convention of 1816, as a general of the state militia, and as a member of the Indiana General Assembly. Shortly after his father's death, Washington entered the county clerk's office at the age of nineteen and was elected clerk three years later. Political office and prominence served young DePauw well, enabling him to win the contract to build the Salem depot of the New Albany and Salem Railroad. In 1850 he opened a small wool carding mill, and soon thereafter a flour and saw mill. On retiring from office in 1853, DePauw started a bank and soon became a leading stockholder in the newly chartered state bank of Indiana. During the war, he supplied the Union Army with grain, though most of his efforts were devoted to banking. Investing heavily in the purchase of government bonds and securities, DePauw emerged from the war as perhaps the richest man in Indiana, paying taxes in 1865 on an income of $207,904.[20]

His involvement in the New Albany economy dated back before the war. In the 1850s he established a branch of the Bank of Salem at New Albany which was managed by his father-in-law. In the 1860s, DePauw developed commercial property, building warehouses and large business blocks suitable for mercantile establishments or modest workshops.[21] After the war he was the financial backer of at least two wholesale businesses. DePauw's importance to these concerns was probably not overstated by the local agent of the R. G. Dunn and Company Mercantile Agency when he advised "as long as he backs the concern, you need have no fear. . . . Mr. DePauw commands unlimited means for any business he may engage in."[22] As early as 1860 he may have entered local manufacturing, backing the small woolen mill run by merchant John Creed and Pennsylvanian textile manufacturer, J. F. Gebhart.[23] However, it was in the years just after the war when he relocated to New Albany, that DePauw began to dominate local manufacturing.

DePauw first seized control of the local iron industry, becoming the chief stockholder in both the Ohio Falls Iron Works and the New Albany Rolling Mill. In the fall of 1866, he was elected president of the newly organized Ohio Falls Nail Works, which very soon after absorbed the Hoosier Rolling Mill. Later that winter, with bankers Jesse J. Brown and John S. McDonald, DePauw bought out John B. Ford's substantial interest in the New Albany Rolling Mill. Both enterprises soon underwent a program of expansion.[24] He had a similar effect on a new woolen mill that began operation in 1867 with fifty workers. Reputed to be a large stockholder in the firm, he was soon elected one of three directors. By 1873, the owners had invested $250,000 into the mill and employed 170 workers.[25]

However, it was the constant capital requirements of the plate glassworks that provided DePauw his greatest opportunity to transform the local landscape. Plate glass manufacturing was distinct from window and bottle glassmaking in that it required no great degree of art or skill, relying on "repetitive rather than discretionary" work processes. Before the establishment of the glassworks in New Albany, plate glass had never been profitably produced in the United States. This fact was, according to an historian of the industry, largely due to an ignorance of the details of the work process and more importantly a "failure to recognize the very factors in plate glass manufacture which forecast its eventual success in the United States . . . the importance of large-scale production."[26]

Whereas Ford had been cognizant of the potential of the industry, DePauw held the means to bring it to fruition. In January 1870, DePauw bought half of the Star Glass Works. Within days the company announced a large expansion of the plate glass department, ordering grinding, polishing, and finishing machines from manufacturers in England. The expense of plate glass manufacture soon exhausted Ford's resources, forcing him to leave the glassworks in the hands of his creditors—chief among them was DePauw.[27] His control of the works became absolute when he purchased the remaining shares of stock in 1879. By 1882 DePauw had invested 1.25 million dollars in the works, which were then producing over 1 million dollars in glass a year and employing about a thousand workers.[28]

In addition to his local manufacturing empire, DePauw retained a substantial interest in banking. In 1873, he held a majority interest in three of the city's six financial institutions and 35 percent of another. As manufacturing took up more of his time and resources, his grasp over the city's banks loosened, yet he remained the largest shareholder in them at least until 1883, and probably until his death.[29]

By the mid 1870s, then, DePauw had taken control of the major sectors of the local economy, a development that did not fail to impress his contemporaries. Under his guidance the city had experienced a steady growth of population until it reached 21,000 in 1890.[30] "Take the glass works out of New Albany," warned the editor of the Louisville *Courier-Journal*,

> and every man, woman, and child who works for a living would feel its loss . . . it is hard to tell whether this loss would be greater than that of DePauw himself, whose money and business tact are used in every great enterprise in this city. Constantly improving his manufactories, never curtailing their capacity, he is, beyond doubt, a great benefactor to New Albany and the nerviest business man in Indiana. Always helping to start some public improvement, or great enterprise, he invests his money as fast as he earns it, giving the workman employment and remuneration for his services. Mr. DePauw has stock in every manufactory in New Albany.[31]

A traveling correspondent to the *National Labor Tribune* agreed, though with a different sensibility, when he wrote: "if there is one man in America entitled to the sobriquet of 'king' it is W. C. Depaw . . . because he comes nearer being able to say 'I am lord of all I survey; my right there is none to dispute!' than any other man I know of."[32]

Due to the efforts of Ford and DePauw, the Gilded Age local economy bore little resemblance to its antebellum predecessor. Factories owned by and large by one merchant-banker, a man who stood opposed to labor as capital personified, employed as many as 2,500 workers, perhaps two-thirds of the local wage-earning population. An older, peripheral economy characterized by smaller units of production and mechanic-manufacturers remained, in which a number of German immigrants opened small workshops. Some older industries prospered and a few of these firms grew to factory proportions. However, they were less important than in Evansville, as class relations locally were influenced largely by the structure of the new industrial economy. For to live and work in New Albany, the odds were, was to be employed by W. C. DePauw.

An Increasingly Integrated Elite

One of the most significant results of this industrial transformation was the rise of a cohesive elite, centering around DePauw, that actively directed both the manufacturing and commercial sectors of the economy. Distinctions between merchant and manufacturer became less evident; the same individual now filled both roles. This was not only true for men like DePauw and William S. Culbertson, the two wealthiest men in New Albany, but it also characterized the stockholders and officers of the corporations.[33] At the same time, the social distance between manufacturer and worker, in most cases, widened considerably. Out of the ambiguous social structure of antebellum New Albany arose a clearly defined class of capitalists.

This confluence of wealth with industrial stewardship has already been suggested. A closer look at the city's wealthiest men solidifies the impression. In 1870, ten were listed in the census as officers of the new corporate manufacturing firms. Most of these men, like Joshua Bragdon or Morris McDonald, had previously engaged in banking or the river trade. Another nine listed themselves as bankers. Each of the nine was closely tied to the new industrial order, either through direct investment in the factories, as was the case with James M. Hains, William N. Mahon, John S. McDonald, Jesse J. Brown, and John B. Winstandley, or through association with DePauw on the board of directors of one of the local banks. Six of the wealthiest merchants had similarly invested large amounts of capital into the manufacture of glass, iron, and wool (four others were closely tied by blood to officers of these firms) and two others served as officers of one of DePauw's banks. Of the forty-six individuals whose net worth was reported to be at least $50,000, no fewer than twenty-one (45.7 percent) were either substantial investors in one of the new manufacturing firms, or were closely tied to DePauw in banking or mercantile ventures.[34]

This elite shared more than a similar function within the local economy; they were uniformly native-born or English. In 1870, every banker, every woolen, iron, and glass mill owner or officer, and thirty-three of the thirty-five wealthiest merchants (the two exceptions were English) involved in either the jobbing or wholesale trade were born in the United States. The ten most prominent and wealthy lawyers, likewise, were native-born.[35]

Bourgeois New Albany was broader than that, however. A wide variety of individuals had accumulated estates worth at least $20,000 by 1870. Fourteen operated retail outlets of some kind, including saloons and grocery stores, and fifteen others owned manufactories. Of this group, nearly half were immigrants—and this proportion would grow during the following two decades—most of whom were German. Among them were Joseph Terstegge, a partner in the National Stove Foundry, and John Shrader, owner of the largest furniture factory in the city.[36] Still, elite New Albany society was mostly native-born.

This new elite possessed the means to live in a style far removed from that of the plebeian masses. Men like DePauw, Sam and William Culbertson, and Jesse J. Brown built themselves huge mansions on Main street, just east of the business district. These two-story homes, fronted by sweeping porches, were characterized by large rooms, high ceilings, and numerous windows. William Culbertson's, which was crowned by a mansard roof covered with purple tiles, cost $50,000 to build.[37] It was not uncommon for the wealthiest men in town to have three or four servants residing in the household, including a hostler to care for the horses. Culbertson's brick stable alone was more than twice the size of the average working-class home.[38]

While most of the local elite lacked either the means or the will to construct such monumental residences, they nevertheless lived in a style very similar to that of the leading bankers, merchants, and manufacturers. For instance, most were able to hire a servant or two. Extant probate records for the widows of furniture manufacturer John Shrader and tannery proprietor August Barth reveal the level of affluence attained by capitalists of the second rank.[39] The homes of both were filled with leather couches, "fancy" sofas, china cabinets, bookcases, tables, upwards of forty chairs, wardrobes, lace and portier curtains, lamps, pianos or organs, three or more stoves, as well as mantle mirrors, fine china, and silverware. The inventory of Margaret Shrader, John's widow, is particularly detailed, revealing parlors and sitting rooms graced by Japanese vases, Indian rugs, oil paintings, and marble-top tables. The dining room housed other luxuries including bisque figures and two candelabra. Upstairs were five rooms, including separate "father's" and "mother's" rooms. Such comfortable and often extravagant living standards clearly set the elite apart from the more common citizenry.[40]

The wealthy played an active role in shaping local affairs, wielding their prestige to persuade local citizens to support ventures designed to increase local trade and industry. Many came together in the early 1870s to urge the council to give money to the proposed Air-Line Railroad, which promised to open markets west of the city to New Albany merchants while providing manufacturers access to cheap coal located near Evansville.[41] Later that decade elites urged the council to grant favors to the glassworks to keep them in the city.

The wealthy figured in less entrepreneurial aspects of life. When much of the city was inundated with water during the flood of 1884, W. C. DePauw and others took a highly visible role in raising money for the relief effort.[42] Many, like DePauw who regularly presided over the Preachers' and Layman's meeting at Centenary Methodist Episcopal Church, played an active role in church affairs.[43] And sometimes sermons directly reflected their interest in disciplining workers. In the winter of 1880-81, the preacher at the John Street Church, located near the glassworks, addressed his mostly working-class congregation with a sermon titled "Work, Work, Work, from Morning Until Evening." Adult Sunday School classes for glass and iron workers were established in the 1880s with DePauw's generous support, and the officers of the school were superintendents in the glassworks.[44]

A New and Heterogeneous Work Force

The effect of the abrupt decline in shipbuilding and the rise of wool, glass, and iron mills was particularly evident in the changing composition of the work force. Unlike the shipyards, where most work had been done by highly skilled journeymen, these new sprawling workplaces incorporated numerous and simultaneous processes that required varying levels of skill.[45] Unskilled laborers, who previously had worked outside manufacturing, now worked in the same establishments in growing numbers with better trained and sometimes very highly paid skilled workers. Some, like the rollers and puddlers of the iron mills, and the blowers in the glassworks achieved a level of control over their work and commanded wages that were well above the standard of even the best paid and most autonomous workers in Evansville. Further, ethnic and religious differences in the factories divided workers in ways that were less evident downriver. Despite these sources of division, postwar industrial development spatially brought together immigrant and native, black and white, Protestant and Catholic, journeyman and laborer, and created an industrial working class that encompassed most of wage-earning New Albany.

Skill and Work in the Iron Mills

Built on the ruins of the shipbuilding community were the Ohio Falls Iron Works and the New Albany Rolling Mill, which between them employed about four hundred workers throughout the 1870s and 1880s. The former primarily produced bar iron while the latter manufactured rails, and in both cases the productive process required the employment of a sizable core of skilled workers in addition to large numbers of common laborers.

Nearly forty puddlers were employed by the two firms to refine pig iron, ridding it of carbon and other impurities. An exacting process, puddling required great strength and skill.[46] Aided by helpers who assisted chiefly in the preparation and maintenance of the furnace, the puddler introduced the correct amount of iron oxides to aid in the decarbonization process. He had to maintain the correct temperature in the furnace for each stage of the process, which was determined in part by the quality of the raw material with which he worked. The puddler required both an understanding, gained in years at the furnace, of the properties of the raw materials under various conditions, and great strength to stir the mixture in order to eliminate the carbon and to remove it wielding tongs in the form of sixty to eighty pound balls.

To shape the iron into rails required a host of skilled workmen. First, the shearsman cut the iron bars while hot into the specific length required for the rolling process. The heater then placed the bars together in "piles" in a furnace to weld them together, taking care that the piles were equally exposed to the fire. After they were removed by the heater with tongs, the piles were taken by the buggyman to the rolling machines where they were passed through by skilled rollers, roughers, and catchers and shaped into rails.[47] As with puddling, these processes required experience and great physical strength. For these reasons skilled ironworkers commanded wages that were two to three times that paid to laborers, a few earning as much as $7 a day.[48]

The high wages skilled ironworkers commanded and their propensity to strike led manufacturers to seek technological innovations that would lessen their dependency on them. Improvements in rolling machinery that permitted rails to be rolled in reverse reduced the time needed to move iron and the number of required heats. Other innovations were introduced that rolled shapes previously requiring the use of the forge hammer.[49] Though they were unable to significantly reduce their dependence on puddlers, rollers, and other skilled workers, manufacturers constantly improved their mills to remain competitive.[50]

Filling the skilled positions was a mix of native whites and British immigrants. Between them, English and Welsh (most of them

Table 6. Iron Industry: Ethnic Composition of Labor Force, New Albany,
          1880

| | Skilled Workers | | | | Unskilled | |
Ethnicity	Puddler	Roller	Heater	Other	Helper	Laborer
N =	37	16	18	34	19	128
Native-white	35.1	31.3	38.9	47.1	68.4	61.7
British Immigrants						
English	27.0	6.3	16.7	20.6	5.3	0.8
2d gen.	10.8	25.0	5.6	8.8	5.3	7.0
Welsh	2.7	18.8	27.8	11.8	—	2.3
2d gen.	—	—	—	—	—	—
Other Immigrants						
Irish	2.7	—	11.1	—	—	1.6
German	—	6.2	—	—	—	2.3
French	—	—	—	—	—	—
Other	2.7	—	—	—	—	—
2d Generation						
Irish	10.8	—	—	—	5.3	2.3
German	—	6.2	—	11.8	5.3	5.5
French	5.4	—	—	—	5.3	1.6
Other	2.7	—	—	—	—	0.8
Native-black	—	6.2	—	—	5.3	13.3
Unknown	—	—	—	—	—	0.8

SOURCE: Tenth Census, population schedules, Floyd County

first generation) accounted for 40 percent of the puddlers and half of
the rollers and heaters. Native whites constituted about 39 percent
of the skilled labor force, while the few remaining positions were
taken largely by second-generation French, German, and Irish immigrants (see table 6).[51] Despite the diversity of the skilled labor force,
workers were by and large unified by language and ties of blood.
Many acquired their skills under the tutelage of a father, uncle or
other relative. Such was the case with the family of puddler Richard
Powell. In 1870, his sons David, nineteen, and George, fifteen, served
as "helpers at furnace" probably under their father. Within a couple
of years, David married and was promoted to "puddler." Meanwhile,
George continued to live at home and work as a helper until he, too,
married. By 1880 each son headed a household, living with his wife
and two children and they, like their father, plied the puddler's trade

at the Ohio Falls Iron Works.[52] For ironworkers, skills were often passed from father to son.

A large and increasing percentage of the labor force, however, was unskilled. In 1873, just under 40 percent of the labor force worked as either a helper or a laborer.[53] Such workers typically tended fires and transported materials through the factory. Their lack of skills made them highly replaceable and their wages reflected this; laborers earned little more than a dollar a day.[54] As firms introduced new methods of production the percentage of unskilled employees grew, so that by 1890 they made up half of the iron mill labor force.[55] Many of them were sons of skilled men. While some were the children of ironworkers, more commonly their fathers worked at the leather and needle trades. Equal numbers were the children of day laborers who found work at the wharf or in the city streets.[56]

While the unskilled were younger than their better trained co-workers, for most the rank of laborer in the iron mills was not a mere waystation on their way up the occupational ladder. An equal number of workers in their thirties and beyond continued to work at that level. While the sons of skilled ironworkers might expect to learn the coveted trade of a puddler and a roller, the majority would have to content themselves with more modest attainments. Laborers generally came from different families than the skilled. Few were British immigrants. About 13 percent were of Irish, German, or French descent, mostly second generation. An equal number were black, and this marked the largest incursion of blacks into manufacturing. Most, however, were native whites (61.7 percent) whose parents were also born in the United States.[57]

Despite differences in ethnicity, skill, wage levels, and age, some uniformity did exist among ironworkers. For one, nearly all were native speakers of English. And since few Irish or German immigrants worked in the iron mills, it is likely that the labor force there was largely Protestant. Located as they were across from the city's two Catholic Churches, the iron mills were eschewed as a source of employment by the local Catholic population in favor of the glassworks and the woolen mill. And unlike the iron mills, these works were divided by ethnicity as well as religion and skill. In these factories, larger numbers of Irish and German Catholic workers worked alongside English and native Methodists than in the ironworks.

The Retention of Craft in Glass Blowing

By 1890, a thousand workers were employed in the glassworks, which stood along the river in the First Ward. Though it was for the

successful manufacture of plate glass that the works were most re-
nowned, window and bottle glass were originally the more important
products, the former accounting for nearly two-thirds of the firm's sales
in 1870.[58] Work in these departments was accomplished in the main by
highly paid glassblowers who formed an elite corps of workers.

Their power to command high wages was rooted in the productive
process. The work of blowing glass commenced after the master teas-
er and his assistants had melted and refined the glass. At this point
the blower and gatherer approached the furnace, taking a position on
one of several raised platforms surrounding the openings in the oven.
The gatherer, who now took charge of the fire and the pots, dipped a
wrought iron blowpipe a few times into the batch and "gathered" the
molten glass with a wavelike motion. He then cooled and shaped the
glass alongside an iron plate. The evenly gathered mass was taken by
the blower, who held the blowpipe at a seventy-five degree angle and
applied it to a wooden mold to further shape it into a globe. Taking
the iron rod to his lips while rotating it in the air, he then, as one
contemporary put it, "blows till his cheeks stand out like red apples,
blows till he is red behind the ears, blows until he becomes of a com-
plexion as blooming as the glass." The skill and art of the blower was
most evident when he raised the blowpipe directly over his head and
blew, then swinging the pipe down into the pit between the platforms up again. This was repeated so often as was needed to properly
elongate the cylinder.[59]

While the glass subsequently required the attention of cutters and
flatteners, work in the window and bottle departments was directed
by the blower, who retained much of the position of the artisan glassmaker.[60] Glassmaking had long been a highly esteemed craft—in
France it was one of the few trades deemed suitable for nobles.[61] The
division of work between blower and gatherer was a recent development that institutionalized traditional relationships between younger and more experienced workers. Until midcentury, it was common
for the young glassmaker, often the son of a master, to gather the
glass and prepare the pipe for blowing. Distinctions were not hard
and fast, and it was not unusual for the younger workman to do some
blowing or for the master to finish the gathering. This grey area persisted as long as blowing retained its salience as a craft.[62]

This task sharing was especially true when gatherers were the sons
of blowers, which was often—the union limited entry to relatives.[63] A
survey of glassblower households reveals that it was highly unusual
for children in their teens to work, except as a gatherer. The genera-
tional component to the work group was reaffirmed by the age of the

Table 7. Glassworks: Ethnic Composition of Labor Force, New Albany, 1880

Ethnicity	Blower	Gatherer	Finisher	Cutter	Other	Laborer
n =	68	28	47	23	30	250
Native-white	45.6	53.6	8.5	39.1	33.3	32.0
British Immigrants						
English	19.1	10.7	68.1	39.1	16.7	14.0
2d gen.	—	—	2.1	8.7	—	2.0
Welsh	1.5	—	—	—	—	—
2d gen.	—	—	—	4.3	—	—
Other Immigrants						
Irish	5.9	3.6	2.1	—	—	3.6
German	7.3	—	2.1	—	3.3	9.6
French	1.5	—	—	—	6.7	0.8
Other	2.9	3.6	—	—	—	—
2d Generation						
Irish	10.3	7.1	8.5	—	13.3	18.0
German	4.4	3.6	6.4	4.3	10.0	12.4
French	—	—	—	4.3	3.3	2.0
Other	1.5	3.6	2.1	—	3.3	0.8
Native-black	—	—	—	—	10.0	4.8
Unknown	—	14.3	—	—	—	—

Note: Column headed by "other" includes workers of varying skills. Among the thirty are eight window glass flatteners, four of whom were native, two French, and two second-generation Irish. The three black workers were teasers, who prepared the furnace for the molten glass mixture.

SOURCE: Tenth Census, population schedules, Floyd County.

workers. Blowers were the oldest of the skilled men, averaging 33.9 years of age in 1880, while gatherers were the youngest, averaging 24.8 years.[64] Though their earnings were equaled by flatteners and cutters, only they were in position to learn the blower's craft.

And a remunerative craft it was. Glassblowers were the highest paid workers in the city, earning as much as $12 a day.[65] Some became prominent. That Otis Roy was building a "fine residence" was noted by the *Ledger*, and the comings and goings of his family as well as those of other blowers were frequently remarked upon by the editor of the local society column. Another blower, Levi Pierce, assumed a position of stature in the Masons and was mentioned by the press as a potential mayoral candidate.[66]

The organization of work in the window house, then, provided the basis for an aristocracy of labor. Collective efforts on the part of the blowers during the 1870s and 1880s were designed largely to protect their position. Union rules limited both production and entry into the craft.[67] So long as glassmaking defied technological improvement, the blowers and gatherers were able to carve out a comfortable position for themselves.

The elite positions at the furnace were held largely by native-born workers (47.9 percent) and a sizeable minority of English immigrants (16.7 percent). Slightly fewer came from the Irish community (9.4 percent from the second generation, and 5.2 from the first), and a small number of Germans (immigrants filled 5.2 percent of the jobs, the next generation took 4.2) found work as either a gatherer or a blower.[68] The largely native composition of this labor aristocracy set them apart from the large numbers of immigrant workers employed in the plate department (see table 7).

Capitalization and the Plate Glassworks

The plate glassworks soon overshadowed the window glass house in importance. The New Albany firm accounted for over 40 percent of U.S. plate glass production in 1880.[69] Rapid growth resulted from large infusions of DePauw's capital, which paid for annealing ovens and the latest in grinding, smoothing, and polishing machines.[70] To house them, DePauw built a factory of huge proportions that was over 600 hundred feet long and between 184 and 240 feet wide.[71]

In plate glass production, labor was far less expensive a factor than machinery and raw material.[72] Aside from finishing, most processes required relatively little in the way of skill. The glass was first mixed and melted, and then it was poured onto an iron casting table. The molten mass was spread evenly by a heavy iron roller and the size was set by adjustable metal strips bolted on to the table. Once the glass solidified, it was speedily moved to the annealing oven, where it cooled for up to five days. Movement of pots and cast sheets of glass did require great care, and up to seventeen men were needed to move the larger sheets and the heavier pots.

After cooling, the glass was ready for the first finishing process—"grinding." One plate was embedded on a large platform in plaster of paris while another was similarly placed on the underside of a platform directly opposite. By means of forward, backward and circular motions, the two plates were continually put in contact with each other, with river sand applied to grind out defects. The glass was then moved to the "smoothing" room where similar machines used fine powders of emery. The last process, "polishing," was also done by machine. Rubbers, covered with a fine felt and applied with rouge, contacted the glass while the table on which the sheet rested was moved back and forth.[73] Despite the mechanized character of these processes, "imperfections" in the machines required that skilled operators run them.[74] Despite their efforts, rarely did a flawless sheet of plate glass arrive in the cutting room. With a diamond the cutter cut the glass to marketable dimensions, circumventing the imperfections. Due to these considerations, cutting required a high level of experience and judgement.[75]

Since the United States lacked a plate glass industry, DePauw recruited skilled English workers to run the finishing departments.[76] In 1880, 75 percent of the polishers and smoothers were English, as were 60 percent of the grinders. Most other skilled finishers were born in the United States (25.5 percent), and were evenly divided between those with native, Irish and German parents (see table 7).[77] Compared to those who worked in the window house, this recruited labor force was relatively low paid. While flatteners and gatherers earned on the average about $4 a day, cutters and polishers earned little more than two.[78]

Aspects of family life reflected this pay differential. Fewer of their children attended school than those of blowers (see table 8), and they more commonly entered the labor force. For example, in 1880 two daughters of cutter Thomas Tagg were hired out—Mary, seventeen, at the glassworks and Caroline, twenty-one, as a servant. For smoothers John Baugh and George Love circumstances were similar. At the age of sixteen Baugh's son Willie worked as a laborer in the glassworks, as did George Love, Jr., who was fourteen. Love's wife, Jane, was also employed there.[79] In general, life was more tenuous for skilled plate glass men than it was for window glassworkers. Their wages were barely sufficient to support families. In times of significant work stoppages sons, daughters, and even wives had to find work outside the home.

For the majority of glassworkers life was more difficult and uncertain. Most work in plate glass production was relatively unskilled, requiring large gangs of men to manipulate hot heavy pots and sheets of glass in and out of the various ovens and on to the finishing machines. At least 56 percent of the employees of the glassworks in 1880 performed unskilled jobs, most of them in the plate glass department. In the following decade the percentage of jobs filled by skilled men declined by half. Increasingly work was done by lesser skilled men, women, and children who received daily wages of $1.50 or less.[80]

Unlike the skilled glassworkers or the ironworkers of the west

Table 8.   School Attendance by Trade of Family Members, New Albany, 1880

Trade	No. in Sample	No. School Age	No. in School	Percentage
Petty Proprietors	27	28	26	92.9
Small Manufacturers	17	24	25	104.2
White Collar	42	32	32	100.0
Skilled Workers				
Nonfactory				
Prosperous Metal and				
Construction Trades[1]	40	36	42	116.7
Leather and Needle				
Trades[2]	15	16	8	50.0
Factory Workers				
Iron Mills				
Puddlers	37	24	21	87.5
Rollers	16	16	12	75.0
Heaters	18	23	18	78.3
Laborers	128	113	87	77.0
Window Glass				
Blowers	68	35	34	97.1
Gatherers	28	21	20	95.2
Flatteners	8	9	9	100.0
Plate Glass				
Polishers	17	15	14	93.3
Smoothers	15	17	15	88.2
Grinders	15	25	21	84.0
Glass (dept. unknown)				
Cutters	23	16	10	62.5
Laborers	250	274	208	75.9
Woolen Workers	320	349	247	70.8

Notes: Data for factory workers include all listed in the census. For other occupational groups, data were derived from a sample of every ten households in the city. The first column presents the number engaged in the occupation on which other columns are based. School age was determined to be between seven and fifteen. As some fifteen-year-olds left school while some six-year-olds entered the classroom, the two columns do not always refer to the same children. This explains figures greater than 100 percent.

1. Includes machinists, molders, engineers, carpenters and painters.

2. Includes tailors, shoemakers, saddlers and tanners.

SOURCE: Tenth Census, population schedules, Floyd County.

end, unskilled laborers in the glassworks were not mostly native or English. Instead they were an ethnic mix that reflected the population of the east side of the city. Native whites accounted for 32 percent, while most of the rest came from the immigrant communities. Second-generation Irish (18 percent) and German (12.4 percent), and first-generation English (14 percent) and German (9.6 percent) immigrants filled the bulk of the positions. A small number of Irish, second-generation French, and native-born black workers rounded out the work force (see table 7).[81]

That a more hierarchical labor force developed in the glassworks was a direct result of the nature of the work process. Though the numbers of unskilled ironworkers were growing, the percentage was higher in the glassworks, especially in the plate glass department. The need for unskilled labor, and the location of the works near the center of the immigrant community, led to the greater employment of Irish and German workers and a more diverse labor force than was found in the iron mills. And due to the persistent salience of glass-blowing as a craft, a labor aristocracy imposed itself atop the occupational ladder in the glassworks. Unlike the shipyards of antebellum New Albany and the manufacturing sector of Gilded Age Evansville, the labor force in the glassworks was riddled with sources of division.

Textile Workers

A few blocks to the northeast, the New Albany Woolen Mill employed a small number of men and an increasing number of women and children. In 1870 the mill engaged 142 workers; 42 were women over the age of fifteen, and 51 others were children.[82] Twenty years later as many as 700 were employed there, and female workers accounted for as much as 70.3 percent of the total.[83] About half of the labor force worked in the weaving or spinning departments where women were most highly concentrated. Spinners and weavers tended steam-driven jacks and looms, turning out yarn and cloth. Young women then took the woven cloth and with tweezers and scissors picked out imperfections. Adult men were largely employed in the dying and sorting rooms as beamers and warpers who prepared the yarn for the looms, as jack and loom fixers, as machinists, and as foremen.[84]

Woolen workers of any kind were not highly paid, and this low pay explains why the children of older male woolen workers worked in the mills. Wage data for woolen workers are scarce, but it appears that the best paid could hope to earn $4.00 a day in the early 1870s. By 1890, men in their thirties working as dyers, finishers, washers,

Table 9. Woolen Mill: Ethnic Composition of Labor Force by Age and by
          Gender, New Albany, 1880

	Male			Female		
Ethnicity	Under 16	16–20	Over 20	Under 16	16–20	Over 20
N=	50	65	69	21	61	54
Native-white	40.0	33.8	31.9	19.0	45.9	51.9
British Immigrants						
English	—	—	11.6	4.8	3.3	1.9
2d gen.	6.0	3.1	2.9	4.8	—	5.6
Welsh	—	—	—	—	—	—
2d gen.	—	—	—	—	1.6	—
Other Immigrants						
Irish	—	1.5	1.4	—	—	1.9
German	2.0	3.1	18.8	4.8	4.9	7.4
French	—	—	—	—	—	—
Other	2.0	—	1.4	—	—	1.9
2d Generation						
Irish	8.0	20.0	4.3	14.3	11.5	9.3
German	40.0	33.8	15.9	42.9	26.2	16.7
French	2.0	1.5	1.4	4.8	6.6	3.7
Other	—	1.5	1.4	4.8	—	—
Native-black	—	1.5	8.7	—	—	—

SOURCE: Tenth Census, population schedules, Floyd County.

and loom fixers earned between $1.25 and $1.35 a day. Two spinners, averaging forty years of age, earned $2.50 and $1.25.[85]

Most of the male workers over thirty years of age were born in Germany (37.1), in England (20.0) or in the United States (22.9). But more importantly, the woolen mills gave work to the sons and daughters of German immigrants, who constituted more than a quarter of the mill's work force and 12.8 percent of all employed second-generation Germans in the city. The woolen mills employed a similar percentage of the progeny of Irish immigrants (12.4).[86] Here, then, as in the glassworks, was a diverse labor force (see table 9).

The Meaning of Unskilled Labor

While expansion and innovation increased the demand for unskilled labor in these industries, the number of day "laborers" in the city declined from 541 in 1860 to only 401 in 1880. The data suggest that many of New Albany's unskilled had exchanged the vagaries of casual labor for the regularity of factory work. Whereas the Irish and Germans in 1860 made up 31.4 and 25.7 percent, respectively, of the city's laborers, twenty years later the percentages had shrunk to 18.2 percent for the Irish and 8.2 percent for the Germans.[87] This was not all pull; the decline of New Albany's port in the 1870s and growing competition from black workers pushed many white laborers into finding new sources of work.[88]

As in Evansville, the movement of significant numbers of immigrant workers into the factories left the city's least remunerative and most irregular work to the growing black population. Largely due to northward migrations of freedmen, the local black community doubled during the war decade, and by 1870 nearly fifteen hundred black men, women, and children made their homes in New Albany and surrounding Floyd County, mostly in the ghetto on the north central side of town near the stockyards.[89]

Less than forty found employment in the mills. Most black males worked at the wharf and on the city streets, constituting just over 30 percent of the day laboring population in 1880. Few black teenagers were listed with an occupation in the census, which deprived black families of a vital source of income. As a result, black women entered the wage-earning labor force in far higher numbers than their white working-class counterparts, usually as full-time servants or as washers and ironers.[90] While jobs were more plentiful for black women than their sons, it is likely that their rate of labor force participation was affected as well by a desire that their children stay in school. Though most black adults (55.2 percent) were illiterate, they sent their children to school at higher rates than did white laborers, behavior consistent with the hunger for education generally displayed by freedmen in the postwar years.[91]

In the factories, many of the unskilled were young white men and women, especially in the glass and woolen mills. Glass workers yet to reach their twentieth birthday numbered 127 in 1880, and more than a third of these were under sixteen. The woolen mill relied even more on the young, hiring 167 teenage boys and girls, 66 of whom were not yet sixteen. Unskilled workers usually lived with their parents, who needed their wages to maintain an acceptable standard of living.[92] Frequently the fathers of such workers were themselves laborers. The portrait of impoverished families as a source of labor is sustained by the small, but significant, number—5.9 percent of the woolen workers and 3.3 percent of the unskilled glassworkers—who were children of men skilled in the declining shoe and needle trades.[93]

Many others came from families headed by widowed mothers; the loss of the primary wage earner necessitated early entry into the labor force. At least twenty unskilled ironworkers and thirty-nine glassworkers lived in such households. It was the woolen mills, however, that most heavily relied on this most desperate stratum of society. Nearly 40 percent of the female workers resided with widowed mothers.[94] The experience of the family of ironworker Major A. Burd is instructive. In 1870, Burd was 48 and owned real property worth $1,000. His eldest son, Wesley, was a painter and Willis, sixteen, and Andrew, fifteen, were employed with him at the Ohio Falls Iron Works while eleven-year-old Daniel attended school. Sarah, his wife, took care of the house and the couple's two-year-old daughter, Dora. Major died sometime in the next five years. In 1880 Sarah lived with her two youngest sons, one a nailer and the other a frequently unemployed painter, and Dora, now twelve and working at the woolen mill. Similarly, the children of deceased tanner John Peterson—John, Jr., seventeen, Mary, fifteen, and Willie, thirteen—were employed in the woolen mill in 1880, leaving only seven-year-old Ida at home with their mother. The mill offered low-paying jobs, as low as fifty cents a day, for families in such straits.[95]

For some, early entry into the work force led to the acquisition of a desirable trade. Certainly this was true for the sons of glassblowers and iron puddlers who entered the work force as gatherers or as helpers. For others the results were mixed. Of the teenage workers in the iron, glass, and woolen mills in 1880, a large majority who remained in New Albany into the early 1890s continued to work in the mills (70.5 percent).[96] Half continued to work as laborers, helpers, or as low paid semiskilled workers. Others worked at one of the skilled trades in the factories. Those that found work outside the mills likewise divided evenly between skilled and unskilled positions, though the former tended to be the sons of skilled workers. Among the youngest workers, then, a modest degree of social mobility within the working class was displayed.

Neighborhoods of Factory Workers

The growing reliance on young, unskilled, and often Catholic workers had a profound structural impact on the working class. When New Albany was a shipyard town, the unskilled lived and worked by and large on the other side of the city from mechanics. Further, skilled carpenters, joiners, and sawyers worked with little help from the unskilled. The growth of large mechanized firms brought the skilled and unskilled together at both the workplace and the community. Where residential, industrial, and ethnic lines were once roughly the same, now arose diverse working-class neighborhoods.

This diversity was first apparent in the west end. As the iron mills opened in the late 1860s, skilled workers gathered in boarding houses nearby. As they settled in, they bought or rented houses or flats in the Sixth Ward between Spring Street and the waterfront—the heart of what had been the shipbuilding community only a few years before—and turned it into a community of wage earners. By the early seventies, this residential pattern was well under way, and by 1890 the area had clearly been turned into an industrial working-class neighborhood (see map 5).[97]

Closer inspection reveals that residency patterns reflected the diversity of the mills. In 1890, on a block of West Seventh Street, native puddlers like Al Worsey and Welsh immigrants like John Jones lived next door to black laborers James Hicks and Henry Thomas. A block further west, on Eighth Street, at successive addresses lived the families of puddler Jesse Dangerfield, railroad worker Cornelius J. Murphy, heater Joseph Owens, rail mill mixer John A. Johnson, roll turners John G. Jenkins and Boyd Gaugh, and railroad fireman William Kemper.[98]

The transformation of the First Ward into a sprawling factory community was nearly as complete. Nearly 40 percent of all households there included at least one person employed in the large corporate firms, primarily the glassworks and the woolen mill. Early in the industrial regime, before the building of the plate glassworks, glassworkers concentrated in boarding houses in the First and Second wards between Main street and the river. Within a few years, a number had moved a few blocks north to the new residential areas north of Spring street. By 1890 the change was complete; what had been largely unsettled thirty years before, was now the city's most populous ward, as most woolen and glassworkers made it their home.[99]

Examination of residency patterns in 1890 on two city blocks shows that despite the occupational diversity of the mills, class was instrumental in the formation of neighborhoods. The first, was in "Bog Hollow," a glassworker enclave. Located, fittingly enough, just on the other side of the railroad tracks and down the hill from the mansions of Main Street, this riverfront neighborhood was home to native whites, blacks, and Irish immigrants.[100] Glassworkers lived in more than half of the houses on Eighth Street, which ran down the middle of Bog

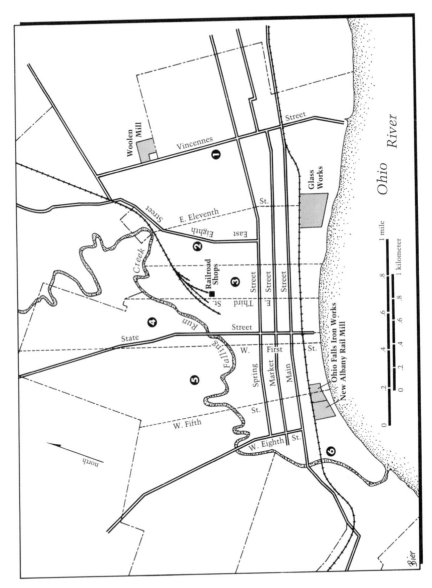

Map 5. New Albany, 1890

Hollow. Among the residents were two blowers, two grinders, three helpers, three "layers," a "snapper," a "bench boy," a "tramper," a glass handler, and a laborer—all employed in the glassworks. Around the corner on Water Street lived a helper, a grinder, a roofer, and a gas producer. Residing amidst these glassworkers were two iron heaters, an engineer, a box maker, a carpenter, and four laborers.[101] This was a working-class neighborhood composed of both skilled and unskilled workers; the swampy nature of the ground and its proximity to the glassworks made it both inexpensive and convenient.

To the northeast, First Ward neighborhoods were more diverse, though still overwhelmingly working class. On the south side of Sycamore Street and the north side of Oak, for instance, resided a variety of skilled workers, including three carpenters, two cigar makers, a glassblower, a cutter, a smoother, a molder, a machinist, a stonemason and a railroad brakeman. Sharing the block were a handful of less-skilled workers, including three female woolen workers, a driver, a watchman, a barkeeper, a laborer and three unskilled glassworkers. A saloonkeeper (whose three sons were skilled workmen), a grocer and four clerks were the only nonworkers on the block.[102]

Most housing in these neighborhoods was of a uniform kind: small one- or two-story cottages with modest gardens and an outbuilding in back. Some residences were divided into upper and lower flats.[103] Most workers, regardless of trade or skill level, ceased boarding on marrying, and they tended to rent their dwellings twice as frequently as they bought them. Different groups paid similar amounts in rent: eight puddlers averaged $7 a month; two heaters paid $8; twenty laborers in the iron mills averaged $7.90; while ten glass cutters, four polishers, four flatteners, and nine unskilled glassworkers paid between $8 and $9 a month. Only glassblowers and gatherers paid significantly more.[104] As in Evansville, the equality of living standards was probably maintained by the labor of teenage children of lesser skilled men.

The growth of working-class neighborhoods reveals how much had changed. In the decade before the Civil War, skilled mechanics in the shipbuilding trades lived far from the mass of immigrant shoemakers, tailors, and day laborers and felt little in common with them. This was particularly evident in the mid-1850s when Know-Nothingism divided the city along the same residential pattern. Now, however, workers from the various departments within the mills came into contact with each other, sharing the same saloons and grocery stores. By 1890, such clear-cut geographical divisions had disappeared, a development symbolically made evident by the pres-

ence in 1890 of nine saloons in the heart of the ironworking community. Thirty years earlier, when the shipyards were active, there had
been none.[105] Here, within the working-class community were some
of the building blocks for the construction of class consciousness.[106]

The Decline of the "Virtuous Middle"

Industrial change had ramifications for the petty bourgeoisie as
well. Growing more slowly than the working class, the "middling
sort" became more pronounced in the white-collar and professional
occupations and less so in manufacturing.[107] Though the small master (employing six or fewer workers) did not disappear, his relative
importance declined as the percentage of the manufacturing work
force that was employed in such shops dropped from 20.3 in 1860 to
7.1 percent in 1880. Equally important was their isolation, occupationally and residentially, from the vast majority of factory workers.
None of the smaller workshops engaged in any aspect of glass, iron
or textile production. Most were marginal producers, characterized
by small capital investment in the needle, shoemaking, and tobacco
trades.

The growth of factories increased the demand for white-collar
workers. The glassworks employed at least twenty such men and
women in 1890, among them a timekeeper, a shipping clerk, a purchasing agent, and a bill clerk. The New Albany Rail Mill employed
four superintendents, two bookkeepers (one was female), and a female stenographer. The nearby Ohio Falls Iron Works employed a
shipping clerk and a bookkeeper. Even smaller firms, like the National Stove Foundry, employed a couple of clerks and a salesman or
two.[108] Overall, the number of white-collar workers increased 64 percent since 1860. Despite the growth in white-collar employment in
the factories, the clerical sector grew more slowly than in Evansville
where it tripled in size between 1860 and 1880.

The geographical expansion of the east side of the city and the
growth of the labor force created opportunities for petty proprietorship. Nearly three hundred men and women operated the city's ho-
tels, saloons, and groceries.[109] Some were related to workers. For instance, Rosa Ziegelbauer, a former employee of the woolen mill, ran
a grocery store just a few blocks from the mill that still employed her
younger sisters. Similarly, Alfred Hinkley's wife operated the family
grocery while he worked as a painter at the railroad car shop. Others,
like blacksmith and one-time glassworks employee Otto Hoffman,

opened groceries only to return to the factories during difficult times.[110]

Aside from grocers and saloonkeepers, most middling types lived separate from the industrial working class. Large percentages of retailers (80.9), salesmen (79.1), bookkeepers (73.9), and clerks (57.3) concentrated heavily in the business district of the city—the Third, Fourth, and Fifth wards—while most woolen, glass and iron workers resided in the First, Second, and Sixth wards.[111]

The growing distance between the middling types and the factory working class is further highlighted by differences in educational attainments (see table 8). Illiteracy among the middling sort was virtually nonexistent, and with the exception of the sons and daughters of grocers and saloonkeepers—those occupations most closely tied to working-class New Albany—their children uniformly attended school.[112] Whereas significant portions of the antebellum working class shared the petty bourgeois propensity to school their children, by 1880 rates of school attendance only served to separate further the factory labor force—with the notable exception of the glassblowers—from the rest of the community.

Still some workers outside the factories retained artisanal ambitions. Children of machinists, carpenters, engineers, painters and iron molders all attended the classroom at high rates. It was not uncommon for such workers, especially the employees of foundries and the railroad car works, to pay more than $10 a month in rent, a figure only equaled by window glassworkers.[113] Most lived outside the factory districts, concentrating in the northern parts of the Second and Third wards just southeast of the railroad depot.[114] Neighborhoods in this area were a diverse mixture of small proprietors, skilled workmen and white-collar workers. One such neighborhood included a newspaper editor, a clerk in the county auditor' office, the deputy county auditor, a marble works proprietor, the cashier of the water works, a railroad baggage agent, a conductor, a foreman at the stove foundry (related to the proprietor of the firm), a grocer, a grain and feed retailer, tanner, four blacksmiths, a railroad engineer, three molders, three carpenters, two painters, a tinner and a harness maker. Housing in this neighborhood was not only more expensive; dwellings were 50–100 percent larger than in the factory neighborhoods.[115] Here, then, were the remains of the "virtuous" middle of New Albany society. Workmen shared neighborhoods and living conditions with petty proprietors and white-collar workers and uniformly sent their children to school. Elsewhere, the working class had become quite isolated from the petty bourgeoisie, further hardening class lines.

Plebeian and Working-Class Associations

With the transformation of the economy, a more complex network of social institutions developed. The old plebeian cross-class pattern of association persisted, bringing workers and the petty bourgeoisie together. However, alongside these interclass fraternal organizations a new pattern emerged from both the experience of the ship carpenters' union and the increasing cleavages between social classes; skilled workers began to associate together.

The old plebeian network remained vital, as skilled workers, particularly those outside the factories, continued to join lodges with the petty bourgeoisie. While the well-heeled still dominated a few of the Masonic lodges in the 1870s, others came to be led by retailers, white-collar workers, and skilled wage earners. By the last half of the following decade, the wealthy had abandoned the leadership of all but Commandery No. 5 of the Knights Templar to the petty bourgeoisie and skilled workers, and one, DePauw Lodge No. 338, was remarkable in that half of its leaders were workers, some of whom worked in either the rolling mill or the glassworks.[116]

As time went on the social composition of the Odd Fellows came to resemble that of the Masons. Odd Fellows still brought together small manufacturers, white-collar workers, and skilled workers, particularly iron molders, machinists, carpenters, and painters. Though they continued to reflect the "virtuous middle" of society, the Odd Fellows of the postwar era had grown more prosperous than their antebellum predecessors. Between 1871 and 1875, as many Odd Fellow leaders claimed estates worth $2,000 or more—including thirteen skilled workers—as those claiming less.[117] Fifteen years later, the social makeup of the Odd Fellows was indistinguishable from that of the Masons.[118]

Less prosperous were the lodges of the Knights of Pythias, whose lore and ritual celebrated nonentrepreneurial values of friendship and sacrifice over that of self-interest, and in that way seem to embody the mutualistic ethos that some historians have attributed to the fraternal network.[119] The Pythians, whose origins date to the waning years of the Civil War, enjoyed great success in New Albany where three lodges were established by the early 1870s. Among the leaders of these new lodges, skilled workers—none of whom were employed in the factories—constituted the largest single group (39.6 percent), followed by white collar workers (26.4 percent) and small masters (17 percent)—nearly all of whom were relatively poor painters and carpenters. The Pythian leadership was poorer than that of its competing fraternal orders as nearly half owned estates worth less than $500 and but 15 percent owned as much as $2,000.[120] Throughout the Gilded Age the composition of the Pythians remained the same, and even more than the Masons and Odd Fellows, continued to lack factory workers of any skill level.[121]

The 1860s and 1870s witnessed the rapid growth of ethnic associations, particularly among the Irish and the German immigrants of the eastern wards. Organizations like the Ancient Order of Hibernians, the Holy Trinity Abstinence Society, the Catholic Knights of America, the St. Joseph Benevolent Society, and the German Joseph-Mary-Jesus Society joined the already existent German Benevolent Society in establishing a network of societies that stressed ethnic and religious ties over those of class. Typically they were led by small retailers and a somewhat larger number of skilled and unskilled workers, particularly iron molders and skilled glassworkers.[122] German lodges of the Odd Fellows and the Knights of Pythias were likewise established. In such organizations a pattern of interclass association that was common during the prewar era prevailed. Still vital in the industrial era, fraternal and ethnic associations served as a cultural bridge connecting the petty bourgeoisie with segments of the working class, allowing for the transmission of values up and down the social hierarchy.

However, more narrowly working-class associations appeared and thrived in the industrial era. Two lodges of the nativist Order of United American Mechanics (OUAM) were founded, and they were led almost entirely by skilled workers, including four employees of the iron mills—two puddlers, a charger, and an engineer.[123] The OUAM had been in existence in cities to the east like Cincinnati, where its emphasis on individual improvement, its strictures against drinking and other forms of undisciplined behavior, and its fierce adherence to producerism made it popular among master craftsmen and journeymen.[124] In such places it drew from the same groups in society that the AOUW did in Evansville, but in New Albany, the OUAM became firmly entrenched in the worker community, leaving masters behind.

A similar organization, the Independent Order of Workingmen (IOWM), was founded in New Albany by skilled workers in 1874.[125] Though eschewing nativist proscription of immigrant workers, the IOWM shared much with its older counterpart, especially its reliance on "honesty, industry, sobriety, intelligence and virtue" to improve the lot of workingmen.[126] And like the OUAM, it offered a mutual aid feature. Yet, the IOWM was intended to be something more. While pledging to "wage no war against Capital," the leaders declared that workers deserved "equality, fairness, equity, and protection." Among their goals was equal political representation for workers and "the just share of benefits in the legislation of the country."[127]

Over the next few years the fledgling association enjoyed success. Early in 1877 the city boasted four lodges with a total of four hundred members. The founders carried the IOWM to neighboring cities, towns and hamlets. In 1877, the order had about 2,000 members in Louisville, and in March of that year a lodge was established in Indianapolis.[128] The order's message, that "the laborer is worthy of his hire," struck a chord with many workers struggling to survive the hard times of the 1870s. "For years we have beheld a perpetual breaking down of labor, and in all departments wages has [sic] been placed at a starving point," a prominent leader reminded the members of one lodge.[129]

Its success was short-lived. Lodges outside New Albany soon became numerically superior and voted to change the name to the Independent Order of Mutual Aid to the disapproval of the New Albany members.[130] The local lodges soon disbanded, some of them reorganizing as Knights of Industry.[131] A few of the order's leaders, like glassblower Isaac Whetsel who served as president of the order's Grand Lodge of Indiana in 1877, would soon turn to the Knights of Labor as the best vehicle to improve the conditions of the working class.[132]

At the same time, social organization among workers in the iron mills and the glassworks appeared. While ironworkers established the National Dancing Club, the workmen of the window glass house formed the Star Glass Works Fishing Club.[133] English glassworkers organized cricket matches between smoothers and polishers, and sometimes against the window glass men.[134] The growth of unions among skilled workers in the iron mills, the glassworks, and the foundries further structured leisure for the workingman. Each union put on its own annual ball, and they and Knights of Labor Assemblies alike indulged in picnics and "moonlight excursions."[135]

A new pattern of skilled worker association had emerged. Yet, like the interclass plebeian network, the meaning of these organizations is ambiguous, for while they could build a common sense of class identity, they also tended to institutionalize ethnic rivalry. Others like the recreational societies and unions brought workers from the same workplace together. From such a wide variety of organizations, different ideas and values were sure to have proliferated. Nevertheless, it would be unwise to build hard and fast cultural types, for instance, by setting up opposing ethnic, fraternal, and union cultures for the very reason that the same men were often active in rival spheres. For workers like puddler John K. Fogle, who held leadership positions in the Good Templars, the IOWM, and the puddler's union, or George Carpenter, an officer of the puddler's union who was active in the OUAM, the conflicting aims of the various organizations seems to have posed little problem. More important was the process of associating together in organizations where counter-hegemonic values could be expressed and developed.

Nevertheless, the old plebeian network persisted, and a few union leaders participated in it as well. Glassblower Levi Pierce and skilled ironworkers George Roberts, Reese Prosser, and James Ogden were members of Oceola Lodge No. 47 of the Knights of Honor.[136] Pierce also was prominent in the Masons. These men may have been more ambitious than others. By 1890 Pierce had left the blower's platform to superintend at the glassworks, while Prosser and Roberts left the factory entirely—the former operating a laundry, the latter a dry goods store.[137] Consequently, even within the unions themselves, workers brought diverse cultural experiences with them.

Building on the experience of the ship carpenters during and immediately after the Civil War, glass and iron workers formed a community that in many respects left the old interclass pattern behind, and that was truly working class. Formative in this process was the concentration of large numbers of workers in factories and neighborhoods, and a widening gap between worker and capitalist. Social forces led many workers to see common concerns and experience. They responded by associating in benefit societies and unions. The following chapter traces the outline of union activity and the effect that it and other more divisive social and cultural forces had on the political life of New Albany.

Workers in Isolation: Militancy and Division in DePauw's Industrial Empire

8 The great increase in class differentiation created by the new industrial regime led to a surge in worker organization and an unprecedented number of strikes during the 1870s and 1880s. Some were long, hard-fought affairs, occasionally breaking out in violence. Militant workers, however, did not receive widespread support from the larger local community and they tended to fight isolated battles. Nor did militancy translate into a working-class presence in the political arena. In New Albany, party politicians rarely catered to working-class aspirations.

There are two reasons for this quiescence at the ballot box. First and foremost was the looming presence of W. C. DePauw. Unlike the classic outsider of Gutman's essays, he moved to New Albany as he transformed its economy and became deeply involved in local cultural life. The press was usually solicitous of him, emphasizing his good works in the church, for temperance, and in charity. But by far the most important basis of DePauw's power was economic. Employing half of the wage-earning population, his capital nourished the city's growth. Local storekeepers, who might have been expected to extend aid to workers in times of strikes, were ultimately dependent on the operation of DePauw's firms. As a result, few of the city's propertied classes had the stomach for making political war on DePauw.

Ethnic diversity also hindered the rise of a working-class political presence. Divisions of skill at the workplace were reinforced by ethnic employment patterns; such rivalries often threatened to dissolve class unity. As no ethnic group comprised a large percentage of the working class, politicians were not tempted to make class appeals, lacking the large voting bloc of German workers that Evansville Democrats used so effectively.

As a consequence of DePauw's dominance and ethnic diversity, New Albany workers found little potential to satisfy their collective aspirations through political action. Politicians certainly made appeals for working-class votes, though instead of framing appeals in terms of class conflict, they emphasized the tariff. Similarly, neither party supported working-class militancy at the workplace. Politics took on a militant flavor only in 1887, with the brief ascendancy of the Knights of Labor and the formation of an independent labor party.

A Confident and Hegemonic Elite

The postwar years were confident ones for the monied men of New Albany who boldly asserted their leadership in local affairs, especially in regard to improving the city's transportation network. When the loss of an important railroad connection threatened to cut the trade of New Albany merchants, the business community mobilized.[1] Soon it united to support the construction of a railroad to St. Louis, known as the "Air-Line" due to its direct route through the coal fields of southeastern Indiana. Meetings of merchants and manufacturers set in motion a petition drive to have the city subscribe to $300,000 of stock. Interest in the road was drummed up in the press; a booster writing under the pseudonym of "enterprise" envisioned that the Air-Line would bring "the hidden and untold wealth of the country." Access to cheap coal would induce capitalists to build factories in New Albany. To this end, the author argued, all classes of the city had a direct interest.[2]

The petition drive revealed a unity of purpose among elites, and their influence over lesser-propertied individuals. More than three-fourths of the city's wealthiest individuals—those worth at least $50,000 in 1870—signed the petition. But support throughout the business community was strong; 53 grocers, 19 saloon and boarding-house keepers, and 118 manufacturers added their names. With the exception of a few in the building trades, who stood to gain from the work generated by construction of the road, workers showed little interest. On receiving the petition, the council unanimously approved the subscription.[3] The signing of the contract between the company and the city revealed that, for the moment, the capitalists of New Albany were able to direct the city with little interference.

At the workplace capitalists promoted warm relations with their employees. The new industrial regime was symbolically inaugurated in October 1867 with a banquet commemorating the opening of the Ohio Falls Iron Works. More than sixty company officers, workers and local notables listened as the firm's vice-president Peter Stoy declared, "however much demagogues may say of the antagonism between capital and labor, these manufactories must prove that their interest [sic] are one and the same." Ironworkers were urged to "bear in mind the fact, that whatever is for the interest of the company by whom you are employed is for your interest." Stoy's exhortations for harmony were echoed by E. M. Hubbert, another member of the firm, who "hailed the kind feelings existing between the company and the men employed," while promising that the company would do nothing to disturb the prevailing calm.[4] Speeches by workers were also amiable, if less sanguine. A committee drafted resolutions thanking the company for the evening's festivities and wishing them success. Puddler Thomas Danks, who had been selected chair of the meeting, reiterated these sentiments, but added that there had always been conflict between capital and labor and that the future would be no different. With "mutual forbearance," however, Danks suggested such strife might be minimized.[5]

That the workers recognized the existence of conflict between capital and labor reflected the experience that they brought with them to New Albany. Most had come from Wales or Pittsburgh and, in either case, learned their trades in an industry that was based on large units of production. The harmony of the artisanal workshop, where labor and capital were unified in the master craftsman, was not a part of their work experience. And they settled, for the most part, in the Sixth Ward, where they came into close contact with ship carpenters who had only recently engaged in their own struggles. Nevertheless, the next three years were calm ones in the city's factories. Disputes between managers and workmen remained minor affairs.

Sources of Dissonance

The prosperity of the early 1870s set in motion increasingly antagonistic relations between workers and their employers. Most significantly skilled workers organized. By 1873 boilermakers, coopers, glassblowers, iron molders, and shoemakers had all established trade unions.[6] The largest surge of organizing occurred among the ironworkers in 1871 when a "forge" of the Sons of Vulcan was founded, enrolling nearly two-thirds of the city's puddlers.[7] The next year the heaters established a union. By the autumn of 1873 other skilled rolling mill men joined the heaters in an amalgamated local incorporating rollers, roughers, and catchers. The common experience of work around the heating furnaces and rollers led the skilled ironworkers only halfway down the path of industrial unionism, however; a helper who attempted to join was "chucked out with surprising suddenness."[8]

Union organizing proceeded amid growing tensions at the workplace. In an effort to force management to abandon a subcontracting arrangement by which they controlled production but also bore many losses, blowers at the New Albany Glass Works left work in July 1871 demanding wage payments. The financially strapped company refused, and the plant lay idle until it burned down in 1875.[9] In 1873 English plate glassworkers engaged in a brief strike to have DePauw forgive a $5 a week debt they had assumed in return for transatlantic passage.[10]

Ironworkers also asserted their power. In October 1871 the management of the New Albany Rolling Mill posted regulations that aimed at disciplining its work force. The new rules forbade workers from leaving the mill during working hours to visit saloons or for any other purpose without the consent of the foreman. Further, off duty workers would not be allowed on the premises where they might disturb the men at work. The workmen bristled at this attempt to control the rhythms of work, a customary prerogative of rollers and heaters, and a strike ensued. When some refused to walk out, the strikers came *en masse* into the mill and prevented them from working. Order was restored by the city police, but the strike continued for a week until the proprietors relented and tore up the offensive rules. The following summer, when heaters held out for a 20 percent increase in the piece rate, management agreed to a compromise within a week.[11]

These disputes were brief. Prosperity gave workers leverage and employers incentive to grant wage increases so as not to lose their share of the market. As the press frequently reported, settlements usually resumed "amicable relations" between workers and employers. More ominous was the hostility of the press and city government. The police had been called out to quell worker protest in both the glass and iron mills. And when the press took sides, it was with management. While workers were portrayed as irresponsible and mendacious, employers came across as well meaning and honorable. The *Ledger-Standard* praised DePauw for going "far beyond the requirements of justice, or even generosity, in his treatment of his employees." The company, the editors maintained, in accord with its agreement with the English workers, had paid wages though the factory had been idle due to an expansion of the works. On opening, two grinders, a polisher, and a smoother "absconded" and the others refused to work. Moreover, some were said to have run up large debts with grocers claiming to be unable to pay. The *Commercial* agreed, declaring the workers "were not acting on the square."[12]

In politics, too, signs of discontent appeared. The success of Air-Line supporters inspired mechanics in the shipbuilding trades to petition the council to subscribe $50,000 toward the establishment of a shipyard. The petition was presented by Joseph St. John, a journeyman ship carpenter and councilmember from the Sixth Ward, and a number of members spoke in favor of it.[13] However, banker John Winstandley, chair of the council finance committee, attacked the proposal. If this petition was granted, he asked, "would [it] not equally justify the city in taking the like interest in any other one or all of the great mechanical and manufacturing industries of the city." Such a policy, Winstandley warned, would bankrupt the city. Further, he denied a shipyard could be "likened to subscriptions to railroad and other public works" which "have long been distinguished from such private works and pursuits."[14]

Reference to the Air-Line struck many nerves. The closing of the shipyards had left many with no choice but to leave their homes and search for work elsewhere. In the minds of many lower-ward residents the proposed shipyard constituted a meritorious and public spirited venture. That Winstandley's report had named a "special power" for railroad support in the city charter only pointed out that they had allowed the elite to control the city for too long.

Soon after the 1870 Cincinnati convention of the National Labor Union came out strongly in favor of forming a labor party, about seventy-five workmen and petty proprietors gathered to form the Workingman's Reform Association (WRA). The meeting adopted articles of association condemning both parties and pledging members to vote only for workingmen. Then George Hipple, a journeyman blacksmith and green grocer, gave a rousing diatribe against the council's subscription to the Air-Line, asking his audience, "you all hear, fellow citizens, of what a fine Council we've got, and how well they attend to our business?" The problem, he told them, was that the council had "voted away our money to build a railroad . . . and now we are paying $21,000 a year interest." Referring to ship carpenters who leave their families, "whom they love as well as the rich man," to take work elsewhere, Hipple argued that it would have done more good "if they had given that money to build up shipyards." The speech was hailed with "immense applause."[15]

Of the twelve active participants at the WRA meeting, two-thirds were workers: puddlers John K. Fogle and J. T. Bell; three glassblowers; a ship carpenter; a blacksmith; and a cooper. Others included

William Seville, a poor master frame maker, and Sam Milligan, a molder who recently had opened a small foundry. They were soon joined by Dummer M. Hooper, leader of the old ship carpenter's union, who was elected vice-president of the organization. Leadership of this movement, then, connected workers in the new industries with those from the shipbuilding community; and it was strongly correlated with unionization. At least four—Fogle, Bell, Hooper, and Isaac Whetsel—were prominent local union figures. Only George Hipple among the working-class leaders plied a trade that had not already organized, or was just about to do so.[16] The Workingmen's Reform Association (WRA) was a product of the aspirations of skilled trade-union men who blended economic organization and frustration with local government into a recipe for political activism.

The new party was treated disdainfully by local Democrats, who saw in it a threat to the dominance they had enjoyed in Floyd County since the end of the war. During the city elections of 1869 and 1870 Democrats carried every ward handily, with the exception of the Fifth. Democratic strength was so overwhelming in the largely German Fourth Ward that Republicans in 1870 failed to nominate a candidate to oppose Democrat Louis Vernia. Only slightly less resolute in their Democracy were the ironworkers and ship carpenters of the Sixth Ward.[17] The WRA, then, posed a substantial threat to Democratic party dominance.

Republicans were less hostile to the new organization, perceiving in it a means to loosen the Democratic stranglehold on local office. The Republican *Commercial* wooed the new party, describing its membership as "mechanics or laboring men, and all of them respectable and useful citizens," while attempting to defuse its class spirit. Though "the design . . . is a good one," the editors advised that "no organization will succeed that makes war on capital and public improvements." Attempting to restore the politics of class harmony, they warned that "the man who tries to mislead mechanics and laboring men into the belief that capital is hostile to labor is a demagogue of the first water . . . Capital and labor are in perfect accord and harmony. One would be useless without the other."[18]

Republicans made a concerted effort to capture the WRA, urging a relaxation of the restrictive articles of association. Once this was done the party was inundated with office seekers.[19] Again the *Commercial* offered advice: "The people of New Albany do not want men in their offices who are co-operators with the disaffected against all public improvements; who are the pets of the whiskey saloons, the favorites of the lower stratum of society."[20]

Their efforts were rewarded when the WRA nominated for mayor prosperous master painter, Thomas Kunkle, a signer of the Air-Line petition. The citywide ticket was filled out by small employers, a foreman at the *Ledger*, and a long-term Republican office holder, George Gresham. But it was in the wards where the Republican strategy truly paid dividends. Four of the WRA's council nominees were wealthy, including John Ford's son, Edward, and rolling mill officer Morris McDonald. And they were all Air-Line supporters.[21] To those questioning McDonald's place on a Workingman's ticket, the *Commercial* replied: "For their benefit we would state that in the past four years, Mr. McDonald has paid out, as wages, to the workingmen of New Albany over five hundred thousand dollars in cash. Let his enemies put this in their pipes and smoke it."[22] Only Joel Cogswell, a former leader of the defunct ship carpenters' union nominated in the Sixth Ward, seemed to embody the original intent of the organization.

Meanwhile, the Democrats were having difficulties. Prominent council incumbent John Winstandley, who had killed the shipyard proposal the previous spring, was soundly defeated by George Kraft, a favorite of the German wing of the party. Similarly, Mayor Hart was defeated in his bid for another term by ship carpenter George Townsend.[23] Results of this primary created such acrimony that Democrats remained divided for well over a year, leading to the establishment of a rival Democratic newspaper, the *Standard*, the following summer. The *Commercial* took advantage of the dissension within the Democratic ranks, and published a letter from "A Glass Blower," accusing the Townsend men of trying to buy glassworker votes with whiskey and money.[24]

This was essential to unite the anti-Democratic forces under the banner of the Workingmen. And it was, perhaps, not the departure that it seems at first glance. Not one of the working-class activists in the WRA was foreign-born. Fogle, Hipple, and Hooper were, or would shortly become, prominent members of temperance societies, and J. T. Bell would soon attain a position of prominence in the nativist Order of United American Workmen. Furthermore, only Hipple was a Democrat; the others had been Republicans. To these activists, fusion with the Republicans may have seemed a relatively painless road to power. That it occurred so readily and that the class rhetoric was dropped to achieve it, suggests that divisions of ethnicity and skill prevented iron and glass workers from thinking, much less acting, as a class. Such divisions, correlating so comfortably with the two major parties were more likely, at this time, to achieve success than attempts to forge class solidarity.

Yet the vote suggests that an explanation relying too much on ethnic antagonisms within the work force ignores the sense of class that pervaded the ironworker and ship carpenter dominated sixth ward. There the nativist WRA was the weakest, as Kunkle received only 37.8 percent of the vote and St. John, the ship carpenter who had introduced the shipyard petition, was the only Democratic council candidate who had an easy time of it. In the city as a whole, however, the rise of the WRA weakened the hold of the Democrats on the electorate. In every other ward, Kunkle handily defeated Townsend. While Democrats won the other city offices, they only split the council races, winning two seats by a total of just fifteen votes.[25]

The WRA survived until the next year's election, when it endorsed merchants or manufacturers who normally ran on one of the major party tickets. The 1872 election was decidedly nonpartisan. Unable to generate any enthusiasm for its survival, the WRA disappeared. Still resentments persisted into the mayoral election of 1873 when, on the third ballot, a divided Democratic convention selected Winstandley as its standard bearer over St. John. The reassertion of the "better element" of the party had poor results at the polls. Kunkle, running now on a "Citizen's ticket," defeated Winstandley in every ward except the Fourth. Significantly, Winstandley ran 8 to 18 percent behind the rest of the Democratic ticket, and in the sixth ward where St. John resided he was beaten by a three to one margin.[26]

The early 1870s witnessed renewed worker organization. As noted in the previous chapter, workers formed sporting and social clubs, fraternal and benevolent lodges, and a cooperative grocery. At the same time they organized unions to defend their interests at the workplace. It is not surprising, then, that working-class activists responded to the call of the 1870 National Labor Union convention and formed a labor reform party. Its original militancy suggests the kind of ideas that flowed through the network of working-class association. The WRA's ultimate inability to wage a campaign on its original premises and to avoid cooptation by the Republicans reveals, however, that the leaders were yet unable to unify workers with an oppositional program. Yet class still retained some salience; the Sixth Ward voted for Democratic ship carpenters Townsend and St. John in 1871, despite the nonimmigrant quality of the ward, and they even more clearly opposed the Democrats when banker Winstandley was offered at the head of the ticket instead of St. John. Thus if ethnic divisions tended to reinforce traditional party lines, which prevented workers from across the city uniting politically, class remained a strong force when the Sixth Ward voter decided which ballot to place in the box.

Strikers and Crusaders

In early 1874, when the severity of the depression was first being felt, an editor acknowledged "considerable suffering among the poorer classes." Many men were out of work and their daughters were forced to sew for "starvation prices." That winter was made all the more difficult by the failure of prices to fall in pace with the loss of income, and landlords were urged to "reduce rents at least in the same proportion that workingmen have been obliged to submit to." Though many workers escaped long-term unemployment, few were able to avoid reductions in wages. Petty proprietors also felt the squeeze of the depression as sources of loan capital dried up.[27] Some, like George Hipple, lost their businesses and returned to the workbench. Hard times were felt by a broad segment of the community, and it let loose a number of competing cultural tensions.

Church members responded to the approach of winter by organizing poor relief. At a meeting attended by the richest men in the city, merchant Joseph Cadwalader, a member of the Second Presbyterian Church, addressed the women whose duty it was to raise and distribute funds and reminded them "not to confine our activities to church members," but to "go outside, and aid the Poor wherever they may be."[28] The "Ladies' Benevolent Society" responded by establishing ward committees to visit the poor and determine whether or not they were "deserving." That such work could be a moving experience was demonstrated in the brief relationship established between Mrs. Marie Graham Grant, a member of the Second Presbyterian Church, and Mrs. Zanhorn, a poor woman taken ill with consumption and resigned to die.[29] Grant found her to be "very intelligent and ladylike," but her life had been ruined by a drunkard husband, and Grant concluded that death would "surely be a happy exchange for her." The woman's misfortune in marriage weighed heavily on her. Death came before winter's end, and Grant attended the funeral, noting that "from extreme suffering and neglect she is at last free." Even the funeral became a stage for conflict when the husband refused to permit his wife to be buried by the Presbyterians. During the service he removed her body from the donated coffin and placed it into one he had brought in a wagon and hauled his wife's remains elsewhere; Grant and her companions were stunned. "Such a scene," Marie Grant wrote, "I never witnessed before, and hope I never shall again."

Though we know little of the Zanhorns, we can surmise what they symbolized for Marie Grant. An alleged frequenter of the saloon, Mr. Zanhorn represented the evils of the undisciplined life so feared by the evangelicals. On the other hand, his wife exemplified the idea of the "deserving poor." Relief workers were always vigilant not to aid "unworthy and trifling people" who turned to the city for charity.[30] For Marie Graham Grant, Mrs. Zanhorn's death must have suggested that poverty—at least in the case of the "deserving poor"— was a matter of gender, in that it was suffered by women and caused by male indolence and vice.

While members of the Ladies' Benevolent Society worked to uncover cases worthy of aid, some of their husbands were taking more business-like measures to cope with hard times by removing some competitive disadvantages. The owners of the Ohio Falls Iron Works, acting in concert with other manufacturers in the Ohio Valley Iron Association (OVIA), posted a notice declaring the adoption of a sliding scale that prevailed in Pittsburgh, which amounted to a 20 percent wage cut. The rolling mill men protested and left work when management proved inflexible. Along with others across the Ohio Valley, they convened at Covington, Kentucky and unanimously rejected the new sliding scale as "not just" and agreed to strike.[31] As the strike entered its second month, the OVIA met in Louisville and raised the stakes, declaring that any workman who refused to accept their terms by February 20 would be discharged and blacklisted, which the National Labor Tribune (NLT) denounced as "obnoxious to all honorable and independent workingmen."[32]

In New Albany, ironworkers maintained a tight discipline that kept the Ohio Falls Iron Works closed well into the spring. Aiming to prevent the operation of the mill with "blacksheep," they addressed readers of the NLT, informing them that they were fighting for their "just rights" and requesting ironworkers to stay away.[33] When management sought to run the mill in late March with the services of strikebreakers from Chattanooga, the union men explained the situation to the new workers, who then refused to go to work. And when a few strikers appeared ready to return to work in mid-April, the more resolute men persuaded them to maintain their defiance of the owners. Two days later, however, the Ohio Falls Iron Works started with nonunion men, despite the presence of a crowd outside the mill. Large placards declaring "no admission except by permission from the office" were posted and those violating the order, warned the Ledger-Standard, "would doubtless be summarily dealt with."[34] Ten days later most of the union men replaced them.[35]

Ironworkers elsewhere waged this strike with the support of the local community. City governments refused to cooperate with manufacturers, and newspapers like the Times of Portsmouth, Ohio, portrayed the members of the OVIA "velvet-lined aristocrats" and challenged their "right" to circulate a blacklist of workers like "the name of a thief is sent from one police station to another."[36] In New Albany it was another matter. At the outset, the *Ledger-Standard* bemoaned the forced idleness of over two hundred wage earners by a small contingent of skilled workers. When the Chattanooga men refused to work, the press of both parties accused the union of plying them with whiskey and then forcing them out of town, a tale denied by the Tennesseans themselves. Later the press condemned the union for foiling the startup in April and suggested that city officials "let a few of these meddlers in other people's business look through the bars of a jail for a few weeks for their unwarrantable interference." The *Commercial* lamented that "a large number of families are compelled to suffer on account of six or eight men who control the strike."[37]

That ironworkers were able to hold out as long as they did was due to the solidarities that they developed at work and in the neighborhoods surrounding the mills. The Sixth Ward had long been a center of hostility to the rich, and so it continued to be in the industrial era. Voters there regularly elected workers, often a former leader of the ship carpenters' union, to council, a practice that distinguished them from the electorate of any other ward. Ironworkers had established their own institutions, including a cooperative grocery and a dancing club during the years of prosperity. A sense of otherness pervaded the working-class community of the west end. Now engaged in a strike and faced with the hardships of a depression, west end workers—mostly employees of the Ohio Falls Iron Works—organized a "Have Nothing" carnival to be held on St. Valentine's Day. Despite the temperance background of many of the organizers like John Fogle, in the spirit of inclusiveness they permitted participants to drink alcohol—though all would be limited to a two quart bottle—and encouraged "all who want to mix a little fun with their poverty" to join the festivities.[38]

These processions, which lasted through the depression, shared with European carnivals a public setting in which antielite sentiments could be expressed. Figures of the day were both praised and lampooned, including Horace Greeley and Boss Tweed. Others portrayed cultural types, like the Carpetbagger, or the "Vivandiere" who was prominent in depictions of the Paris Commune.[39] The poverty that afflicted workers was symbolized by some who wore ragged clothing held together with patches. The most pointed barbs, however, were reserved for local politicians who voted money to railroads and used office to line their own pockets. During the 1876 procession opponents of the Air-Line stood out for the intense crowd support they were given. The popularity of these affairs ebbed and flowed with the depression. In 1875, the *Ledger-Standard* suggested that the "Independent Order of Have Nothings" had grown with reinforcements from the "Dependent Order of Do Nothings." Five years later the paper noted that such parades were "about played out in New Albany." Since many of the carnival organizers had been prominent in the WRA, some believed the Have-Nothings to be the embryo of an independent party. Yet it never was born.[40]

For in the midst of the ironworkers' strike, and just a couple of weeks after the Have Nothing parade, New Albany was caught in a whirlwind of agitation as local women led a sustained drive to close down saloons. The "women's crusade" antagonized Germans, while dislodging workers from the rest of the temperance movement. And the passions it stirred spilled over into the spring elections.

Temperance advocates throughout Indiana were given a boost in early 1873 when the Republican majority in the legislature passed the "Baxter Bill," a local option law that permitted saloons to operate only if a majority of voters in a ward or township signed a petition. In New Albany, supporters of the measure marshalled their forces to assure proper enforcement, and they received cross-class support. This was not surprising for local temperance conventions usually attracted working-class activists like George Hipple and John Fogle.[41]

The nature of the temperance movement dramatically changed the following spring. Beginning in December 1873 in Hillsboro, Ohio, women from bourgeois families confronted saloonkeepers and their customers, singing and praying that proprietors would give up the business. Blessed with great success in Ohio, the women's crusade spread throughout the Midwest during the winter and spring.[42] In February it made its way to New Albany, where the same leading citizens who had led the relief effort just two months before now met to organize against the saloon. Large numbers of women, excited by tales of success elsewhere, came to hear crusader Mrs. Hunt, a Quaker from Indianapolis, exhort them to form praying bands. Hunt brought her audience to tears when she spoke of the misery that wives and children experienced at the hands of drunkard husbands. Marie Grant, and undoubtedly others who had attempted to bury Mrs. Zanhorn just three weeks before, were persuaded.[43]

We need not doubt the sincerity of the participants to find other elements at work. Representing three different churches on the ex-

ecutive board of the first meeting were W. C. DePauw, Peter Stoy, and
E. M. Hubbert, officers of the Ohio Falls Iron Works. A week later,
DePauw donated a large hall as a headquarters for the crusaders. On
the other hand, working-class activists like Fogle and Hipple, so visible in citywide temperance meetings in the past, were nowhere to
be seen.[44] Like elsewhere, the New Albany crusade was a movement
of the well-to-do.[45] Orderly crowds of educated and prosperous wom-
en marched from saloon to saloon, singing hymns and praying for the
salvation of the proprietors.[46] While the class background of the crusaders may have been intimidating, that they were women made
male saloonkeepers all the more uncomfortable. When it was at all
possible they avoided the crusaders, instead sending their wives to
meet them. One band of praying women was met by a Mrs. Futterer,
a large muscular woman who ordered them to be on their way. When
told they intended to sing and pray, she threatened, "I will spill every drop of my blood, right here on this pavement before you shall
sing and pray here." When the women began to pray, speaking of the
"heavenly father," Futterer interrupted with "your father is in hell—
the devil is your father." At other times, the crusaders were deluged
with insults from women leaning out of second-story windows; on
at least one occasion, they were spat upon.[47]

The crusading spirit eventually filtered down to the poor. West
end women, who "complain that they cannot dress well enough to
attend the meetings in the central part of the city," organized praying bands at the Mission Chapel near the ironworks. Here, where the
class background of crusader and saloonkeeper were similar, tensions
remained low. Saloonkeeper George Kramer stood respectfully with
the women as they prayed, and John Livingston told them he wished
he could quit the business, an admission that brought tears to their
eyes.[48]

On one level, the crusade threatened a revolution in gender relations. Though their desire to defend the family was traditional
enough, the crusaders articulated it in new places. Taking the lead in
public meetings and marching from saloon to saloon, they acknowledged a right to act forcefully in the public sphere. One historian has
described the crusade as "a liberating force for a group of church-ori-
ented women who could not have associated themselves directly
with the equal rights or suffrage movements."[49] That such a challenge had been made, however subtly, was grasped by local Presbyterians, who in the middle of the enthusiasm had pledged their support
for the women. Just a year later, the same body approved the sentiments of George C. Heckman of Hanover College, who denied that

women had any public role at all. "Woman cannot depart from her sphere," he warned, "without misfortune to herself and calamity to society."[50]

The crusade polarized New Albany in other ways. Though the movement gained converts for the temperance cause, few saloons were closed, and the effort led much of the German community to close ranks. Many Germans did not consider the drinking of beer to be sinful, and they viewed the Baxter law as an infringement on their civil rights. A letter, written by "An American of German Descent," defended "industrious" members of the community whose consumption of alcohol was "sensibly and moderately enjoyed, in well regulated saloons and gardens, in company with their families, ministers and teachers." Hardly sinful, the beer gardens were filled with a *"true* feeling of gratitude to their creator for the enjoyment vouchsafed them."[51]

The stage was set for a political showdown over temperance. Though cultural and religious enthusiasms had pushed the ironworkers' strike out of the public eye, the language of class was still deemed effective in stimulating political action. While the local Democratic party remained neutral during the spring campaign, it did not prevent a few Democrats from joining a group of political neophytes to protest the crusade. Among them was lawyer James V. Kelso, who renewed his attacks on bondholders, whose exemption from taxation left laboring men "enslaved" to make up the difference. Addressing "bondholder-crusader," Kelso asked: "suppose the good and frugal wives of the taxed yeomanry should move upon the works of the bondholders, and like Jacob of old, wrestle in prayer and song with them until they consented to be taxed like common people, what would you say to that?" Lawyer John S. Davis argued that bankers and capitalists were behind the crusade. "Who pays all their expenses?" Who pats them on the back and says pray on sister?" he inquired."[52] Kelso later warned Sixth Ward voters that temperance men would issue an additional $300,000 in bonds for the Air-Line Railroad.[53]

In a close election, temperance candidates—among them ship carpenter Jacob Alford in the Sixth Ward—won four of six council seats.[54] Party lines were not tightly drawn and the presence of the saloon remained the sole substantive issue. Buoyed by success, DePauw and other wealthy men organized a convention in October to support temperance men for office. This meeting, too, was devoid of working-class leadership.[55] Temperance in New Albany may be understood in context of church women's efforts to remove an evil that they confronted in their benevolent work and to expand their own public role, or as another effort of iron manufacturers to create a disciplined labor force. In either case, the result was that issues of unionization and the iron strike were deeply submerged.

The Structure of Political Opportunity

Unlike their contemporaries in Evansville who had developed a loose alliance with local Democrats, New Albany workers made little impact on the election of 1874. It was not due to a lack of workplace or community organization. Skilled men in the iron trades had unionized before the depression and their counterparts in the various departments of the glassworks had demonstrated the ability to wage successful strikes. In large working-class neighborhoods, workers formed cooperatives and recreational societies. The years to come would bring more organization, and from time to time widespread anticapitalist, or at least antielite, sentiment was evident.

However, party politics offered New Albany workers little. Susceptible as election campaigns were to religious and ethnic rivalries, the division of the working class into blocs of skilled native, British, and German workers, as well as unskilled native, German, and Irish laborers, was an obstacle to political unity. While class and ethnicity reinforced each other in Evansville, in New Albany class unity was frequently destroyed by cultural divisions.

Yet, ethnicity and class could not always be separated. At its inception, the WRA appeared to be the expression of class-conscious unionized workers before Republican politicians deftly guided the movement into accepting both temperance and the Air-Line. Still, workers like John Fogle and George Hipple continued to lead the WRA, indicating that in their minds issues like temperance were not incompatible with antielite politics. On the other hand, in 1874, when ethnic and moral issues seemed so clearly to be the ground on which the battle would be fought, anti-Temperance men drew on class resentments to delegitimate the women's crusade and its offspring, the temperance ticket.

It was no coincidence that the use of anticapitalist rhetoric was made during a campaign in which the traditional party apparatuses remained neutral. Most prominent local Democrats were tied closely to Washington C. DePauw. While iron and glass workers were putting together the original platform for the WRA, the *Ledger* announced it would support a gubernatorial bid by DePauw.[56] Even in the 1880s, after DePauw had changed parties, the *Ledger* treated him gently. Instead of using strikes to political advantage with workers, Republicans and Democrats publicly supported DePauw.

This extended to matters of public policy. In a hastily called meeting during the 1877 railroad strikes, the council granted DePauw's request to appoint a special police force to protect the city's factories, though locally there had been no agitation. When an objection to holding a closed private session was raised, one councilmember retorted that the men who paid three-fourths of the city taxes were "entitled to be heard."[57]

DePauw's extensive power was most clearly unmasked in 1878 when he coerced the city into giving him land and granting him substantial tax advantages. In a petition calling on the city to vacate without compensation the streets that ran between the buildings of the glassworks, DePauw warned that failure to do so would lead him to "hunt acres elsewhere or quit." Expecting hostility, he urged the council to comply only if it was in the city's interest, adding "it is not necessary for anyone to throw mud or use ugly words."[58]

For the next two months the Ledger-Standard urged compliance. The editors argued that granting the petition was better policy than driving 2–3,000 citizens out of the city for want of work. They warned that loss of the glassworks would leave the Air-Line a smaller coal market and, consequently, less motivation to complete the road to New Albany. Such a turn of events would force the iron mills to move to cities with better facilities.[59] And DePauw's threat appeared to be a good one. In late April it was reported that DePauw visited Cleveland and Pittsburgh to inspect sites for a glass factory.[60]

While the council approved the vacating of the streets in mid-April, presentation of the petition to exempt the works from taxation was delayed until after the spring election.[61] The committee on ordinances, comprised of DePauw's business associates, reported favorably on the petition and offered a future expansion of the works as a carrot to the council. By redrawing the city's boundaries and keeping the glassworks in operation, they argued, "the City will thereby have increased her taxable property much more than what is lost," adding that "a failure to do so will result in a loss to the city of these extensive works." When asked what guarantee the city had that expansion would result, the prominent G. C. Cannon and John Winstandley vouched for DePauw. That was good enough for most, and the council decided eleven to one to support the petition.[62]

The decision was greeted with displeasure from those the Ledger-Standard termed "grumblers." A brief campaign was waged by the press to justify it. The Commercial defended the measure as "a matter of policy," and denied it was adopted or asked for "as a matter of right." In its support, the *Ledger-Standard* claimed "we have never known so great unanimity among the business men and taxpayers." DePauw, himself, defended the honor of his intentions, reminding the people of New Albany, needlessly perhaps, that "in every ward and block . . . men live that have borrowed money of me, that have worked for me, that have dealt with me." The Louisville *Courier-Journal* summed up the affair poetically, "like unto the city of New Albany, we will stand or fall with Mr. Washington DePauw."[63]

In this political environment debate by the two parties lacked the charged class rhetoric used by Evansville Democrats. This had not always been so. Years before James Kelso, with the blessings of the *Ledger*, had scoured bondholders and capitalists during the Congressional election of 1866.[64] As late as 1873, Democrats had delved into the antimonopoly tradition to denounce Republican legislation for being "in the interest of capital, favoring the rich manufacturers in certain portions of the country to the detriment of the laboring interests."[65] Democrats were rewarded, particularly in the Sixth Ward, by broad support until the 1873 convention, when banker Winstandley defeated ship carpenter St. John for the party's mayoral nomination.

The depression and the outbreak of industrial conflict changed all that. In increasingly shrill tones, the Democratic press took trade unionists to task. Members of unions "must learn," lectured the *Ledger-Standard*, "they have no right to interfere with others."[66] In the years to come the editors maintained a firm commitment to the free labor contract. "If they don't like their places" the newspapermen suggested, "they can leave." In response to the railroad strikes of 1877, they argued that the workers had "no business . . . to inquire whether the officers' salaries have been cut." Their only concern was whether or not they could accept the wage cut. "If they cannot, they have one simple duty, one and only one, the right to quit and seek employment elsewhere. The strikers have no more right to band themselves together and take charge of the trains and stop the business of the road, than a lot of dead beats would have on the Fourth of July to go to a livery stable and take charge of the stock because the livery man charged them a little more on that day." The strike was blamed on the "Communistic element, the hangers on of society, the men who do not earn their bread by the sweat of their brow." From this element, railroad corporations deserved protection.[67]

In an attempt to restore the relative harmony of the past, the *Ledger-Standard* tried to revive the broadest interpretations of producerism. Noting that "those who style themselves workingmen" often appropriated the term "producer" assuming "that they are about the only persons who work, and that all other people live upon their labor," the editors argued that manualists were "but one class of workers." Retailers and white collar workers provided essential services, they reminded their readers. More to the point, they defended bankers and other capitalists. Such monied men, by accumulating fortunes and then investing them in factories, provided workers with the means to toil. Capital and labor were not inherently antagonistic, they concluded, for "the whole social system . . . is one of mutual dependence" and "the real interests of all classes are harmonious."[68] Here, more defensively stated, were the old assumptions frequently bandied about to celebrate the virtues of the antebellum social order. From this point on, the local leadership of both parties would deny any legitimacy to class conflict.

Working-Class Organization

The point at which labor reformers departed from the political press was in the interpretation of harmony. While politicians argued that it prevailed and that conflict resulted from the instigation of malcontents, workers believed organization was needed to restore any semblance of it. For most of the Gilded Age an uneasy truce existed between these outlooks; workers choosing, for the most part, not to involve their organizations in politics, and politicians threatening them with ruin should they form an independent party.

New Albany proved fertile ground for sporadic working-class organization. In addition to the benevolent Independent Order of Working Men (IOWM), workers from the factory trades organized the Workingmen's Assembly of New Albany. The assembly was born when the glassblower's union admitted a committee of puddlers from the Sons of Vulcan to discuss citywide organization. Most of the participants for whom we have data were married, middle-aged and modestly propertied workmen who recently moved to New Albany. Half of them hailed from Pennsylvania, and both groups of workmen regularly corresponded with John M. Davis, Master Workman of District Assembly No. 3 of Pittsburgh, the most powerful Knights of Labor assembly in the Midwest.[69] On making the necessary arrangements, the blowers and puddlers issued a call for all workers to meet at Woodward Hall in the Fifth Ward.

All the competing strains that constituted the nineteenth-century American labor movement were present in this meeting.[70] A rationalist belief in human progress was juxtaposed with the evangelical's respect for the bounty provided by "the All-wise Providence of God." Glassblower Isaac Whetsel, president of the IOWM and chairman of the meeting, led the three hundred workers in the hall through a revivalistic recitation of the grievances of labor. "Unite in a sold column," counseled Whetsel, "and stand up squarely for the rights of man according to the designs of God." If they failed to cultivate a "fraternal feeling," he warned, then capital surely "would press labor to the wall." The workers argued that capital sought to degrade labor and "to form distinct classes in society." To prevent "these outrages on the part of capital," workers were urged to combine and "as American citizens . . . assert their rights in controlling the destinies of their country." Only by so doing could republican workers "uphold the high rank which labor should maintain in society." The message was endorsed by the audience, which resolved unanimously to form "an associated brotherhood" known as the "———— of the city of New Albany."

The press found the meeting disturbing. The *Ledger-Standard* noted an "earnest spirit" but also a "disposition to complain of the want of proper compensation for their employment." Though they approved of the "moderate" tone of the speakers, the editors noticed "a feeling prevalent among them that they are wronged." Rather than combine against capital, they urged workers to be self-reliant, "leaving their more fortunate neighbors to paddle their own canoe." Moreover, they urged workers to "eschew partizan politics in your organizations." While the *Commercial* did not cover the event, it criticized the leaders for not allowing a black worker to join.[71]

Though the meeting was covered by the *Ledger-Standard*, there are reasons to suspect that this was an attempt to organize an early assembly of the then-secret Knights of Labor. In addition to ties that the leaders had to master workman Davis in Pittsburgh, and the omission of the name of the organization, the structure of membership anticipates the Knights. Though the leaders called for the organization of all trades, each to be represented in united council, men from thirty-one callings (including a master barber and silversmith, both of very modest means) joined a committee on permanent organization, bringing tanners, shoemakers, tailors, and even unskilled laborers in association with highly skilled iron and glass workers. Further, immigrants joined with native-born workmen. Much as the Knights would do in Evansville, the Workingmen's Assembly attempted to strengthen trade unionism without excluding the mass of workers.

Also striking is the continuity displayed in working-class organization. Three of the speakers at the meeting—Whetsel, John Fogle, and Sam Milligan—had been active in the WRA four years before. Whetsel and Milligan were joined by tailor William Shaw, from the IOWM. Throughout the 1870s, the same men worked in different ways to raise the dignity of labor. Beginning in politics, they later confined their activities to the working-class community when the political climate became more hostile.

The need to perfect organization was well understood by even the most highly paid workers. Those in the glass and iron mills submitted to a series of wage cuts during the depression.[72] And workers were plagued by more than wage disputes. When William Rosenbaum, a new superintendent in the window glass house, encouraged blowers to increase their output, some responded with a record-setting pace. During the week ending January 21, 1875, nine men made over sixty boxes of glass, led by twenty-four-year-old Levi Pierce, who blew 85.5 boxes.[73] Such individualistic efforts to expand productivity and earnings divided their ranks and brought censure from glassblowers across the country. The "big blowers" were criticized by the *NLT*, which argued that no "respectable blower" would produce so much. Overproduction threatened the jobs of men who could not keep up such a health threatening pace, they warned, and went on to say that "when a man blows 80 boxes of glass he is unfit to be a man and cannot enjoy life, books, society, or even his victuals."[74] Managers of the firm tried to convince workers that the union was merely jealous of Pierce. A letter was sent to the *NLT* defending Rosenbaum with Pierce's name signed to it. Others accused the superintendent of penning the correspondence and claimed that Pierce had been "prostrated by piles from his overwork."[75]

A visit by a traveling correspondent found the situation had been resolved as the men "pulled up" when Rosenbaum revealed himself as a "nigger driver." The incident demonstrated the role that unions played as a school. "Uneducated" workmen, he claimed, did little but work or "sit in saloons and play cards for beer" without thinking of their interests, or those of their fellow blowers. Young workers needed guidance from lodge members who can "recover" them after making "a false step."[76]

Independent Political Action

The depression continued to hold its grip on the city until the spring of 1879. Times were particularly hard for ironworkers, who since losing the strike in 1874 had experienced periodic unemployment, and once again political opposition to elite rule emanated from the Sixth Ward, this time within the structure of the Greenback movement.[77] The independent path, on which New Albany workers had brief and modest success, was cleared by the hostility of the established party leadership to monetary radicalism.

An attempt was made by James Kelso, long known as "the workingman's friend," to steer the Democrats into the Greenback camp at the county convention of 1876. Presenting a resolution calling for repeal of the resumption act, the printing of more greenbacks, and "taxing the rich man's bond the same as the poor man's cottage," Kelso was denounced by the dominant hard-money wing of the party. Jonathan Peters, proprietor of the *Ledger-Standard*, called him a "ratty Democrat." When John Winstandley denied that this was Democratic doctrine, Kelso replied that he had copied it from the 1872 state party platform, causing a sensation in the room. The Winstandley men stood firm, however, voting to table Kelso's resolution, and Kelso temporarily left for the Greenback party.[78]

The campaign of 1876 was a straight party affair, however, and local Democrats swept the election, promising an end to repression in the southern states, a lower tariff and a return of prosperity.[79] Though a Greenback ticket was nominated, it did woefully in every ward. The pattern held the following spring, as the Democrats swept the city offices based on huge majorities in every ward but the Fifth, which split its vote.[80] The depression had been kind to New Albany Democrats. Without indulging in class rhetoric, they were able to stigmatize the Republicans as the party of depression and corruption.

It was the railroad strikes of 1877 that reawakened the political militancy of the ironworker community. Meetings were held that August at a stable in the Sixth Ward. Joining with workers from other wards, they formed a small section of the socialist Workingmen's party of the United States. Political newcomers like machinist Peter Campbell and glass flattener John Steel joined activists Isaac Whetsel and George Hipple in giving the organization direction.[81] Its status as a purely working-class party was short-lived, for its leaders leaned toward fusion with the Greenback party. By September, the two groups were holding joint meetings.[82]

The revitalized Greenback party entered the Spring campaign with great vigor. With a full slate nominated for the April township election, the leaders warned workers to beware of tricks from the "old parties" and urged them to "vote for workingmen who have the interest of the whole people at heart."[83] Running against the Democrats, the Greenbackers received between 24 and 37 percent of the vote in the upper five wards, and a large majority in the Sixth.[84] Though they lost, they were encouraged and turned their efforts toward the election of a city council ticket.

Election day brought success as the new party, aided by Republican voters, elected three candidates to council.[85] However, two were longtime Republican merchants who, once elected, worked in concert with their former colleagues, ignoring efforts of the Greenback party to control them. The other, wholesale grocer Reuben P. Main, was more closely affiliated with the movement, but worked to defuse the militancy of its working-class constituency, which now provided the majority of the party's activists. Older leaders like Dummer Hooper, George Hipple, and Isaac Whetsel worked with newcomers to politics like molders Fred Bethel and Joseph Taylor in keeping Greenbackers true to the interests of workingmen.[86] In the fall, their candidate, A. E. Long, nearly defeated the Democratic nominee for Congress, losing by less than three hundred votes. Fred Bethel lost by an even smaller margin in his race for state representative. Again, the Sixth Ward, where two-thirds of the voters cast ballots for Long and Bethel, was most resolute in its support for the Greenback-Labor cause.[87]

By the following spring, Greenback support had largely dissolved with respectable totals being tallied only in the Sixth Ward where voters elected ship carpenter Charles Jones in a three-party race.[88] The campaign had been a trying one. Since the party emerged as a force, Democrats had charged it was operating in the interests of the Republican party. The *Commercial* charged the opposite. The result was a schism on the party's central committee. Divisiveness reemerged after the election when councilmember Charles Schively, who had been elected as a Greenbacker in 1878, went into caucus with the Republicans. Greenbackers who previously were Democrats condemned the move, while Republican Greenbackers ignored it.[89] Greenbackers never again mounted a serious challenge to the other parties.

Militance and Division

Inspired by the return of prosperity in 1879, workers responded with renewed organizing and militance at the workplace. Despite the breadth of this activity, they remained deeply divided, with the only intertrade support coming under the auspices of the Knights of Labor. And among the rest of the community, striking workers found little sympathy.

The strike wave was initiated in June by the molders' union, who in concert with workers in Jeffersonville and Louisville, won the restoration of a 20 percent wage cut they had voluntarily submitted to the year before.[90] Four months later, rising prices and increased orders led them to demand a further advance of 15 percent, to which Terstegge and Gohmann submitted.[91] At the same time the cigar makers struck for a raise in the piece-rate of $1 per thousand.[92] By the end of 1881 the molders had successfully waged two more strikes, and the puddlers, rollers, heaters and buggymen in the iron mills had each struck once.[93] It was the strike of English plate glass finishers in the winter of 1880, however, that most fully revealed the class tensions in the community and their relationship to other sources of division within the working class.

The plate glassworkers—including polishers, smoothers and grinders—were ready for a confrontation with DePauw. Most of them were English and had been brought to America by the Star Glass Company. Claiming that they were promised regular work at between $14 and $20 a week, the workers instead found the labor market overflowing. Consequently they made between $5 and $10 a week.[94] The problem was exacerbated when DePauw closed his Louisville glassworks and then discharged some of the workers who had established a local assembly of the Knights of Labor, hiring the Louisville men in their place.[95] In addition, the stress of supporting their families who, in many cases, had remained in England weighed heavily upon them.

The workers waited for what they thought was a opportune moment to recoup some of their losses. The week before DePauw planned to operate the works at full capacity, they demanded a 15 percent advance. Arguing that after the rising costs of raw material and the losses from heavy breakage "there is nothing left for me," DePauw adamantly refused, though he promised a share of any rise in the price of glass.[96] On January 29 he and his family left for Florida and two days later the strike commenced.[97]

The press was used from the start against the strikers. The *Commercial* immediately conjured up the specter of the removal of the works, suggesting that they may never open again.[98] From Florida DePauw issued a reply to the grievances of the strikers that was published in the *Ledger-Standard* and which set the tone for the rest of the strike. Chastising the workers for their "dense ignorance" of trade conditions and their carelessness in handling cast glass, DePauw questioned their status as skilled workers. He also attacked their independence, suggesting they had been paupers in England. In a blatantly inaccurate article, the *Ledger-Standard* announced that Joseph Keehner, a 23 year old English polisher and strike leader, had stated that "DePauw's letter was unanswerable," and that the strike was forced on him and other "old hands" by the men newest to New Albany.[99] The attempt to divide workers and portray the strike as a cabal of a small number of men roused the ire of the union men and led to a boycott of the Democratic organ.

The effort continued through the course of the strike. An attempt to intimidate a strikebreaking glass cutter by three men led to their arrest by the city police. Ed Cutler, a 38 year old English glassblower, was convicted by the city court and fined $12.60. Also arrested was Matt Scanlan, probably an English glassworker as well, who met the $100 bail.[100] The *Ledger-Standard* predictably responded by labeling strikers as "Molly Maguires," but the incident also suggests the importance of ethnic bonds between English workers in different crafts, especially since the predominantly native glassblowers' union remained neutral during the strike.

Plate glassworkers fought with the aid of the Knights of Labor. After three weeks, the strikers found themselves running out of provisions and turned to Otto Hoffman, a member of Local Assembly 846 and the owner of a small grocery. Hoffman had once sustained a life-threatening injury while employed at the Star Glass Works, and he was anxious to help the union.[101] So that they would not be forced to capitulate to DePauw, whom he termed "the greatest tyrant and labor-crusher on earth," Hoffman sold to the strikers on credit.[102] Some men, still short of money, survived the strike shoveling coal or working on the river.[103]

A few strikers traveled to neighboring cities looking for sources of aid. Much of their support came from Jeffersonville, where an organized labor movement and a sympathetic Democratic press had forged the kind of alliance seen in Evansville. The Jeffersonville *Evening News* was in a particularly militant mood in 1880, and it denounced DePauw to workers as a "heartless capitalist" who "rolls in fatness while they want food." It belittled threats that the glassworks would be moved as "one of DePauw's old tricks." Praising the "gallant fight" of the New Albany men, the editor urged Jeffersonville workers to cut tobacco and liquor expenditures for a month, sending the savings to the strikers.[104]

Emotions intensified in March when the chemical department and the pot house of the glassworks were burned down. The strikers themselves were dismayed by the incident and posted a $500 reward for the arrest and conviction of the perpetrator.[105] This probable act of rage may have cost DePauw money, but it cost the strikers a great deal of public support. Already fighting a boycott, the *Ledger-Standard* responded to the fire with a nativist frenzy. Strikers were now characterized as "cowardly foreign paupers," and were warned that a "well-loaded shot-gun will reach further than the incendiary's torch."[106]

To rally the working-class community, the Knights of Labor organized a mass "indignation" meeting for the evening of March 20. Two railroad cars full of workers from Louisville and another from Jeffersonville joined the New Albany workers, and 1,000 of them crowded into the courthouse. Speakers played to the crowd's resentment of DePauw. One from Louisville, denied he was a benefactor to New Albany, arguing to great applause that twenty-five years before there were "no millionaires, nor soup houses in New Albany . . . the people owned a little money and everybody was contented and happy." But the war had changed all that. After standing "shoulder to shoulder fighting for principles," workers returned to find that a neighbor had amassed a "colossal fortune selling shoddy clothing to the government, or in furnishing damaged wheat to the soldiers." New Albany molder Henry Fecker, an organizer for the Knights, blamed DePauw for creating a "den of misery and destitution of New Albany." Fecker urged workingmen to use the vote wisely to remedy the situation, and in making his argument, spoke to recent city history: "I suppose the honorable city dads are looking for another election, for another grab, to exempt DePauw from another $50,000 taxation. He was to double the capacity of the works. He has doubled the capacity of the paupers. Who pays his taxes? The man alongside of him with his little cottage. If he don't the sheriff comes along."[107]

The *Ledger-Standard* responded with an unprecedented level of vindictiveness, denouncing the meeting as the work of "shameless vagabonds, blatant bummers, and despicable demagogues from the hellholes of Louisville and Jeffersonville." Such men need not be surprised, they warned, "if indignant citizens take them in hand and drown them in the Ohio River as they deserve." Turning to the strikers, the editors ranted "the lousy stinking paupers must go. They cannot run New Albany. The incendiaries need hanging and shooting." The editors encouraged citizens to shoot boycott supporters, and attempts to intimidate individuals were made as in the case of a 25 year old union molder: "Henry Jansing, are you not ashamed of your small action in refusing to buy a half gallon of molasses from a grocer who subscribes and pays for the *Ledger-Standard*. Do you want to be ranked with communists and incendiaries? Can you afford to?"[108]

Some of the clergy joined in the denunciations. The reverend J. L. Pitner spoke at the Methodist Wesley Church and decried the threat to individualism posed by trade unions and the monopolization of skills by workers who "refuse to impart a knowledge of their trade to any but their nearest relatives." Nativism, too, was present in the good reverend's sermon when he asserted that "leaders of the most violent strikes" are often foreign-born and warned "we cannot consent for Europe to skim her slums and dash the scum onto our faces, without a protest."[109]

The strike continued another four weeks as DePauw, busy repairing the damage to the burned buildings, outwaited the union. In the meantime he penned a paternalistic rejoinder to the strikers. He scolded them for not standing by him while his capital employed "directly or indirectly nearly one-half of the population of this city . . . often at a loss." When they were in need, DePauw claimed he never refused aid. Yet the workers inflicted a "heavy loss" on him by waging a "causeless strike," and he asked them "do you wonder that capital is timid, and millions are idle?"[110]

The men surrendered in late April when Otto Hoffman's supplies ran out.[111] To reclaim their jobs, they were forced to sign an agreement renouncing the union and promising to stay away from saloons. Ten strike leaders who were refused employment soon left for the glassworks in Crystal City, Missouri.[112] Those who remained faced harassment from the police, in response to which they formed an organization "for mutual protection and defence against annoying arrests." Paying a dollar a month into a treasury for the hiring of attorneys, the members may well have been sowing the seeds of a new union.[113]

The loss of the strike by the workers is not surprising. In addition to facing a hostile business community and an unpromising political apparatus, workers themselves were divided. This was true even within the confines of LA 846 of the Knights of Labor. Organized in 1878, the assembly was soon plagued by religious rivalries. Catholic Knights complained that some members were also affiliated with the secret "Elephant" society, which was opposed to any political presence by the Catholic church, particularly with regard to the schools.[114] Nativism had long been present in worker organizations like the Order of United American Mechanics, which derived support from a broad cross-section of working-class New Albany.[115] "Elephants" claimed responsibility for the sole Greenback victory during the 1879 council election, and the 1880 Greenback candidate from that ward was also said to be "tainted" with "elephantism."[116]

There may have been some truth to the *Ledger-Standard*'s assertion that local union men were hostile to the English strikers. In any case, between October 1879 and October 1880 the membership of L.A. 846 declined by over 50 percent, and in 1881 it disbanded.[117]

Within the glassworks, itself, divisions were equally visible. There an aristocracy of highly paid glassblowers arose—based on the difficulty of the production process—and their relations with DePauw were strikingly different. The *Ledger-Standard* frequently remarked on this, suggesting that the blowers fondly referred to DePauw as "Uncle Wash."[118] Indeed, during the summer following the plate glass struggle, a minor dispute arose concerning the prompt payment of men before the July 4 holiday. Two conflicting letters to the labor press debated the role of superintendent George F. Penn. But even the angrier of the writers portrayed DePauw as a benevolent protector of the men and the victim of an overly aggressive underling.[119]

Labor relations in the window glass industry had become regularized during the 1880s when wage agreements were arrived at in meetings between committees of manufacturers and of workers, organized in Local Assembly 300 of the Knights of Labor, which served as a national trade union for window glassworkers.[120] Though a long hard fought strike occurred in the fall of 1883, when manufacturers failed in their attempt to lower wages and to eliminate restrictions on output or the number of apprentices, the focus was never local.[121]

The window glassworkers were interested in maintaining limits on production and job security, a matter exemplified in the response to William Rosenbaum in 1875. Essential to that goal was a limit on the number of apprentices who would be taught the craft. The New Albany men were at the forefront of the effort to do so. Representing the New Albany men at the 1883 convention of the national Window Glass Workers' Assembly, Levi Pierce proposed a plan to limit apprentices to 20 percent of the men employed and the establishment of a "Board of Examiners" to individually evaluate all applications to apprenticeship. The plan was adopted by the convention. Protection of the blower's craft led Pierce into the realm of nativist exclusion when he moved that foreign gatherers and blowers pay initiation fees of $50 and $75, respectively. Though the proposal was tabled, it suggests the inward outlook of the largely native-born window glassblowers of New Albany.[122]

Yet the organizing by the Irish of the Davitt Land League of New Albany suggested that ethnic hostility could be overcome. This Irish nationalist society, like many ethnic associations, was led mostly by the ethnic petty bourgeoisie. The message of the Land League, however, put it solidly in the labor reform tradition.[123] Local Protestant activists like George Hipple gave rousing speeches condemning the oppressive land laws imposed by the British on the Irish peasantry. The next week, Irish bricklayer Miles Kehoe, a member of the league's executive committee, and stove molder Tom O'Donnell organized and addressed a meeting of Irish workers.[124] While its existence may have been brief—there is no further mention of it after March by the press—the Davitt Land League demonstrated that ideological bonds could be forged between workers in the native and immigrant communities. And it pointed out the possible alliances that might have been forged in political activity.

Acquiescence Restored

As late as August 1880, molder Henry Fecker mounted an unsuccessful bid to capture the moribund Greenback party for workers. The only opponent to Reuben Main's nomination to the state senate, Fecker stressed the need for labor to be represented directly in the state legislature and not by "figureheads." Later he accused successful candidates of selling out the party.[125] Nevertheless, the energy of the independent movement was already spent.

The next five years were quiet ones in New Albany in that they were devoid of bitter strikes and were marked by party discipline. Democrats and Republicans attacked each other on the tariff and both attempted to capture the working-class vote. This was difficult for the Democrats in 1880, as little water had run under the bridge since the *Ledger-Standard*'s tirades of the previous spring. In the habit of denouncing unions, the paper declared free labor to be "true democratic doctrine," defining it as the absence of "compulsion of a single laborer to work or to abstain from work by organizations or societies of labor."[126]

For the most part, Republicans framed the debate in the glass and iron mill wards. At a Republican meeting in the first ward, Peter Stoy suggested that a Democratic victory and the lower tariff sure to follow would result in the closing of the Ohio Falls Iron Works. DePauw's eldest son, Newland, who only recently had become the business manager of the glassworks, warned workers that a vote for Winfield Scott Hancock, the Democratic candidate for president, was a vote for low wages, as the tariff issue had led his father into the Republican camp.[127] A week later, James Kelso equivocated when he said a Democratic "tariff for revenue only" would still provide "incidental protection as would cover and keep in perpetuity every

American industrial interest."[128] Generally the Democratic response was feeble, harking back to the glories of the steamboat building industry that thrived under Democratic administrations and its subsequent ruin under the Republicans.[129] In any case the Democrats carried New Albany for Hancock, though they lost the First Ward, and nearly the Sixth; the two wards had gone strongly for Tilden four years earlier.[130]

Four years later, the Democrats stepped up their appeals to workers. One Democrat accused the Republicans of pretending to be the special friend of "laboring men," while giving away the public domain to the railroads and refusing to establish labor bureaus and bans on foreign contract labor. On the tariff he said "the Democratic party is more in favor of protecting and encouraging labor than the Republicans, but not in favor of enriching monopolies."[131] At a meeting in the First Ward, Kelso pointed out that woolen mill operatives were on short time, and concluded that the "protected industries" were not giving employment to workers to the degree promised by the Republicans. Such appeals and a depression gave majorities to the Democrats of over 56 percent in every ward but the Fifth.[132]

Political calm reflected relative peace at the workplace. In the iron mills and the window glass house, workers in national unions allowed committees to handle wage disputes.[133] Conflicts were more regularized and less likely to be responses to local conditions. At the same time, party politicians appealed to workers without having to involve themselves in troublesome workplace issues. Workers, themselves, rarely demanded that they do so. And a number of prominent union men, like puddler George Roberts, roller Reese Prosser, and glassblower Levi Pierce, were incorporated into the leadership of the Republican party.[134] When the *Ledger-Standard* and *Commercial* spoke of the moderation of New Albany trade unionists, it was to such men that they referred. In 1883 Roberts won election to the city council, taking a seat that he would not relinquish until 1888.

The Knights of Labor Mobilize a Class

Class feeling reappeared in New Albany with the massive mobilization of workers in 1886. Under the umbrella of the Knights of Labor, local activists brought into the fold less-skilled workers who had previously been unorganized. Further, Protestant and Catholic workers were united under its auspices. Expanding their activities into politics, local Knights ran the most successful labor campaign of the nineteenth century in New Albany.

The movement began with the organization of Advance Assembly No. 3115 in 1884. A mixed assembly, it was largely composed of employees of the Louisville, New Albany, and Chicago Railroad (LNA&C), including skilled shop workers, clerks, brakemen, and laborers. The master workman of the assembly was stove molder John Kerrigan. In January 1886 the assembly included 110 of the 175 employees of the railroad in New Albany, and the *Commercial* noted that it was "in a very prosperous condition."[135] Two months later the Knights experienced phenomenal growth. Knights assemblies across the country were flooded with workers desiring to be initiated into the order, and New Albany was no exception. By the end of March, Knights organizers were forced to turn away two hundred working men and women attempting to join due to the smallness of the hall. Already the *Ledger* termed the Knights of Labor "the strongest labor body that has been formed in New Albany.[136]

The order continued to grow, initiating over five hundred workers on April 11. In 1886, six new assemblies were organized, two of them trade assemblies of furniture and railroad workers. Organizing was aided by visiting lecturers like Richard Trevellick who encouraged workers to join the order and to stay away from saloons. At the May Day parade held in Louisville, New Albany assemblies were able to send a contingent of five hundred Knights of Labor to participate.[137]

So long as they stayed clear of politics and refrained from violence, the *Ledger* had nothing but praise for the Knights. An extreme drop in the number of arrests, especially for drunkenness and disorderly conduct, were attributed by the editors to the Knights who "discourage liquor drinking, inculcate in their teachings the principles of morality, decidedly advocate public education, and enforce obedience to law."[138] There may have been some basis to this. As an alternative to the saloon the Knights organized recreational activities. The benefit drama "Ambition, or Thrown upon the World" was well attended as were picnics, balls, and moonlight excursions.[139] In April 1887, they organized a co-operative association. Enthusiasm for the Knights among the city's workers remained strong well into the spring.[140]

The success of the Knights rearranged political equilibrium. A new breed of politician, like Democrat Charles Jewett, praised the Knights of Labor and trade unions as organizations "worthy of the aid and support of all just men."[141] The Knights, however, endorsed the candidate and not the party, and the fall election of 1886 was a split ticket affair. J. K. Marsh, the labor Republican for Congress, swept the city with a clear majority over his Democratic and Republican rivals. In a race for the state legislature, Jewett barely prevailed after losing the endorsement of the Knights to Republican Tom Clarke, behind whom he ran in the First and Sixth wards by identical margins of 46.3 to 53.7 percent.[142]

Reactions to the election varied. The *Ledger* warned that by entering politics the Knights doomed themselves to failure. As a pressure group, they got a better reception. In the lower state house Charles Jewett introduced a labor bill requiring regular payment of miners, to which one New Albany Assembly adopted a resolution in appreciation, and a number of local Knights left for Indianapolis to lobby for the bill. State Senator John S. Day rewarded the Knights for their efforts by awarding molder Mike Farrell with a clerkship in the Senate.[143]

The success of the fall encouraged the Knights to run a Union Labor ticket in the spring. A newspaper, the *Evening Mail*, was established to serve as an organ, and Knight John Kerrigan was selected to run for the mayor's office.[144] In response, the Democrats ran incumbent butcher John J. Richards, and an independent movement of Republican and Democratic businessmen nominated lawyer Simeon K. Wolfe. The *Ledger* argued that the independent ticket would draw votes away from Richards, thus giving the election to the Knights. "Do thoughtful business men desire Mr. Kerrigan's election?" the editors asked. For the most part, the press ignored the Union Labor campaign, though the *Ledger* sometimes derisively spoke of "the Kerrigan side show."[145]

In a three-way race Kerrigan ran well, gathering 39.5 percent of the vote in the First Ward and 51.5 in the Sixth. The *Public Press*, a Democratic weekly, attributed Kerrigan's strong showing to the support of "nearly the entire labor vote."[146] Yet Richards' strength in the Fourth and Fifth wards was enough to make up the difference and Kerrigan fell short by 343 votes. Yet this was the first attempt by workers to run an independent citywide campaign and the closeness of the returns made Kerrigan and the Union Labor party appear to be a legitimate political force.

Heightened class feeling and increased worker organization led to the largest wave of strike activity yet to be seen in New Albany. In 1886 painters employed on the Kentucky and Indiana Bridge, spanning the Ohio River, quit for an advance of half a dollar a day. Employees of the LNA&C continued to organize throughout 1886, forming a trade assembly in the process. In February 1887 machine shop employees quit work in response to a long-standing grievance— late payment of wages. Citing the "Jewett Labor Bill" (incorrectly, as it happens) the workers refused to return until payment was made.[147] What distinguished this strike wave from others preceding it, however, was the large number by unskilled workers, especially during the last two weeks of March 1887.

The first to strike were the laborers employed in the American Foundry. They were followed three days later by the car washers employed by the Air-Line Railroad. In the days to follow helpers at Charles Hegewald's foundry, laborers at the rail mill, and the seven coal shovelers employed by merchant John Newhouse all demanded higher wages. In most cases wages were advanced. If not elsewhere, class solidarity came to play in the strike at Hegewald's, where the demands of the helpers were bolstered by a threat of the molders to strike.[148] It is no wonder that the *Ledger* thought businessmen should fear a Kerrigan victory.

Opposition to the Knights extended beyond the ballot box as employers assaulted one of the citadels of worker strength, the union shop at the National Stove Foundry of Terstegge, Gohmann & Co. Since 1877, molders had been at the forefront of every local working-class effort and organization that transcended narrow trade interests, and the Knights were no exception. Since the molders had first unionized in 1873, they had maintained a close relationship with the proprietors of the foundry. The Gohmanns themselves were molders, as was Andy Terstegge. At various times the journeyman sons of the owners had belonged to the union. The bonds between employer and employees were also political, as both were Democrats, and during campaigns they were known to demonstrate as a shop.

The trouble originated in a showdown between the Stove Founders' Defensive Association and the Iron Molders' Union. When a St. Louis firm, in the midst of a strike, sent its patterns to other foundries to meet its orders, a strike ensued as the molders at these foundries refused to work on the 'scab' patterns. As of April 14, none of the patterns had reached New Albany, and there seemed to be no reason to doubt the *Ledger* when it said none would in the future, for Terstegge and Gohmann "are in sympathy with their workmen and will always be found ready to do what is right toward them."[149] Four days later the firm introduced the scab patterns. Immediately molders and finishers refused to work until the offensive patterns were removed. In a public statement signed by Kerrigan and four others they explained, "every one of us are union men, and we fully appreciate that an injury to our brother toilers in any section of the country's the concern of us all."[150]

The employers remained intransigent. A local report suggests that the founders' association had lured the union into a strike they could not win.[151] For a month and a half the Gohmanns ran the foundry themselves with five apprentices.[152] In the beginning of June the scab patterns were removed, and the nature of the dispute changed into a battle for the open shop. Employers welcomed the molders to return to work, but as one said "we will keep the men and boys who have stood by us . . . the Union molders cannot complain of our works, for they are included in our offer." The union men vowed to fight on.[153]

It did not go well for the union. John Kerrigan was physically beaten by Andy Terstegge when he refused to retract a remark. And the union was battered too, as the foundry steadily acquired a set of nonunion men from Indianapolis, St. Louis, and Philadelphia. By mid-July, Terstegge, Gohmann & Company was an open shop. Several of its former employees subsequently found work in Hannibal, Missouri, and moved their families.[154]

The defeat crippled the Knights of Labor. With its most militant source of leadership caught up in a battle for survival, the assemblies of the Knights of Labor floundered. The membership of Advance Assembly No. 3115, which was nearly a thousand at the time of the spring election, dwindled to just seventy by November.[155] However, the dissolution of LA 3115 had internal sources as well. It appears that cigar maker John F. Connely and a number of carpenters hid the resources of the assembly, which soon became depleted of funds. At the same time, one of the carpenters, Peter Tellon, "raised a cry of the order being run by the Catholics."[156] Knowing that master workman John Kerrigan would be late, they packed a meeting and dissolved the assembly, leaving its property in their own hands. This was not a case of pure theft, however, for Tellon and fellow carpenter, P. H. McKamey, wrote Grand Master Workman of the Knights of Labor Terence Powderly to gain his blessing for the transfer of authority. Unaware of the nature of the factions, Powderly granted them the right to hold the assembly's charter, a decision he was soon to reverse.[157] It came too late; months of divisiveness had already done its work. By the end of 1888 a local of the United Brotherhood of Carpenters was organized, and the members elected P. H. McKamey financial secretary.[158]

The fall of the Knights of Labor left New Albany firmly in the grips of its businessmen. Politicians focused more than ever on the tariff. Woolen, glass, and ironworkers from local factories demonstrated at rallies, bearing their products and mottos like "free trade means low wages," "no competition with Pauper Labor," "Harrison, Morton and Protection means Roast Beef and Pie," and "Workingmen, Stand Together."[159] The following spring, the *Ledger* called for Democrats to nominate "the best business men as candidates." The Republicans, however, nominated the better businessman, banker, and manufacturer Morris McDonald, for mayor and he handily won.[160]

By the end of the year, local businessmen had united in a joint stock association known as the Commercial Club. Members were required to pay an initiation fee of $5, and the new organization soon included what the *Ledger* termed "the representative young business men of the city."[161] The selection of Newland T. DePauw as president was widely acclaimed.[162] The weekly meetings were given large play by the press, and the organization mainly worked to boost New Albany and to improve its facilities for manufacturing, like a scheme to pipe natural gas to the city.

End of an Era

Perhaps the most significant event for New Albany during these years was the death of DePauw in May 1887. He was glowingly eulogized by the *Ledger*. Employees and business associates drew up resolutions of tribute to the man, and fifteen thousand people were said to have attended his funeral and procession. One in a crowd of workingmen was heard to say "Washington C. DePauw was one of the best friends the poor men of New Albany ever had." Another, according to the *Ledger*, added "I would willingly have died myself if by doing so I could have prolonged his life; for it would have been spent in helping to give employment to the workingmen of New Albany."[163]

DePauw's death left his manufacturing empire in the hands of Newland and his brother Charles, who responded to the natural gas boom by relocating much of the glassworks to the gas belt in northern Indiana. The DePauws failed during the depression of the 1890s, and the effect on New Albany was enormous. During that decade the amount of capital invested in the city declined by 44 percent, the number of manufacturing establishments by 30 percent and the number of wage earners by 42 percent. Among the largest cities in Indiana in 1890 New Albany was the only one not to experience *any* industrial growth in the 1890s.[164]

During the last fifteen years of his life, Washington Charles DePauw dominated New Albany. In him, we have an example of the industrialist who did wield an extraordinary degree of power by forcing the city to grant him favors, by stifling the terms of political debate, and by acquiring the backing of the local judicial apparatus.

Few local politicians were willing to defend striking workers, for neither party saw it in its interest to antagonize DePauw. Without allies, workers of New Albany were forced to rely entirely on their own resources.

For the most part, that was not enough. Except for the persistence of a few ship carpenters, the industrial workers of New Albany were not long rooted in the community. Neither were they particularly homogeneous. In most of the larger works, native workmen worked alongside British immigrants and the second generation of the Irish and German community. Ethnic divisiveness frequently emerged from local worker organizations, and this was readymade for politicians who desired working-class support without legitimating class hostility.

Only the Knights of Labor broke this pattern. First present in 1878, they too succumbed to religious and ethnic antagonisms. However, in 1886 the revitalized Knights unified the New Albany working class. The Knights organized skilled and unskilled, Protestant and Catholic, and thereby unleashed the most significant strike wave to hit the city in the nineteenth century. Unlike their counterparts in Evansville, and probably a reflection of the general isolation of unions in New Albany, these assemblies were composed solely of workers. And it had the effect of briefly transforming the status of electoral politics. The mobilization of the local working class as a potential voting bloc led Republican and Democrat alike to appeal to worker aspirations. Yet without the long-term alliance building that had occurred in Evansville the formation of the Union Labor party was strenuously opposed by both parties with all the class fervor that their leaders could muster; nevertheless the resentments that the Knights mobilized gained the ULP a very strong showing in the working-class wards of the city. For a brief moment, ethnic divisions disappeared and politics assumed a class character. In New Albany, the movement of the Knights of Labor was as Leon Fink has suggested, "a break with the past."[165] It was a momentary break from political impotence.

Conclusion:
Industry, Culture, and Politics
in the Gilded Age Community

I arrived in New Albany ninety-seven years after W. C. DePauw's funeral. Though in the intervening years it has been engulfed by greater Louisville, the city retains the character of a town where face-to-face relations between people prevail, and many residents continue to maintain long-held local attachments. An interest in its past is evident in the restoration of the Culbertson mansion, and there is talk of restoring the equally impressive, if less tasteful, DePauw home a few doors down the street. It was at a meeting of the local historical society that an older gentleman, who had heard that I meant to examine the role of the labor movement in community affairs, sought me out. There was nothing of that sort here, he told me, for when labor agitators came to town to stir things up, "we threw them in the river."

When English glassblowers appeared before the local justice of the peace and were fined for threatening a strikebreaker, it shows up in court records and often in the press. However, if a union supporter was beaten there is likely to be no historical record of it, unless someone brought the case to court. The gentleman who approached me could not remember back into the nineteenth century; if he is correct, it was a more recent era of labor organizing to which he referred. Yet, after examining the historical experience of the city in the Gilded Age, it comes as no shock that such a repressive atmosphere might have developed in New Albany.

For it was during the DePauw era that an antilabor policy was effectively implemented by the local elite. When DePauw began to seize control of local industry, a tradition of worker militancy, rooted in the antebellum shipyards and which found outlet in partisan politics, was drastically weakened. While the press in places like

Paterson, New Jersey, Portsmouth, Ohio, and Evansville utilized the language of republicanism to challenge the power of the "aristocratic" employer, no such thing happened in New Albany where the "lord" actually made his home.[1] There the press and politicians supported the prerogatives of the capitalist. During the railroad strikes of 1877, the city council granted DePauw the police force that he requested to protect his property, even though there was no mass activity in New Albany at the time. When DePauw blackmailed the city council into vacating streets and redrawing the city limits to exclude the glassworks from municipal taxation, the *Ledger-Standard* urged compliance and termed dissenters "grumblers."[2] To find nonworker critiques of DePauw, one must look outside the city to the harsh anticapitalist language of the Jeffersonville *Evening News*.

It was during the strike in the plate glass department in 1880, however, that the repressive climate was most fully revealed. The editors of the *Ledger-Standard*, responding to mass meetings held by the Knights of Labor, to the burning down of a glassworks department, and to a boycott of their product, encouraged citizens to shoot strikers, whom they labeled "incendiaries" and "paupers," and warned that agitators might be drowned in the river.[3] There is no evidence that this advice was taken.

However, there is a chilling individual possibility, that of Henry Jansing. A young molder imbued with the cause of unionism, Jansing took an active role in leading the boycott against the *Ledger* during the plate glassworker strike. The editors singled Jansing out, and on March 23 asked him if he, as a young husband and father, could "afford" such a militant posture. The strike was crushed in late April, and Jansing would be involved in no others. For on July 21, Henry G. Jansing died; the cause of death remains unknown. His union brethren sent into the *Iron Molders' Journal* the usual resolutions of respect honoring the deceased, but on this occasion they offered an additional eulogy that portrayed Jansing as a fallen saint in the church of labor. Jansing died "without one blemish on his noble character." He was "devoted to his wife and child, to his mother and his kindred." And he was unswervingly committed to the fight against injustice. His union brothers remembered him as "ever impulsive and quick to aid the oppressed," and "devoted to his beloved Union" for which "manfully he ever fought." Jansing was escorted by procession to the burial ground by the union; their banner lofted above his remains.[4] We do not know if Jansing was murdered, but the personal threat levied at him in the local press just four months earlier is a haunting reminder of just what was at stake in the political realm.

For if the workers of Evansville failed to address power relationships at work by electing their own and sympathetic Democrats from
the middling sort, they did legitimate trade unions and other worker
organizations. In response to worker militancy and to challenges on
the left by socialists, Democratic politicians in convention and the
party press stressed their support for workers in their efforts to organize, and urged them to vote against the wealthy. The result is that
in Evansville the ebbs and flows of worker militancy went hand-in-
hand with Democratic power. And unions have maintained a significant role in Democratic party politics to the present day. If nothing
else workers in Evansville, by casting their ballots, created some
breathing room for themselves. Few workers were threatened with
violence; if they had, it would have been grist for the party mill.

But there was no inexorable bond between the unions and the
Democratic party in Evansville. Often workers failed to support
Democrats, and by the end of the century the local labor movement
had been infused with significant socialist influence. In 1904 the first
district, of which Evansville was a part, registered the largest vote for
a Socialist candidate for Congress in the state.[5] This too may have
been made possible by the loose long-term alliance between Democrats and workers. At times, the effort to build a coalition led the
editors of the *Courier* to open their pages to socialists and they refrained, usually, from denouncing them. Even militia units of socialists brought comment, but no condemnation from the editors. And
in the socialist-influenced *Trades and Labor Directory*, put out by
the Central Labor Union in 1895, the continuities with Democratic
discourse (which was infused with the American radical languages of
producerism and republicanism) were striking.[6] It is hard to escape
the conclusion that party politics in Evansville helped nourish the
culture of worker opposition.

Most historical writing in the past thirty years has ignored this connection. When historians have focused on politics, it has been the independent labor party that they have had in mind. In his excellent re-
interpretation of the Knights of Labor, Leon Fink has refocused
attention on the electoral challenge that they posed to traditional
elites and concludes that the movement "at least raised a critique of
corporate power and an affirmation of popular rights that would play
an abiding role in the political culture."[7] An independent culture—
that of the Knights—however, remains central for this challenge to
have been made. That mainstream party politics might have had some
effect seems not to have been the case in the cities that Fink examined.

Instead the emphasis has been on discovering the roots of an independent working-class culture. At the workplace and in association and saloons, workers gathered together to make sense of industrial change. Drawing on expectations from their own artisanal experience, or perhaps that of their parents, they put together a worldview that opposed the legitimacy of capitalist authority.[8] Out of this working-class culture arose a fiercely egalitarian form of republicanism, and the producerist notion that the manual worker who creates all value should receive the full rewards of labor. Historians like Herbert Gutman, Steven Ross, Alan Dawley, Sean Wilentz, and Nick Salvatore have enriched our understanding of the growth of capitalism in the United States by making it abundantly clear that Americans were not unqualified proponents of liberal individualism.[9] Out of this vital working-class culture arose a challenge to capital; it was that "justice" be meted out to workers.

This was also the case in the cities studied here. Both the shipyards of New Albany and the artisanal workshops of Evansville nourished similar traditions despite different ethnic components of the two work forces. If culture was all that mattered, the historian would have good reason to expect New Albany to have been a hotbed of working-class unrest in the Gilded Age. The essential question, then, is how do these traditions get politicized and transported to later periods.

Gutman thought that it was the smaller industrial city that allowed for the spread and persistence of militancy. There, he argued, the industrialist was "more vulnerable than in the larger complex metropolis." Face-to-face relationships between residents had a strong guiding effect. Moreover, "the closeness of the middle class and the old resident population to the new industrialism gave such persons the opportunity to judge the industrial city's social dislocations and social conflicts by personal experience, and not simply through the opaque filter of ideologies such as laissez-faire liberalism and Darwinism."[10]

Such *Gemeinschaft* conditions certainly had some effects in associational patterns and in politics. That common men, like ship carpenter Dummer Hooper or molder Conrad Muth, were more likely to achieve political office in the small industrial city where wards were small only confirms Madisonian logic regarding the stature of leaders and the size of republican units.[11] However, whether or not face-to-face relations led others in the small city to sympathize with workers is another thing entirely.

The debates over unemployment relief in Evansville bear out the point. The Republican *Journal* quickly labeled such schemes as communistic, and wealthy men like Republican banker John Hopkins and Democratic manufacturer John Reitz opposed relief measures in similar fashion to their counterparts in the large, more *Gesellschaft*-like cities. Other voices were heard, but to ascribe their sympathetic postures merely to a sense of community ignores the possibility that such support was part of the long-term process of building political coalitions. Thus, when John Kleiner and William Rahm backed the measure, they took care not to alienate workers, their strongest base of support. And the small size of the city did not stop the *Journal* in the spring of 1886 from denouncing boycotts and strikes as "un-American."

The examples of New Albany and Evansville suggest that power, in all its economic and political manifestations, was important in the creation and transmission of any culture of opposition. That political action did not lead workers to seize the state and use it to restructure local economies is true, and if that remains the measure by which we judge political activity, then the focus of previous writers is enough. However, this would have gone against the grain of working-class republicanism, which maintained the notion of the neutral state.[12] As a consequence, much worker political activity was defensive, aiming primarily to restrict capitalists from using that state for their own purposes. Accordingly, in some instances the most important local political issue for labor activists was the misuse of the police and the courts by hostile politicians to protect strikebreakers, and in the wake of the Buzan trial in 1874 and the use of city police to repress a strike outside the city boundaries in 1878 these issues proved salient.[13] However, workers challenged the ability of the elite to use local government as they wished in broader terms, and they did battle in the political arena over expensive railroad projects, tax policy, poor relief, liquor licensing, and the ability to form and sustain unions. With the exception of poor relief, which even in the hardest of times was framed by workers and their allies as an effort to maintain the independence of working-class men and the viability of their families, these were primarily efforts to deprive their social betters of the instrumentality of the state, and it proved a powerful incentive for workers to become involved in politics. It was this very appreciation for the proper role of the state that made republicanism such a viable vehicle for negotiations between politicians and working-class constituencies.

Furthermore, the effort to distinguish between the political and cultural sources of radicalism assumes an imperviousness of the former to the latter. Instead, we should strive to see in both battlegrounds over the meaning of "justice." For this, the Italian Marxist, Antonio Gramsci is particularly useful. Gramsci tells us that power in capitalist states is diffuse, that it is not concentrated in any one institution, but is interspersed throughout the culture. Control by workers of any one institution, therefore, does not necessarily lead to class victory; rather it is but one small battle in a series of small battles, and it is for this reason that Gramsci's allusion to trench warfare is so suggestive.[14] Battles over "justice" are waged throughout the culture. When workers and small producers dominated the Odd Fellows in New Albany, the organ of the order assailed the rich in producerist fashion. At that moment, the fraternal order was infused with the world view of the artisanal workshop. And, as demonstrated by New Albany's fire companies, voluntary associations could be centers of discipline as much as the focal point for rowdier, preindustrial types of behavior.

When workers acted politically, voting was by no means the most significant element. Political life, in meetings and conventions, was a year-long phenomenon. Less-structured participation surely occurred in the lodges and in the saloons; whether it involved the "buying" of votes and whiskey, or just informal discussion, it served to make politics a significant part of cultural existence. The long and reasoned discourse in the partisan press about measures before Congress, the state legislature, or the city council suggest that common men took their politics seriously. To make broad distinctions between culture and politics is to ignore the important role that the latter played in everyday life in the nineteenth century.[15] It was this heavy involvement of ordinary men—of workers—as much as the corruption of the urban "machine" with which elites were so concerned in the Gilded Age.

In a larger sense, it is inescapable that politics did submerge class interests. But it is not to the local level that we should look for this, but to the state and the national arenas. For the American political system has traditionally given rural areas more power than their share of the population would warrant in a strictly democratic apportionment. Consequently, industrial workers, a minority in the nineteenth century, were unable to dominate national parties, which found it necessary to build coalitions among diverse social strata and geographical interests. To better understand the complex interaction between workers and political parties we need to know what happened to the workers sent to the state legislature and who they associated with once they were there. While our focus is local, however, we should recognize that political life probably reflected much that was present elsewhere in the community.

That the ultimate problems facing workers were extralocal has already been suggested. Daniel Walkowitz, who found that Troy nourished a radical worker response to employer initiatives, argued that by relocating capitalists were able to escape the limitations of the local community, something that New Albany councilmembers were confronted with in the spring of 1878. Similar conclusions were drawn by John Cumbler: "As long as the companies were locally oriented and owned, and in competition with others locally and nationally, a local union movement could effectively unite its community against the company and last out the strike. When the companies became part of national organizations, they overcame the community efforts of union men." Ultimately Cumbler argued that the local community in the age of corporate capitalism was not enough to defend traditional rights against employer encroachments.[16] A focus on politics does not change the equation.

There is a certain incongruity in the local experiences of these cities. One might have expected workers in New Albany, due to greater levels of proletarianization and the rise of working-class associations, to have maintained a stronger labor movement than in Evansville. Certainly shops were larger in New Albany, and there was a greater reliance on unskilled labor. Further, workers—skilled and unskilled—tended to congregate in distinctly working-class neighborhoods around the glass and iron works, whereas workers and the smaller proprietors lived next to each other in Evansville.

The militancy of Evansville workers and ship carpenters in antebellum New Albany as well as the relative lack of militancy in "proletarianized" New Albany suggests it was the old artisanal community that nourished opposition and not proletarianization.[17] And to a certain extent that was the case, though we should be careful not to make too much of this. Artisans in Evansville experienced de-skilling and downward pressure on wages that in many cases, like that of coopers and cabinetmakers, reduced living standards toward that of families headed by common laborers. Though these workers were no longer artisans, they continued to benefit from continuity of leadership and the strength of community support. On one level, again the personal nature of the city appears to be crucial.

Nevertheless, it is political life and peculiarities of social structure that explains the differences. The lack of community support in New Albany suggests the inadequacy of face-to-face relationships as a causal explanation. Since New Albany was a small place, the rise of working-class neighborhoods alone seems hardly a powerful enough explanation for the growing isolation experienced by workers there.

Instead, it was in politics that workers there were most alone, and this isolation was fostered by naked economic power. Retailers and small producers feared the closing of lines of credit or the collapse of the local economy if DePauw relocated. They knew that the closing of factories meant fewer customers. They were equally aware that bonds for railroads still needed to be paid off, even if their primary intended beneficiary moved on. Consequently, there was little incentive for the middling sort to support political initiatives that promised to raise class tensions.

A hundred miles downstream the situation was different. Industry was diverse and units of production were smaller. On the one hand this situation suggests that workers had not been fully proletarianized, that they retained some vestiges of the artisan, of the producer. If we focus on the totality of social relations within the industrializing city, it becomes evident that other accompanying developments were equally, if not more, important. Due to the structure of its economy, Evansville depended on no one manufacturer for its prosperity. No single industrialist could blackmail the city council as DePauw had done in New Albany. This is not to say that elites wielded little influence—far from it. However, rival politicians could attack them for it by using the language of class. This is precisely what happened. Elite Democrats like the Shanklins constantly reaffirmed aspects of working-class radicalism as they challenged William Heilman and other Republicans for local power. As a consequence, by the time the Knights arrived they offered little that was new in the political realm; consequently the importance of the "Noble Order" in Evansville was primarily the economic solidarity that it inspired.

Evansville Democrats were encouraged in this course politically by the existence of vital trade union and socialist movements, and sociologically by the persistence of a vital middle element in the social structure. The city was distinctly more important than New Albany as both a retail and wholesale center, and the growth of small outlets and the numbers of white-collar workers increased the numbers of citizens who could be rallied to make war on the rich "bondholder" or the exploiter of labor. It is probably no mere coincidence that the most radical voice during the unemployment debate of the 1870s came from Benjamin Jewett, a clerk employed in an iron foundry. Nor is it surprising that workers found a friend in John Kleiner, a man who trained boys from the working class and petty bourgeoisie for clerical positions within the expanding local economy.

Thus, it was more the interrelationship between social structure and political competition than any vague sense of community that explains the existence or lack of support for strikers in these two cities. Of course, because of local deviations—no one town is representative, nor any two—this may not have been the case elsewhere. But it is important that the question of political competition has rarely been posed.

In his studies of strikers during the 1870s, Gutman used the press as an important barometer of local opinion. In an account of the Ohio Valley ironworker strike of 1874, the Ironton *Register* is cited for expressing regret that "'warm and old associations' had been sacrificed 'to the cold demands of business.'"[18] When discussing the decision of the employers to blacklist strikers, Gutman offers the query of the Portsmouth *Times*, "Is this to be the reward for men who have grown gray in the service of these velvet-lined aristocrats," as evidence of community disapproval of the course set by the industrialist.[19] Nowhere appears the suggestion that this support might have been seasoned through political alliances and conflict.

That such conflict may have been more political than the mere expression of community disapproval of capitalist behavior is embedded in the same article and is revealed by the position of the Cincinnati press. Cincinnati is just across the Ohio River from Newport and Covington, Kentucky, and is less than a hundred miles downstream from Portsmouth, Ohio; proximity to the strike centers led the editors to cover it. While the Republican *Commercial* "complained of the 'power' of the strikers" and warned its readers that "Cincinnati had 'the horrors of the Sheffield [England] unions . . . at our door,'" the coverage of the Democratic *Enquirer* was more favorable to the strikers. A reporter condemned attempts by iron master Alexander Swift to obtain state troops to protect his strikebreakers as "little else than a clever piece of acting intended to kindle public sentiment against the strikers." The paper also saw fit to print a letter from strikebreakers in Portsmouth who claimed that management had misled them, and that "'as men of honor and principle' they could not 'go to work under the circumstances.'"[20]

Surely the favorable position of the Cincinnati *Enquirer* was not a reflection of the personal nature of the small industrial city. It is a distinct possibility that the approaches taken by the two party organs were a response to local party positions and efforts to build workable political coalitions in Cincinnati. But if this was the case in the large city, why not the smaller city as well? Is it not possible that when the Portsmouth *Times* opposed iron manufacturer Benjamin Gaylord, it was investing political capital? If so, then it along with the historical record of Evansville and New Albany suggests that politics *could* nourish militancy and that the realm of electoral politics was an important part of working-class culture. It was in the constant meetings and processions that classes negotiated with each other, sharing and disputing meanings about citizenship and justice.

Notes

Chapter 1: The Ballot Box and Industrialization

1. Karl Marx and Frederick Engels, *Letters to Americans, 1848–1895* (New York, 1953).

2. *Nation*, Aug. 2, 1877.

3. Quoted in David Montgomery, *Beyond Equality: Labor and the Radical Republicans, 1862–1872* (Urbana, 1981), 339.

4. On reformer disenchantment with political democracy, see Michael E. McGerr, *The Decline of Popular Politics: The American North, 1865–1928* (Oxford, 1986).

5. John R. Commons and associates, *History of Labour in the United States*, 4 vols. (New York, 1921–35); Selig Perlman, *A Theory of the Labor Movement* (New York, 1928).

6. Louis Hartz, *The Liberal Tradition in America* (New York, 1955).

7. For labor history, see Alan Dawley, *Class and Community: The Industrial Revolution in Lynn* (Cambridge, Mass., 1976); Daniel Walkowitz, *Worker City, Company Town: Iron and Cotton-Worker Protest in Troy and Cohoes, New York, 1855–84* (Urbana, 1978); John T. Cumbler, *Working-Class Community in Industrial America: Work, Leisure, and Struggle in Two Industrial Cities, 1880–1930* (Westport, Conn., 1979). On ethnocultural history, see Lee Benson, *The Concept of Jacksonian Democracy* (Princeton, 1961); Richard Jensen, *The Winning of the Midwest: Social and Political Conflict, 1888–1896* (Chicago, 1971); Paul Kleppner, *The Cross of Culture: A Social Analysis of Midwestern Politics* (New York, 1970).

8. McGerr, *Decline of Popular Politics.*

9. See Herbert Gutman, *Work, Culture and Society in Industrializing America* (New York, 1977), 234–60; "The Buena Vista Affair, 1874–1875," in *Workers in the Industrial Revolution*, ed. Peter Stearns and Daniel Walkowitz (New Brunswick, N.J., 1974); "The Workers' Search for Power," in *The Gilded Age: A Reappraisal*, ed. H. Wayne Morgan (Syracuse, N. Y., 1963). For a critique that places more importance on wage differentials between skilled and unskilled workers (which is consistent with the evidence of this study), see Sari J. Bennett and Carville V. Earle, "Labour Power and Locality in the Gilded Age: The Northeastern United States, 1881–1894," *Historie Sociale—Social History* 15 (Nov. 1982): 383–405.

10. This outlook on economic affairs presumed that individuals would not enrich themselves at the expense of the community as a whole and drew its strength from the moral economy of preindustrial village life. See E. P. Thompson, "The Moral Economy of the English Crowd in the Eighteenth Century," *Past and Present* 50 (1971): 76–136. For a discussion of this in the American context see Herbert Gutman, "Work, Culture and Society in Industrializing America, 1815–1919," in *Work, Culture and Society*, 3–78.

11. Gutman, *Work, Culture and Society*, 243.

12. Bruce Laurie, *Working People of Philadelphia, 1800–1850* (Philadelphia, 1980); Paul Faler, *Mechanics and Manufacturers in the Early Industrial Revolution: Lynn, Massachusetts* (Albany, 1981); Eric Foner, *Tom Paine and Revolutionary America* (London, 1976).

13. John Ashworth, 'Agrarians' and 'Aristocrats': Party Political Ideology in the United States, 1837–1846 (Cambridge, Eng., 1983), esp. chaps 1, 2.

14. Gordon S. Wood, *The Creation of the American Republic, 1776–1787* (Chapel Hill, 1969), 49–77. See also Drew McCoy, *The Elusive Republic: Political Economy in Jeffersonian America* (Chapel Hill, 1980).

15. Gutman, *Work, Culture and Society*, 50.

16. Sean Wilentz, *Chants Democratic: New York City and the Rise of the American Working Class, 1788–1850* (New York, 1984); Steven J. Ross, *Workers on the Edge: Work, Leisure, and Politics in Industrializing Cincinnati, 1788–1890* (New York, 1985); David Montgomery, "Labor and the Republic in Industrial America, 1860–1920," *Movement Social* 111 (1980): 201–15; Linda Schneider, "The Citizen Striker: Workers' Ideology in the Homestead Strike of 1892," *Labor History* 23 (Winter 1982): 47–66; Dawley, *Class and Community*.

17. See Sean Wilentz's discussion of the proletarian politician, Mike Walsh in *Chants Democratic*, 326–35.

18. Alexander Saxton, *The Rise and Fall of the White Republic: Class Politics and Mass Culture in Nineteenth Century America* (London, 1990); idem, *The Indispensable Enemy: Labor and the Anti-Chinese Movement in California* (Berkeley, 1971); David Roediger, *The Wages of Whiteness: Race and the Making of the American Working Class* (London, 1991).

19. Bruce Laurie, "Fire Companies and Gangs in Southwark: The 1840s," in *The Peoples of Philadelphia: A History of Ethnic Groups and Lower-Class Life, 1790–1940*, ed. Allen F. Davis and Mark H. Haller (Philadelphia, 1973), 77–91; Wilentz, *Chants Democratic*; Ross, *Workers on the Edge*. On worker and plebeian neighborhoods, see Cumbler, *Working-Class Community*; and Francis Couvares, *The Remaking of Pittsburgh: Class and Culture in an Industrializing City, 1877–1919* (Albany, 1984).

20. Michael Cassity, *Defending a Way of Life: An American Community in the Nineteenth Century* (Albany, 1989), 125–31; David Thelen, *Paths of Resistance: Tradition and Dignity in Industrializing Missouri* (New York, 1986), 156–72. Mary Ann Clawson stresses the fraternal society's construction of a male sphere of mutuality and brotherhood based on the memory of the artisanal workshop as "compensation for the dislocations of capitalist

development." *Constructing Brotherhood: Class, Gender, and Fraternalism* (Princeton, 1989).

21. Cumbler, *Working-Class Community*, 10.

22. Dawley, *Class and Community*, 70. Dawley argues that early acquisition of the vote by American workers was the formative influence away from revolutionary politics, and that it was electoral politics—and not social mobility or the frontier—that served as the true safety-valve for American working-class discontent.

23. Daniel Walkowitz claims "the dominant liberal social and political ideology of progress undermined labor's class consciousness, while social mobility and the political process both provided experiences that confirmed that ideology." *Worker City, Company Town*, 253–54. Bruce Laurie concludes that "while the Democracy drained off the cream of radical working-class leadership, it resisted their ideas." *Working People of Philadelphia*, 115. Though Sean Wilentz's portrait of Mike Walsh and the "shirtless democracy" of New York suggests the potential relevance of politics for workers he too argues that the process coopted radicalism. *Chants Democratic*, 326–35, 383–86.

24. While historians influenced by E. P. Thompson have dropped essentialist categories of class consciousness, most continue to apply the distinction between revolutionary (or "true") and reformist ("false") politics. For a critique, see Iver Bernstein, "Expanding the Boundaries of the Political: Workers and Political Change in the Nineteenth Century," *International Labor and Working-Class History* 32 (Fall 1987): 59–75. For a critical discussion of the use of ideal models of class conscious and loyal workers, see Friedrich Lenger, "Class, Culture and Class Consciousness in Ante-Bellum Lynn: A Critique of Alan Dawley and Paul Faler," *Social History* 6 (Oct. 1981): 317–32.

25. See Amy Bridges, *A City in the Republic: Antebellum New York and the Origins of Machine Politics* (Cambridge, Eng., 1984); Martin Shefter, "Trade Unions and Political Machines: The Organization and Disorganization of the American Working Class in the Late Nineteenth Century," in *Working-Class Formation: Nineteenth-Century Patterns in Western Europe and the United States*, ed. Ira Katznelson and Aristide R. Zolberg (Princeton, 1986), 197–276.

26. Iver Bernstein, *The New York City Draft Riots: Their Significance for American Society and Politics in the Age of the Civil War* (New York, 1990); Grace Palladino, *Another Civil War: Labor, Capital, and the State in the Anthracite Regions of Pennsylvania, 1840–68* (Urbana, 1990). Historians of crowd behavior during the colonial and revolutionary eras, unencumbered by the antibureaucratic bias of the literature on the later periods, have more easily recognized this process of bargaining between elites and plebes that was implicit in political and extrapolitical behavior. See Gary B. Nash, *The Urban Crucible: Social Change, Political Consciousness, and the Origins of the American Revolution* (Cambridge, Mass., 1979); Charles G. Steffens, *The Mechanics of Baltimore: Workers and Politics in the Age of Revolution, 1763–1812* (Urbana, 1984).

27. Daniel Walker Howe, *The Political Culture of the American Whigs*

(Chicago, 1979); Jean H. Baker, *Affairs of Party: The Political Culture of Northern Democrats in the Mid-Nineteenth Century* (Ithaca, 1983); Saxton, *Indispensable Enemy.*

28. Gareth Stedman-Jones, *Languages of Class: Studies in English Working Class History, 1832–1982* (Cambridge, Eng., 1983), 1–24, 90–178.

29. John Ashworth, '*Agrarians' and 'Aristocrats.'* On the influence of the "Country party" in England, see Bernard Bailyn, *The Ideological Origins of the American Revolution* (Cambridge, Mass., 1967). On the Jeffersonian commitment to a natural order, see Joyce Appleby, *Capitalism and a New Social Order: The Republican Vision of the 1790s* (New York, 1984).

30. Eric Foner, *Free Soil, Free Labor, Free Men: The Ideology of the Republican Party before the Civil War* (New York, 1970); Michael F. Holt, *The Political Crisis of the 1850s* (New York, 1978).

31. Richard Franklin Bensel, *Yankee Leviathan: The Origins of Central State Authority in America, 1859–1877* (Cambridge, Eng., 1990); Eric Foner, *Reconstruction: America's Unfinished Revolution, 1863–1877* (New York, 1988); Montgomery, *Beyond Equality.*

32. Bernstein, *The New York City Draft Riots*; Palladino, *Another Civil War.*

33. Joel Silbey, *A Respectable Minority: The Democratic Party in the Civil War Era, 1860–68* (New York, 1977); Robert P. Sharkey, *Money, Class, and Party: An Economic Study of Civil War and Reconstruction* (Baltimore, 1959); Irwin Unger, *The Greenback Era: A Social and Political History of American Finance, 1865–1879* (Princeton, 1964).

34. Leon Fink links this radical tradition to the by and large negative posture of the Knights of Labor toward an activist state. However, he argues that this tradition ceased to be relevant within the party system after the Civil War as an increasingly militant labor movement began making claims of its own for "class legislation," most notably the eight-hour day. While recognizing the importance of political behavior, he limits his discussion to the independent parties that arose out of the Knights of Labor. *Workingmen's Democracy: The Knights of Labor and American Politics* (Urbana, 1983). In this he follows the important work of Eric Foner and David Montgomery, who discuss the Republican party as representative of a coalition of social forces. However, the collapse of that alliance did not negate the political value of a radical language, and in many localities the Democrats continued to be the bearers of this tradition.

35. See Brian Greenberg's discussion of the Odd Fellows in *Worker and Community: Response to Industrialization in a Nineteenth-Century American City, Albany, New York, 1850–1884* (Albany, 1985), 89–101. For a description of ethnic fraternal societies as a rival to a developing "working-class subculture of opposition," see Richard Jules Oestreicher, *Working People and Class Consciousness in Detroit, 1875–1900* (Urbana, 1986).

36. Based largely on developments in Philadelphia and New York City, Stuart Blumin argues that a "middle-class" formed itself in the nineteenth century. *The Emergence of the Middle Class: Social Experience in the American City, 1760–1900* (Cambridge, Eng., 1989). While much of his material

is excellent, especially with regard to the changing nature and location of nonmanualist work and the rise of a distinct standard of living, I am reluctant to define the middle as a "class" or to use Blumin's manual/nonmanual split as the basis of any such demarcation. For one, in smaller cities the level of residential segregation that marked the metropolis was not necessarily evident until the very end of the century. There, divisions between nonmanual and manual neighborhoods often reflected the difference between merchants and artisans rather than the attempt of a group of clerks or modest storekeepers to define themselves, and such a division cannot take into account the significant number of sons of workers who entered clerical professions, but still maintained residence within the manual community. And second, so much of Gutman's work suggests that in such places it was precisely the lack of such hard and fast boundaries that made broad community support for unions possible.

37. Jonathan M. Wiener, "Marxism and the Lower Middle Class: A Response to Arno Mayer," *Journal of Modern History* 48 (Dec. 1976): 666.

38. Albert Soboul, *The Parisian Sans-Culottes and the French Revolution, 1793–94* (Oxford, 1964); William Sewell, Jr., *Work and Revolution in France: The Language of Labor from the Old Regime to 1848* (Cambridge, Eng., 1980).

39. In New Albany, however, where workers were politically isolated, the Knights of Labor did mark the first significant move by workers into the political realm since the Civil War. See Fink, *Workingmen's Democracy*.

40. T. J. Jackson Lears, "The Concept of Cultural Hegemony: Problems and Possibilities," *American Historical Review* 90 (June 1985): 567–93, quote on 568.

41. Thomas Bender, "Wholes and Parts: The Need for Synthesis in American History," *Journal of American History* 73 (June 1986): 120–36.

42. David Montgomery, "Gutman's Nineteenth Century America," *Labor History* 19 (Summer 1978): 416–29, quote on p. 428.

Chapter 2: Last Days of the Mechanic

1. *History of the Ohio Falls Cities and their Counties*, v. 2 (Cleveland, 1882), 140–44; Victor M. Bogle, "Nineteenth Century River Town: A Social-Economic Study of New Albany, Indiana" (Ph.D. diss., Boston University, 1951), 3–5; Mary Scribner Davis Collins, "New Albany, with a Short Sketch of the Scribner Family," *Indiana Magazine of History* 17 (Sept. 1921): 213–16.

2. *History of the Ohio Falls Cities*, 2:143.

3. Samuel R. Brown, *The Western Gazetteer; or, Emigrant's Directory* (Auburn, N.Y., 1817), 63.

4. Issac Reed, *The Christian Traveller* (New York, 1828), reprinted in Harlow Lindley, ed., *Indiana as Seen by Early Travelers* (Indianapolis, 1916), 473.

5. Richard Lee Mason, *Narrative of Richard Lee Mason in the Pioneer*

West, (New York, 1819), 34; William Cobbett, *A Years Residence in the United States of America,* part 3 (London, 1819), 492.

6. C. Bradford Mitchell, *Merchant Steam Vessels of the United States, 1790–1868: "The Lytle-Holdcamper List"* (New York, 1975).

7. Edmund Dana, *Geographical Sketches on the Western Country Designed for Migrants and Settlers* (Cincinnati, 1819), 121–22; Timothy Flint, *The History and Geography of the Mississippi Valley,* v. 1 (Cincinnati, 1832), 377; H. McMurtrie, *Sketches of Louisville and Its Environs* (Louisville, 1819), 165–68.

8. Richard C. Wade, *The Urban Frontier: Pioneer Life in Early Pittsburgh, Cincinnati, Lexington, Louisville, and St. Louis* (Chicago, 1967).

9. Mitchell, *Merchant Steam Vessels.*

10. Evansville Daily *Journal,* Nov. 4, 1857. The "A. L. Shotwell" and the "Eclipse" established the antebellum record for the trip between Louisville and New Orleans in a celebrated race, finishing in identical times of four days, nine hours, and thirty minutes. Louis C. Hunter, *Steamboats on the Western Rivers: An Economic and Technological History* (Cambridge, Mass., 1949), 23.

11. United States Census Bureau, *Seventh Census, Statistical View of the United States* (Washington, 1854), 371; *Eighth Census, Population of the United States in 1860* (Washington, 1864), 116–17.

12. *The Commercial and Manufacturing Advantages of New Albany, Ind.* (New Albany, 1857), 25–28.

13. New Albany Daily *Ledger* (hereafter *Ledger*), Apr. 2, 1857.

14. Ibid., Feb. 2, 1854.

15. The amount of $10,000 is used here as a line dividing elites from the rest of local society. Eighth Census, population schedules, Floyd County.

16. Ibid. Quote is from Bogle, "Nineteenth Century River Town," 203.

17. For example, see *Ledger,* Feb. 15, 1856, and the description of the "splendid new craft," the "James Montgomery."

18. Eighth Census, manufacturing schedules, Floyd County.

19. United States Census Bureau, *Eighth Census, Manufacturers of the United States in 1860* (Washington, 1865), 120.

20. Eighth Census, population schedules.

21. The other large concentration of servants, where 22.9 percent worked, was on the northern edge of the business district of the Third Ward, just south of the recently built railroad station. *New Albany Directory, City Guide and Business Mirror, for the Year 1860* (New Albany, 1860).

22. Bogle, "Nineteenth Century River Town," 227; First Presbyterian Church record book (1858), Robert L. Breck Collection, Indiana Historical Society Library; Eighth Census, population schedules.

23. *History of the Ohio Falls Cities,* 2:177–78.

24. *Proceedings on the Occasion of the Opening of Indiana Asbury Female College* (New Albany, 1852), 12.

25. *Ledger,* Jan. 5, 1861.

26. Seventh Census, manufacturing schedules.

27. Betty Lawson Walters, "Furniture Makers of Indiana," *Indiana Historical Society Publications* 25 (Indianapolis, 1972).

28. *Gabriel Collins' Louisville and New Albany Directory and Annual Advertiser for 1848* (Louisville, 1848); Seventh Census, manufacturing schedules.

29. Seventh Census, manufacturing schedules.

30. *Ledger,* Jan. 1, 1854, and Feb. 18, 1857; *Directory* (1860).

31. Eighth Census, manufacturing and population schedules.

32. Seventh Census and Eighth Census, manufacturing schedules.

33. Eighth Census, population schedules. An exception was William Sanderson who opened his house to manufacturer Peter Tellon, his father-in-law.

34. Eighth Census, manufacturing schedules.

35. Ibid.

36. For Hood's status in 1848, see *Directory* (1848). An advertisement appears in *Groom's and Smith's New Albany City Directory and Business Mirror* (1856), 36.

37. Eighth Census, manufacturing schedules.

38. *Ledger,* Sept. 21, 1855.

39. Eighth Census, manufacturing schedules.

40. *Ledger,* June 5, 1857.

41. Workshop data was found in the manufacturing schedules of the Eighth Census; that reflecting the ethnicity and wealth of the work force was culled from the population schedules of the Seventh Census and Eighth Census. Each individual listed with an occupation was tallied according to age, marital status, occupation, level of property holding, and nativity. This tally informs much of the discussion that follows.

42. Seventh Census and Eighth Census, population schedules.

43. Wilentz, *Chants Democratic,* 119–29.

44. Mary Blewett, *Men, Women, and Work: Class, Gender, and Protest in the New England Shoe Industry* (Urbana, 1988); Ava Baron and Susan Klepp, "'If I Didn't Have my Sewing Machine': Women and Sewing Technology," in *A Needle, A Bobbin, A Strike: Women Needleworkers in America,* ed. Joan M. Jensen and Sue Davidson (Philadelphia, 1984), 20–59.

45. Eighth Census, population schedules. The enumerators for the upper three wards in 1860 did not distinguish between masters and journeymen. Yet it is evident that the ratio was high due to the large number of shops listed in directories and the manufacturing census.

46. Eighth Census, manufacturing schedules.

47. Eighth Census, population schedules. The percentage of older propertyless house carpenters, for instance, was double that number.

48. Iorwerth Prothero, *Artisans and Politics in early Nineteenth Century London: John Gast and His Times* (Folkestone, Kent, 1979), 63.

49. Wilentz, *Chants Democratic,* 134–37.

50. *Fincher's Trades' Review* (*FTR*), Jan. 27, Feb. 10, Mar. 3, 1866. Harley was careful to choose his master well for he knew that cruel and indiffer-

ent masters were plentiful, and they generally trained "third or fourth rate workmen." As his account suggests, artisanal relations and traditions were no guarantee against mistreatment and exploitation. See Robert Darnton's recounting of the symbolic revolt against such mistreatment by a group of printers in a Parisian workshop in *The Great Cat Massacre* and *Other Episodes in French Cultural History* (New York, 1985), 75–104.

51. Thomas Humphrey Account Books, Humphrey Family Papers, New Albany–Floyd County Public Library.

52. Humphrey Account Books, "Steamer Diana."

53. Ibid.; Eighth Census, population schedules.

54. Prothero, *Artisans and Politics*, 63.

55. Work on the "Trio" and the "Baltic" was minor and was completed by these two journeymen and the two partners of the firm.

56. Humphrey Account Books.

57. Ibid., "Captain Richardson's boat."

58. On subcontracting, see Joseph A. Goldenberg, *Shipbuilding in Colonial America* (Charlottesville, 1976).

59. Humphrey Account Books, "Captain Spott's boat."

60. Ibid., "Captain Richardson's boat."

61. The total is 19.4 percent, but this does not account for family members with different last names, as would have been the case, for instance, with a widowed sister or an in-law. Therefore, the actual figure was probably lower. Eighth Census, population schedules. Data for the families of each ship carpenter and joiner were taken from the pages of the census.

62. Ibid.

63. Ibid.

64. *Directory* (1848, 1856, 1859, and 1860); Seventh Census and Eighth Census, manufacturing schedules.

65. Diary of William Hooper, pp. 8, 12, New Albany—Floyd County Public Library.

66. Eighth Census, population schedules.

67. Susan and Annabella were officers of Integrity Lodge No. 99 of the Independent Order of Good Templars. *Directory* (1859), 177. Dummer, who would later take an active role in the Know-Nothing movement, joined the Sons of Temperance while in San Francisco. Letter of D. M. Hooper addressed to "Wife, Children, and Friends," dated June 24, 1850, Hooper family folder, New Albany-Floyd County Public Library. The family's temperance posture also appeared in the diary of minister William.

68. Eighth Census, population schedules. By 1872, David was a contractor while Shadrach was employed as a railroad ticket agent. Letter of Dummer Mitchell Hooper to Elizabeth Hooper Chandler, June 2, 1872 (typescript copy), Hooper Family Folder.

69. Eighth Census, population schedules. Unlike data on ship carpenters concerning family structure and education, data for other occupations was arrived at by a sampling of every ten household in the population schedules of the Eighth Census. The size of this sample is 244 households.

70. Laborers working on street repairs for the city earned a dollar a day in 1857. *Ledger,* June 2, 1857.

71. *Ledger,* Feb. 4, 1856, Nov. 15, 1857, Feb. 25, 1858.

72. Eighth Census, population schedules.

73. Ibid. On domestic labor, see Christine Stansell, *City of Women: Sex and Class in New York, 1789–1860* (New York, 1986), 155–68. On immigrant family strategies, Stephen Thernstrom, *Progress and Poverty: Social Mobility in a Nineteenth-Century City* (Cambridge, Mass., 1964).

74. *Ledger,* Nov. 11, 18, 1857.

75. Eighth Census, population schedules.

76. Oliver MacDonagh, "The Irish Famine Emigration to the United States," *Perspectives in American History* 10 (1976): 357–448; William V. Shannon, *The American Irish* (New York, 1964), 28–29.

77. *Ledger,* Mar. 18, 1854, and Apr. 7, 1857.

78. Letter fragment written by Jos. W. Gale, Jan. 1860 (precise date unknown), Wakefield Gale Papers, Folder 2b, Indiana Historical Society Library.

79. Eighth Census, population schedules.

80. *Directory* (1865, 1868, 1871, and 1873). Due to a tendency to omit young propertyless boarders, the names of many clerks and bookkeepers who appear in the census do not appear in the city directory. For this reason, most occupations were better represented in the census than in the directories.

81. *Directory* (1860); Eighth Census, population schedules; and *Edwards' Annual Director to . . . the Cities of New Albany and Jeffersonville* (New Albany, 1865).

82. *Directory* (1865, 1868, 1871, and 1873).

83. In 1854, clerks urged merchants to agree to close their stores at eight in the evening. *Ledger,* June 6, 7, 1854.

84. Clyde Griffen and Sally Griffen, *Natives and Newcomers; The Ordering of Opportunity in Mid-Nineteenth-Century Poughkeepsie* (Cambridge, Mass., 1978), 36.

85. Eighth Census, population schedules.

86. Bruce Laurie and Mark Schmitz, "Manufacture and Productivity: The Making of an Industrial Base, Philadelphia, 1850–1880," in *Philadelphia: Work, Space, Family, and Group Experience in the Nineteenth Century,* ed. Theodore Hershberg (New York, 1981), 85–86.

87. Eighth Census, manufacturing schedules.

88. For a sophisticated use of residency patterns, see Olivier Zunz, *The Changing Face of Inequality: Urbanization, Industrial Development, and Immigrants in Detroit, 1880–1920* (Chicago, 1982).

89. This analysis was informed by use of the 1860 city directory and the population schedules of the eighth census.

90. M. W. Carr, *History of Catholicity in New Albany and Jeffersonville* (Indianapolis, 1890), 31; *History of the Ohio Falls Cities,* 2:210.

91. It was rare for an Irish or German neighborhood to take up more than two pages of the census schedule.

92. *History of the Ohio Falls Cities,* 2:157–59.
93. Eighth Census, population schedules.
94. *The Remaking of Pittsburgh: Class and Culture in an Industrializing City, 1877–1919* (Albany, 1984), 31.
95. *Western Odd Fellows' Magazine* 3 (July 1854), 6.
96. Ibid.
97. *Directory* (1859), 175–76; Eighth Census, population schedules. On the Masons, see the author's "Producers, Proletarians and Politicians: Opposition and Accommodation in the Small Industrializing City, 1850–1887 (Ph.D diss., University of Los Angeles, California, 1989).
98. E. W. Brabrook, *Provident Societies and Industrial Welfare* (London, 1898), 63; J. M. Baernreither, *English Associations of Working Men,* trans. Alice Taylor (London, 1891), 217–25; P. H. J. H. Gosden, *The Friendly Societies in England, 1815–1875* (Manchester, 1961), 1–12.
99. Mary Ann Clawson, *Constructing Brotherhood: Class, Gender, and Fraternalism* (Princeton, 1989), 118–23.
100. On artisanal sources in the construction of the concept of self-made men, see Mary Ryan, *Cradle of the Middle Class: The Family in Oneida County, New York, 1790–1865* (Cambridge, Eng., 1981).
101. *Western Odd Fellows' Magazine* 1 (Dec. 1852), 177.
102. Ibid., 1 (Oct. 1852), 110.
103. Ibid., 3 (July 1854), 1–2,
104. Ibid., 2 (Aug. 1853), 51.
105. Ibid., 2 (Mar. 1854), 277.
106. Ibid., 2 (July 1853), 14.
107. Ibid., 3 (July 1854), 1–2.
108. Arno Mayor argues that the petty bourgeoisie "has a compliant but also strained relationship with the upper establishment which it both aspires to and resents." "The Lower Middle Class as Historical Problem," *Journal of Modern History* 47 (Sept. 1975): 409–36. Quote on 423.
109. Laurie, *Working People of Philadelphia,* 60.
110. Bogle, "Nineteenth Century River Town," 275–76.
111. *Ledger,* Aug. 19, 20, 1858. Also see June 19, 1857.
112. *Directory* (1856), vii–viii; *Directory* (1859), 163–64; Eighth Census, population schedules; *Ledger,* May 5, 1856, Jan. 1 and Dec. 23, 1859, Jan. 11, 17, and 24, May 8, July 11, 1860.
113. Five of the nine were ship carpenters and joiners, two were steamboat blacksmiths, one was a caulker, and one a mill sawyer.
114. *Bye-Laws of the Hook and Ladder Company,* adopted Nov. 30, 1844 (New Albany).
115. *Directory* (1859), 177; Eighth census, population schedules. On the rise of a plebeian temperance movement, see Ian R. Tyrell, *Sobering Up: From Temperance to Prohibition in Antebellum America, 1800–1860* (Westport, Conn., 1979).
116. *History of the Ohio Falls Cities,* 2:186–91.
117. E. P. Thompson, *The Making of the English Working-Class* (New York, 1966), 350–400; Steffen, *The Mechanics of Baltimore,* 253–73.

118. *Western Odd Fellows' Magazine* 2 (Mar. 1854), 232.
119. Ibid., 1 (Dec. 1852) 192.
120. Ibid., 193.
121. Gutman, *Work, Culture and Society*, 257.
122. Glenn Porter and Harold Livesay, *Merchants and Manufacturers: Studies in the Changing Structure of Nineteenth Century Marketing* (Baltimore, 1971), 116–17.
123. See Sean Wilentz's description of what he calls the "bastard workshop," in *Chants Democratic*, 107–42.

Chapter 3: From "Mechanic" to "Worker"

1. *Ledger*, July 23, 1860.
2. Michael E. McGerr, *The Decline of Popular Politics*, 33.
3. Louisville *Courier*, Mar. 25, 1854; *Ledger*, Mar. 25, 1854.
4. *Ledger*, July 24, 1854.
5. Ibid., Mar. 29, 31, 1855, and Apr. 2, 1855.
6. New Albany *Tribune* (hereafter *Tribune*), July 25, 1857.
7. *Ledger*, Sept. 14, 1857.
8. *Tribune*, Oct. 16, 1857.
9. *Ledger*, May 14, 1858.
10. Ibid., May 21, 1858. Seventy-two of the one hundred fifteen men listed were identified in the 1856 or the 1859 city directory.
11. Ibid., July 17, 1856; *Tribune*, July 21, 1856.
12. *Ledger*, Mar. 16, 1854.
13. *Constitution and Bye Laws of New Albany Beneficial Association of Steamboat Engineers* (New Albany, 1853), 12.
14. *Ledger*, Aug. 12, 1857.
15. *Tribune*, July 21, 1857.
16. *Ledger*, May 2, 1854. Background material on Kelso was found in the population schedules of the Seventh Census, and in *Gabriel Collins' Louisville and New Albany Directory and Annual Advertiser* (Louisville, 1848).
17. *Tribune*, May 20, 1854.
18. *Ledger*, Aug. 30, 1854.
19. Ibid., Oct. 14, 1854.
20. Michael Fitzgibbon Holt, *Forging a Majority: The Formation of the Republican Party in Pittsburgh, 1848–1860* (New Haven, 1969); Dale Baum, "Know-Nothingism and the Republican Majority in Massachusetts: The Political Realignment of the 1850s," *Journal of American History* 64 (Mar. 1978): 959–86.
21. *Tribune*, Oct. 4, 1854. See also *Ledger*, Oct. 3, 1854.
22. *Ledger*, Oct. 11, 12, 1854; New Albany Daily *Morning Herald*, Oct. 11, 12, 1854.
23. The editor of the *Tribune* had this to say: "when attempts are made to destroy the purity of the ballot-box, as was the case yesterday, and threats of personal violence used in case any citizen should exercise his *right* to chal-

268 Notes to Pages 51–54

lenge certain voters, it arouses a spirit in *American* breasts that is not easily subdued, and which prompts them to take the remedy in their own hands without pausing to consult the *law* . . . there was a determination that not one illegal vote should pollute the ballot-box—that its purity should be kept inviolate at all hazards—and that the *rights of American Citizens* should be trampled on no longer." Oct. 11, 1854.

24. The Irish rarely appeared as officers in the plebeian associations discussed in the previous chapter.

25. Bogle, "Nineteenth Century River Town," 241–42.

26. Emma Lou Thornbrough, *Indiana in the Civil War Era, 1850–1880,* (Indianapolis, 1965), 59–60.

27. The local German community was the target of nativist rowdies on Christmas Eve, 1855 when a "mob . . . paraded the streets, entering coffee houses, whipping bar keepers, breaking decanters and glasses. . . . Houses were broken open, doors kicked in, barrels and other missiles were hurled against them, and many a poor German heard the whizzing of glass or stone as it passed his head or felt its force tumble him to the ground." *Ledger,* Dec. 26, 1855.

28. *Ledger,* Oct. 14, 1854, and Aug. 21, 1855.

29. Eric Foner, *Free Soil, Free Labor, Free Men,* 149–85.

30. *Ledger,* Jan. 17, 31, 1854.

31. Ibid., Mar. 14, 1854.

32. Ibid., Mar. 11, 1854.

33. Ibid., May 26 and Aug. 26, 1854.

34. Ibid., Feb. 24, 1855. The original subscription was rendered void by a decision of the Indiana Supreme Court; ratification of that subscription was enabled by a subsequent act of the state legislature. Mar. 9, 1855.

35. Ibid., Mar. 9, 1855; *Tribune,* Mar. 5, 1855.

36. New Albany Common Council Proceedings, Book 5, Mar. 7, 1855, pp. 148–53.

37. *Tribune,* Mar. 14, 1855.

38. *Ledger,* Apr. 17, 20, and 21, 1855; *Tribune,* Apr. 21, 1855.

39. *Ledger,* Dec. 7, 1855; *Tribune,* Mar. 27, 1856.

40. *Ledger,* Nov. 10, 1855.

41. Council Proceedings, Book 5, Nov. 26, 1855, pp. 321–28.

42. *Ledger,* Nov. 15, 1855.

43. For example, see *Ledger,* Feb. 25, 1856, and Apr. 19, 1856; *Tribune,* Dec. 8, 1855, Mar. 24, 1856.

44. Council Proceedings, Book 5, Nov. 26, 1855, pp. 321–28. The *Ledger* argued small property owners were being duped into bearing "the brunt of the expense" of a legal challenge that stood primarily to benefit the wealthy. Dec. 8, 1855.

45. *Ledger,* Dec. 6, 24, 1855. *Tribune,* Dec. 8, 1855, attributes opposition to "a certain section being chagrined because they imagine they may not be as much benefited by the railroad as another section."

46. *Tribune,* Apr. 28, 1856.

47. Ibid., May 5, 1856.

48. *Ledger*, Feb. 19 and Mar. 20, 22, 1856; *Tribune*, Mar. 18, 1856.

49. *Ledger*, Mar. 20, 1856.

50. Ibid., Mar. 21, 24, 1856; *Tribune*, Mar. 21, 1856.

51. See David Montgomery, "The Shuttle and the Cross: Weavers and Artisans in the Kensington Riots of 1844," *Journal of Social History* 5 (1972): 411–46.

52. *Tribune*, Mar. 21, 1856.

53. Ibid., May 7, 1856.

54. Ibid., Nov. 12, 1855. See also Dec. 8, 1855, Apr. 28, 1856; *Ledger*, Dec. 24, 1855.

55. *Tribune*, Apr. 30, 1856.

56. Ibid., June 11, 1856.

57. Ibid., July 11, 1856.

58. Kenneth M. Stampp, *Indiana Politics during the Civil War* (Indianapolis, 1949), 95.

59. *Tribune*, Aug. 25, 1856.

60. Ibid., July 14, 1856; *Ledger*, July 14, 1856.

61. *Ledger*, Nov. 7, 1856.

62. Ibid., Aug. 6, 1860.

63. Ibid., Aug. 2, 3, and 4, 1860.

64. Ibid., Aug. 7, 1860; Thornbrough, *Indiana in the Civil War Era*, 15.

65. *Ledger*, Aug. 8, 1860.

66. *Tribune*, July 17, 1860.

67. *Ledger*, July 27, 1860. For comparative purposes, the offices and committee positions of the "Lincoln Campaign Club" were held by professionals (5), extremely wealthy merchants and bankers (4), a well-to-do master, a wealthy manufacturer, and a marble dealer of relatively modest means. No journeyman held a position of leadership in this political association. Nine of the twelve lived in the upper wards; the only one to hail from the Sixth Ward was James V. Kelso, a teacher. *Tribune*, July 16, 1860; Eighth Census, population schedules.

68. *Ledger*, Nov. 5, 8, 1860.

69. Ibid., Nov. 26, 28, 1860.

70. Ibid., Nov. 30, 1860. Similar meetings were held in cities and towns across the state. Stampp, *Indiana Politics during the Civil War Era*, 55.

71. Philip S. Foner, *History of the Labor Movement in the United States*, v. 1 (New York, 1975), 298–99.

72. *Ledger*, Jan. 5, 1861. The "workingmen" selected Cash to represent them at the National Workingmen's Convention at Philadelphia on January 22. Ibid., Jan. 19, 1961.

73. Ibid.

74. Stampp, *Indiana Politics during the Civil War*, 95.

75. Following one of many flag presentations that were held in April and May, seventeen different militia companies participated in a procession up Main Street, led by the Cornet Band. *Ledger*, May 9, 10, 1861.

76. Exactly 116 men joined Home Guards No. 1, and 23 were mentioned

by the *Ledger* as officers or committee members of one kind or another. Occupational data is available for 21, all of whom were self-employed. Of the 17 for which property data has been found, 7 owned estates worth at least $15,000. For the membership of the Independent Home Guards, the figures are similar. Of the 91 members, property data was found for 53, and 27 (50.9 percent) owned over $10,000 in property. Eighty-nine percent owned at least $2,000, and of the five who did not, all were either master craftsmen, holders of city office, or white-collar workers. Occupational data alone was found for 26 others, and only 2 of them, engineers, were manualists who were not self-employed. *Ledger,* Apr. 20, 22, 1861; Eighth Census, population schedules; *Directory* (1860).

77. *Ledger,* Apr. 22, 1861.

78. Ibid., Apr. 29, 1861.

79. Ibid., Apr. 25, 1861.

80. Ibid., Feb. 11, May 15, July 3, Aug. 8 and 9, 1861.

81. Ibid., Sept. 21, 1861, Feb. 13, 27, 1862, May 21, 1862; Lieut. W. L. Lenan, Camp Nessly, to Mess. Nunemacher & Shaw, New Albany, Dec. 9, 1861, Nunemacher Family File, New Albany Public Library.

82. *Ledger,* Apr. 4, Dec. 22, 1862.

83. Ibid., Apr. 22, 1863.

84. Ibid., Aug. 5, 1863. On November 20, the following appeared in the *Ledger:* "houses for rent are getting scarcer every day and landlords are piling on the tariff in proportion."

85. Ibid., Apr. 22, 1864. A steak that formerly sold for twenty to twenty-five cents went in April 1864 for fifty to sixty cents. April 26, 1864.

86. Ibid., July 15, 16, 1862.

87. This was a common practice, and the consequence was that volunteers were lured to locales offering the highest bounties. Stampp, *Indiana Politics during the Civil War,* 215–16.

88. *Ledger,* Dec. 18, 1863, and Jan. 14, 1865.

89. Ibid., Feb. 10, 1865.

90. Ibid., Oct. 10, 1865. On the political expediency of exempting one's constituency, see Iver Bernstein, *The New York City Draft Riots: Their Significance for American Society and Politics in the Age of the Civil War* (Oxford, 1990).

91. See Stampp, *Indiana Politics during the Civil War,* 146.

92. *Ledger,* July 22, 1862. The white men were said to have been between the ages of eighteen and twenty-one. None of them are listed in the city directory, though they may have been related to journeymen with the same last name who lived near where the incident occurred.

93. Ibid.

94. Ibid., July 23, 1862. This remained a prominent theme until May of the following spring. The *Ledger* customarily criticized union army officers who sent freedmen to New Albany. See Oct. 25, Nov. 10, 1862.

95. Ibid., Aug. 4, 1862.

96. Ibid., July 24, 29, 1862.

97. Rev. John G. Atterbury, *God in Civil Government: A Discourse Preached in the First Presbyterian Church, New Albany, Nov. 27, 1862* (New Albany, 1862), 8–9, 12.

98. *Ledger,* July 22, 1862; *Directory,* 1863; John Madden, New Albany, to C. J. Madden, Clarksville, Tennessee, May 19, 1863, Madden Papers, Indiana Historical Society Library.

99. *Ledger,* May 7, 1863.

100. Ibid., Nov. 19, 1863.

101. *FTR,* Jan. 14, 1865.

102. *Directory* (1848, 1856, 1859, and 1860); Eighth Census, population schedules; Thomas Humphrey Account Books, Humphrey Family Papers, New Albany Public Library.

103. *FTR,* Feb., 18, 1865.

104. Ibid., May 27, 1865.

105. Ibid., Jan. 14, 1865.

106. Ibid., Apr. 29, 1865; *Ledger,* Apr. 3 and July 1, 1865.

107. *Ledger,* Apr. 7, 1865.

108. Ibid., June 17, 1865, June 25 and 30, July 5, 1866.

109. David Montgomery, *Beyond Equality,* 260.

110. *FTR,* Feb. 18, 1865.

111. *Ledger,* Apr. 11, 15, 1865; *Directory* (1865).

112. *Ledger,* Apr. 15, 1865.

113. Ibid., Apr. 29, May 3, 1865.

114. *FTR,* Dec. 16, 1865; *Ledger,* Nov. 25, 1865.

115. *FTR,* Dec. 16, 1865.

116. *Ledger,* Dec. 9, 16, 1865; *Commercial,* Dec. 5, 16, 1865; *Directory* (1865).

117. *Ledger,* Dec. 4, 1865.

118. *Commercial,* Dec. 9, 1865.

119. Ibid., Dec. 9, 1865.

120. Ibid., Oct. 21, 1865.

121. *Ledger,* Oct. 24, 1865.

122. Ibid.

123. *Commercial,* Oct. 26, 1865.

124. Ibid., Dec. 16, 1865.

125. Ibid., Dec. 23, 1865.

126. *Ledger,* Jan. 3, 1865.

127. *FTR,* Feb. 3, 1866; *Commercial,* Jan. 11, 17, 1866.

128. *Ledger,* Feb. 12, 1866.

129. There is no mention of subsequent eight-hour day activity in New Albany in either the local press or the correspondence of local activists to the national labor press.

130. *Ledger,* Aug. 11, 1866. The February county convention appears to have been the last time that Kelso worked in concert with the Republican party.

131. Ibid.

132. Ibid., Aug. 16, 1866.
133. Ibid., Sept. 4, 1866.
134. Ibid., Oct. 12, 1866, May 8, 1867, Aug. 5, 1868; *Commercial*, May 5, 1869.
135. *Ledger*, July 9, 1866.
136. Hunter, *Steamboats on the Western Rivers*, 481.

Chapter 4: Continuity and Transformation

1. William Cobbett, *A Years Residence in the United States of America*, part 3 (London, 1819), 329; Edmund Dana, *Geographical Sketches of the Western Country Designed for Emigrants and Settlers* (Cincinnati, 1819), 128.
2. United States, Census Office, *The Seventh Census of the United States* (Washington, 1853), 177; Idem, *Statistics of the Population of the United States at the Tenth Census* (Washington, 1883), 155.
3. Theodore Dreiser, *Dawn* (New York, 1931), 117.
4. This figure includes all residents with an occupation in the 1860 census. Eighth Census, population schedules, Vanderburgh County.
5. *Annual Report of the Board of Trade of Evansville, Indiana, for 1867* (Evansville, 1868), typewritten copy in Willard Library, Evansville, 4; The Seventh Census of the United States, 177.
6. *Western Odd Fellows' Magazine* 1 (Nov. 1852), 166.
7. Seventh Census, population schedules.
8. *History of Vanderburgh County, Indiana* (Madison, Wis., 1889), 147–49; *History of Walnut Street Church* (Evansville, 1891), 96–100. The experiences of Samuel Orr, wholesale grocer and iron merchant, also from Ulster, were similar.
9. *Annual Report*, 4–5; Daniel W. Snepp, "Evansville's Channels of Trade and the Secession Movement, 1850–1865," *Indiana Historical Society Publications* 8 (1928): 325–91.
10. Evansville *Journal*, June 24, 25, July 7, 1857.
11. Bernard H. Schockel, "Manufacturial Evansville, 1820–1933" (Ph.D. diss., University of Chicago, 1947), 116.
12. Logan Esarey, "Internal Improvements in Early Indiana," *Indian Historical Society Publications* 5 (1912): 145–51.
13. Evansville *Enquirer*, June 8, 1855.
14. Ibid., June 13, 1855; *Journal*, June 14, 1855.
15. *Enquirer*, June 18, 1855.
16. *Journal*, June 14, 1855. The drying up of the lower part of the canal left Terre Haute as the southern terminus of the canal. Also see *Enquirer*, June 25, 1855.
17. Esarey, "Internal Improvements in Early Indiana," 150.
18. *Journal*, June 30, 1855.
19. Esarey, "Internal Improvements in Early Indiana," 150.

20. Shockel, "Manufactural Evansville, 1820–1933," 118.

21. *Annual Report*, 21.

22. Snepp, "Evansville's Channels of Trade and the Secession Movement," 332; *Journal*, May 22, 1865.

23. Shockel, "Manufactural Evansville, 1820–1933," 118–19; *Journal*, Feb. 24, 1864, July 28, 1870.

24. Use of $20,000 as the dividing line to identify the elite in 1870 takes into account the inflation of the war years.

25. Eighth Census and Ninth Census, population schedules.

26. Ninth Census, population schedules.

27. Tenth Census, population schedules.

28. Eighth Census and Ninth Census, population schedules.

29. This is corroborated by totaling the personal and real property holding held by the wealthy, as listed in the census schedules. In 1870, they collectively owned $10,921,900 in real estate, and $6,874,550 in personal. Tax assessment information was taken from Charles E. Robert, *Evansville: Her Commerce and Manufactures* (Evansville, 1874), 473.

30. *Annual report*, 11.

31. Lamasco, situated just north of Division Street, was annexed by Evansville in 1857, though the less-populated area west of Pigeon Creek known as Independence remained outside the city until the early 1870s.

32. Seventh Census, population and manufacturing schedules.

33. Seventh Census, population schedules.

34. The names of masters listed in the 1850 manufacturing schedules were linked to the population rolls of the same year.

35. Seventh Census, population and manufacturing schedules.

36. *Journal*, June 16, 1854, and Apr. 9, 1855.

37. Robert, *Evansville*, 417–18.

38. Eighth Census, manufacturing schedules.

39. *Journal*, July 27, 1859, and Apr. 21, 1860.

40. Seventh Census, Eighth Census, and Tenth Census, manufacturing schedules.

41. Seventh Census, Eighth Census, Ninth Census, and Tenth Census, manufacturing schedules.

42. Edward White, ed., *Evansville and its Men of Mark* (Evansville, 1873), 25–26; *History of Vanderburgh County*, 146; *Journal*, Nov. 22, 1855.

43. Seventh Census, manufacturing schedules.

44. *Journal*, Nov. 22, 1855.

45. Eighth Census, manufacturing schedules.

46. Ninth Census and Tenth Census, manufacturing schedules.

47. Tenth Census, manufacturing schedules.

48. *Industries of Evansville: Trade, Commerce and Manufactures* (Evansville, 1880), 85; Betty Lawson Walters, "Furniture Makers of Indiana."

49. Robert, *Evansville*, 355; Ninth Census, manufacturing schedules; *Industries of Evansville*, 85–86.

50. *The Sanborn Fire Insurance Maps*, Indiana, 1884, reel 7.

51. Tenth Census, manufacturing schedules; *Industries of Evansville*, 85–86.

52. Robert, *Evansville*, 350; Tenth Census, manufacturing schedules.

53. *History of Vanderburgh County*, 17; *Industries of Evansville*, 156; Eighth Census and Tenth Census, manufacturing schedules.

54. Eighth Census, manufacturing schedules; *Journal*, June 10, 1858.

55. Donald E. Baker, "Willard Carpenter, Eccentric Philanthropist: The Life and Times of the Founder of Willard Library," in *Where There's a Willard: The First 100 Years of the Willard Library of Evansville, Indiana*, ed. Selma Schaperjohn, (Evansville, 1986), 14.

56. *Industries of Evansville*, 75; Robert, *Evansville*, 404–5; Ninth Census, manufacturing schedules; Journal, Jan. 13, 1875.

57. Eighth Census and Tenth Census, population schedules.

58. Eighth Census and Ninth Census, population schedules. A drawing of Heilman's residence and its grounds can be found in *Griffing's Atlas of Vanderburgh County, Indiana* (Philadelphia, 1880), 41.

59. The 1880 census differs from preceding enumerations in that it provides a column indicating the relationship of individuals to the head of the household. As a result, in data bases derived from earlier censuses in-laws and other distant kin are sometimes counted as unrelated boarders. For the sake of consistency, this data for 1880 has been excluded from this analysis. If it is taken into account, the percentage of employer households without unrelated members other than servants rises to 89.2. Eighth Census and Tenth Census, manufacturing and population schedules.

60. Eighth Census, manufacturing schedules; Thirteenth Annual Report of the Commissioner of Labor, *Hand and Machine Labor*, v. 2 (Washington, 1899), 1106–9.

61. This sketch was compiled with the *Sanborn Fire Insurance Map*, 1884; and *Hand and Machine Labor*, 2:1106–9.

62. Tenth Census, manufacturing schedules.

63. *Hand and Machine Labor*, 2:1106–9.

64. Eighth Census and Ninth Census, population schedules.

65. Evansville *Courier*, Sept. 17, 1886.

66. Indiana, *Fourth Biennial Report of the Department of Statistics for 1891–92* (Indianapolis, 1892), 99.

67. *Courier*, Oct. 6, 1876, and Oct. 3, 1877; United States Census Bureau, *Report on the Statistics of Wages in Manufacturing Industries*, by Jos. D. Weeks (Washington, 1883), 341. The last year that the wages of male weavers were listed by Weeks was 1870, when they reportedly earned $4 a day, substantially more than any other manual worker in the mill.

68. *Report on the Statistics of Wages*, 384–85.

69. Eighth Census and Ninth Census, population schedules.

70. *Courier*, Sept. 26, 1878, and Oct. 4, 5, 1879; Tenth Census, manufacturing schedules.

71. *Fourth Biennial Report*, 116.

72. *Hand and Machine Labor*, 1:371, and 2:1439–57.

73. Ibid., v. 1, 371.

74. *Harness* 2 (Mar. 1888), 16.

75. Ninth Census, manufacturing schedules.

76. Eighth Census and Ninth Census, populations schedules; *Journal,* May 11, 1871; Tenth Census, manufacturing schedules.

77. David Montgomery, *The Fall of the House of Labor: The Workplace, the State, and American Labor Activism, 1865–1925* (Cambridge, Eng., 1987), 180.

78. Eighth Census and Ninth Census, population schedules; *Report on the Statistics of Wages,* 6, 184, 191.

79. Montgomery, *Fall of the House of Labor,* 191–213.

80. *Fourth Biennial Report,* 63.

81. Frank T. Stockton, *The International Molders' Union of North America* (Baltimore, 1921), 188; Daniel Walkowitz, *Worker City, Company Town,* 35.

82. *Fourth Biennial Report,* 116.

83. Ibid. 347–49

84. For a comparison with workers in Pittsburgh, see Peter R. Shergold, *Working-Class Life: The "American Standard" in Comparative Perspective, 1899–1913* (Pittsburgh, 1982), 179

85. This assumes that the $40 that childless couples averaged on meat purchases was close to a standard. Though no information is available for 1891, data on Evansville retail meat prices in 1880 exist. Most cuts of mutton, pork, and beef cost about ten cents a pound. These prices were 33 percent less than prevailing prices in 1870. Assuming that prices in the 1880s did not increase, $20 would buy 200 pounds of meat, which averages 3.8 pounds a week. For prices, see Jos. D. Weeks, "Report on the Necessaries of Life in the United States," Tenth Census, 20:54.

86. *Sanborn Fire Insurance Maps,* 1884.

87. Weeks, *Statistics of Wages,* 341.

88. *Fourth Biennial Report,* 347–49.

89. Records of Inventory, Circuit Court, Vanderburgh County, August 1885–August 1889.

90. *Fourth Biennial Report,* 347–49.

91. On the connection between poverty and the life cycle in three nineteenth-century English towns, see John Foster, *Class Struggle and the Industrial Revolution* (London, 1974), 94–99.

92. Circuit Court, estate inventories of William Tieman, p. 185, Philip Woehler, p. 249, and Christian Hobell, p. 373.

93. A sample of every ten families reveals that only five of 117 working-class families sent their children under the age of sixteen to work. One was a cooper—the fifteen-year-old in question was employed as a cooper's apprentice. Eighth Census, population schedules.

94. The discussion that follows is based on a survey of every household in which a cooper, cabinetmaker, harness maker or molder resided. Tenth Census, population schedules.

95. *Fourth Biennial Report*, 347–49.

96. This analysis is based on an attempt to link cooper, molder, cabinetmaker and harness maker heads of households and their employed children as they appeared in the 1880 census, with their listings in the 1890 city directory.

97. Hartmut Keil warns against viewing occupational designations as static categories, arguing that "their relative importance and status were considerably affected by fundamental economic transformations." "Chicago's German Working Class in 1900," in *German Workers in Industrial Chicago, 1850–1910: A Comparative Perspective*, ed. Keil and John B. Jentz (DeKalb, Ill., 1983), 27.

98. Mack Walker, *Germany and the Emigration, 1816–1885* (Cambridge, Mass., 1964), 47–53; Wolfgang Köllmann and Peter Marschalck, "German Emigration to the United States, *Perspectives in American History* 7 (1973): 524–31; Bruce Carlan Levine, "'In the Spirit of 1848': German-Americans and the Fight over Slavery's Expansion" (Ph.D. diss., University of Rochester, 1980), 29–30; Toni Pierenkemper, "Labour Market, Labour Force and Standard of Living: from Agriculture to Industry," in *Population, Labour and Migration in 19th and 20th-Century Germany*, ed. Klaus J. Bade (Hamburg, 1987), 39–40.

99. Walker, *Germany and the Emigration*, 72–73; Levine, "'In the Spirit of 1848,'" 28–55.

100. Seventh Census, population schedules.

101. Eighth Census, population schedules.

102. The discussion of the occupational structure of the German community that follows is based on a tally of all persons listed with an occupation in the population schedules of the tenth census.

103. Kathleen Neils Conzen, *Immigrant Milwaukee, 1836–1860: Accommodation and Community in a Frontier City* (Cambridge, Mass., 1976), 153.

104. *History of Vanderburgh County*, 277–303; *Directory* (1890), 18–20; Darrell E. Bigham, *Reflections on a Heritage: The German Americans in Southwestern Indiana* (Evansville, 1980), 4–10.

105. Tenth Census, population schedules. "Work force" refers to all persons listed in the census with an occupation.

106. *Sanborn Fire Insurance Map, 1884*; Tenth Census, population schedules.

107. Tenth Census, population schedules.

108. Ninth Census, population schedules.

109. Tenth Census, population schedules.

110. *History of Vanderburgh County*, 297.

111. Tenth Census, population schedules. For a thorough treatment of black society in Evansville, see Darrel E. Bigham, *We Ask Only a Fair Trial: A History of the Black Community of Evansville, Indiana* (Bloomington, Ind., 1987).

112. Tenth Census, manufacturing schedules, Vanderburgh County. Bigham finds that about 45 percent of black women in the city worked, compared with only 10 percent of white immigrant women and 25 percent of

native white women. *We Ask Only a Fair Trial,* 66. This supports Claudia Goldin's argument that black women participated in the labor force on an average of three times the rate of white women. Differences between married women of the two races were even greater. "Female Labor Force Participation: Origin of Black and White Differences, 1870 and 1880," *Journal of Economic History* 37 (Mar. 1977): 87–108.

113. Bigham, *We Ask Only a Fair Trial,* 21–34, 56–60.

114. Tenth Census, manufacturing schedules.

115. Robert, *Evansville,* 130.

116. See the letters written by George Vickery in Rockport to Samuel Vickery in Evansville, October 24 to November 29, 1873, Vickery Brothers Folder, Vanderburgh County Miscellaneous Materials, Indiana Historical Society Library.

117. *Courier,* June 18, 1880.

118. Eighth Census and Tenth Census, population schedules.

119. James H. McNeely to Hon. Conrad Baker, May 11, 1867, Box 3, Conrad Baker Papers, Indiana Historical Society Library.

120. Tenth Census, population schedules.

121. White, *Evansville and its Men of Mark,* 120.

122. Eighth Census and Tenth Census, population schedules.

123. Circuit Court, estate inventories of George Nolte, 5, and Peter Blend, 341. Those of butcher John Schmitt, 337, bank clerk Reinhold F. Schor, 549, ex-baker Jacob Sinzich, 81, and in Records of Inventory, Court of Common Pleas, traveling agent B. F. Norton, 97, reveal similar lists of goods.

124. *Journal,* Mar. 30 and Sept. 29, 1871, Mar. 5 and Dec. 28, 1872, Mar. 4, 1873, Jan. 3 and 10, 1874, Jan. 2, 1875; *Directory* (1871 and 1874).

125. *History of Vanderburgh County,* 390–92. Ancient Order of United Workmen, *Proceedings of the Supreme Lodge,* 1879–1882; Walter A. Legeman, comp., *Directory of Subordinate Lodges of the Ancient Order United Workmen, Located in Evansville, Indiana* (Evansville, 1894), esp. 157, 171–89. See also Cassity, *Defending A Way of Life,* 125–31. On the Knights of Honor, see *Courier,* July 1, 1886.

126. *Courier,* Jan. 22, 1886, July 1, 21, 1886, Dec. 29, 1886, June 23, 26, and 30, 1887, Dec. 29, 1887, July 11 and Dec. 5, 7, 1888, Dec. 7, 1889; *Directory* (1886 and 1890).

127. Legeman, *Directory of Subordinate Lodges.*

128. Circuit Court, estate inventory of John Bobinger, p. 249.

129. Ancient Order of United Workmen, *Proceedings of the Supreme Lodge* (Cincinnati, 1882), 518–41.

130. Much of the literature tends to focus on this likely result, portraying these associations as a cultural system that competed with unions for the loyalty of workers. For a good example, see Oestreicher, *Solidarity and Fragmentation: Working People and Class Consciousness in Detroit, 1875–1900* (Urbana, 1986), 30–75. It is not my intention to overturn this interpretation, for in many cases I believe it to be correct, but rather to suggest other possibilities of looking at this material.

131. On the relationship between the plebeian community and working-class power, see Couvares, *The Remaking of Pittsburgh*.

Chapter 5: The Search for a Majority

1. See the discussion of the literature in chapter one.

2. *History of Vanderburgh County, Indiana* (Madison, Wis., 1889), 67–69.

3. Evansville *Journal*, Mar. 10, 18, 1854.

4. Eric Foner, *Free Soil, Free Labor, Free Men*, 11–39.

5. Dietsch is alleged to have called the *Enquirer*, the Democratic paper, "an infamous hunker sheet, slavery and Nebraska swindle paper." Evansville *Enquirer*, June 26, 1855. He is briefly mentioned in Carl Wittke, *Refugees of Revolution: The German Forty-Eighters in America* (Philadelphia, 1952), 67, 269, and in Karl J. R. Arndt and May E. Olson, *German-American Newspapers and Periodicals, 1732–1955* (Heidelberg, 1961), 116.

6. *Journal*, June 27, 1854.

7. *Journal*, Oct. 13, 1854.

8. *Enquirer*, June 27, 1855.

9. *Journal*, Mar. 15, 17, 1856; *Enquirer*, Mar. 15, 17, and 21, 1856.

10. *Enquirer*, Mar. 26, 1856. The reference was to violence aimed at Germans in other cities, among them New Albany.

11. *Journal*, Apr. 9, 1856.

12. Ibid., Aug. 29, 1856.

13. This analysis is derived from the convention proceedings that appeared in the press between 1856 and 1860, from which the names of 125 activists were culled. Eighty of them were located in the population schedules of the Eighth Census.

14. *Journal*, Sept. 1, 1856; Holt, *The Political Crisis of the 1850s*, 163–69.

15. *Enquirer*, Oct. 17 and Nov. 7, 1856.

16. For biographical details, see Baker, "Willard Carpenter, Eccentric Philanthropist, 1–145; *A Biographical History of Eminent and Self Made Men of the State of Indiana* (Cincinnati, 1880), 12–15.

17. *Journal*, Nov. 10, 1856; *Enquirer*, Dec. 8, 1856.

18. John Ingle, Jr., president of the rival railroad line, was elected president of the association. *Enquirer*, Jan. 7, 1857.

19. *Journal*, Mar. 2–7, 10–12, 1857.

20. Ibid., Mar. 12, 1857.

21. Ibid., Mar. 17, 23, and 24, 1857.

22. Ibid., Apr. 6, 1857.

23. Ibid., Apr. 22 and July 13, 1857.

24. Quoted in Baker, "Willard Carpenter," 28.

25. Ibid., July 8, 13, 1857.

26. Ibid., July 11, 1857; *Enquirer*, July 14, 1857.

27. *Journal*, July 16, 17, 1857.

28. *Enquirer*, Oct. 30, 1857; *Journal*, Nov. 3, 1857.

29. *Journal*, Nov. 5, 1857.

30. *Journal*, Nov. 7, 1857.

31. Thornbrough, *Indiana in the Civil War Era, 1850–1880* (Indianapolis, 1965), 472–73.

32. *Journal*, Feb. 15, 16, and 17, 1858.

33. *Enquirer*, Feb. 12, 16, 18, and 20, 1858.

34. *Journal*, Feb. 20, 1858.

35. *Enquirer*, Feb. 25, 1858.

36. *Journal*, Feb. 22, 1858.

37. Eric Foner, *Free Soil, Free Labor, Free Men*.

38. For example, see *Journal*, Mar. 1, 25, 1858.

39. Ibid., Mar. 17, 1858.

40. *Journal*, Apr. 7, 1858

41. Democrats had opposed high schools as "aristocratic institutions . . . in which the children of the rich find easy admission and from which the children of the poor man . . . [are] excluded." *Enquirer*, Mar. 24, 1858.

42. *Journal*, Apr. 6, 7, 1858.

43. Ibid., Apr. 7, 1858.

44. Ibid., Oct. 15, 1858.

45. Like many a good Whig, Carpenter actively supported religion and reform. Prominent in the temperance movement, he bequeathed large donations on Protestant churches and reform agencies. In the 1850s, he chaired "bleeding Kansas" meetings, and his name appeared at the top of appeals for aid to free-soil forces (*Journal*, June 16 and Sept. 13, 1856). He is also believed to have been a "conductor" on the underground railroad. In his declining years, he stipulated that the local library he endowed be open to all races. Carpenter was not Democratic material. Baker, "Willard Carpenter," 13, 46.

46. *Enquirer*, July 18, 1856. Compare with Evans: "It is a dangerous thing to sneer at universal suffrage in this republican country. In France, it is tolerated to speak of the 'canaille,' and in England to talk of the 'mob' and the 'swinish multitude'; but this is neither France nor England." New York *Workingman's Advocate*, Nov. 7, 1829.

47. *Enquirer*, Aug. 25, 28, 1860.

48. *Journal*, Aug. 27, 1860.

49. Ibid., Nov. 9, 1860.

50. *Journal*, June 10, 1858. On the impoverishment of coopers, see the previous chapter.

51. Ibid.

52. Ibid., May 28, 1860. Twenty-nine individuals were identified as participants at a meeting of the "Mechanical and Working Classes" on May 24, 1860. The nativity of twenty-four has been determined from the census. Nine were German; all but one of the rest were native-born. The occupations of twenty-seven were identified in the census and city directory. Only two appear to have been journeymen.

53. *Enquirer*, May 31 and June 15, 1860; *Journal*, June 11, 12, 1860.

54. *Enquirer*, June 21, 1860.

55. This account of the celebration is based on reports of the *Enquirer* and the *Journal*, July 6, 1860.

56. *Journal*, July 9, 1860. On domesticity, see Nancy F. Cott, *The Bonds of Womanhood: "Woman's Sphere" in New England, 1780–1835* (New Haven, 1977); Mary Ryan, *Cradle of the Middle Class.*

57. *Journal*, July 7, 1860.

58. Ibid., July 6, 1860

59. Thornbrough, *Indiana in the Civil War Era*, 118.

60. *Gazette*, Feb. 14, 1862.

61. Ibid., Aug. 30, 1862.

62. Ibid., Oct. 11, 1862.

63. For local Republican support for black rights, see Bigham, *We Ask Only a Fair Trial*, 15–18.

64. *Journal*, Aug. 20, 1864.

65. Ibid., Feb. 4, 1863.

66. Ibid., Aug. 1, 2, 1864. Frank L. Klement, *The Copperheads in the Middle West* (Chicago, 1960), 134–69.

67. See *Journal*, Mar. 22 and Apr. 1, 2, 4, and 5, 1862.

68. *Gazette*, Mar. 15, 1862.

69. Ibid., Apr. 4, 1863; *Journal*, Apr. 4, 1863.

70. *Journal*, Apr. 9, 1862; *Gazette*, Apr. 11, 1863.

71. *Journal*, June 1, 1864.

72. Ibid., June 7, 1864.

73. Daniel W. Snepp, "Evansville's Channels of Trade and the Secession Movement," *Indiana Historical Society Publications* 8 (1928): 339. Quote is from *Journal*, Apr. 17, 1862.

74. Letter of C. Denby, Evansville, to Capt. J. L. Orr, Dec. 15, 1863, Correspondence of James L. Orr, Indiana Historical Society Library.

75. *Journal*, July 29, 1863.

76. Between 1861 and 1864, the price of roasting beef rose from 7.5 to 15 cents a pound, soup pieces climbed from 6 to 10, veal and mutton experienced similar jumps, and the price of pork tripled. *Tenth Census*, "Report on the Average Retail Prices of Necessaries of Life in the United States," v. 20; see also *Gazette*, May 24, 1862, Feb. 7 and July 25, 1863.

77. *Gazette*, Jan. 17, 1863.

78. *Journal*, May 2, 1864, and Sept. 18, 1861.

79. *Ledger*, Apr. 20, 23, 1860.

80. *Journal*, Oct. 24, 1863.

81. Ibid., May 4, 1860; *Iron Molder's International Journal*, Apr. 11, 1864.

82. *FTR*, Apr. 2, 1864; *Journal*, Apr. 5, 1865.

83. *FTR*, Feb. 13 and Aug. 20, 1864.

84. *Directory* (1863 and 1866).

85. Carpenter J. L. McCutcheon sent $42 to help the Review in 1863 and John Wilkinson of the machinists' union responded to a later crisis by canvassing "among the lawyers and merchants," emerging with $100.32. *FTR*, Nov. 28, 1863, and Sept. 23, 1865.

86. Ibid., July 15, 1865.

87. This analysis is based on names listed in *FTR* during 1865.

88. *Directory* (1863 and 1866).

89. Philip S. Foner, *History of the Labor Movement*, 328; David Montgomery, *Beyond Equality*, 100.

90. *FTR*, July 9, 1864; and *Journal*, June 29, 1864.

91. *FTR*, July 9, 1864.

92. *FTR*, Sept. 10, 1864.

93. *Journal*, June 28, 1864.

94. Ibid., June 30, 1864. There are no extant copies of the *Times*, or substantial runs of any English Democratic paper until the mid-1870s. However, positions can be gleaned from the columns of the *Journal*, which was in the practice of reprinting articles from rival papers, then dissecting them, line by line.

95. *Journal*, July 22, 1864.

96. See the proceedings and resolutions of the Vanderburgh County Convention in *Journal*, July 25, 26, 1864.

97. Evansville *Weekly Demokrat*, Oct. 5, 1864.

98. *Journal*, Oct. 10, 1864.

99. For gubernatorial results, see *Journal*, Oct. 1, 14, 1864; for the presidential tally, see *History of Vanderburgh County, Indiana* (Madison, Wis., 1889), 68.

100. Montgomery, *Beyond Equality*, 113.

101. *Directory* (1860, 1863, and 1865).

102. On the establishment of a stemmery, see *Journal*, Jan. 30, 1865; on the discharging of white workers, see Ibid., Apr. 5, 1869, when long-smoldering passions regarding the event were dragged into a city election.

103. Darrel E. Bigham, *We Ask Only a Fair Trial*, 39.

104. *Ibid.*; letters of Conrad Baker to Governor Morton, Aug. 9, 1865, J. Jones to O. P. Morton, Aug. 2, 1865, and Alvah Johnson to Oliver P. Morton, Aug. 8, 1865, Conrad Baker Papers, Box 1, Indiana Historical Society Library.

105. Jones to Morton; and Baker to Morton.

106. *Journal*, Aug. 3, 1865.

107. Record Book of the First Presbyterian Church, Session minutes, Feb. 28, 1866. First Presbyterian Church of Evansville, Records, 1821–1926, reel 1, Indiana State Library.

108. Vine Street Presbyterian Church Session Book, Dec. 21, 1868, Feb. 17, 1869. First Presbyterian Church of Evansville, Records.

109. Carroll Smith-Rosenberg, "Beauty, the Beast, and the Militant Woman: A Case Study in Sex Roles and Social Stress in Jacksonian America," *American Quarterly* 23 (1971): 562–84.

110. *History of Vanderburgh County*, 399; First Presbyterian Church, session minutes, Nov. 24, 1866.

111. *Annual Report of the Vanderburgh Christian Home* (Evansville, 1872).

112. *Journal*, Sept. 26, 1865.

113. *FTR*, July 15, 1865.

114. Ibid., July 22, 1865.

115. *Journal*, Aug. 24, 25, 1865.

116. Ibid., Aug. 25, 1865.

117. Ibid., Dec. 7, 1865.

118. Ibid., Dec. 15, 1865.

119. Ibid., Dec. 15, 1865.

120. *FTR*, Feb. 10, 1866. Niblack also received praise from the machinist's and blacksmith's union whose officers assured him that his name "will be [engraved] on the hearts of the toiling millions." Jan. 20, 1866.

121. *Journal*, Feb. 14, 1866.

122. Ibid., Feb. 16, 1866.

123. Ibid., Feb. 17, 20, 1866. The *Courier* was the most recent local Democratic newspaper.

124. Ibid., Mar. 19, 1866. The meeting was called to order by Robert H. Hunter, who moved that George T. Cochran be named chair. Both were officers of the machinist's union.

125. Ibid., Mar. 24, 1866.

126. *FTR*, Mar. 31, 1866; *Journal*, Mar. 26, 1866.

127. *Journal*, Mar. 21, 23, 1866.

128. Ibid., Apr. 5, Oct. 12, 1866, Apr. 4, 1867.

129. Ibid., Apr. 13, 1866.

130. Ibid., Apr. 30 and May 31, 1866.

131. Ibid., Dec. 21, 1866.

132. Irwin Unger, *Greenback Era*, 68–85. See also the discussion of the Democratic convention in Journal, Dec. 16, 1867.

133. *Journal*, Jan. 27, 1868.

134. *Demokrat*, Apr. 5, 1868.

135. *Weekly Demokrat*, Apr. 7, 1868.

136. *Journal*, Feb. 12, 1868.

137. *Demokrat*, Apr. 5, 1868.

138. *Journal*, Apr. 1, 1868.

139. Ibid., Apr. 4, 1868.

140. Ibid., Apr. 6, 1868.

141. Ibid., Apr. 8, 1868.

142. *Demokrat*, Aug. 21, 1868.

143. *Journal*, Oct. 16, 1868.

144. Ibid., Mar. 23, 1867.

145. Ibid., Apr. 19, 1866, and Dec. 24, 1868.

146. Ibid., Mar. 28, 1870.

147. Ibid., Apr. 7, 1870.

148. *Weekly Demokrat*, May 10, 1870. See also the daily issues of May 12 and 13.

149. Quoted in *Journal*, May 25, 1870.

150. Ibid., Sept. 25, 1865.

151. Ibid., Mar. 20, 1867.

152. Ibid., Apr. 3, 1868.

Chapter 6: Class Conflicts as Political Opportunity

1. For the turners, see *Journal*, Jan. 31, Feb. 22, 1870; for the chair makers, Feb. 19, 28, 1870; and for the printers, Feb. 18, 19, 21, and 22, Mar. 7, 1870.

2. Ibid., May 7, 1872.

3. Central Labor Union, *Trades and Labor Directory, Evansville, Ind., 1895–96*, 61; *Journal*, Mar. 20, 1872.

4. *Demokrat* and *Union*, Mar. 2, 1872.

5. *Journal*, Dec. 28, 1870.

6. *Iron Molders' Journal*, Apr. 11, 1864, May 10, 1864, July 1, 1870; Ninth Census, population schedules. The total of eighty-four molders included those employed in the machine shops, which at this time remained unorganized.

7. On the International's position, see Frank T. Stockton, *International Molders' Union*.

8. *Journal*, Jan. 30, 31, 1873, Mar. 4, 1873.

9. Ibid., Feb. 14, 1873. See also Feb. 26 and 27.

10. Ibid., Feb. 27, 1873.

11. Evansville, Council Proceedings, Mar. 10, 1873; *Journal*, Mar. 18, 1873; *Demokrat*, Feb. 26, 1873.

12. The following narrative of events was culled from newspaper reporter's account of the inquest and the trial. *Journal*, Mar. 18 and 19, Apr. 30, May 1 and 2, 1873; *Weekly Demokrat*, Mar. 18, 25, 1873.

13. This was no small matter. The trial revealed that nonunion as well as union men frequented saloons. Along with Roelker's presence on the day of the murder it made it difficult to correlate union intimidation with a proclivity toward drink.

14. *Journal*, Mar. 19, 1873.

15. Ibid., Mar. 18, 1873.

16. Ibid., May 1, 1873.

17. Ibid., May 2, 1873.

18. Ibid.

19. *Weekly Demokrat*, Mar. 25, 1873; *Journal*, Apr. 30, May 1 and 2, 1873.

20. *Iron Molders' Journal*, Mar. 31, 1873.

21. *Demokrat*, May 6, 1873; *Journal*, May 5, 15, 1873. On the petition, see *Journal*, Apr. 2, 1874.

22. *Journal*, June 26, 27, 1873.

23. Ibid., May 30, 1873.

24. Ibid., Aug. 6, 1873.

25. *Demokrat*, Mar. 20, 1873.

26. *Workingman's Advocate*, July 19, 26, 1873.

27. *Journal*, Oct. 17, 1873.

28. Council Proceedings, Dec. 22, 1873; *Journal*, Dec. 23, 1873.

29. Council Proceedings, Dec. 29, 1873.

30. *Journal,* Jan. 15, 1874; see also Jan. 22 1874.

31. Quoted in *Journal,* Jan. 23, 1874.

32. On the Van Riper council, see Baker, "Willard Carpenter."

33. *Journal,* Apr. 4, 6, 1871, and Apr. 3, 4, 1872, Apr. 9, 1873.

34. *Journal,* Jan. 26, 1874.

35. Edward White, *Evansville and its Men of Mark,* 119–20. Also, *Journal,* Apr. 9, 1873.

36. *Journal,* Apr. 1, 1874.

37. Ibid., Apr. 2, 1874.

38. Ibid., Apr. 4, 1874.

39. Ibid., Apr. 3, 1873. Perhaps Kleiner's inexperience meant that he would have fewer debts to pay to the party, a thought that might have concerned the Democratic leadership.

40. *Demokrat,* Apr. 2, 1874.

41. *Journal,* Apr. 2, 1874.

42. *Demokrat,* Apr. 5, 1874; *Workingman's Advocate,* Apr. 11, 1874.

43. *Journal,* Apr. 6, 1874.

44. Ibid., Apr. 8, 1874.

45. *Workingman's Advocate,* Apr. 11, 1874; *Journal,* Apr. 9, 1874.

46. *Journal,* Apr. 8, 1874.

47. Ibid., Apr. 11, 1874.

48. Ibid., May 19, 1874.

49. *Journal,* June 5, 1874.

50. Thornbrough, *Indiana in the Civil War Era,* 289–90; Unger, *Greenback Era,* 242.

51. *Journal,* Aug. 31, 1874.

52. Ibid., Sept. 17, 1874. For Heilman's position on the currency debate, see the issue of Mar. 16, 1874.

53. Ibid., Oct. 16, 1874.

54. Ibid., Mar. 29, 1875.

55. Ibid., Feb. 1, 1875.

56. Ibid., Mar. 29, 1875.

57. Ibid., Apr. 6, 1875.

58. Ibid., Apr. 12, 1875.

59. Quoted in Ibid., Apr. 12, 1875.

60. *Courier,* June 8, 1875.

61. Ibid., June 11, 1875.

62. "Supplement" to the *Courier,* Nov. 7, 1875.

63. *Journal,* Apr. 6, 1876.

64. *Courier,* Feb. 22, 1876; *Journal,* Feb. 24, 1876; *Demokrat,* Feb. 24, 1876.

65. *Courier,* Dec. 12, 1875.

66. Ibid., Jan. 29, Feb. 1, 1876.

67. *Journal,* Dec. 27, 1854, Jan. 18, 1856, Feb. 4, 1860, Dec. 18, 1860; Paul Boyer, *Urban Masses and Moral Order in America, 1820–1920* (Cambridge, Mass., 1978).

68. *Courier,* Dec. 12, 1875.

69. Ibid., Jan. 29, 1876.

70. Ibid., Dec. 5, 1876.

71. Ibid., Dec. 6, 1876.

72. *Journal* and *Courier*, Dec. 8, 1876.

73. *Journal*, Dec. 8, 11, 1876; *Courier*, Dec. 8, 1876.

74. *Courier*, Dec. 10, 1876; *Journal*, Dec. 9, 11, 1876.

75. *Courier*, Dec. 9, 10, 1876.

76. Ibid., Dec. 10, 1876.

77. Ibid., Dec. 12, 1876.

78. Ibid., Dec. 19, 1876.

79. *Courier*, Aug. 23, 1876; *Journal*, Jan. 31, 1877.

80. Robert, *Evansville*, 319–20, 352–53; Tenth Census, manufacturing schedules. The "employees" of the Evansville Furniture Company thought about joining a general strike in July 1877, and the Evansville Foundry Association aligned itself with other foundries in opposing a demand for a wage increase by the molders' union (*Courier*, Oct. 15, 1879). It is likely that competitive pressures forced them to emphasize profits at the expense of cooperative principles. Philip S. Foner, *History of the Labor Movement*, 420.

81. Lawrence Goodwyn, *The Populist Moment: A Short History of the Agrarian Movement in America* (Oxford, 1978).

82. *Journal*, Jan. 31, Feb. 14, Apr. 18, 1877; *Courier*, Apr. 15, 19, 1877.

83. For example, see *Journal*, July 21, 1877.

84. *Journal*, Mar. 17, 1877.

85. Ibid., Apr. 5, 1877.

86. *Courier*, June 2, 1877.

87. Ibid., June 27, 1877.

88. Philip S. Foner, *The Great Labor Uprising of 1877* (New York, 1977).

89. *Journal*, July 24, 1877.

90. *Courier*, July 22, 24, 1877.

91. Ibid.

92. Ibid., July 24, 1877; *Journal*, July 24, 1877.

93. *Journal*, July 25, 1877.

94. *Journal* and *Courier*, July 26, 1877.

95. *Journal* and *Courier*, July 27, 1877. A "Bush Taylor" is listed in the 1880 population census as a barber.

96. *Journal* and *Courier*, July 27, 1877.

97. *Journal* and *Courier*, July 28, 1877.

98. *Courier*, July 29, 1877.

99. Ibid., July 28, 1877. Italics are mine.

100. *Journal*, July 27, 1877.

101. Ibid., July 30, 1877.

102. Matilda Gresham, *Life of Walter Quintin Gresham, 1832–1895* (Chicago, 1919), 394–97; *Journal*, July 27, 1877.

103. *Journal*, July 30, 1877.

104. This account was culled from the reports in the *Journal*, the *Courier* and the *Weekly Demokrat*, July 31, 1877.

105. *Courier*, Aug. 3, 1877.

106. Ibid., Sept. 6, 1877.

107. Ibid., Nov. 12, 1877.

108. Ibid., Aug. 27, 1877, and May 10, 1878. On a socialist militia in Chicago, see Christine Heiss, "German Radicals in Industrial America: The Lehr-und Wehr-Verein in Gilded Age Chicago" in Hartmut Keil and John B. Jentz, eds., *German Workers in Industrial Chicago, 1850–1910: A Comparative Perspective* (DeKalb, Ill., 1983), 206–23.

109. Evansville *Union*, May 11, 1878. The German and Republican *Union* identified the militia members as members of "socialist workingmen's parties" and expressed disapproval of "loud-mouths" who offered slogans like "down with the rich." In the *Courier*, May 10, 1878, a local socialist claimed to be in contact with an unspecified Chicago military society.

110. *Courier*, May 10, 1878. Newspaper reports are too vague to identify the affiliation of these groups with any precision.

111. *Demokrat*, May 11, 1878.

112. *Courier*, July 12, 1878.

113. Ibid., Aug. 19, 1877.

114. Ibid., Nov. 13, 1877.

115. *Journal*, Aug. 27, 1877; and *Courier*, Aug. 30, 1877.

116. *Courier*, Sept. 10, 1879.

117. *Courier*, Oct. 2, 3, and 4, 1877; *Demokrat*, Oct. 3, 1877; *Journal*, Oct. 2, 3, 1877.

118. *Courier*, Feb. 3, 1878.

119. *Journal*, Mar. 24, 1878; *Courier*, Mar. 26, 1878.

120. *Courier* and *Journal* Mar. 26, 1878.

121. *Courier*, Mar. 27, 30, 1878.

122. *Journal*, Mar. 8, 1878.

123. *Courier*, Aug. 2, 4, 6, 8, 9, and 13, 1878.

124. *Journal*, Apr. 3, 4, 1878.

125. Tenth Census, population schedules. Analysis of persons listing occupations reveal that blacks were concentrated in the First, Second and Sixth wards, where they comprised 25.2, 17.3 and 12.8 percent of the work force. The Fourth and Fifth had the smallest black workforce, both in absolute and relative terms (6.0 percent in the Fourth, and 4.8 in the Fifth).

126. *Courier*, Oct. 10, 1878, Oct. 15, 1880.

127. Ibid., Sept. 30, 1879.

128. On the revival of trade, see *Journal*, Oct. 1, 1879.

129. Ibid., Oct. 6, 10, 1879; *Courier*, Oct. 5, 9, 10, and 21, 1879.

130. Ibid., Oct. 21, 1879.

131. *Courier* and *Journal*, Oct. 23, 1879.

132. *Courier*, Oct. 21, 1879. Ritz was identified as a socialist during the railroad strikes of 1877. Ibid., July 24, 1877.

133. *Journal*, Oct. 7, 1880. The association of Roelker with Heilman is made in *Courier*, Sept. 24, 1880.

134. Ibid., Oct. 12, 1880.

135. *Courier*, Oct. 29, 1880.

136. Ibid., Oct. 30, 31, 1880; Ted C. Hinckley, "The Politics of Sinophobia: Garfield, the Morey letter and the Presidential Election of 1880," *Ohio History* 89 (1980): 381–99.

137. *Courier*, Nov. 4, 1880.

138. *Journal*, Nov. 8, 1884.

139. *Courier*, Oct. 1, 1884.

140. Ibid., Mar. 17, Apr. 2, 1882

141. Ibid., Mar. 23, 24, 1882.

142. Ibid., Mar. 26, 1882.

143. Ibid., Apr. 4, 1882.

144. *Journal*, Nov. 14, 1882.

145. For example, see *Journal*, Dec. 20, 1882, Feb. 28, Mar. 3 and 10, 1883.

146. Ibid., Mar. 10, 1883. Italics are mine.

147. Ibid., Mar. 25, 1883.

148. *Courier*, Mar. 30, 1883.

149. *Journal*, Apr. 3, 1883.

150. Record of the Proceedings of the General Assembly of the Knights of Labor, Sept. 7–11, 1880, p. 210, Powderly Papers, reel 65; *Journal of United Labor*, June 15, 1880; *Journal*, Jan. 1, 1884; Jonathan Garlock, "A Structural Analysis of the Knights of Labor: A Prolegomenon to the History of the Producing Classes" (Ph.D. diss., University of Rochester, 1974).

151. *National Labor Tribune* (hereafter *NLT*), Aug. 7, 1880.

152. Ibid., Nov. 20, 27, 1880; *Journal of United Labor*, Nov. 15, 1880.

153. *Courier*, Nov. 29, 1881.

154. R. D. Ramsay to T. V. Powderly, Sept. 12, 1882, Powderly Papers, reel 4; Tenth Census, population schedules; *Directory* (1883).

155. Gregory S. Kealey and Bryan D. Palmer, *Dreaming of What Might Be: The Knights of Labor in Ontario, 1880–1900* (Cambridge, 1982).

156. *Journal*, Aug. 6, 13, 1882.

157. *Journal*, Aug. 20, 1882. Those attending the meeting were listed by name and have been identified in the populations schedules of the Tenth Census. Only 27.2 percent were of German (or Swiss, as in the case of Lutz) background. Well over half were native-born, and the rest were British immigrants.

158. Ibid., Aug. 6, 1882. Lutz's shop was capitalized at three hundred dollars. Tenth Census, manufacturing schedules.

159. George A. Klenck to T. V. Powderly, July 7, 1887, Powderly Papers, reel 22.

160. *Journal*, Jan. 27, 1883.

161. Phillip S. Foner, *History of the Labor Movement*, 2:55, 158.

162. *Journal*, Jan. 1, 1884.

163. John Commons, et al., *History of Labour in the United States*, v. 2 (New York, 1946), 368–75.

164. *Directory* (1886), 29; Emil Levy and Charles Spalding to T. V. Powderly, Mar. 9, 1886, Powderly Papers, reel 14.

165. *Courier*, 1885: Dec. 8 (plasterers); Dec. 17 (furniture workers) 1886:

Feb. 9 (shoemakers, tailors and saddle and harness makers); Feb. 19 (machinists and blacksmiths); Feb. 24 (painters); Mar. 17 (coopers); Mar. 24 (musicians); Apr. 4 (bakers); and Apr. 13 (stonecutters). *John Swinton's Paper,* Apr. 18, 1886 (brick makers).

166. Garlock, "A Structural Analysis." The role of organizers Levy and Spalding is displayed in press reports. *Courier,* Feb. 19, 1886 (railroad workers), Feb. 24 (hod-carriers), Mar. 5 (saw mill workers), Mar. 17 (miners), Mar. 19 (collarmakers), and Mar. 20 (tinners).

167. *Demokrat* and *Courier,* Mar. 10, 1886.

168. *Courier,* Mar. 10, 13, 14, 15, 1886.

169. Ibid., Mar. 11, 20, and 22, 1886.

170. Ibid., Mar. 14, 23, 1886

171. Ibid., Mar. 27, 1886.

172. Ibid., Feb. 21, 1886.

173. Ibid., Feb. 23, 24, 1886.

174. *John Swinton's Paper,* Mar. 7, 1886.

175. *Courier,* Feb. 5, 1886. Presumably this was a ratification of the International Union's boycott that extended to the label of the Progressive Cigarmakers' Union. Commons, *History of Labour,* 2:401.

176. *Courier,* Apr. 16, 28, 1886.

177. Ibid., Apr. 13, 18, 1886.

178. *Courier,* Mar. 9, 16, 1886.

179. Ibid., Apr. 4, 1886; *John Swinton's Paper,* Apr. 18, 1886.

180. *John Swinton's Paper,* Mar. 21, Apr. 18, 1886 (bricklayers and carpenters); *Courier,* Apr. 8, 1886 (furniture workers).

181. *Courier,* Apr. 27, 1886.

182. Ibid., May 2, 1886.

183. Ibid., May 4, 8, 1886.

184. Ibid., May 7, 1886.

185. Commons, *History of Labour,* 2:396–97.

186. *Courier,* May 8, 1886.

187. *Courier,* May 8, 16, 1886.

188. *Journal,* Apr. 18, 19, and 20, 1886.

189. *Courier,* Apr. 24, 1886.

190. Ibid., Apr. 26, 1886.

191. Ibid., Apr. 30, 1886.

192. Ibid., Mar. 26, 1886.

193. Ibid., Apr. 4, 1886.

194. *Journal,* Apr. 2, 1886.

195. Ibid., Apr. 7, 1886.

196. *Courier* and *Journal,* Apr. 6, 1886.

197. Emil Levy and Chas. A. Spalding to T. V. Powderly, Mar. 9, 1886, Powderly Papers, reel 14.

198. H. J. Maser and Augustus Eltonhead to T. V. Powderly, Jan. 26, 1887, Powderly Papers, reel 21.

199. *Courier,* Nov. 18, 1886.

200. James C. Smith to T. V. Powderly, Feb. 15, 1887, Powderly Papers, reel 21.

201. See Commons, *History of Labour*, 2:399–401.

202. T. V. Powderly to J. C. Smith, Feb. 21, 1887, Powderly Papers, reel 48.

203. *Courier*, Feb. 23 and Mar. 15, 25, 1887; *Directory* (1886). A similar change in leadership is noted in Richard Jules Oestreicher, *Solidarity and Fragmentation*, 177–78.

204. Clerks also mounted demands for shorter hours, and would in June of 1887 form their own assembly of the Knights of Labor. *Courier*, May 8, 1886, and June 17, 1887.

205. *Courier*, Mar. 25, 1887.

206. Ibid., Feb. 23, 1887.

207. Ibid., Mar. 25, 1887.

208. Steven Ross, "The Culture of Political Economy: Henry George and the American Working Class," *Southern California Quarterly* 65 (Summer 1983): 145–66, esp. 150.

209. *Courier*, Mar. 27, 1887.

210. *Demokrat*, Mar. 22, 1887; see also *Courier*, Mar. 28, 1887.

211. *Demokrat*, Mar. 29, 1887.

212. *Journal*, Apr. 3, 1887.

213. Ibid., Apr. 5, 1887.

214. *Courier*, Apr. 6, 1887.

215. Montgomery, *Beyond Equality*, 215–19.

216. On Keichle, see *Iron Molders' Journal*, May 10, 1864 and on Gorman see the same, Oct. 31, 1882.

217. See chapter four.

218. Central Labor Union, *Trades and Labor Directory*, 65.

219. Ibid., 27, 29, 39.

220. Nick Salvatore, *Eugene V. Debs*, 37–45. Salvatore emphasizes the nonconflict aspect of Debs's years as a Democrat while setting Debs's vision within the American language of republicanism.

Chapter 7: The Industrial Barony of W. C. DePauw

1. C. Bradford Mitchell, *Merchant Steam Vessels*; Ninth Census, manufacturing schedules, Floyd County.

2. Louis C. Hunter, *Steamboats on the Western Rivers*, 481–88, 498–504; Victor M. Bogle, "Nineteenth Century River Town," 315.

3. Allen Johnson and Dumas Malone, eds., *Dictionary of American Biography*, v. 5, (New York, 1930), 516–17; "History of Plate-Glass Manufacture and of Captain John Baptiste Ford," *Bulletin of the American Ceramic Society* 18 (July 1939), 262–67.

4. Eighth Census, Ninth Census, and Tenth Census, population schedules.

5. Eighth Census, population schedules; and *Directory* (1871).

6. Among those who resided in New Albany in 1871, 57.1 percent were listed as "carpenter"—only 8.3 percent listed "ship carpenter." Occasionally the press bemoaned the inability of ship carpenters to find work locally. *Ledger*, Oct. 19, 1866, Sept. 28, 1871. Also see letter of "Ship Carpenter," Jan. 26, 1870.

7. Ninth Census, and Tenth Census, manufacturing schedules.

8. Eighth Census, and Tenth Census, population schedules.

9. *Biographical and Historical Souvenir for the Counties of Clark, Crawford, Harrison, Floyd, Jefferson, Jennings, Scott and Washington, Indiana* (Compiled and published by John M. Gresham & Co., Chicago, 1889), 89; D. P. Robbins, *New Albany, Ind.: Its Advantages and Surroundings* (New Albany, 1892), 55–56; Betty Lawson Walters, "Furniture Makers of Indiana," *Indiana Historical Society Publications*, 25 (Indianapolis, 1972), 191; Ninth Census and Tenth Census, manufacturing schedules.

10. *Commercial*, July 30, 1866.

11. Glenn Porter and Harold Livesay argue that changes in national capital markets, inflation, and the cash economy all combined to liberate the manufacturer from indebtedness to the distributing merchant, and also served to create greater ties between manufacturers and the growing number of bankers. *Merchants and Manufacturers*, 116–30.

12. *Ledger*, Sept. 19, 1864.

13. Ibid., Oct. 13, 1865, Mar. 1, 1867.

14. Ibid., Feb. 7 and June 28, 1867; *Commercial*, Sept. 15, 1867.

15. *Ledger*, Jan. 9, 16, 1869.

16. Ninth Census, manufacturing schedules.

17. Bogle, "Nineteenth Century River Town," 359; *Ledger*, Feb. 15, 1865.

18. *Ledger*, Feb. 11, 1870; Ninth Census, manufacturing schedules.

19. Ninth Census, manufacturing schedules.

20. The next highest income reported was William Culbertson's—$59,400. *A Biographical History*; Thornbrough, *Indiana in the Civil War Era*, 427; Johnson and Malone, *Dictionary of American Biography*, 5:244; Michael F. O'Brien, "A Nineteenth Century Hoosier Businessman: Washington C. DePauw" (Master's thesis, DePauw University, 1966), 22–23; *Ledger*, Dec. 23, 1864; *Commercial*, July 30, 1866.

21. *Ledger*, May 15, 1854, and Aug. 11, 1866.

22. Entry for F. A. Hicks & Co., Oct. 17, 1867, New Albany Mercantile Record, Indiana Division, Indiana State Library.

23. *Ledger*, May 7, 1859, noted that a "gentleman from an adjoining county who had considerable means at his disposal" would be interested in backing the venture.

24. Bogle, "Nineteenth Century River Town," 359–60; *Ledger*, Dec. 11, 1866, Jan. 4, Mar. 29, Apr. 1, Oct. 18, 1867.

25. Bogle, "Nineteenth Century River Town," 356; *Ledger*, May 28, 1867, Jan. 24, 1870, Jan. 7, 1871; C. W. Cottom, *New Albany, Indiana: Location and Natural Advantages for Manufacturing, Mechanical, Mercantile, and General Trade Enterprises* (New Albany, 1873), 29.

26. Pearce Davis, *The Development of the American Glass Industry* (Cambridge, Mass., 1949), 165.

27. *Ledger*, Jan. 22, 25, 1870; Bogle, "Nineteenth Century River Town," 368. Ford later manufactured plate-glass in Louisville, Jeffersonville, and then most successfully, in Creighton, Pennsylvania. Johnson and Malone, *Dictionary of American Biography*, 6:516–17; "History of Plate-Glass Manufacturing," 265.

28. *Ledger*, Jan. 7, 1879; *Directory* (1880), 253; *Report of the Tariff Commission*, v. 1 (Washington, 1882), 937, testimony of N. T. DePauw, Sept. 6, 1882.

29. Bogle, "Nineteenth Century River Town," 375; *Ledger-Standard* (hereafter *LS*), Feb. 15, 1879; *Ledger*, July 23, 1873.

30. United States, Census Office, *Report on the Population of the United States*, v. 1 (Washington, 1895).

31. Quoted in *History of the Ohio Falls Counties*, v. 2 (Cleveland, 1882), 224.

32. *National Labor Tribune*, Dec. 15, 1877.

33. Peter Stoy, for instance, served as the vice-president of the Ohio Falls Iron Works while he ran his wholesale hardware and cutlery business. *Directory* (1873).

34. Ninth Census, population schedules.

35. Ibid.

36. Ninth Census, population and manufacturing schedules.

37. Sanborn Fire Insurance Map, New Albany 1891, New Albany Public Library; *Directory* (1890); *Ledger*, Oct. 2, 1867.

38. Ninth Census and Tenth Census, population schedules; Sanborn Map, 1891, New Albany.

39. This discussion is based on the first full set of local extant inventories. The estates belonged to men and women who died during the first four or five years of the twentieth century. It is unlikely that as a group their economic situations dramatically improved during the nineties, which were generally bleak for the local economy.

40. Probate Inventories and Sales Bills, no. 6, estates of August Barth, 156; of Margaret Shrader, 161; and of Ezekiel R. Day, 10.

41. *Ledger*, Feb. 18, 1869.

42. *Flood of 1883: Brief History of its Rise, Progress and Decline* (New Albany, 1883).

43. *Standard*, July 29, 1872; *LS*, Jan. 20, 1873.

44. *Ledger*, Mar. 3, 8, 1884, Apr. 12, 1884, May 28, 1884, Mar. 15, 1885. DePauw was generous with the church even when it did not serve his economic interests. In his will he agreed to grant Asbury University an endowment of $210,000. One student who has examined the matter argues that the endowment depended on the name of the school being changed to DePauw University. O'Brien, "A Nineteenth Century Hoosier Businessman."

45. For a general treatment that focuses largely, but not exclusively, on the metals industry, see David Montgomery, *Fall of the House of Labor*.

46. The following discussion relies heavily on J. Arthur Phillips, *Elements of Metallurgy: A Practical Treatise on the Art of Extracting Metals from their Ores* (London, 1891), 309–12.

47. Ibid., 331–42.

48. This figure is suggested in Cottom, *New Albany, Indiana*, 47. A group of ironworkers responded to inquiries by the Indiana Bureau of Statistics with totals of up to five dollars daily for skilled trades. *Fourth Biennial Report of the Department of Statistics for 1891–92* (Indianapolis, 1892), 55.

49. Peter Temin, *Iron and Steel in Nineteenth Century America: An Economic Inquiry* (Cambridge, Mass., 1964), 103–5; Victor S. Clark, *History of Manufactures in the United States* (New York, 1929), 261–63.

50. For examples of improvement at the New Albany mills, see *National Labor Tribune*, Apr. 8, 1876, June 29, 1878.

51. Tenth Census, population schedules.

52. Ninth Census and Tenth Census, population schedules; *Directory* (1871, 1873, 1877, and 1880).

53. *Directory* (1873). This figure was arrived at by listing all workers and their trades who were designated as employees of the iron firms.

54. Cottom, *New Albany, Indiana*, 47; *Fourth Biennial Report*, 55; Montgomery, *Fall of the House of Labor*, 58–65.

55. *Directory* (1890). According to the census, the percentage of unskilled was higher.

56. Tenth Census, population schedules.

57. Ibid.

58. Ninth Census, manufacturing schedules.

59. *Scientific American* 52 (Aug. 22, 1885): 392. Also Jos. D. Weeks, "Report of the Manufacture of Glass," in Census Office, *Report on the Manufactures of the United States at the Tenth Census* (Washington, 1884), 1088; *Commercial*, Sept. 15, 1867.

60. Technological innovation, particularly the closed mold, in the early 1870s, reduced the art of the bottle blower's craft. *Ledger*, Mar. 21, 1874. For a detailed description of work in a bottle house, see Joan Wallach Scott, *The Glassworkers of Carmaux: French Craftsmen and Political Action in a Nineteenth-Century City* (Cambridge, Mass., 1974), 72–83; Michael P. Hanagan, *The Logic of Solidarity: Artisans and Industrial Workers in Three French Towns, 1871–1914* (Urbana, 1980), 93–105.

61. Scott, *Glassworkers of Carmaux*, 34–35.

62. Davis, *Development of the American Glass Industry*, 79–80; Scott, *Glassworkers of Carmaux*, 23–34.

63. Davis, *Development of the American Glass Industry*, 129.

64. Tenth Census, population schedules.

65. *Fourth Biennial Report*, 322; Cottom, *New Albany, Indiana*, 47.

66. *Ledger*, July 6, 1887; *Commercial*, Mar. 30, July 19, 1887.

67. Davis, *Development of the American Glass Industry*, 126–32.

68. Tenth Census, population schedules.

69. Weeks, "Report of the Manufacture of Glass," 1047–54. Total U. S. and Indiana production is provided. Only two glass factories were listed for

Indiana; the other in Jeffersonville was listed with output figures. It was possible to derive the New Albany total by subtracting the Jeffersonville total from that of Indiana as a whole.

70. Davis, *Development of the American Glass Industry*, 166.
71. *LS*, Mar. 21, 1874.
72. Weeks, "Report of the Manufacture of Glass," 1049–54.
73. Ibid., 1083–84.
74. Davis, *Development of the American Glass Industry*, 169–70.
75. *Scientific American* 53 (Aug. 22, 1885): 120.
76. *LS*, May 3, 1874; *Commercial*, May 13, 1876. For the most part, immigration of skilled English workers ceased with the onset of depression. This effort to recruit plate glass men was an exception. See Rowland Tappan Berthoff, *British Immigrants in Industrial America, 1790–1950* (Cambridge, Mass., 1953), 65, 76–77.
77. Tenth Census, population schedules.
78. *Fourth Biennial Report*, 332.
79. Tenth Census, population schedules.
80. Ibid.; *Directory* (1880 and 1890); *Fourth Biennial Report*, 322.
81. Tenth Census, population schedules.
82. Ninth Census, manufacturing schedules; Robbins, *New Albany*, 47.
83. In 1890, the directory listed 538 employees of the woolen mills. Of those listed, 239 were clearly female, and 139 others probably were. Robbins, *New Albany*, 47, suggests the labor force was 700 strong, "largely females." This figure is probably closer to the truth, as directories tend to underrenumerate working women and minors.
84. *Ledger*, Oct. 16, 1867; *Directory* (1890).
85. For the 1870s, see Cottom, *New Albany, Indiana*, 47. For 1890, *Fourth Biennial Report*, 188. The Department of Statistics received so few responses from woolen workers that data from New Albany was merged with those from Lafayette and Goshen,
86. Tenth Census, population schedules.
87. Eighth Census and Tenth Census, population schedules.
88. Bogle, "Nineteenth Century River Town," 328–29.
89. Census Office, *Report on the Population of the United States at the Tenth Census* (Washington, 1883) 149.
90. In 1880, 132 black women worked in such a capacity. Tenth Census, population schedules.
91. Leon Litwack, *Been in the Storm So Long* (New York, 1980).
92. Tenth Census, population schedules; 68.4 percent of unskilled glassworkers were single and 66.8 percent lived in the parental household; 72.8 percent of male woolen workers were single, as were 88.2 percent of the females. Altogether, 69.4 percent of woolen workers lived with their parents.
93. Ibid.
94. Ibid.
95. Ninth Census and Tenth Census, population schedules; *Directory*, (1871, 1873, 1877, and 1880); Cottom, *New Albany*, 47.
96. *Directory* (1890 and 1892). If a name appeared in both, the occupation

for the latter edition is used. The persistence rate was 38.3 percent for woolen workers, 35.4 percent for glass workers, and 60.5 percent for iron workers. The greater stability of iron workers is surely due to the smaller number of younger workers employed in 1880 relative to skilled workers. Since over 40 percent of the youngest woolen workers in 1880 were female, linkage was often prevented by the difficulties of tracing women of marriageable age.

97. *Directory*, (1868, 1873, and 1890).

98. Sanborn Insurance Map, 1891; *Directory* (1890).

99. Ward boundaries were moved eastward in the early 1870s in response to growth in the First Ward. The new first and second wards fit within the geographical area of the old first.

100. Tenth Census, population schedules.

101. Sanborn Map, 1891; *Directory* (1890).

102. Ibid.

103. Ibid.

104. *Fourth Biennial Report*, 55, 322.

105. *Directory*, (1860 and 1890).

106. Cumbler, *Working-Class Community*, emphasizes the role of neighborhoods in the building of class solidarities.

107. Between 1860 and 1880, the number of workers employed in manufacturing increased by 144 percent. The combined number of professionals, white collar workers, small master craftsmen, and storekeepers rose 61.6 percent during the same years. Eighth Census and Tenth Census, population and manufacturing schedules.

108. *Directory (1890)*.

109. Tenth Census, population schedules.

110. Tenth Census, population schedules; *Directory* (1890). On Hoffman, see *Journal of United Labor*, May 15, 1880.

111. Tenth Census, population schedules.

112. Ibid.

113. *Fourth Biennial Report*, 55, 153, 323.

114. *Directory* (1890).

115. Sanborn Insurance Map; *Directory* (1890).

116. *Ledger*, Feb. 25, 1871; *LS*, Oct. 24, 1871, Dec. 16, 22, and 24, 1871, Apr. 11, 1873, Dec. 19, 24, 1873, Dec. 15, 16, 22, 23, 26, 29, and 31, 1874, Mar. 2 and 26, Apr. 17 and 22, Dec. 14, 21, 24, 28, and 29, 1875; Ninth Census, population schedules; *Directory* (1871 and 1873).

117. *Ledger*, Mar. 24, 25, 28, 30, and 31, May 29, 1871; *LS*, Sept. 20, 28, 29, and 30, 1871, Mar. 20 and 28, Apr. 6, 1872, July 1, Dec. 26, 1873, Jan. 2, June 26, 27, and 30, Dec. 17 and 29, 1874, Jan. 2 and 7, June 16, 25, 26, and 29, Dec. 22 and 28, 1875; Ninth Census, population schedules; *Directory* (1871 and 1873).

118. For Masons, see *Ledger*, Dec. 14, 15, 18, 22, 24, and 26, 1886, Dec. 13, 16, 21, 23, and 27, 1887, Dec. 11, 14, 19, 21, and 26, 1888, Dec. 19, 20, 24, 26, and 27, 1889, Dec. 9, 17, 19, 23, 24, and 26, 1890. For Odd Fellows, see Jan. 8, Dec. 28, 1886, Jan. 1, Dec. 31, 1887, June 30, Dec. 29, 1888, Jan. 1 and

11, June 29, Dec. 18, 27, and 28, 1889, Apr. 23, June 27, Dec. 27 and 31, 1890; *Directory* (1886 and 1890).

119. H. K. Shackleford, *The Knight's Armor: A History of the Early Origins of the Order of Knights of Pythias* (New Haven, 1869), 21; Hugh Goold Webb, *A History of the Knights of Pythias* (Anaheim, 1910), 4; Cassity, *Defending a Way of Life*, 125–31; David Thelen, *Paths of Resistance*, 156–72.

120. *LS*, Sept. 8, Dec. 28, 1871, Jan. 6, June 26 and 27, 1872, Apr. 19, June 26, July 2, 1873, Jan. 2, June 30, 1874, July 1 and 3, Dec. 31, 1875.

121. *Ledger*, Jan. 1, 1886, Feb. 17, 1886, Dec. 28, 1886, Jan. 1, 1887, Dec. 28 and 29, 1887, Feb. 15, 1888, Jan. 2, 1889, June 25, 1889, Dec. 30 and 31, 1889, Feb. 12, 1890, July 2, 1890, Dec. 30, 1890; *Directory* (1886 and 1890).

122. *LS*, Jan. 11, 1873, July 13, 1874, Mar. 18, Sept. 16, Dec. 13, 1875; Ninth Census, population schedules; *Directory* (1871 and 1873).

123. *LS*, Mar. 19, June 22, 1872, Dec. 29, 1874, July 3, 1875; Ninth Census, population schedules; *Directory* (1871 and 1873).

124. Steven J. Ross, *Workers on the Edge*, 185–86

125. For leaders of the IOWM, see *LS*, June 20, 1874, July 27, Dec. 31, 1875; Ninth Census, population schedules; *Directory* (1873 and 1877).

126. *LS*, June 20, 1874.

127. Ibid.; *Commercial*, June 21, 1874.

128. *LS*, Jan. 6 and Mar. 14, 1877.

129. Ibid., Jan. 7, 1876.

130. Ibid., July 22, 1878; *Commercial*, Mar. 9, 1879.

131. *LS*, Mar. 5, 1879, Sept. 6, 1879.

132. Ibid., Feb. 21, 1877.

133. *LS*, Jan. 16 and 19, 1874, Feb. 27, 1875.

134. Ibid., July 3, 14, and 27, 1875.

135. For examples see *Ledger*, May 16, 1868, July 5, 1869, Jan. 1, July 28, 1887; *LS*, Aug. 12, Sept. 22, 1873, Feb. 11, Nov. 26, 1875, and Oct. 6, 1876; *Commercial*, July 11, 1887.

136. "List of members," Oceola Lodge No. 47, Knights of Honor, ca. 1886, Lodges folder, New Albany/Floyd County Library.

137. *Directory* (1890).

Chapter 8: Workers in Isolation

1. New Albany *Commercial*, Oct. 23, 1867; New Albany *Ledger*, Oct. 23, 26, 1867; Bogle, "Nineteenth Century River Town, 331–33.

2. Bogle, "Nineteenth Century River Town," 336; *Ledger*, Jan. 5, 26, Feb. 19, and Mar. 2, 5, 1869.

3. New Albany, City Council Proceedings, v. 9, Mar. 15, 1869; *Directory* (1868 and 1871); Ninth Census, population schedules.

4. *Ledger* and *Commerical*, Oct. 18, 1867.

5. Ibid.

6. Louisville *Commercial*, May 5, 1871 (coopers); *LS*, Aug. 12, 1873

(molders) and Sept. 12, 1873 (blowers); New Albany *Standard*, Jan. 20, 1872 (boilermakers).

7. *Ledger*, Apr. 7, 1871; Ninth Census, population schedules.

8. *LS*, May 27, 1873, Oct. 1, 1873.

9. Ibid., Apr. 29, 1874; *Commercial*, June 25, 1875.

10. *LS*, July 10, 1873.

11. *Standard*, Oct. 30 and Nov. 6, 1871; *Ledger*, July 17, 23, 1872.

12. *Ledger* and *Commercial*, July 10, 1873.

13. *Ledger*, Jan. 20, Feb. 10, Apr. 26, May 2, 1870.

14. Council Proceedings, v. 10, May 16, 1870; *Ledger*, May 17, 1870.

15. *Ledger* and *Commercial*, Feb. 23, 1871.

16. Ninth Census, population schedules; *Directory* (1871). This local correlation between political and workplace activism affirms observations made by David Montgomery of the nature of the National Labor Union and its political wing, the National Labor Reform Party. *Beyond Equality*, 195.

17. *Ledger*, May 5, 1869, and May 4, 1870.

18. *Commercial*, Mar. 1, 11, and 17, 1871.

19. Ibid., Apr. 3, 1871

20. Ibid., Mar. 30, 1871

21. Ibid., Apr. 8, 1871; *Ledger*, Apr. 8, 21, 1871.

22. *Commercial*, Apr. 27, 1871.

23. *Ledger*, Apr. 15, 1871.

24. *Commercial*, Apr. 14, 15, and 24, 1871.

25. *Ledger*, May 3, 1871.

26. *LS*, Apr. 24 and May 7, 1873; *Commercial*, Apr. 25, 1873.

27. *LS*, Jan. 3, Feb. 26, Mar. 9, 1874; New Albany Mercantile Records, 1867–78, Indiana State Library. Proprietors who previously had received recommendations for loans were now considered bad risks.

28. *LS*, Dec. 5, 1873.

29. The following account is taken from the Diary of Marie Graham Grant, entries of Dec. 17, 1873, Jan. 1 and 3, 1874, and Feb. 15, 1874, John Kennedy Graham Papers, Indiana Historical Society Library.

30. *LS*, July 28, 1874.

31. Ibid., Dec. 16, 1873; and Herbert G. Gutman, "An Iron Workers' Strike in the Ohio Valley, 1873–1874," *Ohio Historical Quarterly* 68 (Oct. 1959): 354–56.

32. *LS*, Feb. 11, 1874; *NLT*, Feb. 14, 1874.

33. *NLT*, Feb. 14, 1874.

34. Louisville *Courier-Journal*, Mar. 23, 1874; *LS*, Apr. 20, 23, 1874; *Commercial*, Apr. 21, 1874; *NLT*, Apr. 25, 1874.

35. *NLT*, May 9 and July 11, 1874. Some, like roller Peter Baltes, refused to return to work. *Commercial*, June 22, 1875.

36. Quoted in Gutman, "An Iron Workers' Strike," 361.

37. *LS*, Dec. 23, 1873, Mar. 23, Apr. 20, 1874; *Commercial*, Mar. 24, Apr. 22, 1874.

38. *LS*, Feb. 6, 11, 1874.

39. *LS*, Feb. 14, 1874. The female vivandiere sold wine and food to French military units as a petty entrepreneur. Eugene Weber kindly informed me of her significance.

40. *LS*, Feb. 14, 1874, Feb. 14, 1876, Feb. 14, 1880; *Commercial*, Feb. 15, 1876. By 1875 businessmen had begun to take an active role organizing the carnivals, presumably because they perceived in them an opportunity to draw people from the countryside into town where they might spend money.

41. Emma Lou Thornbrough, *Indiana in the Civil War Era, 1850–1880*, (Indianapolis, 1865), 263; *LS*, Mar. 20, 1873. On Hipple and Fogle, see *LS*, Feb. 25, 1873.

42. Jack S. Blocker, Jr., *"Give to the Winds Thy Fears": The Women's Temperance Crusade, 1873–1874* (Westport, 1985); Ruth Bordin, *Women and Temperance: The Quest for Power and Liberty, 1873–1900* (Philadelphia, 1981), 15–33; Barbara Leslie Epstein, *The Politics of Domesticity: Women, Evangelism and Temperance in Nineteenth-Century America* (Middletown, Conn., 1981), 194–214; Jed Dannenbaum, *Drink and Disorder: Temperance Reform in Cincinnati from the Washingtonian Revival to the WCTU* (Urbana, 1984).

43. *LS*, Mar. 9, 1874; Diary of Marie Graham Grant, entry for Mar. 7, 1874.

44. Hipple and Fogle remained active within their Good Templar lodges. *LS*, May 4, 1874, and Oct. 29, 1875.

45. Blocker, *"Give to the Wind Thy Fears,"* 121–23. Norman H. Clark, *Deliver Us from Evil: An Interpretation of American Prohibition* (New York, 1976), 68–73, suggests that such women were attempting to stave off social disintegration threatened by economic change and depression.

46. For over two months, beginning on Mar. 11, the crusade was the main news story in the *Ledger*. See also Diary of Marie Graham Grant, entry of Mar. 20, 1874.

47. *LS*, Mar. 24 and May 2, 1874. The paper's support of the crusaders tended to reduce Mrs. Futterer and others like her to caricatures, but the reports convey the real hostility between the two groups.

48. *LS*, Apr. 8, 16, 1874.

49. Bordin, *Women and Temperance*, 33.

50. Minutes, New Albany Presbytery, spring meeting, 1874, 11; Geo. C. Heckman, *An Address on Women's Work in the Church, before the Presbytery of New Albany*, (Madison, Ind., 1875), 26.

51. *LS*, Mar. 26, 1873.

52. Ibid., Apr. 9, 1874.

53. *Commercial*, Apr. 29, 1874.

54. Ibid.; *LS*, May 6, 1874.

55. *LS*, Oct. 2, 1874.

56. *Ledger*, Mar. 27, 1871.

57. *LS*, July 25, 1877; *Commercial*, July 26, 1877.

58. Council Proceedings, v. 11, Feb. 18, 1878.

59. *LS*, Mar. 2, 12, 1878.

60. Ibid., Mar. 1 and Apr. 22, 1878; *NLT*, Apr. 6, 1878.

61. Council Proceedings, v. 11, Apr. 15, 1878.

62. Ibid., May 8, 1878; *LS*, May 8, 1878. The one dissenting vote objected to the speed of the process rather than the policy.

63. *LS*, May 9–11, 1878; *Commercial*, May 10, 1878; *Courier-Journal*, May 9, 10, 1878.

64. See chapter three.

65. *Ledger*, Jan. 8, 1872, and May 28, 1872.

66. *LS*, Jan. 3, 1874.

67. Ibid., July 21, 25, 1877.

68. See *LS*, Sept. 6, 1878, and Nov. 11, 1880.

69. Ninth Census, population schedules.

70. The following account is based on the report in *LS*, Apr. 2, 1875.

71. Ibid.; *Commercial*, Apr. 3, 1875.

72. *LS*, Nov. 13, 1873, Feb. 1, Oct. 24, 1876, and Apr. 13, 1877; *NLT*, Jan. 26, 1878; *Commercial*, Dec. 17, 1875.

73. *LS*, Jan. 27, 1875.

74. *NLT*, Feb. 13, 1875. On the effort of skilled workers to prevent such individualistic excesses, see David Montgomery, *Workers' Control in America: Studies in the History of Work, Technology, and Labor Struggles* (Cambridge, Eng., 1979), 9–31. The threat to health faced by glass blowers is described by Scott, *The Glassworkers of Carmaux*, 42–43.

75. *NLT*, Feb. 27 and Apr. 3, 1875.

76. Ibid., May 1, 15, 1875.

77. On employment in the iron mills, see *NLT*, May 19 and 26, Aug. 11, 1877, June 19, Dec. 14, 1878, Jan. 4, 1879.

78. *Commercial*, Apr. 9, 1876. Kelso played a prominent role at the Greenback Convention, held in a nearby village. *LS*, July 24, 1876.

79. *LS*, Aug. 15, 1876, Sept. 1 and 13, 1876, Oct. 14, 1876, Nov. 9, 1876.

80. *LS*, May 7, 1877.

81. *Commercial*, Aug. 8, 11, and 25, 1877; *LS*, Aug. 13, 17, and 24, 1877. The New Albany supporters of the new party were influenced by its success in neighboring Louisville. See Philip S. Foner, *The Great Labor Uprising of 1877*, 220–24.

82. *LS*, Aug. 27 and Sept. 27, 1877; *Commercial*, Sept. 1, 1877.

83. *LS*, Apr. 1, 1878.

84. *LS*, May 7, 1878.

85. Ibid., May 7, 8, 1878; *NLT*, May 18, 1878.

86. For report of the Greenback Party county convention, *LS*, May 11, 1878; for the congressional convention, July 20, 1878.

87. Ibid., Oct. 11, 1878.

88. Ibid., May 7, 1879.

89. *LS*, Apr. 14 and 16, May 10, 1879.

90. *NLT*, June 28, 1879.

91. *LS*, Oct. 6, 23, 1879; *Commercial*, Oct. 8, 1879.

92. *LS*, Oct. 10, 1879.

93. *LS*, June 3, 4, 1880, July 26, 1881, Mar. 2, 17, 1881, Oct. 10, 1881.

94. *Courier-Journal*, Feb. 1, 1880; *Commercial*, Feb. 1, 1880; *LS*, Feb. 2, 1880; Jeffersonville *Evening News*, Mar. 15, 1880.

95. Henry Fecker to T. V. Powderly, Nov. 26, 1879, Powderly Papers, reel 1.

96. *Commercial* and *LS*, Jan. 27, 1880.

97. *Courier-Journal*, Jan. 30, 1880; *Commercial*, Feb. 1, 1880.

98. *Commercial*, Feb. 1, 1880.

99. *LS*, Feb. 10, 1880. Two half-hearted apologies followed Keehner's visit to the newspaper's office. See Feb. 13, 16, 1880.

100. Ibid., Feb. 18, 19, 1880. The census and 1880 directory list William Scanlan, a twenty-three-year-old English glass cutter. Scanlan's trial went unnoticed by the press. The identity of the third alleged assailant is unknown.

101. *Commercial*, Mar. 28, 1875.

102. *Journal of United Labor*, May 15, 1880.

103. *News*, Feb. 28, 1880.

104. Ibid., Feb. 2, 28, 1880.

105. *LS*, Mar. 5, 1880; *Commercial*, Mar. 6, 1880.

106. *LS*, Mar. 19, 20, 1880.

107. *News*, Mar. 22, 1880.

108. *LS*, Mar. 22, 23, 1880. Henry Jansing died four months later, though the cause is unknown.

109. *LS*, Mar. 23, 1880.

110. *LS*, Apr. 17, 1880.

111. *Journal of United Labor*, May 15, 1880. Hoffman's case was given priority by the General Assembly of the Knights of Labor primarily due to a family tragedy. His sixteen-year-old daughter had lost both her arms in a railroad accident. *LS*, Apr. 12, 27, 1880. His fortunes improved dramatically soon after, as he became a prosperous coal merchant, probably as a result of a settlement of a $100,000 lawsuit he had brought against the Pennsylvania railroad. *LS*, Apr. 30, 1880.

112. *LS*, Apr. 27, 1880.

113. *LS*, July 22, 1880.

114. U. S. Stephens to Henry Fecker, Feb. 6, 1879, and U. S. Stephens to Thomas Wybrant, Feb. 6, 1879, Powderly Papers, Letterpress books, vol. B, 508–09, reel 44. On the Elephants, *LS*, Mar. 13, 20, 1880. On the spread of such organizations throughout the northern states, see John Higham, *Strangers in the Land: Patterns of American Nativism, 1860–1925*, (New Brunswick, 1955), 28–29.

115. *Standard*, Sept. 2, 1871, and June 6, 1872.

116. *LS*, Mar. 20, 1880, and May 5, 1880.

117. *Record of the Proceedings of the General Assembly*, 210, Powderly Papers, reel 65; Garlock, "A Structural Analysis."

118. See, for example, *LS*, Sept. 3, 1880.

119. *NLT*, July 10, 24, 1880.

120. LA 300 was led by blowers, though it also included gatherers, flatteners, and cutters.

121. Minutes, LA 300 of the Knights of Labor, 1882–86, meetings of Aug.

24, Sept. 14, Oct. 19, Dec. 21, 1883, Feb. 1, 1884, in Box 1, Folder 2, Joseph Slight Papers, Ohio Historical Society Library.

122. *Report of the 2nd National Convention of the Window Glass Workers' Assembly No. 300, Knights of Labor* (Pittsburgh, 1883), 22, 27.

123. Eric Foner, "Class, Ethnicity and Radicalism in the Gilded Age: The Land League and Irish America," in *Politics and Ideology in the Age of the Civil War*, (New York, 1980).

124. *LS*, Mar. 7, 12, 1881; *Commercial*, Mar. 7, 14, and 21, 1881.

125. *LS*, Aug. 4, 1880.

126. Ibid.

127. *LS*, Sept. 24, 1880; Clifton J. Phillips, *Indiana in Transition: The Emergence of an Industrial Commonwealth, 1880–1920*, (Indianapolis, 1968), 12.

128. *LS*, Sept. 29, 1880.

129. *LS*, Sept. 25, 27, 1880..

130. *LS*, Nov. 3, 1880, and Nov. 9, 1876.

131. *LS*, Sept. 24, 1884.

132. *LS*, Oct. 6, 1884.

133. For the iron workers, see *LS*, June 2, 3, and 15, 1880, May 31, 1883, and June 1, 1883.

134. *Ledger*, Apr. 25, 1883, and Mar. 12, 1884.

135. John Kerrigan and Frank Sinex to Hon. T. V. Powderly, Jan. 14, 1886, Powderly Papers, reel 12; *Commercial*, Jan. 31, 1886.

136. *Ledger*, Mar. 28, 1886.

137. *Ledger*, Apr. 12, 16, 1886, and May 1, 1886; Garlock, "A Structural Analysis."

138. *Ledger*, Apr. 30, 1886. With regard to politics, see Apr. 26, 1886. On the Knights and drink, see David Thomas Brundage, "The Making of Working-Class Radicalism in the Mountain West: Denver, Colorado, 1880–1903" (Ph. D. diss., University of California Los Angeles, 1982).

139. *Ledger*, Apr. 28, 1886, Jan. 1, Feb. 22, June 27, July 28, 1887; *Commercial*, May 1, 1886, and July 11, 1887.

140. *Commercial*, Apr. 5, 1887; *John Swinton's Paper*, Mar. 20, 1887.

141. *Ledger*, Oct. 18, 1886.

142. Ibid., Nov. 5, 1886.

143. Ibid., Jan. 7, 13, and 20, 1887.

144. *John Swinton's Paper*, Apr. 3, 1887; *Public Press*, Apr. 6, Sept. 21, 1887. There are no extant copies of the *Evening Mail*, and the *Ledger* and *Commercial* completely ignored the organizing efforts by the Knights. Of denunciations, however, there was no shortage.

145. *Ledger*, Apr. 28, May 2, 1887.

146. *Public Press*, May 11, 1887.

147. *Ledger*, Apr. 28, 1886, and Feb. 26, 1887; See also John Kerrigan and Frank Sinex to T. V. Powderly, Jan. 14, 1886, Powderly Papers, reel 12.

148. *Ledger*, Mar. 21, 22, and 28, 1887; *Commercial*, Mar. 28, 1887. The strike wave seems to have bypassed the woolen workers who ignored a strike

of Louisville woolen mill operatives. This may be a result of the molder strike of that summer and the resources it drained. Nancy Schrom Dye, "The Louisville Woolen Mills Strike of 1887: A Case Study of Working Women, the Knights of Labor, and Union Organization in the New South," in *Register of the Kentucky Historical Society* 82 (Spring 1984): 136–50.

149. *Ledger*, Apr. 14, 1887.

150. Ibid., Apr. 19, 1887.

151. *Public Press*, Apr. 20, 1887.

152. *Ledger*, Apr. 25, 1887; *Commercial*, May 2, 10, 1887.

153. *Ledger*, June 2, 4, and 6, 1887.

154. Ibid., July 14, 16, 1887; *Commercial*, June 22, July 10, 15, 1887; *Public Press*, Aug. 24, 31, 1887.

155. *Commercial*, May 15, 1887; *Ledger*, Nov. 4, 1887.

156. Lawrence B. Huckeby to T. V. Powderly, Jan. 25, 1888, Powderly Papers, reel 24.

157. The above account is taken largely from the letter cited above, and *Directory* (1884 and 1886). Also *Public Press*, Nov. 9, 1887; *Ledger*, Nov. 4, 1887; and the following letters from the Powderly Papers: Peter Tellon, P. H. McKamey and J. H. Hall to T. V. Powderly, Nov. 9, 1887, reel 23; Powderly to L. B. Huckeby, Feb. 2, 1888, reel 49; Powderly to Alfred P. Farabee, Nov. 30, 1887, reel 50.

158. *Ledger*, Dec. 15, 1888.

159. New Albany *Evening Tribune*, Oct. 17, 1888.

160. *Ledger*, Mar. 16, May 8, 1889.

161. Ibid., Nov. 27, 1889.

162. Ibid., Dec. 7, 1889.

163. Ibid., May 6, 1887. Also May 5, 7–10, 1887.

164. George King Davis, "The Industrialization of Indiana, 1860–1920" (Ph. D. diss., Indiana University, 1963), 190.

165. Leon Fink, *Workingman's Democracy: The Knights of Labor and American Politics* (Urbana, 1983).

Conclusion: Industry, Culture, and Politics in the Gilded Age Community

1. Herbert G. Gutman, "An Iron Workers' Strike," 353–70; Gutman, "Class, Status and Community Power in Nineteenth-Century American Industrial Cities," in *Work, Culture and Society in Industrializing America* (New York, 1977), 234–60.

2. *LS*, May 10, 1878.

3. Ibid., Mar. 19, 20, 22, 1880.

4. *Iron Molders' Journal*, July 31, 1880.

5. Clifton J. Phillips, *Indiana in Transition*, 93.

6. Central Labor Union, *Trades and Labor Directory*.

7. Fink, *Workingmen's Democracy*, 227.

8. Among the first and most powerful works to focus on the artisan as the source of opposition was E. P. Thompson, *The Making of the English Working Class.*

9. Gutman, *Work, Culture and Society;* Wilentz, *Chants Democratic;* Steven Ross, *Workers on the Edge;* Alan Dawley, *Class and Community;* Nick Salvatore, *Eugene V. Debs.*

10. Gutman, *Work, Culture and Society,* 257.

11. Gordon S. Wood, *The Creation of the American Republic, 1776–1787* (New York, 1972), 505–14; Edmund S. Morgan, *Inventing the People: The Rise of Popular Sovereignty in England and America* (New York, 1988), 263–87.

12. See Fink, *Workingmen's Democracy,* 30–32.

13. On the importance of the police, see Terrence J. McDonald, *The Parameters of Urban Fiscal Policy: Socioeconomic Change and Political Culture in San Francisco, 1860–1906* (Berkeley, 1986), 229–30.

14. Antonio Gramsci, *Selections from the Prison Notebooks,* ed. and trans. by Quinton Hoare and Geoffrey Nowell Smith (New York, 1971), 234–35.

15. Morton Keller, *Affairs of State: Public Life in Late Nineteenth Century America* (Cambridge, Mass., 1977), 239–49; Jean H. Baker, *Affairs of Party: The Political Culture of Northern Democrats in the Mid-Nineteenth Century* (Ithaca, 1983).

16. John T. Cumbler, "Labor, Capital, and Community: The Struggle for Power," *Labor History* 13 (Summer 1974): 395–415, quote on p. 414; Daniel Walkowitz, *Worker City, Company Town.*

17. Craig Calhoun, *The Question of Class Struggle: The Social Foundations of Popular Radicalism during the Industrial Revolution* (Chicago, 1982).

18. Gutman, "An Iron Workers' Strike," 358.

19. Ibid., 361.

20. Ibid., 360 (*Commercial*), 365, 368 (*Enquirer*).

Index

LAWRENCE M. LIPIN received his doctorate in history from UCLA in 1989, has taught at Lewis and Clark College, and is currently assistant professor of American history at Pacific University in Forest Grove, Oregon.

Books in the Series The Working Class in American History

Worker City, Company Town: Iron and Cotton-Worker Protest in Troy and Cohoes, New York, 1855-84
Daniel J. Walkowitz

Life, Work, and Rebellion in the Coal Fields: The Southern West Virginia Miners, 1880-1922
David Alan Corbin

Women and American Socialism, 1870-1920
Mari Jo Buhle

Lives of Their Own: Blacks, Italians, and Poles in Pittsburgh, 1900-1960
John Bodnar, Roger Simon, and Michael P. Weber

Working-Class America: Essays on Labor, Community, and American Society
Edited by Michael H. Frisch and Daniel J. Walkowitz

Eugene V. Debs: Citizen and Socialist
Nick Salvatore

American Labor and Immigration History, 1877-1920s: Recent European Research
Edited by Dirk Hoerder

Workingmen's Democracy: The Knights of Labor and American Politics
Leon Fink

The Electrical Workers: A History of Labor at General Electric and Westinghouse, 1923-60
Ronald W. Schatz

The Mechanics of Baltimore: Workers and Politics in the Age of Revolution, 1763-1812
Charles G. Steffen

The Practice of Solidarity: American Hat Finishers in the Nineteenth Century
David Bensman

The Labor History Reader
Edited by Daniel J. Leab

Solidarity and Fragmentation: Working People and Class Consciousness in Detroit, 1875-1900
Richard Oestreicher

Counter Cultures: Saleswomen, Managers, and Customers in American Department Stores, 1890-1940
Susan Porter Benson

The New England Working Class and the New Labor History
Edited by Herbert G. Gutman and Donald H. Bell

For Democracy, Workers, and God: Labor Song-Poems and Labor Protest, 1865-95
Clark D. Halker

Dishing It Out: Waitresses and Their Unions in the Twentieth Century
Dorothy Sue Cobble

The Spirit of 1848: German Immigrants, Labor Conflict, and the Coming of the Civil War
Bruce Levine

Working Women of Collar City: Gender, Class, and Community in Troy, New York, 1864-86
Carole Turbin

Southern Labor and Black Civil Rights: Organizing Memphis Workers
Michael K. Honey

Radicals of the Worst Sort: Laboring Women in Lawrence, Massachusetts, 1860-1912
Ardis Cameron

Producers, Proletarians, and Politicians: Workers and Party Politics in Evansville and New Albany, Indiana, 1850-87
Lawrence M. Lipin

Date Due

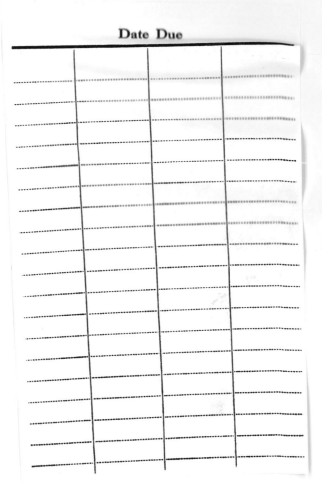